Income Distribution and Economic Inequality
Edited by Zvi Griliches, Wilhelm Krelle,
Hans-Jürgen Krupp, and Oldrich Kyn

Income Distribution and Economic Inequality

Edited by Zvi Griliches, Wilhelm Krelle,
Hans-Jürgen Krupp, and Oldrich Kyn

Campus Verlag
Frankfurt/Main

Halsted Press
John Wiley & Sons
New York – Toronto – Chichester

CIP-Kurztitelaufnahme der Deutschen Bibliothek

Income distribution and economic inequality / ed. by
Zvi Griliches ... - 1. Aufl. - Frankfurt/Main :
Campus Verlag; New York (New York) : Halsted Press,
1978.
  (Campus : Special studies)
  ISBN 3-593-32218-8
NE: Griliches, Zvi (Hrsg.)

Library of Congress Cataloging in Publication Data

Main entry under title:
Income distribution and economic inequality.
1. Income distribution — Addresses, essays,
lectures. I. Griliches, Zvi, 1930–
HC79.I5I48 1978 339.2 78-2390
ISBN 0-470-26331-8

ISBN Campus edition: 3-593-32218-8
ISBN Halsted edition: 0-470-26331-8

Copyright © 1978 Campus Verlag GmbH, Frankfurt
Published 1978 in Frankfurt, West Germany by Campus Verlag
Schumannstraße 65. 6000 Frankfurt, West Germany
Published in the USA, Canada, Latin America, U.K.
and Japan by Halsted Press, a Division of John Wiley & Sons, Inc., New York

Printed and bound in West Germany

CONTENTS

Foreword 7

A. The Distributional Impact of Macroeconomic Policy 9

1. *Edward C. Budd and T.C. Whiteman*
   Macroeconomic Fluctuations and the Size Distribution
   of Income and Earnings in the United States 11

2. *Wilhelm Krelle and Ralf Pauly*
   Distributional Impacts of Public Expenditure Programs
   and Tax Changes 28

3. *Martin Pfaff and Wolfgang Asam*
   Distributive Effects of Real Transfers via Public Infra structure:
   Conceptual Problems and some Empirical Results 66

4. *Jan Pen*
   Tax Policies and Transitory Income: Some Comments 97

B. Paradigms in the Theory of Income Distribution 101

1. *Dennis W. Carlton and Robert E. Hall*
   The Distribution of Permanent Income 103

2. *D.G. Champernowne*
   The Place of Stochastic Models of Income Distribution
   amongst other Models of it 113

3. *Horst Albach, Thomas Fues and Bernd Geisen*
   Approaches to a Theory of Income Distribution in
   the Firm 132

4. *Carl Christian von Weizsäcker*
   A small contribution to the theory of wage structure
   in collective bargaining 155

5. *Hans-Jürgen Krupp*
   The Contribution of Microanalytic Simulation Models to
   the Theory of Income Distribution 160

C. Accounting for Inequality of Earnings:
   The Human Capital Approach 173

1. *George J. B o r j a s and Jacob M i n c e r*
   The Distribution of Earnings Profiles in Longitudinal Data 175

2. *Robert E. B. L u c a s*
   Variances in Return to Human Capital 198

3. *Zvi G r i l i c h e s*
   Earnings of Very Young Men 209

4. *P. T a u b m a n, J. B e h r m a n and T. W a l e s*
   The Roles of Genetics and Environment in the Distribution
   of Earnings 220

5. *Richard B. F r e e m a n*
   The Effect of the Increased Relative Supply of College Graduates
   on Skill Differences and Employment Opportunities 240

D. Income Inequality in its Political Environment 257

1. *Gustav F. P a p a n e k*
   Economic Growth, Income Distribution and the Political Process
   in Less Developed Countries 259

2. *Oldrich K ý n*
   Education, Sex, and Income Inequality in Soviet-type Socialism 274

3. *Michael W a g n e r*
   Income Distribution in Small Countries: Some Evidence
   from Austria 290

4. *Jiri S l á m a*
   A Cross-Country Regression Model of Social Inequality 306

5. *Frank K l a n b e r g*
   Facts, Figures, and Syndromes of Income Distribution:
   Some Notes in Retrospect 324

List of Contributors 334

FOREWORD

This volume contains the revised and extended versions of papers originally presented at a symposium held in the summer of 1976 at Bad Homburg, West Germany. Of course, there have been many conferences focussing on the theme of income distribution during the past 15 years or so. In the past such efforts dealt primarily with the distribution of aggregates and with the distributive consequences of economic growth. More recently, however, the emphasis has moved away from theories that account solely for changes in aggregates toward explanatory paradigms whose focal point is the behavior of microanalytic decision units such as groups, familes or even individuals, and its response to variables of government policies.

There are a good many reasons why this has come about. Among them is the large body of empirical evidence indicating that, in many industrialized countries, the overall picture of income distribution figures has changed surprisingly little since, say, 1960, despite sometimes substantial efforts of governmental agencies to reduce inequality of income by taxation and direct transfers, and despite the often heavy investments in human capital which have occured during the last 20 years. All questions of measurement apart, difficult and sometimes controversial as they are, it is fairly clear that some rethinking of theoretical concepts as well as empirical experimentation is called for.

Since it is unlikely that a single grand design will provide definitive answers to the numerous and recalcitrant problems confronting us, the organizers of the symposium have attempted to select papers which taken together provide a rather comprehensive view of the many facets of current research on income distribution, as well as an outline for research paths to be followed.

The idea to hold the Bad Homburg symposium sprang from various sources. A first inititive was developed by Oldrich Kyn who discussed the prospects with the other editors. Credit must also be given to Professor Hans Moeller, member of the Bavarian Academy of Sciences in Munich, whose valuable advice during the gestation period is gratefully acknowledged. From this a close cooperation developed between Sonderforschungsbereich 21 at Bonn University and the Sozialpolitische Forschergruppe (SPES-Project) at Frankfurt. The local organization of the symposium was largely in the hands of the latter group. Financial support was generously given by the Werner-Reimers-Stiftung at Bad Homburg, which also provided its facilities which are so conducive to hard work in a relaxing and plesasant atmosphere at the foot of the Taunus mountains. The editors take great pleasure to express their gratitude to the Werner-Reimers-Stiftung, especially to its general manager, Professor Konrad Müller, as well as to the members of his staff.

Zvi Griliches   Wilhelm Krelle   Hans-Jürgen Krupp   Oldrich Kyn

A. The Distributional Impact of Macroeconomic Policy

Edward C. Budd and T. C. Whiteman

Macroeconomic fluctuations and the size distribution of income and earnings in the United States

Introduction

While there was early recognition of the possible relation between cyclical fluctuations and income size distribution in the U.S., it was not until time series on size distribution were developed over a quarter of a century ago that this relationship was adequately documented. In his monumental study of upper income groups Kuznets found a tendency for overall inequality to move inversely with the cycle in the interwar period (1919—39), with an upper income group (not always inclusive of the top 1 or 2 percent) gaining at the expense of a lower group comprising the vast majority — probably no less than 85 to 90 percent — of the recipients [Kuznets, pp. 57—8]. For the decline into the Great Depression (1929—33), according to an earlier study of urban families by Mendershausen, this upper group, comprising as much as 30 percent of the recipient unit population, gained not only at the expense of the lower part of the distribution, but the top 2 or 3 percent as well.[1]

The pattern of increasing inequality in recessions and reduced inequality in subsequent recoveries has persisted in the postwar period, although in a somewhat less extreme form, at least according to annual data on the size distribution of total money from the Current Population Survey of the Bureau of the Census. While spacing is lacking to develop this relationship fully, that between a single-valued measure of inequality, the Gini concentration ratio (for families and unrelated individuals), and the overall unemployment rate is portrayed in Figure 1.

The next section examines the theoretical case for supposing that variations in income inequality are related to variations in economic activity and in the unemployment rate in particular. In the final section we develop a simulation model to measure the effects of changes in unemployment on the size distribution of earnings and describe briefly its relation to similar studies.

Theoretical Explanations of the Cyclical Behavior of Income Inequality

While the inverse relation between the size of the property share in personal income and the business cycle may be one possible explanation of the inverse

11

Figure 1 Relation between the Gini concentration ratio for families and unrelated individuals in total money income, and the overall unemployment rate, 1947–1974

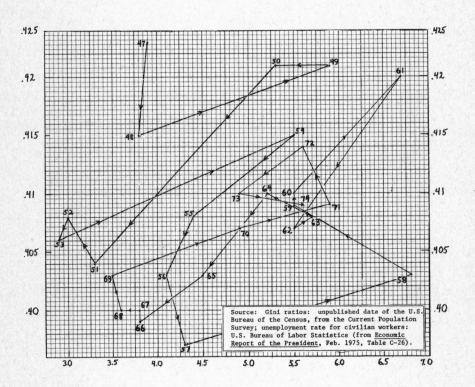

Source: Gini ratios: unpublished data of the U.S. Bureau of the Census, from the Current Population Survey; unemployment rate for civilian workers: U.S. Bureau of Labor Statistics (from Economic Report of the President, Feb. 1975, Table C-26).

Unemployment rate (all civilian workers)

relation between the level of economic activity and income inequality, the major sources of the relation must be sought in the cyclical behavior of the earnings distribution. The effect of unemployment on earnings inequality was recognized even in the early literature. Mendershausen was one of the first to offer an explanation [pp. 68—73]. Even if workers who lost their jobs were drawn proportionately from all parts of the distribution, he noted, they would be pushed into zero or very low income positions compared to those retaining their jobs, serving to increase the extent of the income gap between the un- and underemployed on the one hand and those with relatively full-time employment on the other. Second, all workers do not have the same probability of becoming unemployed in a recession; the incidence of unemployment tends to be greater among the less skilled and lower paid. Supervisory and skilled workers, Mendershausen argued, are more in the nature of fixed assets to their employers, since their services are necessary even for relatively low levels of production. Third, wage differentials between low and high paid workers can be expected to widen, partly as a result of the greater excess supply of lower paid workers created by unemployment.

That short-run fluctuations in demand for lower paid and less skilled workers will be greater than for the higher paid and more skilled in recessions has been rationalized by Oi in therms of human capital theory.[2] Employers incur a fixed cost in hiring workers and in providing them with specific on-the-job training (i.e., training which raises the productivity of a worker to a specific employer, but not to others), and they must expect to be able to recoup these costs (in terms of the difference between the worker's specific marginal product and his wage rate) over the worker's tenure with the firm. The ratio between this cost and the wage rate (the degree of fixity), Oi argues, is greater for those with larger investments in human capital, hence more skilled and more highly paid. During periods of declining product demand the employer thus has more of an incentive to retain such workers and to concentrate layoffs among those with little specific training. The results are larger increases in unemployment among the unskilled and/or widening of wage differentials (assuming relatively inelastic labor supplies and sufficient wage flexibility). If specific training is directly related to general on-the-job training, such socioeconomic characteristics as age, race, and sex should be related to differential changes in labor demand resulting from variations in product demand, since women, blacks, and the young have less invested in such training [Mincer, 1962]. In addition, greater variations in the demand for older workers could be explained by their shorter expected periods of tenure with firms.

Reder [1955, 1962, 1964] has developed a somewhat different model to account for essentially the same phenomena. Instead of laying off both skilled and unskilled workers in a recession, he argues, employers use their underemployed skilled workers for less skilled jobs and concentrate layoffs on the less skilled. More precisely, employers tighten hiring standards in recessions and relax them in subsequent expansions. In recessions they are able to hire experienced workers, many of whom are unemployed, without bidding up their wage rates. But as labor markets tighten, the marginal cost of hiring such workers (relative to inexperienced ones) rises as employers try to »pirate« them away from their current jobs and thus incur the risk of having to increase the wage rates of their existing employees in accordance with the premiums granted new recruits. Difficulties in recruiting, with resulting lengthening of vacancy periods for the more skilled or experienced positions, will at some point make the direct costs of hiring experienced workers great enough so that the employer would minimize his costs by relaxing standards, promoting from within, and hiring less experienced persons to replace those promoted. The theory is essentially one of »hoarding« of skilled or experienced labor in recessions because of the costs of rehiring such workers in subsequent recoveries.

It should be noted that both of these models account for differential shifts in demand for different grades of labor by the same employer; they do not take account of shifts in the composition of demand for workers occasioned by corresponding shifts in the composition of demand for final products as the result of a change in aggregate demand. It is possible, for example, that cyclical variations in the demand for low paid, unskilled workers in service trades would be less, say, than in industries such as durable goods manufacturing, where skill levels may be higher, simply because of a smaller relative decline in the demand for services. Creamer, for example, found that the smallest amplitude in fluctuations of labor income were in service industries and the largest in commodity-producing industries [pp. 111–12].

The preceding theories are also not applicable to the self-employment (business, professional, and farm) income component of earnings. It is well known that this share is subject to more cyclical variability than wages and salaries. For contractual wage payments Creamer's findings were consistent with the theories just discussed: wage payments in manufacturing industries fluctuated more than payments to general salaried personnel, and the latter fluctuated more than the salaries of executive and professional personnel. The greatest fluctuations of any share in personal income, on the other hand, were in the net income of farm and nonfarm proprietors [pp. 111–12]. A good part of the reason for this, of course, is the inability, at least in size distributions, to exclude the property or profit component from such income, so as to make it more nearly equivalent to wage and salary income, as earnings from human labor. Since self-employment income is concentrated in the upper part of both the earnings and income distributions,[3] its greater cyclical variability tends to mitigate increased inequality in the distribution of (contractual) labor incomes.

Earnings Inequality and Unemployment: A Simulation Model

The last decade has seen a considerable amount of empirical work on the relation between inequality and such macroeconomic variables as the level of employment, the rate of inflation, and the rate of growth of total output. The studies differ considerably in conceptual framework, methods used, and data sources employed, making comparisons of results difficult. While space is lacking for a complete review of such literature, examination of some of the similarities and differences as they relate to our own study may serve as a useful introduction.

1. *The recipient unit:* Some studies are concerned with inequality among families (or subcomponents of families [Metcalf]) or consumer units (families plus unrelated individuals); others, with persons, or sometime persons with income or

earnings [Schultz]. While it is easier to interpret a family distribution in terms of welfare than a persons distribution, there are problems in adjusting consumer unit distributions for differences in family size and composition, particularly over time, although such adjustments have been carried out by some investigators [Gramlich]. Our results are presented both for persons (with earnings) and for consumer units, without an adjustment for differences in family size.

2. *The income concept:* Some authors use the income concept implied in the data source, usually current money income [Schultz] or some simple extensions of it [Budd and Seiders]; others try to adjust it to some longer run measure of economic status or »permanent« income [Nordhaus]. Some adjustment is called for if a longitudinal study is used as the data base [Gramlich; Mirer (1973A)]. Our study is limited to the earnings component (wages and salaries plus self-employment income) of total money income as reported in Census field surveys; no attempt was made to convert the resulting measure of annual earnings to some »permanent« concept. Adjustment for underreporting of income so characteristic of field surveys was not attempted either in our study or in the others cited, although underreporting of earnings is a much less serious problem (except possibly for farm income) than for property income or transfer payments.

3. *Concept of inequality:* Some studies are confined to relative changes in distribution in a Lorenz curve sense [Schultz]; others encompass both changes in mean (dollar) incomes of groups and changes in relative inequality. Sometimes the two elements are distinguished and shown separately [Budd and Seiders; Mirer (1973B)]; in others the two are lumped together, sometimes implicitly. For example, studies of the number moving out of poverty as a result of a reduction in unemployment [Hollister and Palmer] combine the effect of a reduction in inequality at the lower end of the distribution with the effect of a general rise in personal income as a result of the expansion of output. In our study, the focus is on relative inequality and relative earnings: the earnings of recipient units and the mean earnings of groups relative to the mean for the distribution as a whole (or relative mean earnings).

4. *Measurement of inequality:* Some investigators use only one or two summary measures of inequality, such as the Gini concentration ratio (GCR) and the log variance [Schultz], or the proportion in poverty [Hollister and Palmer]; others present a broader set of measures or show their results for a whole set of different quantile groups [e.g., Beach; Nordhaus; Budd and Seiders]. Our results are presented in terms of changes in the relative mean incomes of selected quantile groups, as well as in GCR's.

5. *Ranking of recipient units:* In most studies recipient units in a given year are ranked by size of income in the same year; indeed, the data are usually available only in this form, e.g., CPS distributions for different years. In studies employing longitudinal data or using a simulation approach, it is often possible to determine how much difference the reranking of units makes to measuring the change in inequality [Budd and Seiders] or to provide a separate measure of how individual recipient units are moved about in the distribution as the result of a change in a macro variable [Nordhaus]. Separate measures of the reranking effect are not available for our study.

6. *Unemployment vs. inflation:* While most studies try to encompass the effect of both variables on income distribution, some concentrate on measuring only

one, e.g., Budd and Seiders are concerned only with changes in the inflation rate, with the level of employment held constant. In this study we examine only the effect of variations in the unemployment rate, with the inflation rate held constant.

7. *Research design:* Some investigations are confined to time series regression [Schultz; Metcalf; Beach; Hollister and Palmer]; others use time series regressions or other techniques to estimate a model of the economy or the income structure, and the parameters obtained are then used to simulate the effect of unemployment and/or inflation on a micro data file [Budd and Seiders; Nordhaus; Mirer (1973B)]; two other studies utilize the results of a longitudinal survey as well as employing a simulation technique [Gramlich; Mirer (1973A)].

It may be useful to present a brief summary of our own procedures before discussing each of the steps in more detail. First, the individual adults with earnings in the microdata file used for the simulation (the 1967 Survey of Economic Opportunity or SEO for income year 1966) were classified into some 160 groups or cells based on selected socio-economic characteristics (sex, race, age, and occupation) and the relative mean earnings of each was computed. Second, a time series covering the postwar period for frequencies and total earnings for each cell was estimated from published CPS tabulations. Since for most years data for only the margins or rims (distributions cross-tabulated by fewer than the four characteristics used) were available, a method had to be developed for estimating the frequencies and earnings for the missing cells and the estimation carried out. Third, relationships between changes in unemployment and relative mean earnings for each cell were estimated by regressing percentage changes in such earnings on the unemployment rate and the percent change in the implicit price deflator for GNP. Fourth, the effect of an assumed change in the unemployment rate on the distribution of relative mean earnings was estimated by applying the appropriate coefficients or »realization rates« obtained in the preceding step to the earnings of each adult in the SEO file. Fifth, earners were reranked by size of earnings, and relative mean earnings by selected quantile groups (deciles and the top 1 percent) for the simulated distribution were calculated and compared with those for the initial distribution. Earners were also assembled into their respective families and the distributions of consumer units before and after the simulation were compared. The accompanying flow chart (Figure 2) may make the sequence easier to visualize.

The two major data sources used in construction of the model were the Survey of Economic Opportunity for 1967, covering among other things the work experience and incomes during the year 1966 of those surveyed, and published tabulations from the Current Population Survey for the postwar years, 1948–1970. There are a number of problems and limitations in the use of such surveys in economic research which will not be explored here, although problems for our own research were the absence in the CPS of data for all postwar years on years of schooling and on work experience in the year preceding the survey, and the absence of tabulations of earnings (exclusive of property income and transfers) as distinguished from total money income. Indeed, it would be useful on conceptual grounds to have drawn distinctions among the effect, on annual earnings, of changes in unemployment, part-period employment, part-time work, and changes in wage rates or average hourly earnings, since each has its own

16

Figure 2 Illustrative flow diagram for simulation model of the effects of changes in unemployment on the size distribution of earnings

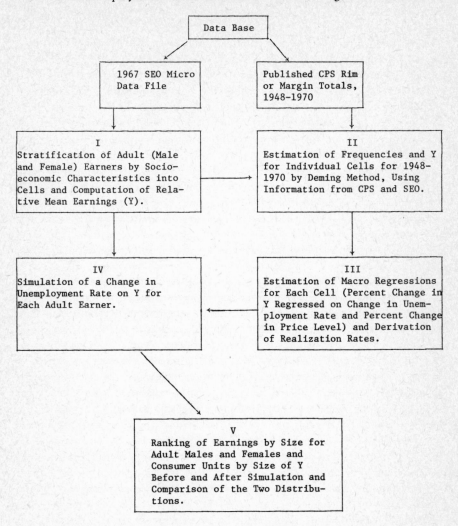

effect on the cyclical variability of earnings. Although there are some data on weeks worked and on full- or part-time for longest job held last year in the CPS and/or SEO, it is difficult, if not impossible, to unscramble these separate effects from the data provided in either. Our study was therefore confined to their combined effect on annual earnings. Most of the unemployed are covered in the study, since it is unlikely they would have been unemployed for a full calendar year and hence report zero earnings in the field survey.

Turning next to the problem of stratifying cells, perhaps the best method of estimating the cyclical variability of earnings at different points in the size distribution would be to classify workers initially by size of earnings and follow those workers by means, say, of a longitudinal study through the course of a cycle to determine the variation in their earnings, an approach analogous to that of Mirer [1973 (A)] and Gramlich [1974]. Such an approach is ruled out if data from surveys covering different samples of individuals in different years are to be used. An alternative is to group earners in each year's survey on the basis of those common socio-economic characteristics that would capture differences in earnings levels and in their sensitivity to cyclical fluctuations. Earning power is clearly related to such factors as ability and aptitude; personality traits such as motivation, perseverance, and habits of work; education and training (both formal and on-the-job); and experience. [Lydall, 1968, ch. 4] Unfortunately, there are no characteristics in the CPS which can directly capture a number of these factors, e.g., on-the-job training and experience, although age and occupation might provide indirect measures of the latter. Data on years of schooling do not go back sufficiently far in the CPS to permit the use formal education as a classifying variable.

The stratifying variables selected were sex, race, age, and occupation, each being defined in the same way in the SEO and the CPS. Adult earners in the SEO were divided into male and female subpopulations and cross-classified by race (the ith characteristic), age (the jth characteristic) and occupation (the kth characteristic). For both subpopulations two race and five age groups were used, plus nine occupations for males and seven for females, producing a total of 90 cells for males and 70 for females, 160 in all.

The effect of sex on the level and variability of earnings is generally recognized, even apart from its evident relation to discrimination. Because of family responsibilities, working wives and female heads tend to be restricted more to part-time and/or part-period work and hence to lower paying occupations. Temporary withdrawals from the labor force associated with childbearing also tend to restrict the extent of their experience and the amount of their investment in human capital via on-the-job training. The relation between race and differentials in earnings and in unemployment rates is also relatively clear. The simple constancy of the nonwhite/white unemployment ratio through the cycle implies that employment fluctuates by a greater proportion for nonwhites than whites. Early environmental factors, the quality and quantity of schooling available to nonwhites, discrimination both before and after entering the labor force, all tend to limit the amount nonwhites are willing to invest in human capital and to restrict the majority of them to relatively low skill jobs requiring only limited experience.

The importance of age as a predictor of earnings levels and their cyclical variability is fairly obvious. Age is an indicator of, indeed often used as a proxy for, the amount of experience and the extent of on-the-job training. Levels of ability and degrees of responsibility are undoubtedly a function of age, making an employer less willing to lay off such workers in recessions. Older workers, on the other hand, are faced with a shorter expected employment span and may be more vulnerable to layoffs. In terms of the underlying rationale, there seemed to be little value in retaining both the 35—44 and 45—54 age classes, and they were therefore combined into one group, resulting in five age classes: (1) 14—24; (2) 25—34; (3) 35—54; (4) 55—64; (5) 65 years and older.

Finally but by no means least, is the importance of stratification by occupation. It should help to pick up the influence of the basic factors referred to earlier, such as education and on-the-job training, insofar as these help to determine occupational choice and attainment. Cyclical variations in aggregate demand will affect different occupations differently, resulting in variations in the relative earnings of different occupational groups.

The occupational classes used by the Bureau of the Census in its annual tabulations of the CPS, however, are broadly defined and include workers of varied skill, educational achievement, and hierarchical status, thus limiting the usefulness of occupation as a stratifying variable. For this reason, it would have been preferable to have subdivided occupations by such variables as earnings size or self-employment status, but such further cross-classifications were not available in the tabulations with which we had to work. Furthermore, because of small sample sizes in certain classes, it was necessary to collapse the 11 major classes used by the Census into 9 for males and 7 for females. For males, private household workers and service workers were combined into one class, and farm and nonfarm laborers into another. For females, on the other hand, craftsman and operatives were consolidated into one group, while farm and nonfarm laborers, service workers, farmers and farm managers were all combined into another.

Finally, we excluded a 12th occupational category employed by Census — unemployed and not in the labor force — which includes those unemployed during the week preceding the survey week in the CPS and those unemployed during the entire calender year in the SEO, as well as persons, such as housewives and students, who are not active participants in the labor force. While the exclusion of the latter was consistent with the purposes of our study, it would have been preferable, had we had a method and the data for doing it, to have assigned the temporarily unemployed in this category to their normal occupations.

While the mean earnings for each of the 160 cells relative to the mean of the distribution as a whole could easily be computed from the SEO tape, data for estimating the time series of relative mean earnings for postwar years that was used in the subsequent regression analysis could be obtained only from CPS tabulations of money income by selected socioeconomic characteristics. Certain difficulties in using the CPS data should, however, be pointed out. First, while earnings (wages and salaries plus self-employment income) were directly available from the SEO file, the CPS distributions are tabulated by size of money income, which, in addition to earnings, includes transfer payments and property income. CPS money income therefore had to be accepted as a proxy for the earnings variable we were interested in. This may not be as bad a proxy as one might think. Differential underreporting of property and transfer incomes tends to convert the CPS into a distribution of earnings. In the 1973 CPS, for example, 95 percent of all earnings, but only three-quarters of all transfer payments, and well under one-half of property income — perhaps only a third of interest and dividends — were reported (or assigned to nonrespondents) [Current Population Reports, P-60, No. 97, p. 180]. While earnings in the same year were 75 percent of personal income as measured in the national income accounts, they were 80 percent of the Census total money income control and 85 percent of the money income actually reported in the 1973 Survey. Property income, on the other hand, was 13 percent of personal income, 9 percent of the money income control, and a little over 4 percent of income actually reported.

Another problem relates to the frequencies used in the occupational classification. In the SEO each earner is classified on the basis of his longest job in the preceding year, whereas the corresponding information in the CPS is available back only to 1958. It was therefore necessary to substitute the CPS tabulations on occupation last week. The occupation at which a person was employed in the week prior to the survey may not necessarily have been the longest job last year in which his primary earnings were obtained, and the frequencies tabulated on the two different bases need not correspond. In general, frequencies based on the last week definition in the CPS for 1966 were less than those based on the longest job held last year in the SEO. While such an underestimate might result in an overestimate of the mean earnings of a cell, it would affect estimates of cyclical variability of such earnings only if the degree of understatement of frequencies itself showed a cyclical pattern. To check this possibility, we compared the CPS occupational totals for 1970 (a year of recession) with those for 1969 (a year of prosperity) for both the last week and the last year definitions. The results were mixed, with the last week definition showing a greater proportionate decline in frequencies relative to the last year definition in five occupations, and a smaller decline, in four. The results lend some support to our procedure, although the potentiality for error remains.

A final problem was the absence in the published CPS tabulations for persons of cross-tabulations of income and frequencies by all the characteristics we wished to use, other than the male-female breakdown, e.g., only $Y_{i..n}$ or $Y_{..kn}$ is published (the nth characteristic being sex). An estimating method was therefore required which would allow us to infer the cross-classified frequencies and incomes for the postwar years by using the available information in the CPS and the SEO. The end product of the method employed should be a set of cell frequencies or income aggregates that when summed will equal the controls provided by the published CPS rim totals.

Deming (1943) gives a normal equation estimation which provides a solution to the present problem.[4] What is desirable about this method is that it allows one to estimate the CPS population and income aggregates for a given cell, given only the frequencies and income aggregates for each characteristic taken by itself, e.g., the rim total $f_{i..}$, separately for males and females, as well as complete knowledge of rim totals and cross-classified cell frequencies and earnings in the 1966 SEO. After the estimation was carried out, the CPS cell estimates agreed with the constraints given by ratios of cross-tabulations to the totals (rims) available in the SEO.

The problem and its solution can be described for our three dimensional estimation. Here the frequencies F_{ijk} and the rim totals $F_{i..}$, $F_{.j.}$, $F_{..k}$ are obtained from the SEO data file while only $f_{i..}$, $f_{.j.}$, $f_{..k}$ are known from the published CPS with the crossed cell frequencies f_{ijk} to be estimated. The three constraints to be met are:

$$\sum_{jk} f_{ijk} = f_{i..}\,, \qquad \sum_{ik} f_{ijk} = f_{.j.}\,, \qquad \sum_{ij} f_{ijk} = f_{..k}\,. \tag{1}$$

The sum of squares to be minimized is

$$S = \sum \frac{\left[f_{ijk} - F_{ijk}\right]^2}{F_{ijk}} \tag{2}$$

Solving the following normal equations (3) for the Lagrange multipliers, λ's, the crossed cell frequencies can be determined by substitution into equation (4).

$$F_{i..}\lambda_{i..} + \sum_j F_{ij.}\lambda_{.j.} + \sum_k F_{i.k}\lambda_{..k} = f_{i..} - F_{i..} \qquad (3)$$

$$\sum_i F_{ij.}\lambda_{i..} + F_{.j.}\lambda_{.j.} + \sum_k F_{.jk}\lambda_{..k} = f_{.j.} - F_{.j.}$$

$$\sum_i F_{i.k}\lambda_{i..} + \sum_j F_{.jk}\lambda_{.j.} + F_{..k}\lambda_{..k} = f_{..k} - F_{..k}$$

$$f_{ijk} = F_{ijk}(1 + \lambda_{i..} + \lambda_{.j.} + \lambda_{..k}). \qquad (4)$$

The same method was employed to estimate the frequency of dollar income aggregates for each of the cross-classified units for the same postwar years. Here the unknow values, Y_{ijk}, were estimated given the information on rim total earnings from CPS and SEO sources and the cross-classified earnings information from the SEO.[5] These estimates gave us the necessary information to calculate relative mean earnings for each of the 160 cells for the 1948–1970 period.

The next step was to specify and run the regressions needed to obtain estimates of the realization rate for each cell. The dependent variable used in the regression was the percentage change in the relative mean income of each cell, $\%\overline{dy}_{ijkn}$, where

$$\overline{y}_{ijkn} = \frac{Y_{ijkn}}{\overline{Y}} \quad (5) \text{ and} \quad \frac{\left[\dfrac{\overline{Y}_{ijkn}}{\overline{Y}}\right]_t - \left[\dfrac{\overline{Y}_{ijkn}}{\overline{Y}}\right]_{(t-1)}}{\left[\dfrac{\overline{Y}_{ijkn}}{\overline{Y}}\right]_{(t-1)}} = \%dy_{ijkn}, \qquad (6)$$

$\overline{Y}$ being the mean for males and females combined.

In the regressions percentage changes in the relative mean income for a cell ($\%\overline{dy}_{ijk}$) was specified to be linearly related to the percentage point change in the unemployment rate (dU) and the percent change in the implicit price deflator for GNP $(\%dP)$, resulting in the following first difference equation:

$$\%dy_{ijkn} = A_o + B_1(dU) + B_2(\%dP), \qquad (7)$$

which was estimated by ordinary least squares.

Regression results obtained for the price variable were unsatisfactory. Nearly all of the B_2 coefficients lacked significance at any arbitrarily selected confidence level, and they were therefore not used as realization rates for simulating the effect of changes in the inflation rate on the earnings distribution. The significance tests came out considerably better for the unemployment variable. A time trend variable introduced into the initial equation was dropped, since it had only a negligible effect on the B_1 coefficients or their significance and did not improve the results for the B_2's.

21

The signs of the B_1 coefficients, used for the unemployment realization rates, in most cases were consistent with theoretical expectations, although there were some exceptions. For white males the coefficients were, as expected, positive for professional workers, clerical workers, and craftsman, and negative for sales workers, operatives, and laborers. The negative coefficients for the managerial class can probably be accounted for by the rather large proportion of self-employed in the class and the greater cyclical variability of self-employment incomes. Some of the results for nonwhite males, on the other hand, are puzzling. While the professional, managerial, and craftsmen classes all had positive realization rates, those for laborers and operatives were also positive, and for sales workers, mixed. While better results for these latter groups might have been obtained had we been able to exclude transfers from the CPS income concept, they suggest that race is not as good a predictor of earnings variability for males as we had anticipated. Since the theory, as noted earlier, is not really applicable to service workers, the negative coefficients for whites and the positive ones for nonwhites can be accepted, although it is surprising that they did not both have the same sign.

The results for females also tended to support theoretical expectations. Professional and clerical workers had strong positive realization rates, and sales workers and operatives, negative ones. Unlike their male counterparts, female craftsman had negative coefficients, and laborers, positive ones, although these results should not be taken too seriously in view of the smallness of the underlying sample sizes for these two groups. Coefficients for service and private household workers were positive. As noted already, there is no theoretical presumption as to what sign the coefficients for these two occupations should have. A positive sign would suggest less cyclical sensitivity in the demand for service workers and a smaller impact from increased competition for jobs at the bottom of the labor market due to excess labor supply generated by increased unemployment in other occupations.

Realization rates for cells covering over 60 percent of the males and 80 percent of the females were significant at a one tail 75 percent confidence level. So far as statistical acceptance was concerned, there were several alternatives open to us. One was to accept all coefficients passing the above confidence level and accept the hypothesis that the others were zero. A second was a substitute for a rejected cell coefficient, a coefficient for one of the rim totals contiguous to the cell, e.g., the .jkth rim for the ijkth cell, if, say, the nonwhite coefficient was not significant and the rim coefficient was. A final alternative was to use all coefficients in the simulations, regardless of their significance levels. Rather than settle the matter on a priori grounds, we carried out simulations for all three alternatives. There was virtually no difference among them, each method producing about the same after-simulation Lorenz curve. The tables containing our results are for the first alternative.

For the simulations, the earnings of each adult in the SEO file was adjusted in accordance with the following equation,

$$Y' = Y [1 + B_1 dU], \qquad (8)$$

where Y is the SEO earnings of the adult worker; dU, the assumed change in the unemployment rate for simulation purposes; B_1, the realization rate for the cell applicable to the individual earner; and Y', the person's earnings after simulation. Two different increases in the unemployment rate — 2.2 and 4.2 percentage points — were assumed. Since the overall rate in 1966 was 3.8 percent, this amounted to assuming rates of 6 and 8 percent respectively.

After simulation, earners were reranked by size of Y' and the corresponding Lorenz distributions derived. The results, shown separately for males and females, are given in Table 1 for deciles and the top 1 percent of recipients, together with the Gini concentration ratio (GCR). (The table is expressed in terms of levels of, changes in, and percent changes in relative mean incomes; decile shares and changes in shares can be read off simply by moving the decimal point one place to the right. The relative mean income and the share of the top 1 percent are, of course, identical.) For the consumer unit distributions shown in Table 2, adult earners who were members of families were combined into their appropriate families and their earnings summed to obtain the family's earnings. Families and unrelated individuals were then ranked by size of earnings (before and after simulation) and divided into the same quantile groups as used in Table 1.

The simulation of increased unemployment on the distribution of male earnings produced an increase in overall inequality, at least as measured by the GCR. There is, on the other hand, evidence of a Lorenz curve intersection: the bottom three deciles and the top decile gained at the expense of the 4th through 9th deciles, whose relative mean incomes declined. In addition, inequality within the top decile was reduced slightly, since the relative mean income of the 91st through 99th percentiles increased by greater percentages (.45 and .85) than did that of the top 1 percent (.32 and .55). The relative gain of the bottom deciles in these simulations is difficult to account for; part may simply reflect our inability to exclude the cushioning effect of transfers from the CPS.

For females there was an outward shift of the Lorenz curve, with no evidence of intersection, the bottom 90 percent losing relative to the top 10 percent. These results are consistent with the hypothesis that lower paid and less skilled female workers suffer greater percentage declines in earnings during a recession than the best paid, most skilled.

Finally, the effect of increased unemployment on the earnings distribution for consumer units are quite similar to those for the distribution of male earners: an increase in overall inequality as measured by the GCR; a Lorenz curve intersection, with the fourth through eighth deciles losing relatively to the bottom three and the top two; and a small reduction in inequality within the top decile. While our inability to exclude fully the effects of transfer payments may partially account for the relative gain of the bottom groups in two of our simulations, another possibility may be that earners at the bottom of the distribution, characterized by part-period and part-time employment even in good times and concentrated in low paid but cyclically less sensitive employments such as service trades, are not as much affected by recessions as those immediately above them in the distribution.

Our findings of an overall increase in inequality associated with an increase in unemployment are consistent with other studies of the relation between income distribution and unemployment cited earlier [e.g., Schultz; Metcalf; Hollister and Palmer; Beach], but the Lorenz curve intersection found for male earners and for consumer units is not.[6] The latter results more nearly parallel

Table 1 Simulation results for the Gini concentration ratio (GCR) and relative mean earnings ($\overline{y}$) for each decile and the top one percent of earners

MALES	1	2	3	4	5	6	7	8	9	10	TOP 1%	GINI
BASE	.02660	.17998	.42270	.66790	.85150	1.00387	1.16505	1.33517	1.60753	2.73965	5.8840	.41463
dU = 2.2	.02685	.18131	.42350	.66700	.84850	1.00046	1.16154	1.33372	1.60578	2.75120	5.9030	.41531
dU = 4.2	.02712	.18230	.42428	.66518	.84557	.99685	1.15770	1.33170	1.60403	2.76327	5.9168	.41623
Δ/dU = 2.2	.00025	.00133	.00080	−.00090	−.00300	−.00341	−.00351	−.00145	−.00175	.01155	.0190	.00068
Δ/dU = 4.2	.00052	.00232	.00158	−.00272	−.00593	−.00702	−.00735	−.00347	−.00350	.02362	.0328	.00160
%Δ/dU = 2.2	.93	.73	.19	−.13	−.35	−.34	−.30	−.11	−.11	.42	.32	.16
%Δ/dU = 4.2	1.92	1.27	.37	−.41	−.70	−.70	−.63	−.26	−.11	.86	.55	.38
FEMALES												
BASE	.01880	.11622	.24788	.43010	.66980	.95777	1.25463	1.56030	1.92606	2.81844	4.76300	.47922
dU = 2.2	.18662	.11600	.24726	.42856	.66807	.95383	1.24273	1.55610	1.92486	2.83975	4.82700	.48081
dU = 4.2	.01855	.11566	.24659	.42667	.66603	.94910	1.23920	1.55120	1.92227	2.86470	4.89970	.48256
Δ/dU = 2.2	−.00014	−.00022	−.00062	−.00154	−.00173	−.00394	−.01190	−.00420	−.00120	.02131	.06400	.00159
Δ/dU = 4.2	−.00025	−.00056	−.00129	−.00343	−.00377	−.00867	−.01543	−.00910	−.00379	.04626	.13670	.00334
%Δ/dU = 2.2	−.74	−.19	−.25	−.36	−.26	−.41	−.96	−.27	−.06	.75	1.33	.33
%Δ/dU = 4.2	−1.35	−.48	−.52	−.80	−.57	−.91	−1.25	−.59	−.19	1.62	2.79	.70

Key:
INITIAL = GCR and $\overline{y}$ for the initial (1967 SEO) distribution.
dU = GCR and $\overline{y}$ for the simulated distributions based on assumed increases in unemployment rate (dU) of 2.2 and 4.2 respectively.
Δ/dU = The change in GCR and $\overline{y}$ from the initial to the simulated distributions.
%Δ/dU = The percent change in GCR and $\overline{y}$ from the initial to the simulated distributions.

24

Table 2 Simulation results for the Gini concentration ratio (GCR) and relative mean earnings ($\bar{y}$) for each decile and the top one percent of consumer units

CONSUMER UNITS	1	2	3	4	5	6	7	8	9	10	TOP 1%	GINI
BASE	.08705	.33414	.53737	.69585	.83659	.97630	1.13262	1.32307	1.58722	2.48979	4.86900	.36497
dU = 2.2	.08823	.33622	.53828	.69389	.83436	.97346	1.12996	1.32083	1.58875	2.49602	4.87120	.36521
dU = 4.2	.08906	.33792	.43881	.69190	.83166	.97083	1.12712	1.31940	1.58975	2.50405	4.87340	.36578
Δ/dU = 2.2	.00118	.00208	.00091	-.00196	-.00223	-.00284	-.00266	-.00224	.00153	.00623	.00220	.00024
Δ/dU = 4.2	.00201	.00379	.00144	-.00395	-.00493	-.00547	-.00550	-.00367	.00254	.01426	.00441	.00081
%Δ/dU = 2.2	1.34	.62	.17	-.28	-.27	-.29	-.24	-.17	.1	.25	.05	.07
%Δ/dU = 4.2	2.26	1.12	.27	-.57	-.59	-.56	-.49	-.29	.16	.57	.09	.22

Key:
INITIAL = GCR and $\bar{y}$ for the initial (1967 SEO) distribution.
dU = GCR and $\bar{y}$ for the simulated distributions based on assumed increases in unemployment rate (dU) of 2.2 and 4.2 respectively.
Δ/dU = The change in GCR and $\bar{y}$ from the initial to the simulated distributions.
%Δ/dU = The percent change in GCR and $\bar{y}$ from the initial to the simulated distributions.

those of Mirer in his two studies of this problem [1973A and 1973B], although the intersection points and the size position of quantile groups gaining or losing relative to others differ from ours, as well as between his two studies. While Gramlich's longitudinal and simulation study suggests a uniform increase in inequality for male-headed families (black and white), his results for female heads indicate that »increases in overall unemployment...result in slightly larger percentage losses of income for middle-income families with female heads than for either poor or rich ones.« [Gramlich, p. 321.] Lorenz curve intersections have also been found in models simulating the effects of inflation on size distribution [e.g., Budd and Seiders; Mirer (1973B)].

While our study is consistent with the hypothesis that increased unemployment results in greater inequality in the distribution of income and earnings, the distributive effects seem small — a result this study has in common with some of those cited above. Part of the problem may well lie in the quality of the data bases with which we have to work, particularly the time series of CPS distributions [Budd, 1970, pp. 256–258], and the tenuous nature of some of the assumptions underlying the statistical methods employed. While a policy maker might choose to ignore these findings on the grounds that the distributional effects of recession appear to be so small, he should be reminded of the very substantial costs associated with the loss in real output itself. In any case, whatever the magnitude of the distributional effects, they appear to reinforce rather than offset the welfare loss from reduced output.

Notes

[1] Estimated from Mendershausen's Chart 8 by a method described briefly by Budd [1970, pp. 247–8]. Cf. Mendershausen, p. 42.

[2] See also Mincer [1962].

[3] In the BEA size distribution of personal income for 1964 (fully corrected for underreporting of income in the CPS) the top 1 percent of consumer units received 21 % of all self-employment income; the top 5 percent, 45 %; the top quintile, 66 %. The figures for non-farm self-employment income are 25 %, 50 % and 71 % respectively; for farm income, 5 %, 23 %, and 49 %. [Based on unpublished estimates of the Bureau of Economic Analysis; the data based on dollar income size brackets rather than quantiles can be approximated from Radner and Hinrichs, 1974, Tables 3, 5 and 12.]

[4] See also Scheuren [1973].

[5] In the computer program, an incremental estimation command was written so that the SEO was used to estimate stratified frequencies and dollar earnings for the 1966 and 1967 CPS cells. The estimated 1966 CPS cells were then used to estimate the 1965; the 1965 cells used to estimate the 1964; and so on back to 1948. Similarly, the estimated 1967 CPS cells were used to estimate the 1968 cells, with the incremental method carried forward to 1970.

[6] To be sure, the methods of some of the above investigators, e.g., Schultz, Hollister and Palmer, could not have detected such an intersection had it existed.

References

Beach, C. M., »Cyclical Impacts on the Personal Distribution of Income,« *Annuals of Economic and Social Measurement*, Winter 1976, v. 5 (1), 29–52.

Budd, E. C., »Postwar Changes in the Size Distribution of Income in the U.S.,« *Am. Econ. Rev.*, May 1970, v. 60 (2), pp. 247–60.

Budd, E. C., and Seiders, D. F., »The Impact of Inflation on the Distribution of Income and Wealth,« *Am. Econ. Rev.*, May 1971, v. 61 (2), pp. 128–138.

Budd, E. C., Radner, D. B., and Hinrichs, J. C., *Size Distribution of Family Personal Income: Methodology and Estimates for 1964*, Bureau of Economic Analysis Staff Paper No. 21, U. S. Department of Commerce, 1973.

Creamer, Damiel, *Personal Income During Business Cycles*, Princeton University Press, 1956.

Deming, W. E., *Statistical Adjustment of Data*, Wiley and Sons, N.Y., 1943.

Gramlich, E. M., »The Distributional Effect of Higher Unemployment,« *Brookings Papers on Economic Activity*, 1974 (2), pp. 293—336.

Hollister, R. G., and Palmer, J. L., »The Impact of Inflation on the Poor,« *Redistribution to the Rich and the Poor*, K. E. Boulding and M. Pfaff, ed.'s, Wadsworth Publishing Co., Belmont, Calif., 1972.

Kuznets, Simon, *Shares of Upper Income Groups in Income and Savings*, National Bureau of Economic Research, N. Y., 1953.

Lydall, Harold, *The Structure of Earnings*, Oxfort University Press, London, 1968.

Mendershausen, Horst, *Changes in Income Distribution During the Great Depression*, National Bureau of Economic Research, N. Y., 1946.

Mincer, Jacob, »On-the-Job Training: Costs, Returns, and Some Implications,« *Journal of Political Economy*, Oct. 1962, v. 70 (5; Part 2), pp. 50—79.

Mirer, T. W., »The Distributional Impact of the 1970 Recession,« *Rev. Econ. & Statistics*, May 1973 (A), v. 55 (2), pp. 214—224.

Mirer, T. W., »The Effects of Macroeconomic Fluctuations on the Distribution of Income,« *Review of Income and Wealth*, Dec. 1973 (B), series 19 (4)

Metcalf, C. E., »The Size Distribution of Personal Income During the Business Cycle,« *Am. Econ. Rev.*, Sept. 1969, v. 59 (4), pp. 657—668.

Nordhaus, W. D., »The Effects of Inflation on the Distribution of Economic Welfare,« *Journal of Money, Credit, and Banking*, Pt. II, Feb. 1973, v. 5 (1), pp. 465-504.

Oi, Walter, »Labor as a Quasi-Fixed Factor,« *Journal of Political Economy*, Dec. 1962, v. 70 (6), pp. 538—55.

Radner, D. B., and Hinrichs, J. C., »Size Distribution of Income in 1964, 1970, and 1971,« *Survey of Current Business*, Oct. 1974, pp. 19—31.

Reder, M.W., »The Theory of Occupational Wage Differentials,« *Am. Econ. Rev.*, Dec. 1955, v. 45 (5), pp. 833—852.

Reder, M. W., »Wage Differentials: Theory and Measurement,« *Aspects of Labor Economics*, H. G. Lewis, ed., Princeton University Press, 1962, pp. 257—317.

Reder, M. W., »Wage Structure and Structural Unemployment,« *Rev. Econ. Studies*, Oct. 1964, v. 31, pp. 309—22.

Scheuren, F. J., »Ransacking CPS Tabulations: Aplications of the Log Linear Model to Poverty Statistics,« *Annals of Economic and Social Measurement*, April 1973, v. 2 (2), pp. 159—182.

Schultz, T. Paul, »Seçular Trends and Cyclical Behavior of Income Distribution in the United States: 1944—1965,« *Six Papers on the Size Distribution of Income and Wealth*, Lee Soltow, ed., Studies in Income and Wealth, v. 33, 1969, pp. 75—100.

U. S. Bureau of the Census, *Current Population Reports, Consumer Income*, Series P—60, various issues.

U. S. Department of Commerce, Bureau of Economic Analysis, *Survey of Current Business*, various issues, and *The National Income and Product Accounts of the United States, 1929—1965*, a Supplement to the *Survey of Current Business*, 1966.

Wilhelm Krelle and Ralf Pauly
**Distributional Impacts of Public Expenditure Programs
and Tax Changes**

1. Introduction. The Problem

Most governments use fiscal policy i.e., changes of public expenditures and of
differential tax rates, as the main instrument to handle unemployment problems.
No doubt, this is effective as far as unemployment is concerned. However,
relatively little attention has been paid so far to the possible income distributional
effects of fiscal policy. Keynes, who initiated the use of this instrument, paid
little, if no attention to this problem; this was perhaps appropriate for the time
of the great depression. However, in our recent history, fiscal policy is still very
much appreciated as an instrument for maintaining (near) full-employment in
the face of fluctuating (private) economic activities. This, then introduced the
problem of income distributional questions, since the impact of a fiscal policy
measure affects the economic sectors in different ways. But in contrast to
Galbraith's belief (see [3], page 82) people are more concerned with real or
imaginary injustice of income distribution when the average income is higher then
when it is lower. In more industrialized economies the use of fiscal policy to cure
unemployment may soon become socially intolerable if it changes income distribution too much in favor of profit income, since the labor unions may react by
enforcing higher wages. Thus, at the end, fiscal policy may induce higher prices
rather then more employment.

This raises the following question: *How does fiscal policy influence the income
distribution?*

This problem should be analysed in the framework of an interdependent model
in order to take into account the effect of other variables (related to changes of
fiscal policy, e.g. of tax changes) on income distribution[1]. In this paper, the
functional distribution is the main topic. Of course, it would be highly desirable
to study the impact on the personal income distribution, too. But this is a task
to be taken up later. In the functional distribution, *gross distribution* between
wage and non-wage income (before taxes and transfer payments) and *net distribution* (after taxes and transfer payments) has to be differentiated. In gross as
well as in net distribution all profits may be considered (including those belonging
to the government) or only profits accruing to private capitalists or only profits
as far as members of the society in question are entitled to them (i.e., profits
going to foreign owners are excluded). Moreover, since the number of employed

and of selfemployed people might change as a result of changes in taxes and in government expenditures, gross and net distribution may be measured as the relation of gross or net wage income per employed person to gross or net non-wage income per selfemployed person.

This relation as a measure for the personal income distribution makes only sense if the »vertical distribution« (= »Querverteilung«, see Stobbe (7)) is insignificant, i.e., if in the average the wage income is the dominant part of the total income of an employed person and if in the average the profit is the dominant part of the total income of a selfemployed person. In the case of West Germany this holds true (see table 2 and the comment belonging to it, page 36).

Another interesting figure related to income distribution is the relative tax burden of wages and profits, and how will it be affected by fiscal policy.

The different measures of income distribution may not react in the same way on fiscal policy. For example, gross distribution may change little, but net distribution and the relative tax burden may change substantially. That is why we use several concepts of income distribution.

Economic theory gives conflicting answers to our problems depending on the assumptions made within the model. We review these answers in the next section 2. In section 3 the model used in this paper will be represented and outlined; it is an econometric forecasting model of 214 equations, called model 9.1 from now on.

In section 4 the simulations carried out by means of this model are explained in detail.

Section 5 presents the results.

2. What Do Economic Theory and Special Investigations Tell Us About the Distributional Effects of Fiscal Policy?

Unfortunately there are no clear cut answers to be derived from present day economic theory. We shall now outline the answers provided by the premises underlying first the neo-classical static theory, next the neo-classical growth theory, and finally the (perhaps more relevant) Keynesian type of distribution theory.

a. Neo-classical Static Theory

In this type of theory only gross distribution can be considered. The starting point is a neo-classical homogeneous of degree one production funktion

(1) $y = f(\pi A, K)$, $f' > 0$, $f'' < 0$, where

   y = net domestic product at factor cost (= NDP)
   A = labor
   K = capital
   π = technical progress factor

or

(1a) $\dfrac{y}{\pi A} = \varphi(k)$, $k = \dfrac{K}{\pi A}$, $\varphi' > 0$, $\varphi'' < 0$

29

By assuming perfect competition in all markets and profit maximizing of the entrepreneurs it is easily seen that the share V of gross wage income in NDP equals the elasticity of production ϵ_A with respect to labor:

$$(2) \quad V = \frac{\partial y}{\partial A} \cdot \frac{A}{y} = :\epsilon_A$$

For a Cobb-Douglas production function, $V = \epsilon_A$ is a constant fixed by technology. Generally, in neoclassical theory:

$$(3a) \quad \epsilon_A = 1-k \frac{\varphi'(k)}{\varphi(k)}, \quad \frac{d}{dk} [\varphi'(k)/\varphi(k)] > 0$$

and (because of cost minimization)

$$(3b) \quad k = \Psi(\tfrac{w}{r}), \quad \Psi > 0, \quad \text{where} \quad w = \text{real wage rate}$$
$$r = \text{real interest rate.}$$

Thus

$$(4) \quad V = \epsilon_A = \phi(\tfrac{w}{r}), \text{ and } \phi' \gtreqless 0.$$

Summing up: in the case of a Cobb-Douglas production function distribution cannot be changed by any sort of fiscal policy influencing aggregate demand, and $\phi' = 0$.

In all other cases fiscal policy may only influence the distribution of income if it changes the ratio of the real wage rate to the real profit rate. If there is no effect of this kind (which seems to be very likely in case of unemployment[2]), income distribution is not changed either. Otherwise there is an influence, but without further specification of the production function one cannot tell the direction of income distributional changes[3].

b. Neo-classical Growth Theory

In the simplest case with malleable capital and a given savings ratio s, the share V of wages in NDP on the equilibrium path is:

$$(5) \quad V = 1 - s\frac{r}{g}$$

where $r = \frac{\partial y}{\partial K}$ the rate of interest and g the equilibrium growth rate. We shall only consider equilibrium paths. If additional government expenditure is used to guarantee that demand equals supply on the full employment path — which is implied in neo-classical growth theory — there should be no effect on income distribution. Only if fiscal policy influences the saving which is used for extending productive capacity an effect on income distribution would occur. In general, only this (in relation to y) is meant by s. The effect is generally a negative one with respect to expenditure, because government spending, as a rule, would increase s. As may be seen from the above results neo-classical theory in its general form is not very well suited for our problem. It does not cover short run disequilibrium situations and does not include taxes and the government expenditures explicitely. It is more a supply oriented theory where demand is only rudimentary dealt with.

c. A Keynesian Type of Distribution Theory

Kaldors well known distribution formula may be extended to cover taxes and government expenditures explicitely. It is demand oriented but does not treat the supply side explicitely — just the opposite of the neo-classical type of theory. Let

$$(6a) \quad Y = L + Q + T_{ind} = C_{pr} + I_{pr} + G$$

be net domestic product at market prices (= NDP), where L = wage income, Q = profits, T_{ind} = indirect taxes, C_{pr} = private consumption, I_{pr} = private investment, G = government expenditure on goods and services.

Let indirect taxes be proportional to NDP, direct wage and profit taxes be proportional to wage and profit income (respectively), and let private consumption be proportional to net wage and net profit income. Let government expenditure G equal government income plus (or minus) an additional part $\overline{G}$ and let private investment be exogenous: $I_{pr} = \overline{I}$. The ratio $(\overline{I}+\overline{G})/Y$ is considered as a political decision variable independent of tax rates. We thus write

$$(6b) \quad T_{ind} = t_{ind} \cdot Y; \; C_{pr} = (1-s_L)(1-t_L)L+(1-s_Q)(1-t_Q)Q,$$
$$G = t_{ind} \cdot Y+t_L L+t_Q Q+\overline{G}, \text{ and } s_Q(1-t_Q) > s_L(1-t_L).$$

Using expressions (6a) and (6b) we obtain the share $\overline{V}$ of profits in NDP after some algebraic manipulations:

$$(7) \quad \overline{V}: = \frac{Q}{Y} = -\frac{s_L(1-t_L)(1-t_{ind})}{s_Q(1-t_Q)-s_L(1-t_L)} + \frac{1}{s_Q(1-t_Q)-s_L(1-t_L)} \cdot \frac{\overline{I}+\overline{G}}{Y}$$

From (7):

$$(7a) \quad \frac{\partial \overline{V}}{\partial(\overline{G}/Y)} = \frac{1}{s_Q(1-t_Q)-s_L(1-t_L)} > 0,$$

$$(7b) \quad \frac{\partial \overline{V}}{\partial t_{ind}} = \frac{s_L(1-t_L)}{s_Q(1-t_Q)-s_L(1-t_L)} > 0:$$

Higher government expenditures (relative to NDP) and higher indirect tax rates deteriorate the income distribution for labor.

But, unfortunately, no definite answer can be reached with respect to changes in the direct tax rate on wage and profit income. The effect of these changes on income distribution depends on the difference of the net savings ratios $s_Q(1-t_Q)(1-t_{ind})$ or $s_L(1-t_L)(1-t_{ind})$ (respectively) and the investment and surplus government expenditure ratio $(\overline{I}+\overline{G})/Y$:

$$(7c) \quad \frac{\partial \overline{V}}{\partial t_L} = \frac{s_L}{N^2} [s_Q(1-t_Q)(1-t_{ind}) - \frac{\overline{I}+\overline{G}}{Y}] \gtrless 0$$

$$(7d) \quad \frac{\partial \overline{V}}{\partial t_Q} = -\frac{s_Q}{N^2} [s_L(1-t_L)(1-t_{ind}) - \frac{\overline{I}+\overline{G}}{Y}] \gtrless 0,$$

31

where N: $= s_Q(1-t_Q) - s_L(1-t_L)$

Though this type of distribution theory gives some answers one may be in doubt to what extent they may be applicable in reality since the supply side is neglected, the theory is static, the tax system is oversimplified, private investment cannot be considered to be exogenous and so on.

d. Special Investigations

Recently Hake [4] has measured the redistributional effects of the government budget during a period of one particular year (1963) in the Federal Republic of Germany. He comes to the conclusion that government revenue as well as government expenditure reduce the income concentration.

Albers [1] shows that the redistribution of income intended by the tax rates as such is considerably reduced by tax-free parts of income, which results from tax evasion, deductions and exemptions. At best, the theories provide some qualitative statements on the direction of changes in income distribution due to fiscal policy. In many cases even this direction of change remains doubtful. Thus it appears disirable to analyse empirically such effects as the special investigations do. In our approach distributional impacts of public expenditure programs and tax changes are studied within the framework of an econometric model.

3. The Econometric Model 9.1 of the German Economy

Model 9.1 has been constructed with the special purpose in mind to simulate changes in the tax system and the system of transfer payments and government expenditures.[4] The main features of the model are described in the following subsections.

a. Model 9.1 in Outline

The economy is divided into a private and a government sector. Gross domestic product (GDP) is defined as the sum of private consumption, private fixed investment, private inventory investment, government consumption and investment and exports minus imports. The government sector is subdivided into the federal, state and local governments and into the social insurance system. The latter comprises seven subsystems, e.g. pension insurance and health insurance. Exports are subdivided into goods and services, imports into four categories of goods and into services. On the labor market employed as well as selfemployed persons in the private sector, and government employees are accounted for separately. Employed persons are categorized into blue collar workers and white collar workers and the blue collar workers into Germans and foreign workers. We distinguish within our model between employed persons as well as hours worked. The labor demand functions are derived from CES-type production functions. The consumption function is based on the permanent income hypothesis. The investment function follows the proposals made by Coen [2] which in turn takes up ideas from Jorgenson [5]. There are several price functions based on the assumptions of a representative monopolistic firm. As to the tax system, the model reproduces the tax laws as exactly as possible. It distinguishes six types of taxes:

  I. on wages (Lohnsteuer),
  II. on profit income of households (Einkommensteuer),
III. on profits of companies (Körperschaftsteuer),
IV. on wealth (Vermögensteuer),
  V. on consumption goods (Verbrauchssteuern),
      and
VI. other indirect taxes (mainly: the value added tax = Mehrwertsteuer).

The model comprises functions explaining the contribution of employed and self-employed persons to the different branches of the social insurance system, and the transfer payments between these branches, the government sectors, and the private households. Thus the public sector of the economy (including the social insurance system) is specified in great detail.

The *exogenous variables* of the model are the world market real demand, the world market prices in US dollar, the population in Germany (excluding foreign labor), labor force (excluding foreign labor), and the nominal wage rate[5]. Tax and government expenditure parameters are to be considered as instruments of the government.

Alltogether, the model consists of 141 definitional and 72 behavioral equations, i.e., 214 equations. Additional definitional equations to consider different concepts of income distribution are not counted.

b. Some Tax and Expenditure Functions in Detail

In order to illustrate the government revenues and expenditure functions, the tax function on wages and the consumption as well as the investment function are reproduced and commented upon here.

ba. Tax Function for Wage Income

Let y be the wage income, h(y) the size distribution of wage income, f(y) a function describing the admissible deductions and exemptions from the wage income y, and let $t(\cdot)$ be the tax rate applicable to the wage income after deductions and exemptions. Using these definitions the tax liabilities T_t of wage earners in period t is given by

$$(8) \quad T_t = \int_0^\infty t_t\left(y_t^{v}(y)\right) h_t(y)dy, \; t = 1,2,..., T,$$

where

$$t_t(y_t^{v}(y)) \; = \text{tax liabilities of a taxpayer with income y}$$

and

$$y_t^{v}(y) \; = \text{taxable income to which the tax rates are applied.}$$

The taxable income equals wage income minus deductions and exemptions[6]:

$$(9) \quad y_t^{v}(y) = \begin{cases} y - f_t(y), \text{ if } y > f_t(y) \\ \quad o \qquad \text{otherwise.} \end{cases}$$

The structure of the German income tax suggests to split up T_t into three parts. This structure may be characterised by the marginal tax rates t_t' $(y_t^V (y))$ at four levels of taxable income y^V:

income levels	$[0,A_t)$	$[A_t,B_t)$	$[B_t,C_t)$	$[C_t, \infty)$
marginal tax rates	0	β_t	progressive	γ_t .

To the limits A_t, B_t and C_t of taxable income y^V correspond limits A_t^f, B_t^f and C_t^f of wage income y. The limits A_t^f, B_t^f, C_t^f are determined by $A_t^f - f(A_t^f) = A_t$, $B_t^f - f(B_t^f) = B_t$ and $C_t^f - f(C_t^f) = C_t$, respectively. Thus (8) may be written as follows:

(10)
$$T_t = [\beta_t \cdot \int_{A_t^f}^{\infty} (y - A_t - f_t(y)) h_t(y)\, dy] +$$

$$+ [(t_t(C_t) - \beta_t \cdot (C_t - A_t)) \cdot \int_{C_t^f}^{\infty} h_t(y) dy + \int_{B_t^f}^{C_t^f} (t_t(y - f_t(y)) - \beta_t \cdot (y - f_t(y) - A_t).$$

$$h_t(y) dy] + [(\gamma_t - \beta_t) \cdot \int_{C_t^f}^{\infty} (y - f_t(y) - C_t) \cdot h_t(y) dy] \, .$$

The first expression in brackets on the right hand side of (10) reproduces the tax liabilities which applies to tax payers according to the marginal tax rate β; the marginal tax rate is multiplied by the total income minus total deductions. The second term additionally accounts for income $y \in [B_t^f, C_t^f)$, under the tax rate difference $t_t(y - f_t(y)) - \beta_t \cdot (y - f_t(y) - A_t)$, and the third term states the tax liabilities applicable to income $y \in [C_f, \infty)$ under the tax rate difference $\gamma_t - \beta_t$.

From equation (10) it is clear that only for the second expression in brackets the deduction function $f(y)$ and the income density function $h(y)$ have to be specified in the income range $[B,C]$. For this range the distribution function $h(y)$ may easily be approximated by the two parametric lognormal distribution.

Substitution of the unobservable variables in (10) by observable variables yields the following regression model:

(11) $TLXLGK_t = a\, R12_t + b \cdot R23_t + c + v_t$
where
$TLXLGK_t = T_t + u_{1t}$ = taxes on wage income

$$a\, R12_t + a' = [\beta_t \int_{A_t^f}^{\infty} (y - A_t - f_t(y))\, h_t(y) dy] + u_{2t},$$

$$b\, R23_t + b' = [\int_{B_t^f}^{C_t^f} t_t (t_t(y - f_t(y)) - \beta (y - f_t(y) - A_t) \cdot h_t(y) dy] + u_{3t},$$

R12 = approximation of the tax liabilities according to the marginal rate β_t

R23 = approximation of the tax liabilities for income $y \in [B^f, C^f)$ under the tax rate difference $t_t(y^V) - \beta(y^V - A)$

c = $a' + b'$, $v_t = u_{1t} - u_{2t} - u_{3t}$,

u_{1t}, u_{2t} and u_{3t} = random errors.

A few comments on the approximation should be added. The first regressor R 12 equals the marginal tax rate ß multiplied by the total income minus that part of deductions which could easily be explained. The part of deductions not taken into account is almost proportional to R12 in the estimation period. According to the proportion the coefficient »a« should be in the neigh-bourhood of 0.85. In the second expression in brackets the income distribution h(y) is approximated by the lognormal function. The deduction function has been neglected. We assumed that each taxpayer with income y greater than B_t has the same amount of deductions. Distribution functions in the estimation period show that only a few taxpayers have a wage income greater than C, so we could neglect the first part of the second term and the third term too. According to this approximation the parameter »b« should be near one and the parameter »c« should be relatively small.

Our (OLS) regression results are (in parantheses below parameter estimates the t-statistics are reproduced):

(12) $\text{TLXLGK} = 0.799 \text{ R12} + 1.292 \text{ R23} + 1.997 \quad R^2 = 0.9996$
$\phantom{(12) \text{TLXLGK} = } (34.42) \quad\quad (14.81) \quad\quad (6.96) \quad \text{DW} = 1.14.$

bb. Expenditure Functions for Consumption and Investment Expenditure of the Government.

The main determinants of government expenditure are the normal government income NE'GK (defined as tax receipts minus interest payments) and the previous expenditure A|1| (habit persistance hypothesis). The OLS regression for these functions of government consumption C'GK and investment I'GK respectively are:

(13) $\text{C'GK} = 0.530 \cdot \text{C'GK|1|} + 0.071 \cdot \text{NED'GK|1|} + 1.667 \quad R^2 = 0.960$
$\phantom{(13) \text{C'GK} = } (2.77) \quad\quad\quad (2.73) \quad\quad\quad\quad (1.039) \quad \text{DW} = 1.83$

and

(14) $\text{I'GK} = 0.655 \cdot \text{I'GK|1|} + 0.064 \cdot \text{NED'GK} + 0.230 \quad R^2 = 0.962$
$\phantom{(14) \text{I'GK} = } (2.90) \quad\quad\quad (1.56) \quad\quad\quad (0.18) \quad \text{DW} = 1.35$

where $\text{NED'GK} = (\text{NE'GK} + \text{NE'GK|1|})/2.$

c. Reliability of the Model

The reliability of the model may be judged under different aspects:

1. From the statistical figures for the fitting of the behavior equations. In general, these figures are quite satisfactory;

2. From the deviations of the actual and the calculated figures in the reference period. These % deviations are reproduced in table 1 for some important economic variables; for more detail we refer to Krelle and Pauly [7];

Table 1 % Deviation of the Observed from the Estimated Value[1]

Variable \ Year	1961	62	63	64	65	66	67	68	69	70	71	72	73
YR = real GDP	4.9	3.2	1.9	2.3	2.6	0.7	-1.2	-3.4	3.1	3.6	4.6	-0.2	1.7
P = GDP deflator for the private sector	1.3	2.3	1.5	0.7	0	-0.9	-3.6	-4.9	-5.1	-1.8	o.7	1.0	0.3
TL'LGK = tax on wages = Lohnsteuer	-2.6	-3.9	-1.9	-2.8	1.5	0.2	-3.7	-1.6	-2.4	0.7	-0.6	2.8	o.4
L = wage bill	1.7	1.7	3.2	1.7	2.3	1.5	-1.5	-3.6	1.1	2.6	4.7	0.6	3.2
Q.PR = profits in the private sector	16.1	11.6	2.5	4.1	3.1	-4.2	-12.9	-14.9	-9.1	1.8	7.8	-0.2	-0.1

[1] The model runs free from 1961 to 1973 without interference and adaptation. The exogenous variables (= world market demand, world market prices, the German population and the nominal wage rate) are set at their actual values.

Table 2 Breakdown of a Private Householder's Income in Germany, 1969[1]

professional classification	Number of householder's (Mill.)	gross income per household per month (DM)	thereof: wage and salary incomes	profit income	rents and income from other sources
selfemployed in agriculture	.765	1884	189	1531	165
selfemployed outside agriculture	1.568	2969	205	2647	117
civil servant	1.229	2117	1837	156	125
white collar workers	3.576	2103	1821	150	131
blue collar workers	6.323	1617	1372	114	131
not gainfully employed	7.079	949	136	124	689
Sum total or average (respectively)	20.540	1614	919	372	323

[1] Source: M. Euler, Zusammensetzung und Verteilung des Einkommens privater Haushalte 1969, Wirtschaft und Statistik, Heft 12 (1972), p. 708.

For further informations see G. Göseke and K.D. Bedau, Verteilung und Schichtung der Einkommen der privaten Haushalte in der Bundesrepublik Deutschland 1950 bis 1975, Deutsches Institut für Wirtschaftsforschung, Beiträge zur Strukturforschung, Heft 31, 1974.

3. From the deviations of actual and calculated figures in a true forecasting period. Forecasts have been made with the model until 1985; see Krelle and Pauly [7]. These forecasts show that the model is stable and produces reasonable results for the future.

In our judgement the ex post-forecasts are sufficiently accurate, so that we place some confidence in the results obtained by using this system.

4. Simulations with Model 9.1

In order to estimate the distributional effects of fiscal policy, Model 9.1 has been solved for 1965 to 1974 under different assumptions on tax and expenditure policy of the government. By comparing the different hypothetical developments of the economic variables under these assumptions, the effects of different fiscal policies are outlined.

The alternative policies analysed in this paper are presented in table 3 (page 38, 39). They are partly motivated by the discussion on indexing taxes and other nominal rates in order to avoid the distorting effects of inflation; see the Beiratsgutachten [9].

As already mentioned in section 1 there are different measures of income distribution. Though a number of other measures have been calculated also, only the measures listed in table 4 (page 41) will be considered in this paper. In order to get an idea how fiscal policy affects the economy as a whole, the impact of fiscal policy on other variables is considered, too.

The proportion of the average income of an employed person to the average income of a selfemployed person is a rough measure for the distribution of personal income. To this measure the wage income per employed person over profit income per selfemployed person is only a good approximation if the »vertical income distribution« (= Querverteilung) is small, i.e. if wage income is in the time period of analysis the dominant part of total income of an employed person and profit income is the dominant part of total income of a selfemployed person. Table 2 gives an idea about the »vertical distribution« for West-Germany in the year 1969. According to this table the employed persons in total receive indeed 21 % of the profits (the selfemployed persons in total receive only 3 % of the wages) but the average monthly wage income 1 623 DM of an employed person only slightly differs by the amount of 89 DM from average income 1 712 DM of an employed person. With respect to a selfemployed person however, the deviation is relative high. The average monthly profit income 2 902 DM deviates by the amount of 421 DM from the average income 2 481 DM. Thus, the approximation should be used with care.

5. Results

Before starting with the distributional impacts of fiscal policy it is appropriate to look at the effects on the gross domestic product (GDP), employment and the total tax burden. These effects coincide with those put forth by economic theory.

Table 3 Alternative Variations of Fiscal Policy

Variation	changes with respect to the normal ex post-forecast	
	verbal description	changes in equations (starting 1965 untill 1974)
[0] = normal ex post-forecast	1)	
[1]	a) The tax rate on wage income is changed in such a way that the deflated tax burden does not depend on the rate of inflation [2)] b) Government expenditure is a function of government income (varied by the changed tax rates) as in the normal ex post-forecast	a) Equation (E.71) $M=LOG(1000 \cdot ML)-0.5 \cdot S^2$ has been replaced by $M=LOG(1000 \cdot ML)-LOG(PC'PR/108.5)$ $-0.5 \cdot S^2$ and E(64) $TLXLGK=0.799 \cdot R12+1.292 \cdot RX23 \cdot \cdot ETU+1.993$ has been replaced by $TLXLGK=0.799 \cdot R12+1.292 \cdot RX23D \cdot \cdot ETU \cdot PC'PR/108.5+1.993$ [2)] b) All expenditure functions remain unchanged
[2]	a) The tax rate on wage income is changed in such a way that it applies to deflated wage income. In this case the deflated tax burden declines with inflation. [2)] b) See variation [1]	a) Equation (E.71) has been changed as in 1 a) and Equation (E.64) has been changed to $TLXLGK=0.799 \cdot R12 \cdot 108.5/PC'PR+ +1.292 \cdot RX23D \cdot ETU+1.993$ [2)] b) See variation [1]
[3]	a) change of the tax rate on wages as in variation [1] b) government expenditures (in current DM) are the observed ones	a) See variation [1] b) Variables L'GK,C'GK,I'GK,ÆB'GKU TRS'GKW,TR'GKSV,VS'GKPR are fixed on their actual values from 1965 to 1974
[4]	a) change of the tax rate on wage income as in variation [2] b) government expenditures (in current DM) are the observed ones	a) See variation [2] b) See variation [3]

[1] Definition of the normal ex-post-forecast, see note 1 to table 1
[2] The indexation of the income tax tarif is explained in detail in the note at the end of table 3

Note to table 3: Indexation of the income tax tarif

Given the income tax tarif $t_d(\cdot)$ the intended direct tax burden for a taxpayer with deflated income y_d in the basic period is $t_d(y_d)/y_d$. With a progressive tarif $t_d(\cdot),(t_d(y \cdot a) \geqslant a \cdot t_d(y), a \geqslant 1)$ the change of the tax burden $\Delta C_t(y_d)$ caused by inflation with the rate $(1+\alpha_t)$ is:

(1) $\qquad \Delta C_t(y_d) = \dfrac{t_d((1+\alpha_t) \cdot y_d)/(1+\alpha_t)}{y_d} \geqslant \dfrac{t_d(y_d)}{y_d}$.

From (1) one can easily determine the adjustment of the tarif such that the inflation will not change the tax burden. The adjusted tarif $t_d^{nb}((1+\alpha_t) \cdot y_d)$ is:

(2) $\qquad t_d^{nb}((1+\alpha_t) \cdot y_d) = (1+\alpha_t) \cdot t_d(y_d).$

In order to lower the inflation rate one may argue that inflation should not increase the government's income. This is automatically insured by the following adjustment:

(3) $\qquad t_d^{ni}((1+\alpha_t) \cdot y_d) = t_d(y_d).$

5	a) change of the tax rate on wage income as in variation **1**. b) government expenditures (in current DM) remain the same as actually observed with the exception of government consumption C'GK and government investment I'GK for the depression years 1966 and 1967. For these years additional government expenditures are supposed.	a) see variation **1** b) Variables L'GK, TRS'GKH, TRS'GKW, TR'GKSV, SB'GKU, VS'GKPR are fixed at their actual values from 1965 to 1974. For the variables C'GK and I'GK the same applies for 1965 and 1968 to 1974. The additional government expenditure in the years 1966 and 1967 are (in bill. DM): 1966 1967 C'GK + 3 + 3 I'GK + 3 + 5
6	a) change of the tax rate on wage income as in variation **2**, b) government expenditures fixed as in variation **5**.	a) see variation **2** b) see variation **5**
7	a) change of the tax rate on wage income as in variation **1** b) government expenditures as in variation **5** with the exception that in the boom years 1970 to 1974 government consumption C'GK and government investment I'GK are reduced.	a) see variation **1** b) variables L'GK, TRS'GKH, TRS'GKW, TR'GKSV, SB'GKU, VS'GKPR are fixed at their actual values from 1965 to 1974. For the variables C'GK and I'GK the same applies for 1965, 1968 and 1969. For the other years C'GK and I'GK has been raised or reduced from their actual values by the following amounts (in bill.DM): 1966 1967 1970 1971 1972 1973 1974 C'GK +3 +3 -1 -2 -2 -4 -4 I'GK +3 +5 -1 -1 -1 -2 -2
8	a) change of the tax rate on wage income as in variation **2** b) government expenditures as in variation **7** with the exception that the cut in expenditure has been increased.	a) see variation **2** b) see variation **7**, the cut in expenditure in bill.DM is: 1970 1971 1972 1973 1974 C'GK -1 -4 -5 -6 -8 I'GK -1 -4 -5 -6 -8

Due to the approximation of the income distribution by the lognormal function, the effects of these adjustments can be analysed without complications. The deflated income $Y_d = Y/(1+\alpha_t)$ is lognormally distributed. For the variable Y_d only the parameter M of the lognormal distribution function $LN_Y(M,S)$ changes to $M_d=M-LOG(1+\alpha_t)$ (Y_d distributed as $LN_{Y_d}(M_d,S)$). If the inflation α_t is measured by

$$1+\alpha_t = PC'PR/108.5$$

where

PC'PR = current price index of consumer goods and 108.5 = price index of consumer goods in the year 1965, the equation (E.71) from model 9.1 changes to $M_d = LOG(1000 \cdot ML) - LOG(PC'PR/108.5) - 0.5 \cdot S^2$.

In order to insure that the inflation does not change the tax burden, the second regressor R23 (R23 = RX23·ETU) of the tax function (11) has been replaced by RX23D·ETU. The distribution function included in RX23D is now defined on deflated income.

In the case that inflation should not increase the government's tax receipts, the income has to be deflated in the first regressor R12 of the function (11), too, this changes R12 to R12·108.5/PC'PR.

Fig. 1a and 1b (page 42, 43) show the effects on real GDP. Variations [1] and [2] do not have much influence: lower tax income of the government is almost perfectly matched by lower expenditure. There is only a substitution of expenditure from the government to the private sector.

In variations [3] and [4] the old expenditure level of the government is maintained which means less total expenditure (and therefore less GDP) some years after a downswing in the business cycle (because government adapts its expenditure with a time lag to its income) and more total expenditure some years after an upswing. A multiplier effect is also at work to strengthen this outcome. Variations [5] and [6] show the effects of an anticyclic expenditure policy in the downswing of 1966/1967, variations [7] and [8] the dampening effects on the business cycle if this type of policy is pursued also in the upswing from 1970 to 1974.

Fig. 2a and 2b (page 44, 45) show the employment effects of the policies considered. Note, that there was an open labor market in Germany in this time: foreign labor flows in if labor demand exceeds labor supply.

All policies considered reduce the tax burden (fig. 3a and 3b, page 46, 47), each of the two types of wage tax reduction approximately in the same way.

As to the gross wage ratio (fig. 4a and 4b, page 48, 49) it is seen that all fiscal policies raising GDP and employment tend to deteriorate the gross income distribution for labor. Given the capital stock, more employment is affiliated with a smaller proportion of GDP going to labor, as a rule. The difference in the gross wage ratios stays in the range of 1 to 2 % points, however. That may not seem very important, but labor unions are very sensitive to it.

Fig. 5a and 5b (page 50, 51) show that effects of fiscal policy on the proportion of wage income per employed person to profit income per selfemployed person are similar to the effects on the gross wage ratio, but less accentuated. The number of selfemployed people does not decline porportionally to the relative decline of profit income as indicated by the rise of the gross wage ratio.

This remains true, if only profits availabe within the country are considered. The gross wage ratio responds even less now (cf. fig. 6a, 6b, 7a, 7b, page 52, 53, 54, 55).

These results are partly reversed if the net wage ratio is considered (fig. 8a and 8b, page 56, 57). If the reduction of taxes on wages is large enough as in the variations [2], [4], [6], [8], the net wage ratio improves with an expansive fiscal policy. If this reduction is too small as in the variations [1], [3], [5], [7] the income distribution for labor may still deteriorate, but only for some periods and only to a small degree. The same applies for the per head ratios (see fig. 9a and 9b, page 58, 59).

To get a fair picture of income distribution not only the gross but also the net distribution ratios have to be considered. The latter are of far greater importance if income distribution should give an impression of the relative net income position of wage and profit earners. As may be seen by comparing fig. 4a and b to fig. 8a and b gross and net wage ratios may move in opposite directions. It goes without saying that the tax burden of wages is reduced by lowering the taxes on wages (see fig. 10, page 60, 61). But it might be surprising to see that the tax burden of wages, without some substantial change in tax policy as indicated by variations [1], [3], [5] and [7], rises in time. This of course, is due to the progressive tax system. But, in contrast it is interesting to note that the tax burden of

Table 4 Measures of income distribution

Nr.	Verbal description	Symbol	Definition	graphically represented in fig.
1	gross wage ratio with respect to gross profits	QL	$QL = L/(L + Q'PR)$ L = gross wages $Q'PR$ = gross profits originating in the private sector	5a 5b
2	gross wages per employed person over gross profits per selfemployed person	QKL	$QKL = \dfrac{L/ETU}{Q'PR/ETS'PR}$ L = gross wages $Q'PR$ = gross profits originating in the private sector ETU = labor force employed $ETS'PR$ = labor force selfemployed	6a 6b
3	gross wage ratio with respect to gross profits available within the country	QLV	$QLV = L/(GVHK + L)$ L = gross wages $GVHK$ = gross profits available within the country	7a 7b
4	gross wages per employed person over gross profits available within the country per selfemployed person	QKLV	$QKLV = \dfrac{L/ETU}{GVHK/ETS'PR}$	8a 8b
5	net wage ratio	QLU1	$QLU1 = \dfrac{LU1}{LU1 + GU1HK}$ $LU1$ = net wages $GU1HK$ = net profits	9a 9b
6	net wages per employed person over net profits per selfemployed person	QKLU1	$QKLU1 = \dfrac{LU1/ETU}{GU1HK/ETS'PR}$	10a 10b

Gross domestic product
(in DM prices of 1962)
YRR

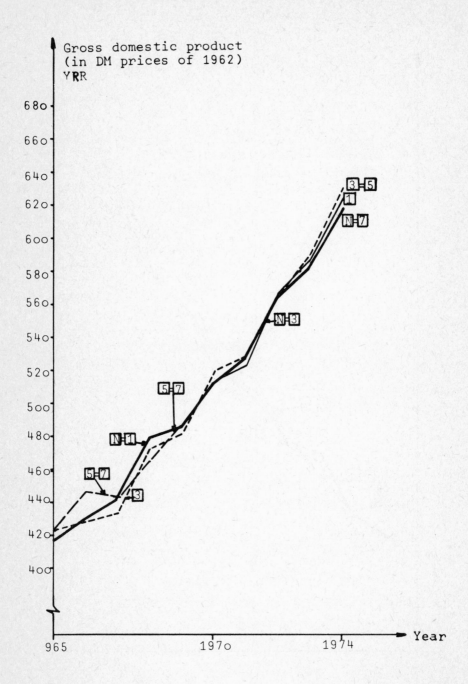

Fig. 1b

Gross domestic product
(in DM prices of 1962)
YRR

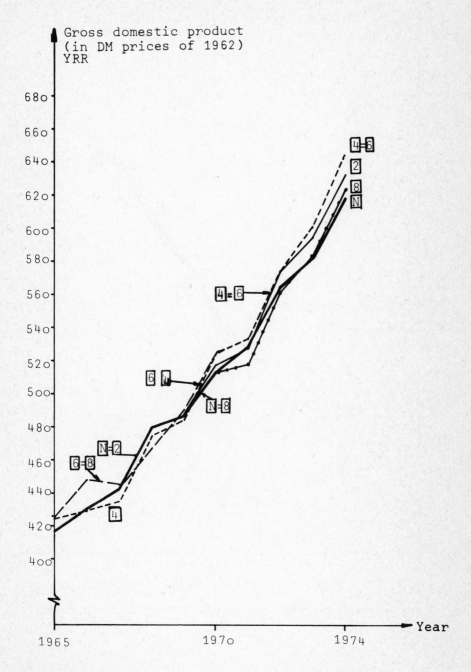

Bill.
working hours
A

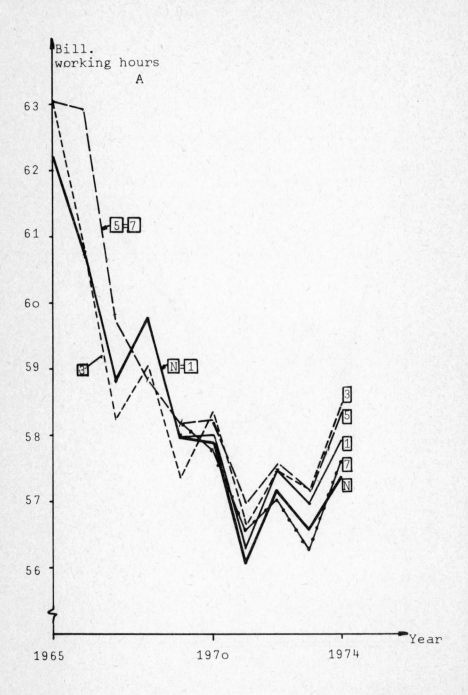

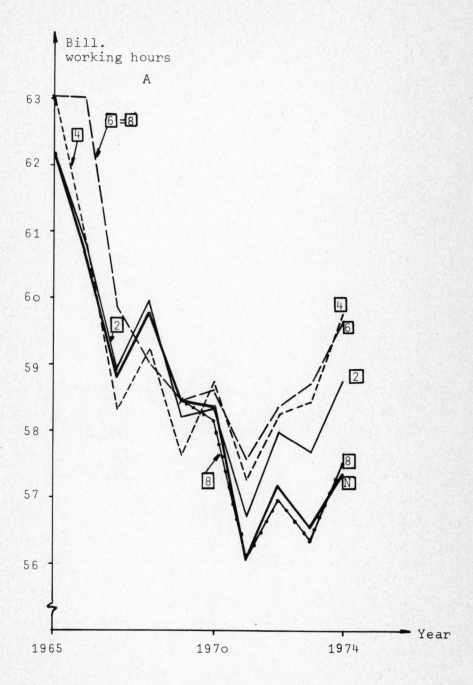

Fig. 3a

tax burden = total taxes
over GDP at current prices
QT = T/Y

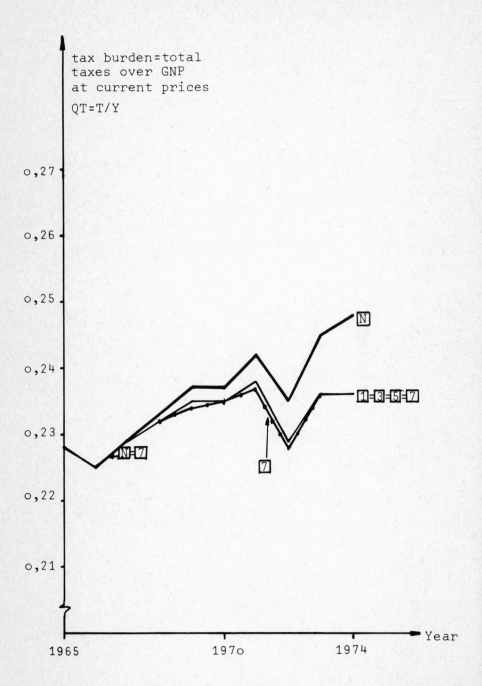

46

Fig. 3b

tax burden = total taxes
over GDP at current prices
QT = T/Y

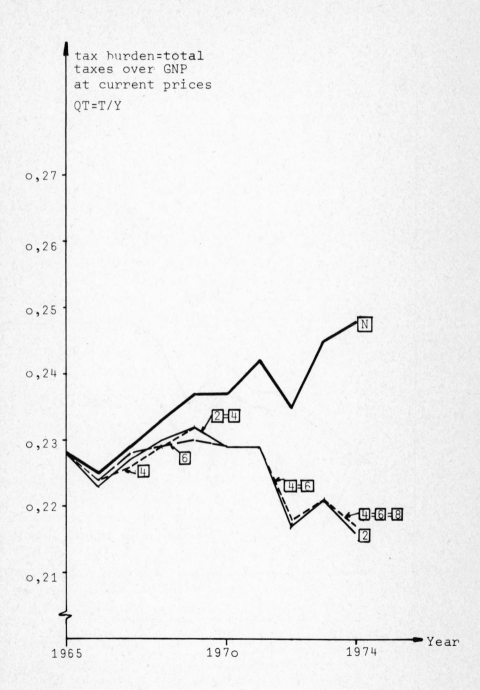

gross wage
ratio

$$QL = \frac{L}{L+Q'PR}$$

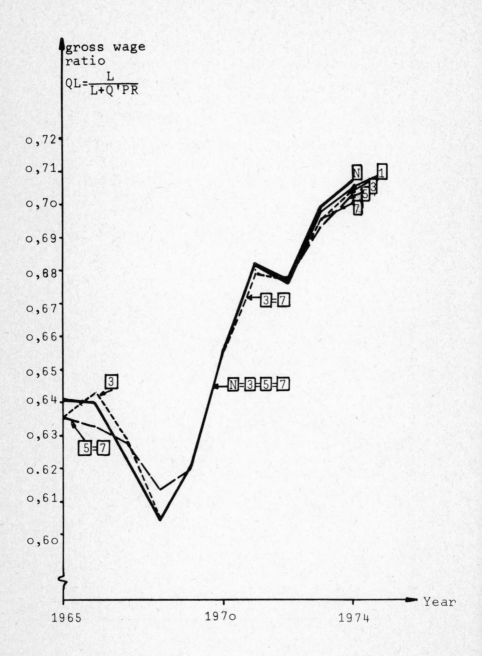

Fig. 4b

gross wage
ratio

$$QL = \frac{L}{L+Q'PR}$$

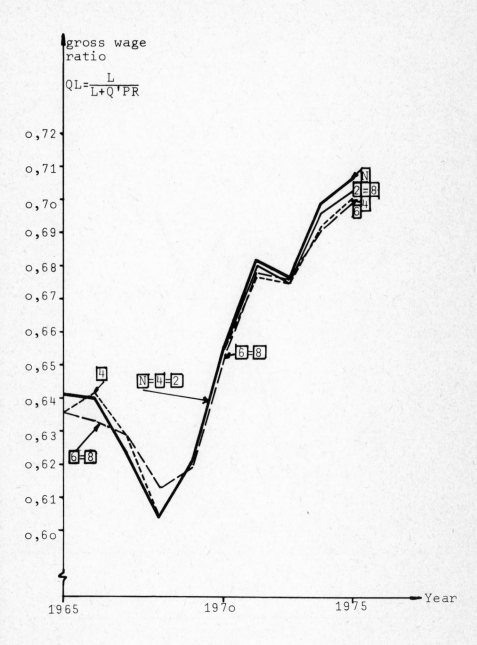

Fig. 5a

gross wages per employed
person over gross profits
per selfemployed person

$$QKL = \frac{L/ETU}{Q'PR/ETS'PR}$$

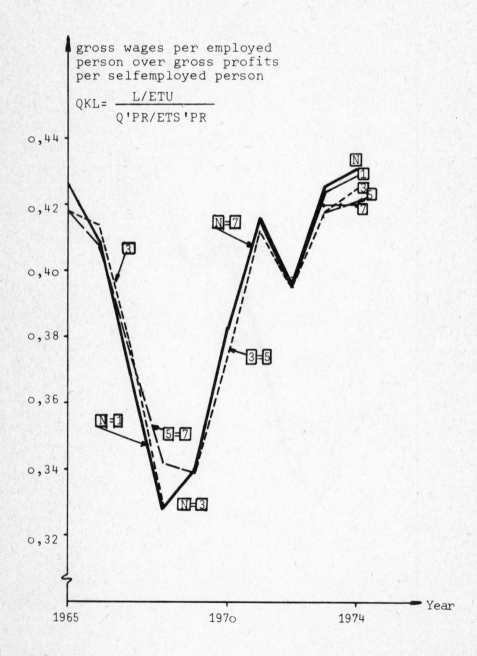

50

Fig. 5b

gross wages per employed
person over gross profits
per selfemployed person

$$QKL = \frac{L/ETU}{Q'PR/ETS'PR}$$

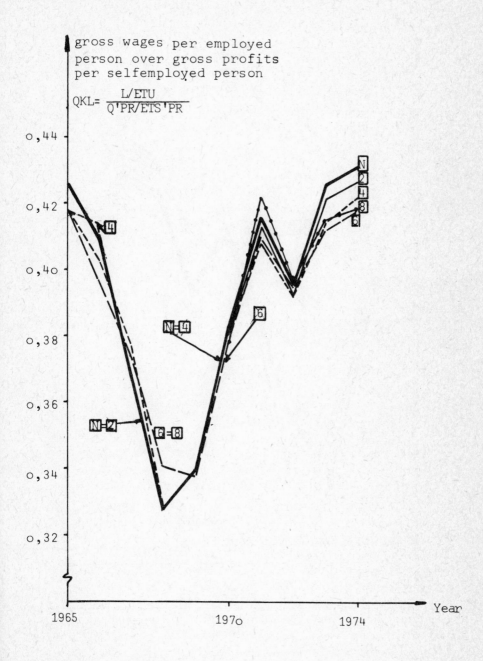

gross wage ratio with respect to gross
profits available within the country

$$QLV = \frac{L}{GVHK+L}$$

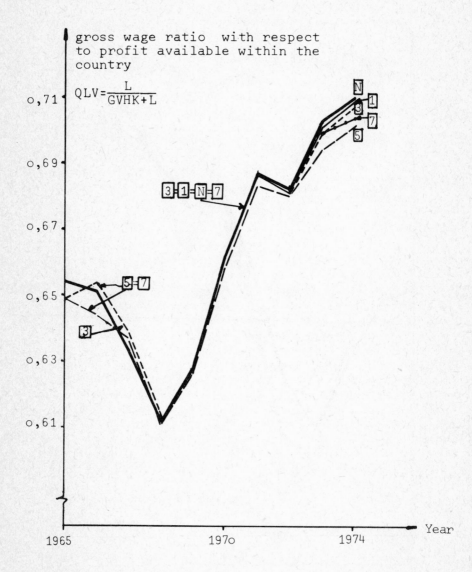

Fig. 6b

gross wage ratio with respect to gross
profits available within the country

$$QLV = \frac{L}{GVHK+L}$$

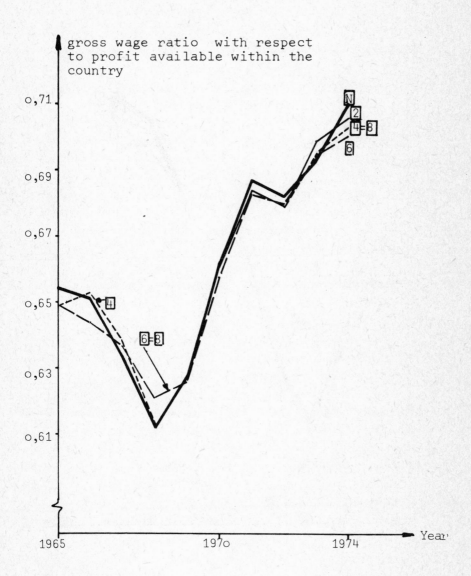

gross wage ratio with respect
to profit available within the
country

gross wages per employed person
over gross profits available within
the country per selfemployed person

$$QKLV = \frac{L/ETU}{GVHK/ETS'PR}$$

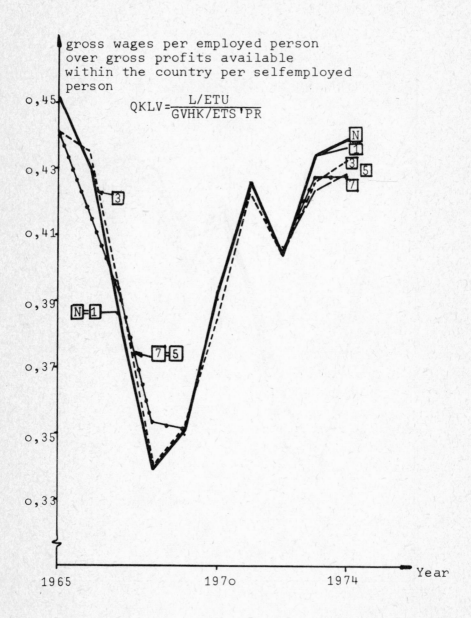

Fig. 7b

gross wages per employed person
over gross profits available within
the country per selfemployed person

$$QKLV = \frac{L/ETU}{GVHK/ETS'PR}$$

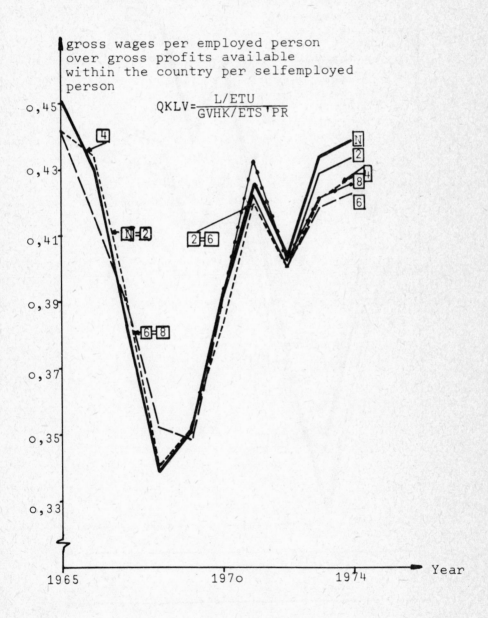

Fig. 8a

net wage ratio = net wages
over net wages + net profits

$$QLU1 = \frac{LU1}{LU1+GU1HK}$$

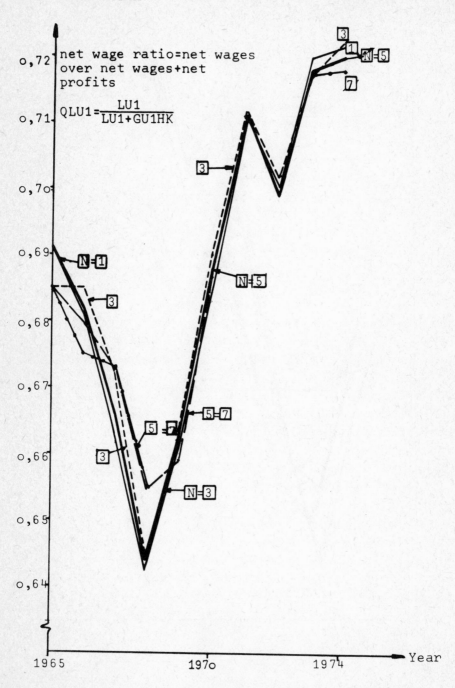

Fig. 8b

net wage ratio = net wages
over net wages + net profits

$$QLU1 = \frac{LU1}{LU1+GU1HK}$$

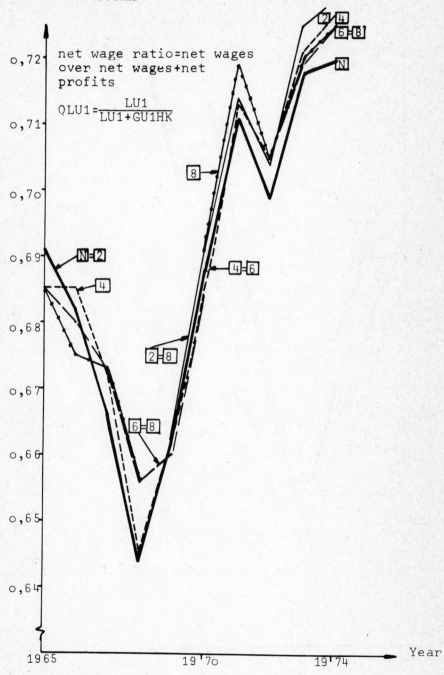

net wages per employed person over
net profits per selfemployed person

$$QKLU1 = \frac{LU1/ETU}{GU1HK/ETS'PR}$$

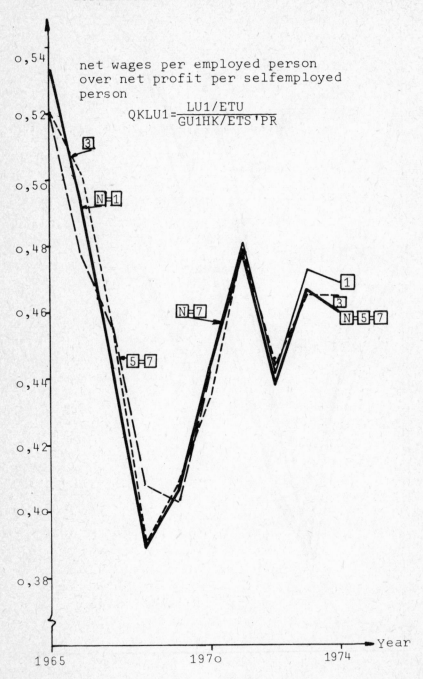

Fig. 9b

net wages per employed person over
net profits per selfemployed person

$$QKLU1 = \frac{LU1/ETU}{GU1HK/ETS'PR}$$

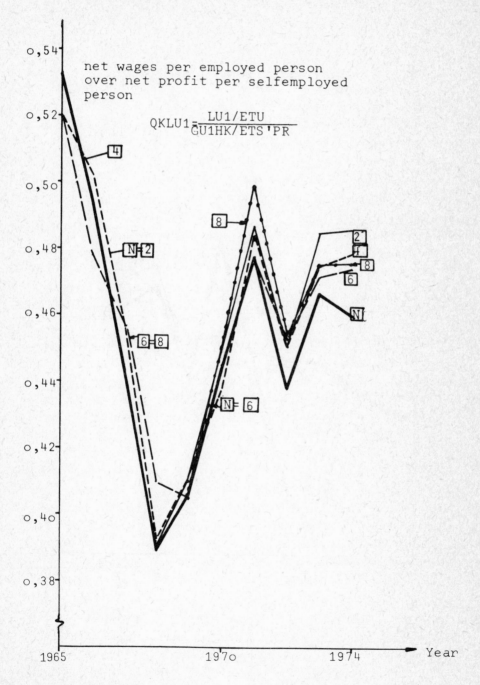

Fig. 10a

tax burden of wages
QTL = (TL'LGK+TI'LGK+TC'LGK)/L
TL'LGK = tax on wage income
TI'LGK = indirect taxes paid from wage earrers
TC'LGK = taxes on consumption goods

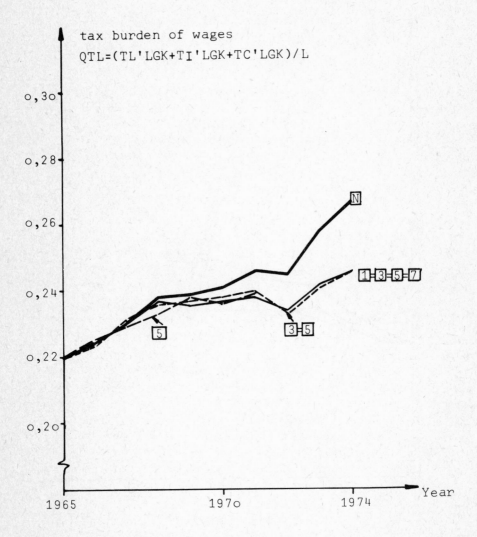

Fig. 10b

tax burden of wages
QTL = (TL'LGK+TI'LGK+TC'LGK)/L

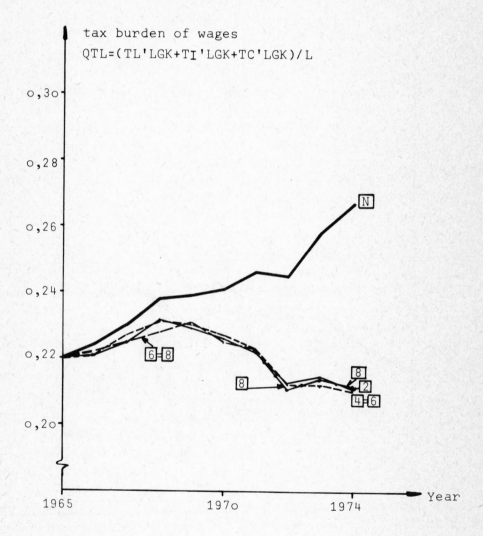

61

Fig. 11a

tax burden of profits

$$QTG = (TI'QGK+TE'QGK+TV'QGK+TK'KGK+TX'KGK)/GVHK$$

$TI'QGK$ = indirect taxes paid from profit income of households
$TE'QGK$ = tax on profit income of households
$TV'QGK$ = tax on wealth paid from households
$TK'KGK$ = tax on profits of companies
$TV'KGK$ = taxes on wealth paid from companies

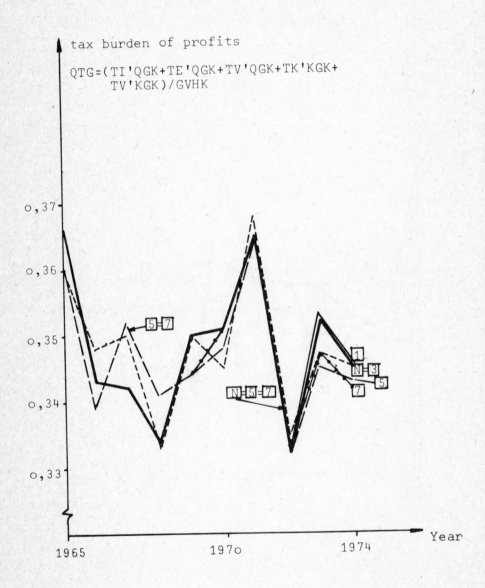

Fig. 11b

tax burden of profits

QTG = (TI'QGK+TE'QGK+TV'QGK+TK'KGK+TV'KGK)/GVHK

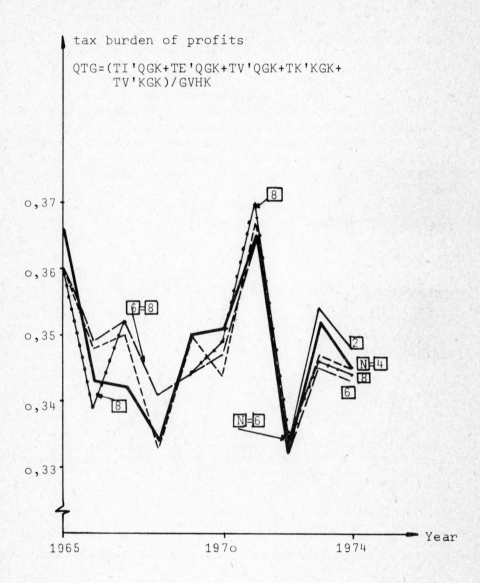

profits in the average shows a declining trend. Of course, it stays constant or even fluctuates with the business cycle (see fig. 11, page 62, 63). It might be also surprising to see that the tax burden of profits may be reduced too by reducing the tax burden of wages though to a much smaller degree. This is due to the expansive effect of this type of fiscal policy.

Summing up, the results of this simulation experiment may be formulated this way: Fiscal policies which tend to raise real GDP also tend to deteriorate the gross wage ratio. But this does not necessarily mean that the net wage ratio deteriorates, too. If the expansive fiscal policy takes the form of a reduction of the tax burden on wages and if this reduction is large enough the net wage ratio may improve. In this case gross and net ratios move in opposite directions. Moreover, the results show that without substantial change in the tax laws, the tax burden of wage income increases in time whereas the tax burden on profits stays almost constant. Taxes on wage income become an always growing part of total tax income of the government. All social reforms which cost money are financed to an always rising proportion by the workers themselves. Considering the rising proportion of employed and the declining proportion of selfemployed persons in the German population and the resulting rising trend of the gross and net wage ratios this seems almost inevitable.

It seems to be interesting to study the consequences of these results with respect to personal income distribution in detail.

Notes

[1] Here we are in accordance with L. Klein [6]

[2] Strictly speaking, static theory is not applicable in short run disequilibrium situations. The statement above should be taken as an approximation in the neighborhood of equilibrium.

[3] In the case of a CES-production function $y = [c_A(\pi A)^{-\delta} + c_K K^{-\delta}]^{-1/\delta}$, $\delta > -1$, $V = \epsilon_A$
$= 1/[1 + \frac{c_K}{c_A} (\frac{K}{\pi A})^{-\delta}] = 1/[1 + \frac{c_K}{c_A} \Psi(\frac{w}{r})^{-\delta}]$

and $\frac{dV}{d(w/r)}$ < 0 for $-1 < \delta < 0$, i.e. $\sigma = \frac{1}{1+\delta} > 1$

> 0 for $\delta > 0$, i.e. $\sigma = \frac{1}{1+\delta} < 1$,

σ = elasticity of substitution. Therefore, it depends on the elasticity of substitution whether an increase of the wage/profit ratio raises or lowers the proportion of wage income.

[4] Model 9 which is almost identical to model 9.1 used here and different forecasts done with model 9 are described in Krelle and Pauly [7]. Model 9.1 and the simulation results are reproduced in an appendix to this paper, which is available upon request.

[5] In other versions of the model the nominal wage rate has been endogenized. In model 9.1 we take the actual wage rate as given in the reference period.

[6] For the sake of exposition we assume that every taxpayer with income y has the same amount of deductions and exemptions.

References:

[1] W. Albers, *Umverteilungswirkungen der Einkommensteuer, Schriften des Vereins für Socialpolitik*, N.F., Bd. 75/II, Berlin 1974, pp. 69–114.

[2] R.M. Coen, *The Effect of Cash Flow on the Speed of Adjustment*, in: G.Fromm (Ed.), *Tax Incentives and Capital Spending*, Amsterdam/London 1971.

[3] J.K. Galbraith, *The Affluent Society*, Boston 1958.

[4] W. Hake, *Umverteilungseffekte des Budgets*, Göttingen 1972.

[5] D.W. Jorgenson, *Anticipations and Investment Behavior*, pp. 35–92, in: J.S. Duesenberry et al (Ed.), *The Brookings Quarterly Econometric Model of the United States*, Chicago 1965.

[6] L.R. Klein, *Econometric Analysis of the Tax Cut of 1964*, pp. 458–472, in: J.S. Duesenberry, G. Fromm, L.R. Klein, E. Kuh, *The Brookings Model: Some Further Results*, Amsterdam–London 1969.

[7] W. Krelle und R. Pauly, *Konsum und Investition des Staates bis 1985*, Göttingen, 1976.

[8] A. Stobbe, *Untersuchungen zur makroökonomischen Theorie der Einkommensverteilung*, Tübingen 1962.

[9] Wissenschaftlicher Beirat beim Bundesministerium für Wirtschaft, *Indexierung wirtschaftlich relevanter Größen*, Studienreihe 9, 1975.

Martin Pfaff and Wolfgang Asam*
Distributive Effects of Real Transfers via Public Infrastructure: Conceptual Problems and Some Empirical Results

1 The Fiscal Residuum as Index of Redistribution?

1.1 The Major Questions

The empirical estimation of the interpersonal distributive effects of expenditures for public infrastructure hinges explicitly or implicitly on a range of assumptions and value judgements. To some these may pose more problems than at present can be answered satisfactorily. To set the stage, therefore, certain major theoretical issues are considered: (1) Which assumptions and concepts may be employed to assess the (re)distributive consequences of expenditures for public infrastructure? (2) What problems arise on the expenditure side when we attempt to evaluate and impute expenditures to socio-economic groups? (3) Which alternative criteria for evaluation and imputation can be applied that allow either an indirect or direct assignment of benefits (or costs) to socio-economic groups?

1.2 Allocation and Distribution Functions of Public Goods

To treat real transfers[1] as pure public goods which in theory are jointly and equally consumed by all[2], appears to fly into the face of empirical evidence pointing to vast differences in the de-facto utilization of public infrastructure facilities. On the other hand, a complete assignment or imputation to individuals or groups appears to neglect such problems as technological and taste externalities, indirect effects, the merit goods character of some goods, and other issues.

We started by pointing to the need for making value judgements and assumptions. To make these more transparent, the following interim steps will be climbed on the staircase of reasoning:

a. The assumptions and concepts implicit in neoclassical public economics — the voluntary exchange-theory of public finance and the value-in-exchange notions employed to evaluate public goods — will be pointed out, and alternative

* The authors wish to acknowledge the advice and contributions of Prof. Anita B. Pfaff, Eberhard Bäuerle, Patricia Burke, Dr. Gerhard Fuchs, Ernst Kistler and Walter Asam (of the University of Augsburg and INIFES).

66

notions — focussing on to the tax-transfer process and on value-in-use as a measure of benefits — will be identified which yield different interpretations of the fiscal residuum.

b. By defining different types of tax-transfer processes and by assuming constant versus diminishing marginal utilities of income, several and more complex interpretations of the fiscal residuum will become evident.

c. Some fundamental questions on the conceptual basis for imputing benefits arise. They have to do with our basic notions of the fiscal process.

Aaron and McGuire employ the former notion when they propose the following procedure for imputing the value of public goods to households:

»Consider a model in which commodities are either pure private goods (goods that are exhaustively apportioned among individuals and produce no external effects) or pure public goods all of which enter the utility function of every person. Assume that some resources are taxed away from households (thereby diminishing each household's consumption of private goods) and are devoted to the production of public goods. The resulting distribution of public and private goods consumption may be analyzed into two conceptually discrete steps: the first step is an implicit redistribution of private goods or income by taxes and transfers; the second is a purchase of public goods paid for by other taxes levied on each household at a rate equal to its marginal rate of substitution between private and public goods (at the final private-public goods position of the household)«[3].

This concept evidently takes off from a particular principle of taxation: Each household engages in »voluntary exchange« for that part of its tax payment which brings it direct benefits; the residual represents — at least implicitly — an »involuntary transfer« of purchasing power to others. Aaron and McGuire, like most contemporary public economists, remain admittedly within the confines of neoclassical exchange and value theory: By using the term »value« in the sense of exchange value — marginal utility times quantity — they exclude infra-marginal utility gains or consumer surplus which would have to be included in the notion of »value in use«. They recognize, however, the limitations of the former only in passing: »of course, in the situation under consideration, individual households cannot exchange the public good«[4].

One need not, however, assume that individuals can exchange the public good, nor that they can make tax contributions based on their marginal evaluation of the benefits received from the government. Rather, the explanation of the fiscal system is based on notions of the tax-transfer process:

1. One need not assume that public expenditures can be analyzed by taking recourse to *either pure private or pure public goods*.

2. One need not assume that there are purchases of public goods possible under present tax systems[5].

3. If we ignore degrees of voluntariness of tax payments, the fiscal residuum can be taken as a measure of the grant-element (positive or negative) and the magnitude of the tax payments or benefits received (whichever is the smaller of the two) as a *quasi*-exchange-element. This provides a classification for distributional analysis.

The grant-element, or the fiscal residuum[6], may be narrowly defined as the difference between taxes paid and the benefits received from publicly provided specific goods.

The fiscal residuum may be defined also more broadly as the difference between taxes paid and the benefits of publicly provided specific goods *plus* some imputed share of public goods, where the latter varies from situation to situation.

The polar extremes — pure public and pure private goods — occur very rarely in real life. More realistically, we have to recognize that all goods provided occupy some intermediate position between these two extremes[7]. This applies almost exclusively to public infrastructure facilities.

1.3 Redistribution under the Assumption of Constant and Diminishing Marginal Utility of Income Relating to Different Tax-Expenditure-Systems

Most studies of the distributive impact of public expenditure have assumed that the marginal utility of income is constant as income rises[8]. On the basis of this assumption we could match all 9 possible combinations of a regressive, proportional, and progressive tax system (T_1 through T_3) with a regressive, proportional and progressive expenditure system (B_1 through B_3).

Table 1 (see page 69) summarizes the joint effects for the case of the balanced budget. Directly paid for benefits are netted out. The combination of tax and expenditure systems represented by the three lower right-hand cells results in a net redistribution to the lower income groups. The converse is true for the combination represented by the three upper left-hand cells. The diagonal from left bottom to right top represents combinations of tax and expenditure systems that may either aggravate or equalize the income distribution, depending on the degree of progressivity or regressivity of revenue and expenditure systems. As long as we maintain the balanced budget assumption the middle cell can only result in a neutral effect. By necessity the proportion of taxes and expenditures has to be equal.

If the assumption of the balanced budget is relaxed, a deficit may arise, i.e., aggregate expenditures may exceed aggregate revenue. Thus we could come up with proportional tax and expenditure systems and still have an aggravative effect on the distribution of income, since the absolute amount of the fiscal residuum could be negative for all and increasing in absolute value as income rises.

If η_{TY} is defined as income elasticity of tax burden $\eta_{TY} = \dfrac{dT}{dY} \dfrac{Y}{T}$ and ϵ_{BY} as income elasticity of publicly derived benefits (public goods benefits) $\epsilon_{BY} = \dfrac{dB}{dY} \dfrac{Y}{B}$, and the fiscal system is defined as having an aggravative effect on the distribution of income if the fiscal residuum T-B declines as income Y rises, then we can write this condition as $d(T-B)/dY < 0$.

We can also write $\dfrac{dT}{dY} - \dfrac{dB}{dY} < 0$ or $\dfrac{dT}{dY} < \dfrac{dB}{dY}$

A fraction remains unchanged in value if multiplied and divided by the same value; therefore

$$\frac{dT}{dY} \frac{YT}{TY} < \frac{dB}{dY} \frac{YB}{BY} \quad \text{or}$$

$$\eta_{TY} \frac{T}{Y} < \epsilon_{BY} \frac{B}{Y} \quad \text{or}$$

$$\eta_{TY} \frac{T}{B} < \epsilon_{BY}$$

Table 1 Redistribution with Regressive, Proportional, and Progressive Tax and Expenditure Systems

tax system / expenditure system		regressive $T_1 = f_1(Y)$ $\dfrac{d\left(\frac{T}{Y}\right)}{dY} < 0$	proportional $T_2 = f_2(Y)$ $\dfrac{d\left(\frac{T}{Y}\right)}{dY} = 0$	progressive $T_3 = f_3(Y)$ $\dfrac{d\left(\frac{T}{Y}\right)}{dY} > 0$
		T_1	T_2	T_3
regressive $B_1 = g_1(Y)$ $\dfrac{d\left(\frac{B}{Y}\right)}{dY} > 0$	B_1	$\dfrac{d(T-B)}{dY} < 0$ aggravative fiscal system	$\dfrac{d(T-B)}{dY} < 0$ aggravative fiscal system	$\dfrac{d(T-B)}{dY} \gtrless 0$ if $d\left(\frac{T}{Y}\right)/dY > d\left(\frac{B}{Y}\right)/dY$ equalitarian if $d\left(\frac{T}{Y}\right)/dY = d\left(\frac{B}{Y}\right)/dY$ neutral if $d\left(\frac{T}{Y}\right)/dY < d\left(\frac{B}{Y}\right)/dY$ aggravative
proportional $B_2 = g_2(Y)$ $\dfrac{d\left(\frac{B}{Y}\right)}{dY} = 0$	B_2	$\dfrac{d(T-B)}{dY} < 0$ aggravative fiscal system	$\dfrac{d(T-B)}{dY} = 0$ neutral fiscal system	$\dfrac{d(T-B)}{dY} > 0$ equalitarian fiscal system
progressive $B_3 = g_3(Y)$ $\dfrac{d\left(\frac{B}{Y}\right)}{dY} < 0$	B_3	$\dfrac{d(T-B)}{dY} \lessgtr 0$ if $\dfrac{d\left(\frac{T}{Y}\right)}{dY} < \dfrac{d\left(\frac{B}{Y}\right)}{dY}$ aggravative if $\dfrac{d\left(\frac{T}{Y}\right)}{dY} = \dfrac{d\left(\frac{B}{Y}\right)}{dY}$ neutral if $\dfrac{d\left(\frac{T}{Y}\right)}{dY} > \dfrac{d\left(\frac{B}{Y}\right)}{dY}$ equalitarian	$\dfrac{d(T-B)}{dY} > 0$ equalitarian fiscal system	$\dfrac{d(T-B)}{dY} > 0$ equalitarian fiscal system

is the condition for a tax-expenditures system to result in an aggravative effect on the distribution[9].

If we assume that the marginal utility of income (i.e. money) declines as income increases, total utility increases or approaches a finite maximum. Thus if $U = f(Y)$,

$$\frac{dU}{dY} > 0 \qquad \text{and}$$

$$\frac{d^2U}{dY^2} < 0$$

In an economic model of the private sector we can assume that the marginal utility of the last DM spent is equal for the purchase of any commodity. This assumption has to be qualified if not dropped when we talk about taxes and public goods. It is even questionable whether the marginal utility of income is the same for different types of income, say factor vs. monetary transfer income or the provision of real income through public goods.

The size of the fiscal residuum is then not necessarily a monotonic function of the extent of change in real welfare. A fiscal residuum which equals zero may entail either an increase or decrease of welfare.

If we assume a redistributive tax-expenditure system, the utility loss due to a given tax (or the utility gain due to a given benefit or increase in real income) is smaller for higher than for lower income recipients, i.e.

$$\frac{dU}{dY_1} \frac{dY_1}{dFR} > \frac{dU}{dY_2} \frac{dY_2}{dFR} \quad \text{if and only if } Y_1 < Y_2$$

Thus an aggravative fiscal system would contribute more to a decline in welfare if marginal utilities of income decline than if they are constant. On the other hand an equalitarian fiscal system would tend to increase total utility of all to a greater extent, if marginal utility of income declines. It does not seem acceptable to apply declining marginal utilities only to the expenditure or only to the tax side.

1.4 Alternatives to the Fiscal Residuum: Indicators of Usage and Life-Time Tax-Transfer Residua

There are two shortcomings other than those pointed out before on grounds of welfare:

1. The benefits conveyed on the expenditure side are not expressed by output measures but by the cost of inputs used to generate these outputs.

2. Fiscal residua are generally computed for a given year to make them compatible with the concept of annual income, annual taxes, and the like. Accordingly, the concept of the annual fiscal residuum can be subjected to the same criticism which applies to all income-distribution measures for a given year and to their use as a yardstick for judging the equity of distributive patterns, i.e. that it is also meaningful to compare patterns of life-time income[10]. Similarly, the usage of public facilities is intimately tied to the stage of the user's life cycle. An analysis which neglects, for example, the changes in the socio-economic structure of the population — including the age structure — will lead to misleading conclusions about the distribution of the real benefits of public activities.

These two added objections can be met at least in part:

1. By relying on indicators of usage, the problem of evaluating benefits on the basis of the cost of inputs used in their production can be obviated. (This neglects, however, inequalities in the financing of these public services).

2. By using life-time tax-transfer residua[11] the intertemporal distributive effect of public infrastructure expenditures can be assessed in a more adequate fashion. In the empirical part of the paper, both of these methods for inferring patterns of (re)distribution will be illustrated by case examples.

2 Alternative Criteria for Evaluation and Imputation

2.1 An Overview of Criteria Used for Imputation

A search of the literature reveals a wide range of criteria and procedures used for imputing real transfers to individuals, households or groups. In Overview 1 a summary view of these criteria is provided. By choosing different assumptions or hypotheses as a basis of imputation one arrives at entirely different distributive impacts. An examination of the implicit assumptions or value premises appears to be in order.

2.2 Assessment of Volume and Evaluation of Real Transfers

We proceed to sketch the most commonly employed methods of determining who receives real transfers and how they are evaluated. As far as the economic approach to this problem is concerned we confine ourselves to an exceedingly brief statement. The non-economic aspects shall be dealt with in more detail, in order to reveal a so far neglected field in the general area of incidence analysis.

The following methods focus directly on the individuals or groups constituting the recipients of — or the demand for — real transfers.

Real transfers attributable to individuals or groups can be directly imputed by

a. pricing (fees for infrastructure usage) differentiated by groups;
b. election procedures;
c. survey and observation;
d. control carried out by the administrating agency.

The first of these alternatives is of little use since in many instances this instrument is not employed for a variety of reasons. The same argument holds for alternatives b. and d. This leaves alternative c. as the mose promising to help establish which groups are users and thus beneficiaries of a real transfer.

Real transfers can also be attributed to individuals or groups indirectly:

a. by establishing the exclusion mechanisms;
b. by analyzing the relationship of public and private goods in consumption[12].

Thus the exclusion mechanisms resulting from characteristics of the user or characteristics of the facility (or public good) can be employed at least in part to establish which individuals or groups benefit from these facilities. In our opinion, however, they are more apt to explain user patterns established by direct methods.

Overview 1: Criteria and Procedures Used for Imputation

Incidence-assumptions according to authors	General expenditures		Specific expenditure					
	Name, Examples		education	health and hospitals	highways	police, fire protection	housing	others
			Allocation alternatives					
Adler (1951)	- indivisible goods - defense, general government	1. per capita 2. income 3. tax burden	- per capita	- inversely to income below $4000	- income	- real property holdings	- consumer units with income below $4000	
Tucker (1953)	- not allocable goods	1. per capita 2. total income or ownership of property 3. total consumption 4. ownership of "capital"	- number of children under 18 in each income bracket	- consumption expenditures (50%) and automobile expenditures (50%) - consumption expenditures (33 1/3 %) automobile expenditures (33 1/3%) and ownership of real estate			- amount of rent (income below $5000) - spending units paying rent (income over $5000)	
Conrad (1954)	- indivisibilities (total benefits) - general government, military services foreign relations expenditures	1. income	- spending units	- low income units	- expenditures on automotive transportation	- property holding		natural resources: - spending units
Musgrave/ Daicoff (1958)			- income of families with school age children	- consumption expenditures and number of families money income capital income property income	- oil and gas expenditures and consumption expenditures	- consumption expenditures and number of families - money income - capital income - residential property tax		public health, sanitation, welfare, recreation, conservation and libraries: - per capita
Brownlee (1960)	- general government and public safety	1. per capita property 2. per capita (50%) 3. per capita (50%) and property (50%)	- per capita (50%) and income of the family with children under 18 (50%) (primary education) - do. but (25%/75%) (secondary education) - distribution of the students according to the income of the household in which they live (higher education)	- inversely to income	- gas expenditures (53%), consumption expenditures (43%) and "foreign drivers" (4%)			public health, sanitation, welfare, recreation, conservation and libraries: - per capita

Musgrave, Case, Leonhard (1974)	- general expenditures	1. total income 2. tax burden	- families with students	- patients in fund-funded hospitals (hospitals) - families (public health)	- households with auto operation expenses (66 2/3%) and consumers in general (33 1/3%)		- public utilities: - spending units public undertaking: - spending units (50%), private expenditures for traffic (35%) and private expenditures for gas and electricity (15%)
Hanusch (1974)	a) - "dominant kollektive Leistungen" - international affairs, defense, general government b) - "Gemeinschaftsleistungen mit diskriminierendem Nutzeffekt" - administration of justice, civilian safety, art, adult education, church, science	a) 1. tax burden 2. personal income 3. private property 4. ownership of capital 5. spending units b) 1. tax burden 2. spending units 3. tax burden/spending units } 50% 4. income/property 5. spending units/property } 50%	- private education expenditures	- private expenditures for hygiene (60%) and private expenditures for health insurance (40%)	- private "Tonnenkilometer" (75,8%), consumption (13,9%) and income of property (10,3%)	- spending units (31%) private amount of rent (55%) and expenditures for "Bausparen" (14%)	- public utilities: - spending units (31%) private amount of rent (55%) and expenditures for "Bausparen" (14%)
Hanusch (communal) (1975)	- "dominant kollektive Leistungen" - general government, general finance economy, general capital-, real- and special property, indivisible debt services reverse position of the budget	1. spending units	- private expenditures for education (schools) - net income of the spending units - private expenditures for education (science)	- private expenditures for hygiene (60%) and private expenditures for health insurance (40%)	- private gas expenditures	- spending units	- public utilities: - spending units public undertaking: - spending units (50%), private expenditures for traffic (15%) and private expenditures for gas and electricity (35%)

Gillespie (1965)	- general expenditures, national defense, general, government control, international affairs and civilian safety, police and prisons	1. families 2. total income 3. capital income 4. disposable income	- families with students	- families (public health services) - short-term hospital patients (general hospitals) - mental patients (institutions for the care of the mentally ill)	- property owner (25%), consumer of transported products (33.7%) and consumer of passenger travels (42,3%)	- total consumption - weighted average of homeowners and renters (civilian safety fire protection and public utilities)	- families with low income	sewage control and other sanitation services: - weighted average of homeowners and renters natural resources, postal services; - total consumption
Bishop (1967)	- general benefits - national defense, international affairs, general government, postal service, civilian safety (police, fire, etc.), transportation, commerce and finance, health and sanitation, natural resources, public utilities	1. number of families and unrelated individuals 2. family money income before taxes (50%) and number of families and unrelated individuals (50%)	- children under 18 (elementary and secondary education). higher education expenditures of families (higher education)		- auto operation expenditures (50%) and total current consumption (50%)			
Hake (1972)	- specific public goods - defense (1.) - public safety (1.,2.) - administration of justice (1.,2.) - rest expenditures, international affairs, general government a.o. (1.)	1. per capita 2. income and property	relative attendance at school of the income groups according to various types of schools the same, but with different cost-benefit-proportion private education expenditures	- private expenditures for hygiene - private expenditures to health insurance - private expenditures for hygiene (42%) and private expenditures for health insurance (58%)	- gas expenditures - gas expenditures (25,1%), consumption (31%) and property (43,9%) - the same, but (25,7%/54,1%/ 20,2%)	see general expenditures	- amount of rent - private expenditures for "Bausparen"	science; - number of students (50%) and consumption (50%)
Eapen/ Eapen (1973)	- general expenditures, police, fire protection, corrections, financial administration, general control	1. families 2. money income 3. families (50%) and money income (50)	- children under 18 (secondary education) proportion to dependent family members, 14 to 34 years of age, enrolled in college (higher education)	- inversely to income			families under $ 7500 income	public health, sanitation and sewage: - families - income

74

List of References to Overview 1:

1. Adler, J.H., The Fiscal System, the Redistribution of Income and Public Welfare, with Appendix by Schlesinger, E.R., in: Poole, K.E. (ed.), *Fiscal Policies and Economy*, New York 1951, pp. 359 – 421.

2. Bishop, G.A., *Tax Burdens and Benefits of Government Expenditures by Income Class, 1961 and 1965*, Tax Foundation (ed.), New York 1967.

3. Brownlee, O.H., *Estimated Distribution of Minnesota Tax and Public Expenditure Benefits*, Minneapolis 1960.

4. Conrad, A.H., Redistribution through Government Budgets in the United States, in: Peacock, A.T. (ed.), *Income Redistribution and Social Policy*, London 1954, pp. 178 – 267.

5. Dodge, D.A., Impact of Tax, Transfer and Expenditure Policies of Government on the Distribution of Personal Income in Canada, in: *Income and Wealth*, March 1975, pp. 1 – 52.

6. Eapen, A.T., Eapen, A.N., Income Redistributive Effects of State and Local Fiscs, Connecticut, A Case Study, in: *Public Finance Quarterly*, 1973, pp. 372 – 387.

7. Franzén, Th., Lörgren, K., Rosenberg, I., Redistributional Effects of Taxes and Public Expenditures in Sweden, in: *Swedish Journal of Economics*, 1975, pp. 31 – 55.

8. Gillespie, J.W., Effects of Public Expenditures on the Distribution of Income, in: Musgrave, R.A. (ed.), *Essays in Fiscal Federalism*, Washington 1965, pp. 122 – 186.

9. Hake, W., *Umverteilungseffekte des Budgets*, Goettingen 1972.

10. Hanusch, H., *Personale Verteilung öffentlicher Leistungen*, Habilitationsschrift, unpublished manuscript, Nuremberg – Erlangen 1974.

11. Hanusch, H., Einkommensverteilung durch kommunale Haushalte. Das Beispiel der Bundesrepublik Deutschland: 1963 and 1969, in: *Archiv für Kommunalwissenschaften*, 1975, pp. 219 – 239.

12. Musgrave, R.A., Daicoff, D.W., *Who pays the Michigan Taxes?* , Michigan 1958.

13. Musgrave, R.A., Case, K.E., Leonhard, H., The Distribution of Fiscal Burdens and Benefits, in: *Public Finance Quarterly*, 1974, pp. 259 – 311.

14. Reynolds, M., Smolensky, E., The Post Fisc Distribution: 1961 and 1970 compared, in: *National Tax Journal*, 1974, pp. 515 – 530.

15. Tucker, R.S., The Distribution of Government Burdens and Benefits, in: *American Economic Review*, 1953, pp. 518 – 543.

Incidence-assumptions according to authors	General expenditures		education	health and hospitals
	Name, examples			
Reyholds/ Smolensky (1974)	- general expenditures - national defense, international affairs, space-research, general government, transportation, commerce and finance, housing and community development, health and sanitation, civilian safety and miscellaneous	1. households and money income (50%)	- children under 18 ("primary, secondary other education") - estimated expenditures on higher education ("higher education")	
Hanusch (communal) (1975)	a) for data of 1963 - "dominant kollektive Leistungen" - general government, general finance economy, general capital-, real- and special property, indivisible debt services, reverse position of the budget	1. spending units	- attendance at school divided into income-class and type of school (schools) - total consumption (culture)	- private expenditures (45%) and private expenditures for health insurance (55%)
	b) for data of 1969	1. spending units	- private expenditures for education (schools) - net income of the spedning units - private expenditures for education (science)	- private expenditures (60%) and private expenditures for health insurance (40%)
Dodge (1975)	a) federal level	1. "broad income"	- children between 5 and 16 yrs. of age (local schools) - students (post secondary education)	- families
	b) state and local level - general expenditures	1. "broad income"	- children between 5 - 16 yrs. of age (primary and secondary education) - students (post secondary education) - families with income below $ 6,000 (other education and training)	- families
Franzén/ Lörgren/ Rosenberg (1975)	- general expenditures - general administration, foreign affairs, judicial institution, defense, general research, parks	1. households 2. total net income	- children 7-16 yrs. of age (students 7-16 yrs. of age) - students 17-18 yrs. of age (students 17-19 yrs. of age) - individuals over 19 (elementary and secondary education for adults) - students receiving educational allowances for higher education (higher education)	- number of days of hospital treatment (hospitals and out-patient care) - children 7-16 yrs. of age (public dental care, children) - public dental care paid by patients (public dental care, adults)

highways	police, fire protection	housing	others
Allocation alternatives			
- automobile ownership			
- private "Tonnen-kilometer" (54,1%), private property (20,2%) and total consumption	- spending units	- private amount of rent	public utilities: - spending units public undertaking - private expenditures for public transportation (private expenditures for gas (and electricity (
- private gas-expenditures	- spending units	- spending units	public utilities: - spending units public undertaking: - spending units (50%), private expenditures for traffic (15%) and private expenditures for gas and electricity (35%)
- expenditures for automobiles (highway transport, passenger cars) - expenditures for transported goods (highway transport, trucks) - expenditures for transported persons (other transport, persons) - expenditures for transported goods (other transport, business)			
- gas expenditures (50%) and disposable income (50%)			Other: child and youth care: - children in day nurseries (day nurseries) - children temporarily cared for at home (day care at home for families with children) - children under 17 yrs. of age (other child and youth care) recreation and cultural services: - household expenditures for recreational services (sports, open-air recreation) - household expenditures for theatre performances and concerts (theatre and concerts) - individuals over 16 yrs. of age (libraries, museums)

The evaluation is based on price, willingness-to-pay and other preference articulation (expectation, pent-up-demand), and use in the demand side; from the supply side indicators of qualitative and quantitative provision of facilities and cost of provision are used to evaluate real transfers.

Even without entering into the familiar problems involved in the application of the various methods, there is little doubt that in an adequate evaluation we have to resort to demand-oriented as well as supply-oriented indicators. As a first step only it may suffice to assign the costs of provision to individuals on the basis of indices of usage. Beyond that, however, it will be necessary to develop welfare indicators on the basis of physical equipment indicators (e.g. infrastructure catalogues), which over and beyond economic factors, such as price and costs, include non-economic effects. Various approaches dealing with problems involved in this endeavor have been developed in recent research projects. These methods seem basically applicable to studying income distribution in the wide context of a broader social framework.

2.3 The Evaluation of Non-economic Benefits

Among the methods for evaluating non-economic benefits we find cost-effectiveness, social indicators and empirical welfare indices formulated on a subjective basis.

2.3.1 Cost-Effectiveness

By applying cost-effectiveness methods we attempt to make transparent the evaluation placed by different groups on particular services rendered. Furthermore, we relate these evaluations to particular attributes of goods and services; and finally, we seek to arrive at a total evaluation on the basis of the partial evaluations associated with particular dimensions or attributes[13]. The use of cost-effectiveness methods yields the following advantages: (1) non-monetary magnitudes can also be assessed; and (2) the multiple effects of public projects can be ascertained and made transparent.

However, the following shortcomings have to be noted: (1) The values arrived at are dependent on the evaluations we make; and (2) problems of participation of individuals and groups arise; their role in determining the criterion base, which is applicable to more complex structures of goals, is of great importance.

2.3.2 Social Indicators

Social indicators can be viewed as problem-oriented indicators to be devised for particular problem areas[14]. Particularly, we can attempt to quantify those intangible effects which are generally associated with benefit-cost-analysis. Within the broad area of social indicators we may distinguish between output and input indicators on the one hand and between subjective and objective indicators on the other. For the purpose of evaluating and imputing the benefits of public infrastructure facilities output indicators are obviously of greater interest: They attempt to assess the result of a public process and thereby also the performance of this process[15]. However, each output indicator should reflect the final place of a cause and effect relationship[16].

There are several problems associated with output indicators: (1) Even if a situation could be described by experts as being objectively identical with another one, there will be substantial differences in the subjective evaluation simply because individuals start from different value assumptions. (2) The results of the evaluation by individuals and groups are influenced not only by the »objective characteristics« of the public facility under consideration (as is the case for most cost-effectiveness analyses) but also on the basis of the information assessed by the evaluator.

Accordingly, we should add, to output indicators also input indicators: They provide an overview over the magnitude and the structure of public infrastructure supply and also the relationship between inputs and expected outputs.

2.3.3 Empirical Welfare Indices Formulated on a Subjective Basis

If it is possible to arrive at a set of indices of consumer and citizen satisfaction which can be regionally differentiated and associated with socio-economic groups, then one could use the indicators as a basis of imputing the benefits of public programs to different individuals and groups.

We have instituted output-oriented subjective methods in order to utilize consumer and citizen satisfaction as measures of the performance of the private and public economy. However, such measures of satisfaction can also be used as proxy indicators of welfare or of benefits conveyed by particular infrastructure facilities.[17].

The attributes of public real transfers or of infrastructure facilities can be viewed as vectors in an attribute space. The individual dimensions of this space measure the individual attributes of the public facilities. The ideal combination of attributes held by a particular individual can also be expressed in the same attribute space in the form of a vector. The greater the difference between the ideal and the actual points the more dissatisfied the individual is likely to be. If ideal and actual coincide the individual is likely to be highly satisfied. Application, of course, requires the methods of representing, scaling, weighting and aggregating subjective responses into an empirical welfare index.

Ultimately, one can test for differences in the evaluations of such facilities by socio-economic groups, by region, and by other classifiers. This then provides an instrument to assess the distributions of the benefits of public infrastructure facilities through the eyes of the beholders and, furthermore, through the eyes of different groups of beholders. When these indices are used in an analysis of distributive impact, shares of the costs of providing particular infrastructure facilities can be allocated to socio-economic groups simply on the basis of the similarities or differences in index values.

2.4 Some Further Problems of Evaluation and Imputation

The presence of merit goods, potential use, material and immaterial bars to usage, and interdependencies of usage, prevents, at least in principle, a simple adding of individual benefits as reflected in cost shares. Some supervening logic appears to be called for which, say, subtracts merit goods from some apparent beneficiaries and adds them to those whose interdependent utility functions have given rise to their provision. Or, actual use may have to be multiplied with a probability vector reflecting likely or potential use. Furthermore, interdependencies imply that a simple addition of the benefits of individual public facilities is not adequate. Similarly, material and immaterial bars appear to warrant a subtraction from actual or potential benefits, and so on.

Any attempt on the part of the investigator to change evaluations is likely to bring us back to the very problem of indirect imputation familiar from the literature. Perhaps here again we should »hear the truth« from the users of public facilities. Again the plea is for nontraditional measures, say, via empirical welfare indices which reflect benefits as perceived by citizens.

2.5 Some Conclusions

Three possible methods can be visualized for determining the incidence of the benefits derived from social goods:

1. The assignment of budget item shares as proxies for costs incurred (input-orientation) according to alternative theoretical assignment criteria;

2. The assignment of expenditure items according to empirically derived global usage patterns;

3. The assignment of specific expenditure items on the basis of preference patterns regarding individual infrastructure facilities.

ad 1. The obvious advantage of this method is that (1) it is operational; (2) the required data are easily accessible; and (3) the analysis is rather simple.

On the other side of the balance sheet we have to point to the following: (1) the incidence structure is rather sensitive to the rather arbitrary choice of hypotheses and assignment criteria; (2) the use of budget items as proxies for input-oriented measurement does not allow for an evaluation based on the preference patterns of users; and (3) employing budgetary items involves problems of separating transfers in cash and real transfers which are lumped together in budgetary items and of applying overhead costs, e.g. general administrative costs to individual services.

The last two arguments are equally applicable to the following methods in as far as they take recourse to using budgetary items as proxies for costs.

ad 2. This method is to be preferred over the first set of methods: (1) the element of arbitrariness in determining assignment criteria is somewhat reduced, and thus (2) the results derived convey more relevant information.

However, the disadvantage involved in using budgetary items as evaluation criterion remains. Furthermore, the quality of the assignment rules depends very crucially on how far methodological problems involved in survey research have been resolved satisfactorily. The same applies for the subsequent methods.

ad 3. This method can take qualitative differences into account. As neither a list of infrastructure facilities nor sufficiently detailed information about usage patterns is available for the entire Federal Republic or the better part of the provinces, such a detailed and rather sophisticated analysis of distributive effects can at best be confined to specific public activities for specific local or regional areas such as individual cities or districts. On the other hand, such case studies may be the only possible approach to overcome the disadvantages of the crude methods mentioned above. It would most probably be possible to include the information on citizen preference patterns in such a method since for some cities and districts surveys of citizen attitudes towards public facilities are available[18]. A great advantage of subjective measures for evaluation is to be found in the fact that contrary to the cost-oriented approach it is also applicable for those services that are not available in sufficient quantity.

The essence of this discussion could be summarized as follows:

1. In the case of *indirect* methods of evaluation and imputation, a value judgement is either explicit or implicit in the analysis. This holds true even if these external, indirect, or joint-consumption effects can be stated more readily in economic terms[19]. At the very least, a value judgement entails some trade-off between efficiency and equity or even between other social norms.

2. If we use *direct* methods of evaluating and imputing benefits, say by asking the affected parties within the context of survey research procedures about their degree of (dis)satisfaction with public programs and their attributes and by a non-metric rescaling of their responses, we obtain an empirical welfare index[20].

3. Objective and subjective indices of the use of infrastructure facilities meet with the least objections. However, the problems touched on before apply thereto: — If we recognize that the same externality may be judged as being »good« by one and »bad« by another individual, then we may rely only on subjective indices of benefits which take note of individual variances. The problem of assessing external effects thus requires the sampling of the population on the basis of a range of socio-economic and social-psychological characteristics.

3. Distributive Effects of Public Infrastructure

This empirical section is devoted to illustrating different methodological approaches on the basis of available data and to provide estimates of benefits accruing to various socio-economic groups from various infrastructure facilities.

The results of the empirical analyses are only valid under the following assumptions discussed more extensively before:

1. the marginal utility of 1 DM spent for public infrastructure is constant and equal for each beneficiary;

2. the marginal disutility of 1 DM paid in taxes is constant and equal for each tax-payer;

3. the marginal utility of the benefits conveyed by 1 DM expended for infrastructure equals in absolute terms the marginal disutility of 1 DM spent in taxes and used to finance the particular infrastructure;

4. material and immaterial bars to usage and interdependencies in usage are reflected indirectly in the empirical pattern of usage, even though they were not identified directly by a set of additional measures.

For the areas health services, recreation and leisure facilities expenditure-analyses were carried out[21]. In assessing the distributive effect of public education, fiscal residua were estimated for school expenditure and the share of taxes paid which can be associated with education expenditures on a life-income-basis.

Annual fiscal residua were computed for the case of transportation but are not reported here.

On the basis of different frequency of usage, assignment weights, were computed which are used to attribute public expenditures, i.e., costs, to the user groups. The data on usage patterns are derived from sample surveys; thus we may dispense with the use of theoretically or deductively derived assignment functions formulated, say, on the basis of assumed relations of complementarity and substitutability between private and public goods. If the distribution of socio-economic characteristics over users is known, an adjustment for the population structures can be made which reflects the differences between users and non-users. Thus expenditures can be assigned to socio-economic groups. (See case study of nursery schools). However, this is not the case for most of the user information since the results are often represented in a matrix of non-cardinal categories of answers. This necessitates the transformation and manipulation of such frequency distributions into group averages.

Usually the survey data appear tabulated as two-dimensional relative frequency distributions over N groups and M possible prestructured (or coded) answer categories $A_m (m = 1,..., M)$. The elements P_{nm} $(n = 1,..., N, m = 1,..., M)$ of the resulting matrix (or vector) indicate which percentage of a group responded in a certain manner. For the n-th group the index value indicating the frequency of usage G_n is arrived at by assigning numerical ranks R_m to the possible answer categories and weighting them with their relative frequency, such that

$$(1) \qquad G_n = \sum_{m=1}^{M} R_m P_{nm}$$

Optimal scales using Lingoe's methods can only be applied to micro-data; therefore, they are not applicable to secondary statistics[22].

A simple and rather crude rank weighting method may be employed which seems, however, to exhibit a relatively high degree of accuracy as indicated by various tests and comparisons.

The pre-structured answers can be cardinal or non-cardinal in nature.

a. Cardinal measures, (e.g., number of visits at the doctor's office during a period (»0, 1—2, 3—5, 5—10«). In this case it is advisable to take as R_m a class median or class average.

b. Non-cardinal measures: (e.g., visit to the doctor's office: »very often, often, sometimes, rarely, never«). In this case arbitrary numerical values chosen in monotonic order to the implied order of the verbal categories are used as R_m such as »4, 3, 2, 1, 0«[23].

We may transform these vectors or matrices (in the case of cross tabulations across more than one socio-economic characteristic) of social goods consumption indices in such a manner that the average value of the index is 1; this yields vectors/matrices in which the average level of consumption of a public service by a certain group is related to the overall average consumption by all groups.

Formally stated:

$$(2) \qquad I_n = \frac{G_n}{(1/N)\sum G_n}$$

The point of crucial importance is not the overall size of expenditure positions but rather the structure of the distributive pattern applicable to these positions.

As far as possible the relative sizes of socio-economic groups were derived from official statistics rather than using the relative shares reflected by the respective samples. The distribution by occupation, however, had to be derived from the respective samples since no better statistics of the distribution of the entire population by these characteristics are available. The official statistics on the distribution of occupations over the members of the labor force cannot be used for this purpose since the survey was not confined to the labor force but covered the entire resident population. Furthermore, using only the labor force as the relevant population to distribute the benefits of public services to, would imply that all those not in the labor force (e.g., housewives, retired people and persons still in schools or in training) would not get any benefits assigned to them. Although we resorted to this treatment of the distribution over occupational groups, the bias involved in the neglect of those not belonging to the labor force could not be avoided completely: Some surveys were not representative of the entire resident population as they did not cover the retired, housewives and/or students. The share of public goods attributed to them by this procedure would be zero; hence no comparison between these groups and groups included in the survey could be drawn. Useful conclusions can still be drawn from these results as far as they apply to the groups included: In distributional analyses often the relative position and not the absolute differences are of major concern.

Furthermore, in the distribution by net income of households the population shares represented indicate the relative number of households and not persons belonging to a group. The distribution of households by income groups was derived from the DIW distribution statistics. We had to refrain from using the official statistics in this context since the group definitions used in the various sample surveys did not correspond to those used in the official statistics.

For the distribution by age we encounter the problem that surveys include individuals only within certain age groups (e.g., between 18 and 80). Attributing shares of social goods only to these groups would evidently have involved the assumption that those younger than 18 or older than 80 did not receive benefits from public services. This is an unrealistic assumption. In order to avoid this draw-back it was assumed that the population groups not included in the sample survey received a share of a service equal to their share in the overall population. That part of the population covered by the survey was then treated separately; and a specific (non-uniform) distribution was derived over that part of the population.

No such problem was encountered when we attempted a distribution by size of residential communities. The classifications covered the entire resident population exhaustively so the share of different sizes of communities in the total number of communities could be derived from the statistical yearbook.

3.1 Imputation of Expenditure Items via Usage Patterns

3.1.1 Health

The analysis of the distributive effects of the health system of the Federal Republic of Germany is based on the assignment of expenditure shares to socioeconomic groups. This assignment takes place for the sub-system of the overall health system, i.e., for the usage of hospitals, doctors' services, frequency of purchase of medicines, and the usage of preventive health examinations. This analysis deals also with the activities of para-fiscal, i.e., non-governmental institutions being part of the system of social security.

From Table 2 (see page 85) the pattern of usage of hospitals can be noted. The benefits accruing to socio-economic groups were derived on a cost basis as derived from the Social Budget[24]. The shares of costs were assigned on the basis of relative frequency of usage of hospital facilities.

Column 1 of Table 2 indicates a deviation from average use resulting from different groups' differential use of hospital facilities.

In a survey, respondents were asked: »Have you yourself used one of the following facilities once, several times, or not at all?« Their answers were recorded into numerical values »1, 2 or 0«. These scores were then used to compute an index of usage which was expressed as a multiple of the overall average of the scores. (Column 1 of Table 2). It is assumed that equal benefits are conveyed to individuals for an equal rate of utilization. Accordingly, in the case of a pure good the costs assignable to a group would correspond to the share of that group in the total population.

Column 2 of Table 2 indicates the cost shares attributable to various socio-economic groups in line with this imputation rule. As the actual rate of usage of hospital facilities differed from group to group as reflected in the index values, the final figure in column 2 represents the benefits accruing to the group on the basis of the differential rate of usage of hospitals by groups. It is derived by multiplying the average benefit accruing to a user (not the total population!) with the number of users in a group.

From Table 2 it becomes evident that women, the elderly, and inhabitants of communities with up to 20,000 residents derive greater benefits from the expenditure of public funds for this type of infrastructure facility. Men, younger persons, and inhabitants of communities with more than 20,000 residents derive fewer benefits on the basis of their relatively less intensive use of these facilities.

In Table 3 (see page 86) similar information is presented for doctors' services, medication, and preventive examinations. The index value derived for Table 3 differs from that of Table 2 as it pertains to the percentage of the groups surveyed who used the facility. Otherwise benefits were assigned as in the case of hospitals.

The following patterns may be noted:

1. Women use doctors' services to a greater extent than men do[25].

2. For the use of medications we note a pattern associated with age and sex: Women buy approximately twice as many medicines as do men. The use of medicines is increased by a factor of six as one moves from the age between 14 and 29 years to the age group 60 and above.

3. Women of the age group 40 − 59 avail mostly of preventive examinations. This applies also to men. Women in the age group 30 − 49 however utilize preventive examinations to the greatest extent.

3.1.2 Leisure and Recreation

To estimate the distributive effect of sports and recreation we again utilize surveys on the pursuit of sports and recreational activities.

Those who appear to derive less benefits are workers, farmers, members of household with income under 600 DM and the older persons. (Table 4, page 87)

Table 2 The Usage Pattern of Hospitals
(by sex, age, size of residential community, and province)*

	J_I [1]	Actual	Hypothetical equal	(2) - (3)	% of population
		Expenditure for Group in Mio DM			
	(1)	(2)	(3)	(4)	(5)
SEX [2]					
Male	0,91	6479	7159	- 680	46,96
Female	1,09	8766	8086	+ 680	53,04
TOTAL:		15245	15245		
AGE					
Under 18	--	4031	4031	0	26,44
18-21	1,04	877	829	48	5,44
22-25	0,81	710	854	- 144	5,60
26-29	1,19	916	750	166	4,92
30-39	0,78	1898	2369	- 471	15,54
40-49	0,81	1561	1877	- 316	12,31
50-59	1,07	1666	1515	151	9,94
60-69	1,22	2128	1698	430	11,14
70 & Over	1,07	1454	1323	131	8,68
TOTAL:		15241	15246		
SIZE OF RESIDENTIAL COMMUNITY (No.Residents) [3]					
less than 2000	1,12	1655	1495	160	9,81
2000 - 20,000	1,12	5687	5139	548	33,71
20,000-100,000	1,00	3551	3595	- 44	23,58
100,000-500,000	1,00	2336	2364	- 28	15,51
500,000 & more	0,77	2016	2651	- 635	17,39
TOTAL:		15245	15246		
PROVINCE					
Bayern	0,86	2355	2666	- 311	17,49
Baden Württemberg	0,86	2006	2270	- 264	14,89
Rheinland-Pfalz/ Saarland	1,41	1709	1180	529	7,74
Hessen	1,00	1409	1371	38	8,99
Nordrhein-Westfalen	0,97	4218	4232	- 14	27,76
Niedersachsen	1,00	1834	1785	49	11,71
Schleswig-Holstein	1,04	678	634	44	4,16
Bremen/Hamburg	0,86	535	607	- 72	3,98
West-Berlin	-	500	500	0	3,28
TOTAL:		15244	15245		

* Computations based on data from Infratest, Repräsentativerhebung, München 1976, Tab. 191 — 199

Based on a sample survey representative of the Federal Republic of Germany (not including West Berlin); October 1975, sample size 2541

Question: »Have you yourself used one of the following facilities in the course of the last few years, once or several times«? (one of the facilities mentioned being hospitals). Prestructure 3 answers: once — several times — never

1. Index computation: The values » 1 — 2 — 0 « were assigned to the answers »once — several times — never«, the index value was computed as multiple of the overall average (multiple vector),

2. Population distribution derived from Statistisches Jahrbuch für die Bundesrepublik Deutschland 1975; p. 58,

3. Population distribution derived, Ibid., p. 57.

Table 3 The Distributive Effects of Real Transfers through Facilities for Doctors' Services, Medication, Preventive Examination (by Sex and Age)*

	Doctors' Services				Medication				Preventive Examinations				% of
	J_n [1]	Actual	Hypothetical equal	(2)-(3)	J_n [1]	Actual	Hypothetical equal	(6)-(7)	J_n [1]	Actual	Hypothetical equal	(10)-(11)	Population [2]
		Expenditures for Groups in mill DM				Expenditures for Groups in mill DM				Expenditures for Groups in mill DM			
	(1)	(2)	(3)	(4)	(5)	(6)	(7)	(8)	(9)	(10)	(11)	(12)	(13)
Sex													
male	0,861	3981	4663	-682	0,667	2420	3702	-1282	0,805	325	408	-83	46,96
female	1,139	5949	5267	682	1,333	5463	4181	1282	1,195	544	461	83	53,04
total		9930	9930			7883	7883			869	869		
Age													
under 14	-	2050	2050	0	-	1627	1627	0	-	179	179	0	20,64
14 -29	0,605	1348	2161	-813	0,301	523	1715	-1192	0,887	175	189	-14	21,76
30 - 39	0,802	1277	1543	-266	0,661	820	1225	- 405	1,026	144	135	9	15,54
40 - 49	1,026	1295	1222	73	1,002	984	970	14	1,178	131	107	24	12,31
50 - 59	1,238	1262	987	275	1,107	878	784	94	1,159	104	86	18	9,94
60 and over	1,329	2699	1967	732	1,930	3052	1562	1490	0,750	135	172	-37	19,81
total		9931				7884	7883			868	868		100
Males-Age													
under 14	-	1051	1051	0	-	834	834	0	-	92	92	0	10,58
14 - 29	0,415	484	1114	-630	0,161	143	884	- 741	0,640	65	98	-33	11,22
30 - 39	0,626	530	810	-280	0,410	266	643	- 377	0,592	44	71	-27	8,16
40 - 49	1,023	646	605	41	0,823	397	480	- 83	0,933	52	53	- 1	6,09
50 - 59	1,317	563	409	154	0,846	277	325	- 48	1,052	39	36	3	4,12
60 and over	1,325	1058	764	294	1,680	1025	606	419	0,844	59	67	- 8	7,69
Females-Age													
under 14	-	999	999	0	-	793	793	0	-	87	87	0	10,06
14 - 29	0,771	844	1048	-204	0,482	404	832	- 428	1,128	108	92	16	10,55
30 - 39	0,979	750	733	17	0,920	538	582	- 44	1,518	102	64	38	7,38
40 - 49	1,056	681	618	63	1,282	632	490	142	1,368	77	54	23	6,22
50 - 59	1,233	745	578	167	1,381	638	459	179	1,218	64	51	13	5,82
60 and over	1,256	1579	1204	375	2,016	1937	955	982	0,707	78	105	-27	12,12
total		9930				7884	7883			867	870		100

Source: Computations based on data derived from Infratest, Werbeerfolgskontrolle 1974 der Maßnahmen der Bundeszentrale für gesundheitliche Aufklärung, München 1975. Sample survey representative of the Federal Republic of Germany and West-Berlin, April, May 1975, sample size: 2017.

1. Group-Index: Multiple of average number of »visits« multiplied by number of people in group.
2. Population distribution based on Statistisches Jahrbuch für die Bundesrepublik Deutschland 1975, p. 58.

Table 4 The Distributive Effects of Real Transfers through Facilities for Recreation and Sports (by occupation, monthly net income, education, age and size of residential community)

	J_n [4] (1)	Actual Expenditures for Groups in mill DM (2)	Hypothetical equal Expenditures for Groups in mill DM (3)	(2)-(3) (4)	% of Population (5)
Occupation [2]					
Proprietor/Manager (large entreprise) professional/propietor	1,00	205	183	22	5,08
higher civil servants & white collar workers	1,27	210	147	63	4,09
other civil servants & white collar workers	1,39	1283	820	463	22,81
blue collar workers	0,88	637	643	- 6	17,89
farmers	0,91	74	72	2	2,00
other	0,61	1187	1730	-543	48,12
total		3596	3596		
Monthly Net Household [3] Income					
under 600	0,18	23	180	-157	5,0
600 - 800	0,36	68	263	-195	7,3
800 - 1000	0,64	168	367	-199	10,2
1000 - 1500	1,23	663	755	- 84	21,0
1500 - 2000	1,68	685	572	113	15,9
2000 and more	1,91	1990	1460	530	40,6
total		3596	3596		
Education [4]					
secondary school	0,64	2308	2797	-489	77,79
intermediate level (10 grades)	1,33	1038	605	433	16,83
high school, colleges university	1,00	250	194	56	5,38
total		3596	3596		
Age [5]					
under 16 and over 80		928	928	0	25,81
16 - 24	1,68	798	445	353	12,38
25 - 34	1,30	714	514	200	14,29
35 - 44	1,15	605	492	113	13,67
45 - 59	0,71	440	579	-139	16,11
60 - 79	0,16	109	638	-529	17,74
total		3596	3596		
Size of Residential Community [6] (No. of Residents)					
less than 2000	1,01	353	352	1	9,8
2000 - 20000	1,01	1218	1216	2	33,8
20000 - 100000	1,08	909	849	60	23,6
100000 - 500000	0,84	464	557	- 93	15,5
500000 and more	1,05	652	626	26	17,4
total		3596	3596		

1. Index: percentage of those who engage in sports.
2. Population distribution derived from sample.
3. Population distribution derived from DIW Wochenbericht 31/75, p. 249.
4. Population distribution derived from Statistisches Jahrbuch für die BRD 1975, p. 57.
5. Population distribution derived from Statistisches Jahrbuch für die BRD 1975, Wohnbevölkerung nach dem Alter, p. 58.
6. Population distribution derived from Statistisches Bundesamt, Fachserie A, Bevölkerung und Kultur, Volkszählung vom Mai 1970 Heft 3, p. 22.

Source: Usage Pattern: DIVO INMAR, Der Westdeutsche Markt in Zahlen, Neubearbeitung 1974, Frankfurt/Main 1974, p. 338.
Sample survey representative of the Federal Republic of Germany, spring 1974, two samples of size 2000.
Expenditures: Statistisches Jahrbuch für die Bundesrepublik Deutschland 1975, p. 402.

3.1.3 Nursery Schools

On December 31, 1972 there were 1,415,541 places in children's day-care facilities available. The places supplied by public nursery schools and semi-public nursery schools (»Träger der freien Jugendhilfe«) amounted to 1,293,456; this represents 93.33 % of the total places in children's day-care facilities which are offered by these institutions. The total expenditures of the public sector for children's day-care facilities amounted to 515.1 Mill. DM. Of these 305.3 Mill. DM were spent for public facilities and 209.8 Mill. DM for subsidies to the semi-public facilities (»Träger der freien Jugendhilfe«). There is no further differentiation of these expenditures for special types of kindergarden (day-care facilities for infants, pre-school and school children).

The problem of estimating the extent of expenditures for nursery schools can be resolved as follows:

The number of places available through public supply and through semi-public supply amount to 93.33 % of all places and nursery schools which are being financed by these institutions. Accordingly, we shall assume henceforth that the expenditures for nursery schools amount to 93.33 % of the total public outlays for children's day-care facilities. Accordingly, we estimated that total expenditures of the public sector made for nursery schools amount to 480.7 Mill. DM. Unlike the previous cases, the potential users of nursery schools are only the pre-school age members of the household. Thus, share of potential users, not the population share, is used in the weighting procedure.

From Table 5 (see page 89) we note the net transfer per child that results to particular groups from their use of nursery facilities[26].

The following results may be noted:

1. In 1972, the socio-economic groups most benefited are also among the upper income groups, specifically households with monthly net incomes of DM 1 800 and more, the self-employed outside agriculture, and those families whose head of household had at least completed high school or an equivalent school.

2. In 1972, the lower income and status groups accordingly received less benefits. This applies particularly for income groups under DM 1 000, for self-employed farmers and unpaid family workers, as well as for others such as unskilled labor, families with head of household who has not completed secondary school (Hauptschulabschluß), and those who have not completed any occupational training.

3. Even in the year 1974 (Table 6, page 90) we note similar patterns of usage: Households with income under DM 300 received less than half of real transfers per child of what households with DM 2 500 and more monthly net income received. When the pattern of usage is differentiated by community size we get a less extreme pattern of distribution.

4. When we compare the increase in real transfers for the periods 1972 and 1974, we note an increasing disparity between high incomes (increase of 8 %) and low incomes (a decrease by 7 %). The highest increase in benefits was obtained by self-employed farmers and unpaid family workers (an increase of 25.9 %). The share of children in this group who attended a nursery school increased from 19.39 to 24.40 %. This increase seems to reflect the structural changes in agriculture which also resulted in the reduction of unskilled workers.

Table 5 Real Transfers Conveyed to Different Socio-Economic Groups through Nursery Schools Use 1972 (by net income of household, labor force status, education, training)

		Real Transfer to the group in million DM	Real Transfer per child in the group
Monthly net income of household (in DM)			
under 1000	0,82	98.967	68,87
1000 - 1400	0,90	179.997	75,66
1400 - 1800	1,15	97.045	96,85
1800 and over	1,21	81.351	101,16
Farmers & unpaid family workers	0,74	18.256	62,09
no answer[1]	1,18	5.124	98,55
TOTAL:		480.740	80,55
Labor force status of head of family			
in labor			
self-employed and unpaid family workers	1,04	69.180	87,46
among these: self-employed (non-agricultural)	1,22	51.885	102,95
civil servants/judges	0,96	45.159	80,93
white collar workers	1,17	150.532	98,46
skilled laborers	0,89	126.190	75,20
other laborers	0,71	71.422	59,77
not in labor force	1,00	18.256	84,13
TOTAL:		480.740	80,55
General education attainment level of head of family			
Secondary school, no answer	0,85	346.863	75,90
intermediate (10 grades)	1,06	77.507	94,64
high school	1,09	56.369	97,36
TOTAL:		480.740	80,55
Occupational training of head of family			
no training, no answer	0,71	74.305	60,86
vocational training	0,94	288.252	80,47
higher vocational training/engineer	1,22	65.978	104,56
vocational schooling technical college/Uni.	1,14	52.206	97,76
TOTAL:		480.740	80,55

Source: Statistisches Bundesamt, Der Besuch von Kindergärten und Sozialstruktur der Kinder und ihrer Eltern, in: Wirtschaft und Statistik, 1974, S. 21 and own computations. We thank the Statistisches Bundesamt for their kind assistance.

Table 6 Real Transfers Conveyed to Different Socio-Economic Groups through Nursery Schools Use 1974 (by size of residential community and monthly net income)

	J_n	Real Transfer to the group in million DM	Real Transfer per child in the group
Size of residential community of head of family (No. of inhabitants)			
less than 2000	0,92	55,376	80,55
2,000 − 10,000	1,09	120,073	95,76
10,000 − 20,000	1,02	62,134	89,26
20,000 − 100,000	0,99	100,600	87,16
100,000 and more	0,99	117,126	86,66
TOTAL:		455,309	88,52
Monthly net income of head of family (in DM)			
less than 300 DM	0,71	256	56,89
300 DM − 600 DM	0,73	2,434	58,51
600 DM − 1.000 DM	0,80	22,516	64,81
1.000 DM − 1.400 DM	0,91	109,440	73,48
1.400 DM − 1.800 DM	1,10	108,959	88,24
1.800 DM − 2.500 DM	1,28	113,027	103,12
2.500 DM and more	1,50	73,280	120,45
unpaid family workers self-employed farmers	0,97	17,038	78,16
no answers	1,01	8,359	81,40
TOTAL:		455,310	88,53

Source: Own computation on the basis of data derived from the census April 1974. We thank the Statistisches Bundesamt for their kind assistance.

5. From these patterns we may conclude that on the basis of the usage of nursery school facilities no equalizing impact can be expected as long as the supply of nursery school places within the proximity of different groups is not enhanced, and secondly, as long as the lower socio-economic groups do not obtain adequate information about the benefits of using nursery schools.

3.2 Life-Time Tax-Transfer Residua (The Case of Education)

The previous case studies indicate that the usage of public infrastructure is dependent on the user's life cycle variables.

In estimating the distributive effects by monthly income levels or even by annual income we neglect wide variances in the distribution of transfers over the life cycle of individuals and groups. The concept of life-time-income, life-time-taxes, and the life-time-transfers therefore offers us a more satisfactory frame of reference for interpreting distributive impacts. This applies particularly to the case of education: »Annual gross income gives completely misleading information on resources available over long periods to individuals with a different profession.«[27]

Accordingly, we estimated the life-cycle distribution of benefits from education facilities by different levels of education of the recipients of these benefits. As a basis for such a simulation of life-time patterns we used the cross-section data of the 1970 census, specifically the monthly net income. For alternative levels of education and different social positions we estimated life-time-net-income.

Monetary and real transfers are provided by the public to those who use public education facilities. Apart from estimating the monetary and real transfers accruing to individuals from the use of different levels of education facilities the educational taxes paid during the life-time of these individuals are also shown in Table 7 (see page 92)[28].

The difference between total taxes paid and total transfers received over one's life-time is reflected in the life-time residuum; it provides an indication of the extent of redistribution which occurs via the system of public education. (See Table 8, page 92).

The analysis of life-time patterns of taxes and transfers as well as of the fiscal residua indicates that life-time-income generally increases with higher levels of education. Furthermore, those whose education entails the highest costs, namely the graduates of university level institutions, are not obliged to repay via taxes the total costs which arose for their education in the first place. Their negative life-time residua correspond to the positive life-time residua of others who utilized lower levels of educational facilities. It can be argued therefore that the latter subsidized the former at least within the sphere of educational finances.

4. Summary and Conclusions

We shall now attempt to formulate brief answers to the basic questions posed at the outset. These may also serve as a summary of the underlying logic of the paper which tends to be obscured at times by the cluster of specific arguments.

Table 7 Net-Life Incomes of Individuals with Different Educational Attainment Level and Occupation.

Educational Level		Type of Occupation			
		Blue Collar Worker	White Collar Worker	Civil Servant	Self-employed
Secondary School	DM	447 470	529 400	603 977	760 897
	%	100	100	100	100
Inter-mediate Level (10 Grades)	DM	459 260	599 712	722 232	1 026 035
	%	103	113	120	135
Gymnasium (High-School)	DM	482 212	746 724	875 141	1 135 386
	%	108	141	145	149
Vocational & Technical Schools	DM	493 822	592 742	730 442	929 700
	%	110	112	121	122
Technical Schools	DM	617 930	968 103	871 200	1 305 586
	%	138	183	144	172
College & University	DM	500 996	891 937	1 115 012	1 401 747
	%	112	168	185	184

Source: INIFES: Verteilungswirkungen des Bildungssystems: computed on the basis of data derived from the census 1970

1. Percentages: 100 % = income of person with secondary school education only

Table 8 Life-Time Tax-Transfer Residua[29]

Educational Level	Type of Occupation			
	Blue Collar Worker	White Collar Worker	Civil Servant	Self-employed
Secondary Schools	+145	+5 236	+5 991	+14 246
Intermediate Level (10 grades)	-454	+5 100	+9 244	+26 981
Gymnasium	-15 297	-1 475	-727	+14 399
Vocational & Technical Schools	-951	+2 998	+6 202	+22 070
Technical Colleges	-9 757	+9 743	-1 754	+27 047
Universities	-75 334	-54 795	-54 685	-17 871

Source: INIFES: Verteilungswirkungen des Bildungssystems: computed on the basis of data derived from the census 1970

1. Percentages; 100 % = income of person with secondary school education only
positive residuum ⇒ Transfer < Tax
negative residuum ⇒ Transfer > Tax

1. Which assumptions and concepts may be employed to assess the (re)distributive consequences of expenditures for public infrastructure?

The assumptions employed either explicitly or implicitly pertain to the very heart of our conception of the fiscal process:

a. If we assume *voluntary or quasi-exchange* to characterize the relations between households and the government, then we may follow Aaron and McGuire in analyzing the distribution of public and private goods consumption in two discrete steps: first, to assume a redistribution of private goods by taxes and transfers, and second, a *purchase of public goods* paid for by the household's taxes at a rate equal to its marginal rate of substitution between private and public goods.

The basis for the valuation in step two is thus *value-in-exchange* — marginal utility times quantity. Intra-marginal utility gains — or consumer's surplus — are excluded.

b. If we reject the notion of voluntary exchanges and assume instead that the tax-transfer-process is fashioned more by political and social relations of groups, particularly by their more complex goals, then we rely essentially on a *transfer or grants* notion: Taxes are extracted by the government from households or individuals (including firms) who view said payments as more or less voluntary transfers of exchangeables; and the benefits they receive as bilateral transfers about whose magnitude they cannot decide as individuals, neither by quoting a higher or lower »price« nor by any other form of bargaining or preference articulation familiar from the market place save by voting. (And even then the extent of impact of any one individual's perception of his marginal rate of substitution between private and public goods is likely to be minimal).

The quasi-exchange-element of the tax-transfer-process may thus be defined as the magnitude of taxes paid and the grant-element as the fiscal residuum, narrowly defined as the difference between taxes paid and benefits received from specific goods, and more broadly, as the difference between taxes paid and benefits received from specific plus public goods.

The use of the fiscal residuum as a first-cut measure of redistribution is not entirely unambiguous: By defining regressive, proportional and progressive tax systems and expenditure systems, respectively, and by assuming either constant or diminishing marginal utilities of income, several more complex interpretations of residuum are possible.

2. Which problems arise on the expenditure side when we attempt to evaluate and impute expenditures to socio-economic groups?

Even after we have refined the index which also reflects our method of evaluation of the share of benefits going to various socio-economic groups, we still face problems on the expenditure side: The presence of merit goods, potential use, material and immaterial bars to usage and interdependencies of usage, prevents, at least in principle, a simple adding of individual benefits as reflected in cost shares. Some supervening logic appears to be called for which, say, subtracts merit goods from some apparent beneficiaries and adds them to those whose interdependent utility functions have given rise to their provision. Or, actual use may have to be multiplied with a probability vector reflecting likely or potential use. Furthermore, interdependencies imply that a simple addition of the benefits of individual public facilities is not adequate. Similarly, material and immaterial bars appear to warrant a subtraction from actual or potential benefits, and so on.

Any attempt on the part of the investigator to change evaluations, so to say from the lofty vantage point of his desk, is likely to bring him back to the very problems familiar from the literature. Perhaps here again we should hear the truth from »the horse's mouth«, i.e., from the users of public facilities. Again the plea is for non-traditional measures, say, via empirical welfare indices which reflect benefits »through the eyes of the beholders«.

3. Which alternative criteria for evaluation and imputation can be applied which allow either an indirect or direct assignment of benefits (of costs) to socio-economic groups?

After all is said and done, three alternative methods are employed for the practical work of empirical estimation and of the incidence of benefits derived from social goods:

a. The assignment of budget item shares as proxies for costs incurred (input-orientation) according to alternative theoretical assignment criteria;

b. the assignment of expenditure items according to empirically derived global usage patterns;

c. the assignment of specific expenditure items on the basis of citizen preference patterns regarding individual infrastructure facilities.

The merit of the empirical results may be sought in the attempt to leave method a. behind as far as possible, given the information on »revealed behavior«, say in the form of global or more detailed usage patterns (method b). On the other hand with the aid of a catalogue of infrastructure equipment in conjunction with detailed user analyses all real transfers and their distribution by socio-economic groups can be assessed through objective and subjective indicators.

None of these methods is likely to be greeted with the unqualified applause of the purist used to contemplate the elegant but abstract categories and structures of economic theory. Nonetheless, in a world in which some information is better than none and where quantitative estimates yield a premium over theoretical speculation, these estimates of the incidence of expenditures for public infrastructure may be of some use for public policy.

Notes

[1] »Real transfers« consist of all goods and services provided to the citizens in a »real«, i.e. non monetary form, by the public sector.

[2] Samuelson, P.A., »Pure Theory of Public Expenditure and Taxation«, in: Margolis, J. a. Guitton, H. (eds.), *Public Economics,* London a.o. 1969, pp. 98—112.

[3] Aaron, H. and McGuire, M.C., »Benefits and Burdens of Government Expenditures«, in: Boulding, K.E. and Pfaff, M. (eds.), *Redistribution to the Rich and the Poor*, Belmont, Calif.: Wadsworth Publ. Co., 1972, pp. 42—43 (»To each household should be imputed a fraction of the total value of public goods proportional to the reciprocal of its marginal utility of income«, p. 45).

[4] *Ibid.*, footnote to p. 43.

[5] In theory each individual could check off in his tax return the purposes for which his taxes may be used, and the proportions in which he wishes them to be allocated among these uses. Such an expression of preferences — which runs contrary to the principle of non-affectation — however, is not generally possible for most national taxes; it is being approximated only in some countries by some taxes (e.g., millage to support education in U.S. cities).

[6] We shall follow the convention established by Buchanan: A positive residuum indicates that an individual has paid more in taxes than the imputed amount of benefits received by him from the fiscal system. A negative residuum, in turn, implies a net benefit received.
Buchanan, J., »The Pure Theory of Public Finance«, in: *Fiscal Theory and Politcal Economy*, Chapel Hill, N.C.: The University of N. Carolina Press, 1960, p. 17.

[7] Pfaff, M. and Pfaff, A.B., »Grants Economics: An Evaluation of Government Policies«, *Public Finance*, 1971, pp. 275—303.

[8] Gillespie, W.J., »The Effects of Public Expenditures on the Distribution of Income. An Empirical Investigation«, in: Musgrave, R.A. (ed.), *Essays in Fiscal Federalism*, Washington, D.C.: Brookings Institution, 1965. Tax Foundation, Inc., *Tax Burdens and Benefits of Covernment Expenditures by Income Class 1961 and 1965*, New York, Tax Foundation, Inc., 1967.

[9] See: Pommerehne, W., Budgetäre Umverteilung in der Demokratie. Ein empirischer Test alternativer Hypothesen, in: *Zeitschrift für Wirtschafts- und Sozialwissenschaften*, 1975, pp. 327. Pommerehne compares marginal utility elasticities derived on the basis of alternative hypotheses on redistribution with the elasticities actually encountered.

[10] See: Boulding, K.E. and Pfaff, M. (eds.), *Redistribution to the Rich and the Poor*, op. cit., pp. 387—389.

[11] See: Pfaff, M. and Fuchs, G., »Education, Inequality and Life Income: A Report on the Federal Republic of Germany«, in: OECD (ed.), *Education, Inequality and Life Chances*, Vol. 2, Paris 1975, pp. 7—128.

[12] See: Hanusch, H., *Personale Verteilung öffentlicher Leistungen*, Habilitationsschrift, unpublished manuscript, Nuremberg-Erlangen 1974, p. 206.

[13] See: Zangemeister, Ch., *Nutzwertanalyse in der Systemtechnik*, 2. edition, Munich 1971, p. 319.

[14] Biervert, B., Subjektive Sozialindikatoren. Ansatzpunkte einer sozioökonomischen Theorie der Bedürfnisse, in: Dierkes, M. (ed.), *Soziale Daten und politische Planung. Sozialindikatorenforschung in der BRD und den USA*, Frankfurt, New York 1975, p. 98.

[15] Thoss, R., Indikatoren für die Qualität des Lebens: Probleme der regionalstatistischen Definition und der regionalpolitischen Interpretation, in: Thoss, R. u.a. (eds.), *Gesellschaftliche Indikatoren als Orientierungshilfe für die Regionalpolitik*, Materialien zum Siedlungs- und Wohnungswesen und zur Raumplanung, Vol. 10, Muenster 1974, p. 13; and: Dietrichs, B., Vor- und Nachteile der Verwendung von Inputindikatoren in der Regionalpolitik, *Ibid.*, p. 71.

[16] Schmidt, V. and Gustafsson, K., Sozialindikatoren: Rationalisierung oder Verschleierung der Willensbildung? in: Pfaff, M. and Gehrmann, F. (eds.), *Informations- und Steuerungsinstrumente zur Schaffung einer höheren Lebensqualität in Städten*, Göttingen 1976, pp. 581—622.

[17] Pfaff, M., »Indices of Consumer and Citizen Satisfaction: Measure of the Performance of the Market and Public Economy«, in: Biervert, B., Schaffartzik, H.J. and Schmoelders, G. (eds.), *Konsum und Qualität des Lebens*, Opladen 1974, p. 343—385. It may be assumed that for repetitive purchases or usage there is a particular relationship between the willingness to pay for goods or services and the level of satisfaction derived from the consumption or use of said good or service. The conceptual questions resulting from this assumption, however, shall not be explored in this paper.

[18] These methods have been applied to three German cities. See: Pfaff, M. »Informations- und Steuerungsinstrumente zur Schaffung einer höheren Lebensqualität in Städten«, in: Pfaff M. and Gehrmann F. (eds.), *Informations- und Steuerungsinstrumente zur Schaffung einer höheren Lebensqualität in Städten*, Göttingen 1975, pp. 13—80.

[19] For example, in the context of the decentralization of government within a metropolitan area, externalities and transaction flows across borders can be identified more readily. The same holds true for the negative externalities or »damages« imposed on people by government programs involving forced sales due to the construction of urban highways or due to urban renewal.
See: Rothenberg, J., »Local Decentralization and the Theory of Optimal Government«, and Downs, A., »Uncompensated Nonconstruction Costs Which Urban Highways and Urban Renewal Impose Upon Residential Households«, both in: Margolis, J. (ed.), *The Analysis of Public Output*, New York: Columbia University Press 1970 1—4.

[20] Pfaff, M., »Indices of Consumer and Citizen Satisfaction: Measure of the Performance of the Market and Public Economy«, *op.cit.*

[21] A method of incorporating such user profiles within an input-output-matrix was suggested by Mackscheidt, K., »Zur Bewertung von Realtransfers in Verteilungsanalysen«, paper presented at the DFG-Symposium »Grenzen der Verteilungs- und Sozialpolitik in einer stagnierenden bzw. wachsenden Wirtschaft«, Augsburg, July 1976.

[22] For the application of such methods, see: Lingoes, J.C. and Pfaff, M., »The Index of Consumer Satisfaction: Methodology«, in: Venkatesan, M. (ed.), *Proceedings of the Conference of the Association for Consumer Research,* Iowa City: University of Iowa Press, 1973. For scaling in general, see for example: Sixtl, F., Skalierungsverfahren: Grundzüge und ausgewählte Methoden sozialwissenschaftlichen Messens, in: Holm, K. (ed.), *Die Befragung,* Vol. 4, Munich 1976, pp. 9.

[23] It is necessary that the answer categories A_m imply an unambiguous order. Assigning the numerical values 8, 6, 4, 2, 0 to the answer categories does not change the results. For the application of such rank weights in the construction of behavioral indices see: Lüdtke, H., *Freizeit in der Industriegesellschaft,* Opladen 1972, pp. 80.

[24] See: *Sozialbericht 1976,* BT Drucksache 7/4953, Bonn, April 1, 1976.

[25] See also: INFRATEST, *Soziale Indikatoren. Repräsentativerhebungen Bundesrepublik Deutschland 1970—1973,* Munich 1974, Table A-18.

[26] Alone the expenditures for nursery schools were estimated on the basis of the ratio of nursery schools to day-care centers. The financing agency — public versus semi-public versus private — was taken into account.

[27] Lindbeck, A., »Inequality and Redistribution, Policy Issues, Principles and Swedish Experience«, in: OECD (ed.), *Education, Inequality, and Life Chances,* Vol. 2, Paris 1975, p. 313.

[28] We assume that for 1970 education taxes amounted to 14 % of individual total taxes since 14 % of the public budget of 1970 was expended for educational purposes. From a juxtaposition of total transfers and taxes we arrive at a life-time tax-trasfer residuum.

[29] In estimating the distributive effect of education we defined the life-time tax-transfer residuum as life-taxes paid minus life-transfers received.

Jan Pen*
Tax Policies and Transitory Income:
Some Comments

In my comments, I would like to focus particularly on two of the conference papers: they are the Pfaff-Asam and the Carlton-Hall papers. Both of these papers display substantial technical skill. Moreover, they deal with related issues.

The work of Pfaff and Asam builds upon a long tradition in economics, but one which has only recently been subjected to substantial empirical research. The basic question is: How are the burdens and benefits of the public sector distributed? Normative positions on this question range widely. Some would argue – Okun, for example, in at least one of his incarnations – that equality under the law implies that all citizens be entitled to the same total benefit from the fisc. He offers as an example the desirability of an equal speed of response by the fire department to all citizens. Others would argue that low income citizens be favored in the distribution of the net benefits of government, and would justify this position by asserting that the marginal utility of income is a decreasing function of income. Aaron and McGuire, among others, have explored the implications of this judgement. For tax policy, the implication is that burdens should be allocated according to citizens' ability to pay, and in addition the tax curve should perhaps have an increasing slope. Indeed, if this principle is applied to what has now become known as tertiary income, net benefits should be negatively related to income, with perhaps an increasing negative slope to the function. Some research has been done on estimating this net benefit function – Vos and Wyngaarden in the 1930's for the Netherlands, Musgrave and Reynolds and Smolensky more recently for the United States.

As is well-known, empirical research on the net benefit function is fraught with difficulties. The fire department might respond with equal speed, but some people have higher incomes and bigger houses than others and, hence, enjoy a larger potential benefit. Some benefits and burdens are shifted and the extent and direction of the shift is not at all well-known. Other benefits are of a public good nature and, the income base on which benefits and burdens are to be levied is not clear cut. These are only some of the problems.

---

* Who thanks Robert H. Haveman for inspiration and editorial help.

However, even though these problems plague such empirical research, such efforts are of great importance. If for no other reason, the accounting framework which they employ insures that the research results will be more reliable than speculation, which is its alternative. Intuition can lead to the conclusion that cultural and education subsidies are pro-rich, while welfare state spending is pro-poor. But such speculation cannot accurately account for the net effect of the entire public sector — including defense, health, transportation, and housing, whose benefits are much less intuitive. It may be U-shaped, but then again it may not. For this reason, then, down-to-earth, data-oriented work of the type that the Pfaff-Asam paper represents is important. While the net benefit function has not yet been completely estimated, a good start has been made.

The tax side of such studies presents less of an estimation problem than the benefit side. Empirical studies of tax incidence have been a good antidote to speculation as well. Those who complain about the high burden of taxation often create the impression that the tax burden rises monotonically with income. Yet when both income and social security taxes are considered together, the tax function may look like the back of a dromedary or even a camel. In the Netherlands, for example, the peak of one hump is at the mean income level (about 30,000 guilders in 1972), and not the modal income level. It is about this level that social security contributions cease. After the average income level, the curve slopes downward slightly and then remains horizontal until about twice this amount. At about 70,000 guilders, the average tax rate again increases until about 500,000 guilders. After this level — a very high income level in the Netherlands — the rate again falls. While the dromedary-shape is not surprising, that of the camel is.

Indeed, in 1975, Halberstadt and de Kam (*Belastingpolitiek en inkomensverdeling, verslag van het Hofstra congres*, Deventer 1975) discovered that income recipients above the level of 500,000 guilders (about 1000 taxpayers) paid an average tax on income (including social security contributions) of 38 percent instead of the 71 percent rate one would expect. These taxpayers had an average income of about one million guilders. While this finding provoked a good deal of speculation, it is clear that the result is not a matter of fraud. The figures are derived from official data and these are based on reported income. Some observers accepted the result at face value, concluding that once an income recipient has passed the 500,000 guilder watershed, his tax rate will go down. This is not so. Others concluded that there exists a small identifiable and permanent group of 1,000 Dutchmen who have these exceedingly high incomes and pay these very low tax rates. This is not true either.

The explanation is an anomaly related to the permanent-transitory phenomena, and this brings me to the Carlton-Hall paper. Halberstadt and De Kam's »1000« are no more a permanent group than the 200 of Berle and Means, or the top decile of Carlton and Hall. The Dutch tax law, as it turns out, contains a special provision for particular forms of capital gain income. This provision applies to profits which have been accumulated in privately-held corporations, taxed by the corporation tax only. When the owner quits his business, or dies, or sells his shares, the income of the firm is taxed under the income tax law but a special rate which may be as low as 20 %. Indeed, the actual rate is often a matter of bargaining between the taxpayer and the tax inspector with the latter exercising a good deal of discretion. While this is not the only loophole in the Dutch tax system, it is by far the most important for those with very high incomes. And this top bracket of a thousand people contains a large transitory component. Indeed, most of these transitory income receivers belong to the top thousand tax payers only once in their life time, and some only reach the top because they are dead.

The question now is: How can the difference between the expected 70 percent tax rate on normal income at this high level and the actual rate of 38 percent be explained? One way of proceeding would be to presume that all transitory income in this high income class is — like this special privately-held corporation income — taxed at a 20 percent rate. This would result in an estimate of about 60 percent as the proportion of the income of this group which is transitory. This pedestrian approach is to be contrasted with that of Carlton and Hall, whose paper I admire for its intellectual purity. These authors address the question of the proportion of income in the tails of the distribution which is transitory. They form an estimate of this proportion, using as little information as possible, employing a highly complex mathematical procedure based on Rao's theorem. Carlton and Hall estimate that transitory income is about $10 - 15$ percent of the total for the top decile in the United States. They do not supplement their estimate based on a quite nonintuitive approach with estimates made by more straightforward, more understandable methods. Indeed, given the availability of panel data in the United States, implementation of more pedestrian approaches — such as that which I have suggested above — would be quite feasible. Such a comparison it seems to me, is necessary if their approach is to gain credibility.

B. Paradigms in the Theory of Income Distribution

Dennis W. Carlton and Robert E. Hall*
The Distribution of Permanent Income

Most economists agree that the distribution of well-being is better measured by the distribution of permanent income than by the distribution of annual measured income, but there have been few attempts to put the idea into practice. Further, those attempts have made questionable assumptions about the relation between permanent income and observed variables, either by following Milton Friedman's suggestion that permanent income could be approximated by a moving average of actual income or by defining permanent income as a function of permanent observed characteristics, notably education. In this paper we take a rather different approach in which permanent income is an unobserved variable that cannot be measured at the level of the individual. Stochastic assumptions about transitory income make it possible to identify the distribution of permanent income within a population on the basis of observations on actual income in two years for each member of the population. Even with these assumptions, permanent income at the individual level remains unidentified.

The questions of greatest interest about the distribution of income relate to its tails. In the United States, the federal government has established a poverty threshold and reports the fraction of the population below the threshold each year. It is widely accepted that the fraction is biased upward by the inclusion of some individuals who are not genuinely poor but have suffered a purely temporary reduction in income from a normally high level. The bias is offset only partially by the exclusion of some of the genuinely poor on account of temporary increases in income. The central question addressed by our work is the magnitude of this bias. It is conceivable that there are almost no genuinely poor individuals and that the reported fraction in poverty is attributable entirely to temporary poverty. Our empirical results show that this is not the case. Though the lower tail of the distribution of permanent income is smaller than the lower tail of the distribution of reported income, it is by no means empty. Similarly, the observation that some fraction of the population has high incomes in a given year does not establish conclusively that there are any genuinely rich individuals, but our results rule this case out as well.

The statistical model of income underlying our work is precisely as stated in Chapter III of Friedman's *Theory of the Consumption Function*, except that we

*This resarch was supported by the National Science Foundation. We are grateful to Gary Chamberlain for valuable suggestions.

deal throughout with logarithms of the variables. Actual log income, y, is treated as the sum of a permanent component, u, and a transitory component, v:

$$y = u + v$$

Our stochastic hypotheses are

1. The expected value of the transitory component, v, is zero. As Friedman points out, this assumption could easily fail within a population for a particular year, because there are transitory influences in the economy at large. Our technique requires only that the transitory component be drawn from a probability distribution with the same mean for all individuals, but in the empirical results presented in this paper we assume that the common mean is zero.

2. Successive transitory components are independent. This assumption is somewhat plausible when the unit of observation is the year, but not if it is the quarter or month. It is a testable assumption within the model. Positive serial correlation of the transitory component will cause us to overstate the dispersion of permanent income slightly.

3. Permanent and transitory components are independent. Friedman assumes only that the two components are uncorrelated; as he says, this assumption has »...little substantive content and can almost be regarded as simply completing or translating the definitions of transitory and permanent components; the qualitative notion that the transitory component is intended to embody is of an accidental and transient addition to or subtraction from income, which is almost equivalent to saying an addition or subtraction that is not correlated with the rest of income.« (Friedman, 1957, pp. 26 − 27). Friedman goes on to point out that zero correlation does not imply independence, and particularly that individuals with large permanent components probably have transitory components that tend to be large in magnitude. Our use of logs takes account of this tendency, perhaps more than adequately. Our technique does depend fundamentally on the full assumption of independence.

It is a remarkable fact that the three assumptions just stated are sufficient to identify the full distributions of the permanent and transitory components, given the joint distribution of observed income in a pair of years. We emphasize that no parametric assumptions about the distributions are required to achieve identification. Distributional questions of central importance such as »What fraction of the population has permanent income below the poverty threshold?« can be answered precisely from the joint frequency distribution of current income in two years for a sufficiently large body of data on individuals. Data on lifetime income are not required.

Statistical theory

Our problem can be formalized in the following way: Let u, v_1, and v_2 be independent random variables, identified as permanent income, transitory income in the first year, and transitory income in the second year, respectively. We know the joint cumulative distribution $F(Y_1, Y_2)$ of observed income in the two years,

$$y_1 = u + v_1$$
$$y_2 = u + v_2$$

We seek the cumulative distribution functions $G(U)$, $H_1(V_1)$, and $H_2(V_2)$ of u, v_1, and v_2. We further specify that v_1 and v_2 have means zero. Then a fundamental theorem due to C.R. Rao (1973, p. 469) assures that G, H_1, and H_2 are uniquely defined by F^1. No further information or assumptions are required.

Rao's theorem establishes the feasibility of determining the distribution of permanent income, but does not lead immediately to a practical technique. Under the further assumption that the various distributions have moments of all orders[2], it is fairly straightforward to calculate the moments of the distribution of permanent income. First we define a_i as the ith moment of y_1:

$$\alpha_i = E(y_1)$$

and β_i as a certain »cross-moment«:

$$\beta_i = E(y_2 y_1^i).$$

Then we let μ_i be the ith moment of permanent income and λ_i be the ith moment of transitory income[3]. These can be calculated from the recursions,

$$\mu_i = \beta_{i-1} - \sum_{j=1}^{i-1} B_{j-1}^{i-1} \mu_j \lambda_{i-j}$$

$$\lambda_i = a_i - \sum_{j=1}^{i} B_j^i \mu_j \lambda_{i-j}$$

Here B_j^i is the jth binomial coefficient of order i. Initial conditions for the recursion are

$$\mu_0 = 1$$
$$\lambda_0 = 1$$

Appendix A establishes the validity of the recursion.

The moments of the distribution of permanent income are not themselves very informative, especially about the tails of the distribution. Our goal is to compute values of $G(U)$ itself for a variety of interesting values of U, including the poverty threshold. The only problem is to find a good way to approximate $G(U)$ on the basis of a finite number of moments. The difficulty is that the obvious methods do not converge very rapidly as the number of moments increases and do not have a rigorous sharp bound on the magnitude of the approximation error. We have adopted a somewhat more roundabout method that provides exact sharp bounds on the approximation error.

The first N moments of G are related to G by the definiton,

$$\mu_j = \int u^j dG(u) \qquad j = 0,...,N$$

This is the classical example of what is termed a Tchebycheff system. Much is known about the information regarding the unknown distribution G that can be extracted from the observed μ_j. The earliest result of this kind is the Tchebycheff inequality which gives a lower bound on $G(\mu_1 + \delta) - G(\mu_1 - \delta)$ in the case of $N = 2$, for arbitrary values of δ. For higher values of N, a powerful theory due to Markov and Krein gives upper and lower bounds on $G(U)$. Many other bounds have been developed for special cases. A unified presentation of results in this area appears in Karlin and Studden (1966). However, the mathematical literature does not contain results on the more general problem of upper and lower bounds $\overline{P}$ and $\underline{P}$ on $P = G(U_2) - G(U_1)$ for arbitrary limits U_1 and U_2 and arbitrary N.

This problem can be set up as one in infinite dimensional linear programming:

$$\overline{P} = \sup \int b(u)dG(u)$$
subject to
$$\mu_i = \int u^i dG(u) \qquad i = 0,...,N.$$

Here $b(u)$ is an indicator function for the interval $[U_1, U_2]$ taking the values one within the interval and zero outside it. We also seek $\underline{P}$, the inf of the same objective function subject to the same constraints. In Appendix B, we show that a modification of a technique due to Dantzig (1963) can be used to solve the infinite dimensional problem through a sequence of solutions of problems of finite dimension.

For any modest number of moments, the bounds $\underline{P}$ and $\overline{P}$ are fairly widely separated — this is the basic source of the slow convergence of methods based on approximating P with a finite set of moments. Our rigorous bounds on the approximation error are unfortunately rather wide. However, the extreme distributions for which $\underline{P}$ and $\overline{P}$ are attained have rather peculiar characteristics. They assign positive probability mass to N+1 points and zero probability elsewhere. In other words, of the many distributions of permanent income consistent with the given set of N moments, the distributions that could cause the largest approximation errors are extremely lumpy — the entire population has only N+1 different levels of permanent income.

There are two ways to reduce the bounds on the approximation error. The first is simply to use enough moments to bring $\underline{P}$ and $\overline{P}$ sufficiently close together. The extreme distributions become less and less lumpy as N increases, and there is always a large enough N to achieve any prescribed level of accuracy in calculating P.

The second approach is to impose additional prior information about the shape of the distribution of permanent income and to calculate $\underline{P}$ and $\overline{P}$ subject to the constraints imposed by this prior information.

In the empirical results presented later in this paper, we made use of two kinds of prior beliefs about the distribution. First, we required that the distribution be unimodal — the probability density must rise below the median and fall above the median. Second, we required that the distribution be smooth in a certain rather weak sense — essentially the derivative of the density must not exceed a prescribed bound. Details about the two restrictions appear in Appendix C. Together they brought about a substantial tightening of the bounds computed on the basis of a given set of moments.

Empirical results

In this section we present the results of a study of the annual incomes of a sample of US families over the period 1967–72. The data were obtained from the Panel Study of Income Dynamics (1972). We restricted the sample to nonrural families with white male heads between the ages of 25 and 64 in order to make it more homogeneous. We also eliminated families whose records of income were incomplete for the six years. Our sample contained 3 048 observations for 508 families. We defined income as total labor earnings of the head deflated by an index of income of men in the total US economy, with 1967 set to 1.000[4]. Since we had six observations for each family rather than just the two assumed in the earlier discussion in this paper, we computed the moments of the distribution of permanent income in a somewhat different way. The ith moment, μ_i, was computed as the average of all possible products of i distinct observations on actual income for each family. According to the permanent income model, the expectation of each such product is the moment, μ_i. It is possible to show that the six moments that can be computed this way are the only ones that can be derived from the data without adjustment for the moments of the distribution of transitory income[5]. We limited our analysis to the six moments because of our concern about the possibly large sampling variation in moments that were estimated by the recursive process outlined earlier. However, we have not so far carried out a formal analysis of the problem of sampling variation.

This procedure yielded the following moments:

$$\mu_1 = 9.0662; \; \mu_2 = .1980; \; \mu_3 = -.0067;$$
$$\mu_4 = .1926; \; \mu_5 = -.0345; \; \mu_6 = .3759.$$

The second and higher-order moments are centered around the mean.

The conventional components of variance analysis reveals that there is an important transitory component of income. The sample variance of the log of annual income is 0.2500, well in excess of our estimate of the variance of the log of permanent income $\mu_2 = .1980$. The difference between them, .0520, is our estimate of the variance of the log of transitory income.

Our next step is to investigate the information about the distribution of permanent income contained in the full set of six moments. Before starting a discussion based on the methods developed earlier in this paper, however, we should point out that one popular model of the income distribution, the log normal distribution, is clearly contradicted by our findings. The normal distribution with variance .1980 should have a fourth moment of .1176 and a sixth moment of .1164. Our estimates exceed these values by margins far larger than could be explained by sampling errors. The distribution of permanent income has tails that are thicker than predicted by the normal distribution.

Table 1 presents the results of applying our techniques to the problem of measuring the fraction of permanent income in each of a set of income categories. The first column shows the distribution of actual income within the sample. Presumably the tails of this distribution are fattened by the inclusion of transitory income. The next column gives the lower bound on the percent of the population having permanent incomes in the category, without imposing the restrictions that the distribution be unimodal and smooth. The third column gives the corresponding upper bound. These two columns can be interpreted as stating all of the information about the distribution across the income categories that is rigorously derivable from the first six moments of the distribution. For example, it is not possible to rule out definitively the possibility that there are no genuinely poor[6] families in this population and that all of those classified as poor on the basis of actual income have negative transitory components. Similarly, the first six

Table 1 Distribution of Observed Income and Derived Distribution of Permanent Income

Income range	Distribution of observed income (percent)	Unrestricted bounds		Restricted bounds (unimodal and smooth)	
		$\underline{P}$	$\overline{P}$	$\underline{P}$	$\overline{P}$
0–2000	1.1	0	2.1	0.3	0.6
0–3335	2.8	0	11.2	1.9	3.1
2000–8000	40.8	6.7	83.0	37.5	45.9
8000–14,000	44.6	0	86.6	39.0	51.0
14,000–20,000	9.1	0	35.3	6.8	12.0
20,000+	4.4	0	14.8	2.7	4.0

moments do not show conclusively that there is any family with a permanent income above $ 20,000. This illustrates just how weak is the distributional information contained in a small set of moments. The large gap between $\underline{P}$ and $\overline{P}$ in every category shows that the problem is the low information content of moments with respect to the class of all possible distributions. The fourth and fifth columns restrict the class of distributions to those that are unimodal and smooth. Within this class, the first six moments are much more informative. $\underline{P}$ is positive in every category, so the existence of genuinely poor and genuinely well-off families is established conditional on the hypothesis that the distribution of permanent income is unimodal and smooth. $\overline{P}$ now yields useful information — no more than 0.6 percent of all families are in the very lowest income category, and no more than 4.0 percent in the highest. The latter conclusion is particularly interesting because it clearly supports the view that the tails of the distribution of actual income are too fat — 4.4 percent of the families have observed incomes in the top category, but at least 0.4 percentage points represent the net effect of misclassification caused by transitory income. On the other hand, the results are not strong enough to demonstrate that a similar overstatement occurs in the official poverty category.

In addition to the values of the bounds in Table 1, our technique yields actual distributions that have the ovserved moments and assign fractions of the population equal to the bounds in the prescribed income interval. Without imposing prior constraints on the shape of the distribution of permanent income, our algorithm gave an upper bound of 11.2 percent of the population with permanent income below the poverty line and a lower bound of zero. The distribution corresponding to the upper bound has 11.2 percent of families with permanent incomes of $ 3315, 36.6 percent with $ 8643, 42.5 percent with $ 8909, 6.5 percent with $ 23,069, and 3.2 percent with $ 23,489. In this world, an important fraction of families have levels of well being just inside the poverty line. The great bulk of the population is around the mean and a minority of around 10 percent have very high incomes. The distribution for the lower bound is very similar except that the low-income group has income just above the poverty line.

Conclusions and suggestions for further work

The accomplishments of this paper are, first, to draw attention to Rao's theorem and the theoretical possibility of identifying fully the distribution of permanent income from limited data, and second, to generalize the existing theory of variance components to higher moments than the second. The growing availability of longitudinal data on individual families should make it possible to refine the information available on the distribution of permanent income using the techniques suggested in this paper. Our results to date are only at the borderline of usefulness. The first step in improving them should be the development of a formal treatment of sampling variation. Then it should be possible to decide whether the recursive calculation of higher-order moments adds additional useful information. It may be possible to compute the desired bounds virtually exactly by using enough moments, in which case the rather tedious and expensive computation of bounds with linear programming could be eliminated. Another approach that we have investigated tentatively is to drop the assumption of the existence of moments and to compute P directly from the joint frequency distribution of successive observations on income. Nothing practical has emerged from our work on this approach to date, however.

Appendix A. Recursion for the moments of permanent and transitory income

First,

$$\alpha_i = E(y_1^i)$$

$$= E(\sum_{j=0}^{i} B_j^i u^j v_1^{i-j})$$

$$= \sum_{j=0}^{i} B_j^i \mu_j \lambda_{i-j} ,$$

where $\mu_j = Eu^j$, and $\lambda_{i-j} = Ev^{i-j}$.

Since $B_0 = 1$ and $\mu_0 = 1$,

$$\lambda_i = \alpha_i - \sum_{j=1}^{i} B_j^i \mu_j \lambda_{i-j}$$

Second,

$$\beta_i = E(y_2 y_1^i)$$

$$= E((u+v_2) y_1^i)$$

$$= E(u y_1^i)$$

$$= E(\sum_{j=0}^{i} B_j^i u^{j+1} v_1^{i-j})$$

$$= \sum_{j=0}^{i} B_j^i \mu_{j+1} \lambda_{i-j} .$$

Since $B_i^i = 1$ and $\lambda_0 = 1$,

$$\mu_{i+1} = \beta_i - \sum_{j=0}^{i-1} B_j^i \mu_{j+1} \lambda_{i-j}$$

Appendix B. Calculating $\underline{P}$ and $\overline{P}$

To solve the infinite dimensional LP problem we solve a sequence of finite dimensional LPs. Since the identical techniques apply to either the upper or lower bound problem, we carry out the discussion for the upper bound only.

Let b(u) be an indicator function that takes on the value 1 when u is in the interval of interest, and zero otherwise. To find the upper bound $\overline{P}$, for any interval, we solve

$$\overline{P}_N = \max_{\{g_n\}} \sum_{n=1}^{N} b(u_n)g_n \tag{B1}$$

subject to

$$\sum_{n=1}^{N} u_n^j g_n = \mu_j, \quad j = 1,\dots,T, \text{ and} \tag{B2}$$

$$\sum_{n=1}^{N} g_n = 1,$$

$$g_n \geq 0 \text{ for } n = 1\dots N.$$

Here $\{u_n\}$ is a gird of points in the range of u and μ_j are the $j = 1\dots6$ moments of permanent income. Next we define

$$\Delta^N = \max_{u} \left[b(u) - \sum_{j=0}^{T} \pi_j u^j \right] \tag{B3}$$

where $\pi_0, \dots, \pi_T$ are the dual variables from the LP problem. Further, let u^{*N} be a value of u where the max in (B3) is attained. With this preparation we define the

Iterative algorithm for calculating $\overline{P}$:

Start with a value of N and a grid such that the LP problem, (B1)–(B2), has a feasible solution. We assume that there exists some probability mass distribution which has the same 6 moments as our underlying continuous distribution. This was the case for all our examples. Define a new grid by appending u^{*N} to the old grid. Iterate until Δ^N is suitably small. The properties of the algorithm are established in the following

Theorem 2. The sequence of $\overline{P}^N$ converges monotonically upward to $\overline{P}$:

$$\overline{P}^N < \overline{P}^{N+1} < \dots < \overline{P} \text{ and } \lim_{N \to \infty} \overline{P}^N = \overline{P}. \text{ Further, the error at any}$$

iteration is bounded by Δ^N: $\overline{P}^N < \overline{P} < \overline{P}^N + \Delta^N$.

The proof parallels Dantzig (1963, ch. 24). Our practical experience with the algorithm has been entirely favorable — with T = 6, we have achieved convergence in fewer than 4 iterations in most cases, where the convergence criterion is $|\Delta^{n*}|$ < .0001.

Appendix C. Restrictions on the shape of the distribution of permanent income

We imposed two restrictions on the distribution of permanent income. First, we required the distribution to be unimodal at the median, increasing before the median, and decreasing beyond the median.

The second restriction imposed smoothness by limiting the slope of the density function. We regard these assumptions about the distribution of permanent income as plausible and very weak. They are designed to rule out the unlikely lumpy distributions that correspond to the bounds reported in the fourth and fifth column of Table 1.

The first constraints are of the form $g_{n+1} - g_n > 0$ when n represents a point to the left of the median income and $g_{n+1} - g_n < 0$ when n represents a point to the right of the median income. The growth constraints are of the form $\frac{|g_{n+1} - g_n|}{|g_n|} \leq 1.3$. Essentially, we are imposing a finite rate at which the probability mass can increase or decrease between adjacent intervals of the log of income.

To obtain an idea of what 1.3 means as a growth rate, consider the normal distribution. For a comparable grid size, the growth rate of the normal would be at most 1.1–1.15. Therefore, our growth rate of 1.3 allows considerable departure from normality in the set of feasible distributions for the log of permanent income.

Once the constraints are imposed, the computation of $\overline{P}$ and $\underline{P}$ becomes more complicated than before. The techniques of Appendix B cannot be used, because whenever an additional point is added to the grid the constraints also change. To calculate $\overline{P}$, we choose a very fine grid size for the log of income. Each interval was .06 units on the log of income scale. For this grid size, N = 200. Using this grid size, we solved the following LP:

$$\overline{P} = \max_{\{g_n\}} \sum_{n=1}^{N} b_n g_n$$

s.t.

$$\sum_{n=1}^{N} g_n u_n = \mu_i \qquad i = 1, \cdots 6,$$

$$\sum_{n=1}^{N} g_n = 1$$

$$g_{n+1} - g_n > 0 \qquad \text{if } u_n < \text{median income}$$

$$g_{n+1} - g_n < 0 \qquad \text{if } u_n > \text{median income}$$

$$\frac{|g_{n+1} - g_n|}{|g_n|} < 1.3$$

$$g_n > 0,$$

111

where all notation has been previously defined in Appendix B.

The solution to such large LP programs can be formidable. The IBM MPSX routine was used to solve this LP.

Except for the obvious modificaions, the solution for the lower bound $\underline{P}$ is identical to that just given for $\overline{P}$.

Notes

[1] Gary Chamberlain called our attention to Rao's theorem.
[2] This is not an entirely innocuous assumption, even with respect to the distribution of the log of income.
[3] For this discussion, we assume the transitory components v_1 and v_2 have the same distribution. Our later empirical results do not rest on this assumption.
[4] This index was constructed from Table 2, Current Population Reports P–60, No. 92, March 1974.
[5] Because such an adjustment is not needed, our results do not require any assumption that the transitory components are identically distributed.
[6] The official poverty line in 1967 for a family of four was $\$3335$. Source: Current Population Reports, P–23, No. 28, August 1969.

References

Dantzig, G., *Linear Programming and Extensions*, Princeton, N.J., Princeton University Press, 1963

Friedman, M., *A Theory of the Consumption Function*, Princeton, N.J., Princeton University Press, 1957

Kagan, A., Y Linnik, C. Rao, *Characterization Problems in Mathematical Statistics*, New York, Wiley, 1973

Karlin, M. and J. Studden, *Tchebycheff Systems with Applications in Analysis and Statistics*, New York, Interscience Publishers, 1966

Survey Research Center — A Panel Study of Income Dynamics, Institute for Social Research, The University of Michigan, Ann Arbor, Michigan, 1972

D.G. Champernowne
The place of Stochastic Models of Income Distribution amongst other Models of it

The place of stochastic models of personal income distribution among other-models of it

1. Characteristic features of stochastic models of income distribution. Stochastic models of income distribution enable one to study the dynamics of the smooth development through time of the frequency distribution of personal incomes. A typical problem is to investigate the sequence of modifications to such a distribution which may result from some specified change in economic policy such as the introduction of a more progressive taxation system, by comparing the two dynamic sequences of personal income distributions to be expected in the event of and in the absence of the change in economic policy.

The typical stochastic model of income distribution lays particular stress on the following features of the dynamic process underlying the change through time of the frequency distribution of personal incomes in an economy.

1. It is convenient to suppose that the distribution is observed at regular intervals which may conveniently be supposed to be one-year intervals.

2. There is likely to be considerable correlation between a person's income in one year and his income in the following year.

3. If one considers the annual change of income and compares the frequency distributions of it for persons in various different income-ranges before the change, these distributions are likely to be far more alike (except in very low or negative income ranges) if the change is measured as a percentage than if it is measured as amounts of money per annum. For this reason it is convenient to measure income along a logarithmic scale and deal with income-power, namely the logarithm of income, as the measure under study rather than deal directly with income.

4. Stochastic models stress the fact that within a family the income of a young man in the early years of his career is likely to reflect the income of his parents. This is both because he will have inherited from them their natural talents and educational advantages and eventually much of their wealth and because he will have obtained through them introductions to the type of people likely to be useful when embarking on a career of a type similar to their own. Thus, just as

113

a man's income is likely to change fairly smoothly from year to year, so may the fortunes and incomes of a family change fairly smoothly from generation to generation. This supposed feature of economic life is represented in the model by establishing links between the income of a man and that of his heir or heirs.

5. Although actual economies contain only moderately large numbers of income-receivers it is convenient for technical purposes to represent them in mathematical models as containing »very large« numbers, so that we can speak equivalently of the *probability* of an income of a certain type and size changing by an amount between a and b and of the *proportion* of such incomes changing by such an amount. Alternatively we should have to refrain from all reference to proportions as such, and pedantically allude instead to the »expected values« of proportions.

6. A central assumption of the stochastic mathematical model is that the probability density functions of change of income-power between now and a year hence from the present income-power level Z, change fairly smoothly as we increase or decrease Z, and for any given level of Z change in a fairly regular fashion from year to year.

7. It is often assumed that the population of income receivers consists of a fairly small number — which may even be only one — of independent groups, within which the level of income-power is the *only* variable affecting the probability density function of change of income power during the next year.

8. It has often but not always been assumed that it is only *this* years income power that affects the probability density of change of income-power. But recently attention has been paid to the two opposite possibilities

    i. that since in any one year a man's income is likely to contain a considerable transitory element which will *not* in general be repeated in the following year, there will be negative serial correlation between the increase of this years income over last year's and the increase of next year's income over this year's.

    ii. that since over a period of several years some individuals — for example those in their early twenties, are likely to be continuously experiencing increasing income whereas others, say in their early sixties, are likely to be continuously experiencing falling income, there will be positive serial correlation between the increase of this year's income over last year's and the increase of next year's income over this year's.

The way that a stochastic model of income distribution works is to consider the frequency distribution of income in two successive years and attribute that in the later year to four things

    i. the distribution in the previous year

    ii. for survivors, the set of changes of income considered separately for each level of income in the previous year

    iii. the deaths at each income level

    iv. the recruits to the body of income receivers at each level.

Set out in this way the model is not so much a theory as an exercise in book-keeping: it must be true if it is executed correctly. It is only of much interest if one can expect to observe regularities in and give some rational account of the determination of the set of changes of income from each level of income in the previous year.

If one can do this and if there is some permanence in these patterns of change of income so that they act as causes more than as effects of change or stability in the characteristics of the frequency distribution of income, then to that extent such a stochastic model of income distribution is likely to be the best available means of developing a theory of the frequency distribution of personal incomes. But if, for some particular group, or worse for the whole population of income receivers, the sets of changes of income are simply a byproduct of the need for the frequency distribution of income to conform to some pattern determined in advance by some exogenous set of causes — if in fact the sets of changes in individual incomes are *determined by* the change in the frequency-distribution instead of *determining* it, then the stochastic model for that group had better be replaced by some other theory.

Having considered the features of income-distribution which are stressed in stochastic models, it is time to examine more closely the nature and uses of such models.

2. The nature and uses of stochastic models of personal income distribution. A stochastic theory of personal income distribution is one which represents the dynamic process of change in an economy's frequency distribution of personal income in terms of a mathematical model which either —

i. traces the process of change in terms of built-in probability density functions for change in income-power by means of difference-equations or differential equations and mathematical or econometric analysis

or

ii. traces the process of change in similar terms by means of computer simulation.

The former method can lead to results in terms of fairly general formulae but depends on keeping the amount of detail allowed for pretty low. The latter method leads to results for selected sets of parameter values only but can be adapted to allow for a great many detailed considerations. The latter method has naturally gained in relative usefulness as a result of the great development of computing facilities in the 3rd quarter of this century.

There may be scope for combining these two techniques and this will be illustrated in a later section by means of a theoretical example. The same example will be employed to suggest various uses to which such stochastic models of income distribution may be put, for instance,

i. at a highly abstract level to provide insight into what circumstances may result in particular types of frequency-distributions of income such as »lognormal« or »asymptotic-Pareto« to which observed frequency distributions of income have approximately conformed,

ii. to classify the economic influences which change incomes into a number of types of influence, to incorporate satisfactory summary measures of the effects of each such type on the frequency distribution of incomes and to provide an analytical and/or computing procedure for deducing the combined effect of all the types on that frequency distribution both in the long run and, more importantly, in the short run,

115

iii. to allow for smooth alteration in these economic influences, both exogenous and »feed-back« alteration in response to change in the frequency distribution of income itself, and

iv. to investigate the effects of hypothetical policy changes in both the long and the short periods.

The expository example which will be used to illustrate these techniques and uses will be based on the following simplified type of stochastic model.

3. A simple type of stochastic model. Let x denote income and let z denot ln(x) the natural logarithm of income, which will be called income-power: for reasons outlined in 3. of section 1 above, it is more convenient to develop the models in terms of the frequency distribution of income-power, z, than in terms of that of income, x.

So let F(z,t) denote the cumulative distribution function of income-power, z, in the year t: it thus gives the proportion of persons whose income-power in that year is any specified amount z or less. Although in real life, F(z,t) is, of course, a step function in z, we shall, in our mathematical model, represent F(z,t) by a differentiable funtion of z and define the density function of income-power in year t as

$$f(z,t) = \frac{\partial F(z,t)}{\partial t} \tag{1}$$

The model is concerned with the dynamics of the change from year to year in this density funtion f(z,t) of the distribution of income-power. Consider 3 types of influences which may change this density function:

1. *The general type* which acts alike to increase (or possibly to decrease) by the same amount the income-power of each person whatever his initial level of income-power — i.e. it acts alike to increase by the same proportion each person's income,

2. *The income-determined type* which increases (or decreases) by the same amount the income-power of each person at any one given initial level of income-power, but where the amount of the change depends on what was the initial level of income-power. When summed over all persons at all levels of income-power, the effects of the income-determined influences cancel out algebraically.

3. The income-independent type which are mainly related to circumstances *other than* income-power and which, although they affect different people's income-power by different amounts according to their circumstances, yet have the property that for the set of persons with income-power initially in any given range, their effects on their total income-power cancel out algebraically.

The general type of influences simply affect the arithmetic mean income-power (and hence affect the geometric mean income) but do not affect the distribution of income-power about its arithmetic mean nor the proportional distribution of income about its geometric mean.

The income-independent type of influence must always act to increase the variance of the frequency distribution of income-power about its arithmetic mean as measured by the variance of the density function f(z,t).

However this effect may be offset by the effect of the income-determined type of influences if these tend to increase an income-power which is low initially more than they affect one which is initially high: stochastic theories of in-

116

come-distribution lay particular stress on this effect of income-determined influences and represent the degree of inequality and the form of the frequency distribution of income-power (and hence also of the frequency distribution of income) as depending in the long run on the balance between the income-independent influences which increase the variance and the income-determined influences, which, under the circumstances indicated above, may act so as to offset this. But if, and for so long as, these circumstances do *not* apply, so that the income-determined influences favour the rich no less than the poor, then they may reinforce the income-independent influences, and then inequality, as measured by the variance of $f(z,t)$ the density function of income-power must increase as t increases.

It will be explained in the Appendix how the interaction of the income-determined and of the income-independent influences may under extreme sets of simplifying assumptions lead in *the very long run* towards an equilibrium frequency distribution of income-power about its arithmetic mean, although that mean is itself likely to be continuously increasing (or decreasing). Since we are more concerned with the dynamics of short-run changes in the frequency distribution, we shall not here pursue the point further.

Stochastic models must allow also for demographic influences such as deaths and inheritance, births and ageing. As a first approximation one might regard the effects of ageing on income-power as income-independent on the grounds that although a person's prospects of increase of income-power are likely to depend to some extent on his age, yet his age cannot be influenced by his income-power. However, certain age-groups will predominate among the rich whereas other age-groups will predominate among the poor with the consequence that the influence of the variation of the prospects of increase of income-power according to age may after all have different average effects on income-power at different initial income-power levels so that the influence of ageing is after all income-determined. Deaths, inheritance and births pose even greater problems than does this life-cycle in the prospects of increase of income-power. The heroic simplifying assumption is to suppose that each person has just one heir who (in the mathematical model) takes over his identity and part of his income-power. Accordingly the persons in the model are rendered immortal and death is transformed into but another economic influence which may alter their income-power. The behaviour of the model is then likely to depend and in the long run to depend rather critically — on whether death and inheritance are to be regarded as an income-independent or as an income-determined set of influences. Since we are here mainly concerned with changes in income-distribution in the short run, this important topic must not, for lack of space, be pursued further here.

There is, of course, no need to make the heroic simplyfing assumption of one-person-one-heir. The mathematical model can be adapted to allow for all such factors as

    i.   those who inherit have already become income-receivers some years before they inherit

    ii. a person may have more than one heir and on the other hand an heir may inherit from more than one person and at different times

    iii. a person may choose to hand over much of his wealth (and hence his income) to his descendant many years before he dies.

To make this manageable, computer simulation will almost certainly be needed in place of mere mathematical analysis. Indeed the whole future study of stochastic models which make any such pretence of realism will assuredly rest on computer simulation.

However for providing insight into the nature of the effects to be expected from particular macro-economic changes and from particular economic policies, there may be a use still for the stochastic model based on simplifying assumptions of the heroic type. There is an even stronger case for considering such highly oversimplified stochastic models when one is studying the relation between such stochastic models and quite different models of personal income distribution. That is the reason why in the following discussion a particular extremely simplified stochastic model will be used for examining some of these theoretical issues.

4. A generalised version of Kalecki's stochastic model of income distribution. Let x_t denote a man's income in year t and let the logarithm of his income be

$$z_t = \ln(x_t) \tag{2}$$

Let $\triangle z_t = z_{t+1} - z_t$ be his increase of income-power by next year and consider the probability density function for $\triangle z_t$ for those at (or in the neighbourhood of) a given level of z_t: denote this probability density function by $g(\triangle z_t, z_t)$.

For simplicity we shall make the following very strong assumptions about $g(\triangle z_t, z_t)$:

    i. $g(\triangle z_t, z_t)$ is a normal density function of mean μ_t and of variance σ_t^2, $\tag{3}$

    ii. μ_t is a linear function of income-power,

        $\mu_t = a_t - c_t z_t \tag{4}$

        where the coefficients a_t and c_t may depend on t but not on z_t

    iii. σ_t^2 may depend on t but not on z_t $\tag{5}$

The first assumption enormously simplifies the analysis and description of the behaviour of the model but is not well suited for handling the effects of death and inheritance.

The second assumption may not be as unrealistic as it may at first sight appear, if the evidence of the U.K. Department of Employment's recent survey of earnings may be relied upon: but it is, of course, a simplifying assumption.

The third assumption is probably systematically biassed in comparison with what facts suggest but is unlikely to introduce serious distortions into one's qualitative conclusions.

Now let A_t and B_t denote the arithmetic mean and variance of the frequency distribution of income-power z_t in year t. Then

$$A_{t+1} = (1-c_t)A_t + a_t \tag{A}$$

and

$$B_{t+1} = (1-c_t)^2 B_t + \sigma_t^2 \tag{B}$$

If we now supplement the model by equations governing the development over time of the three parameters a_t, c_t and σ_t^2 we can derive the development over time of the values of A_t (which is both the arithmetic mean of income-power and the logarithm of the geometric mean of income) in later years, t, and of B_t (which is the variance of income-power in year t) from any initial pair of values of A_O and B_O the arithmetic mean and variance of income-power in year O.

B_t, the variance of income-power in year t, is a measure of the inequality of the frequency distribution of personal income in that year which is quite commonly used although it does not satisfy the Pigou-Dalton criterion.

The model expressed by equations (2), (3), (4) and (5) does not require that the initial distribution of income-power should be normal. However the study of this special case supplies a useful introduction to the properties of the model.

Suppose then that initially in year O income-power, z_O, is normally distributed with arithmetic mean A_O and variance B_O. Then, remembering that $\Delta z_t = z_{t+1} - z_t$ we see that from equations (3), (4) and (5) that z_1, income-power in the following year, is the sum of two independent normal variates

$$y_O = a_O + (1-c_O)z_O \quad \text{and} \quad u_O$$

where y_O has expected value and variance $a_O + (1-c_O)A_O$ and $(1-c_O)^2 B_O$ and u_O has expected value and variance O and σ_O^2.

It follows from these assumptions (3), (4) and (5) that in the special case where z_O is normally distributed with arithmetic mean A_O and variance B_O, z_1 also will be normally distributed and will have arithmetic mean and variance A_1 and B_1 given by

$$A_1 = (1-c_O)A_O + a_O \tag{A'}$$
$$B_1 = (1-c_O)^2 B_O + \sigma_O^2 \tag{B'}$$

which is a special case of equations (A) and (B).

The same argument carries forward from year to year. If the distribution of income-power is initially in year O normal (i.e. the distribution of income is then lognormal) and if in each year t the probability density function for Δz_t, the change in income-power, is governed by equations (3), (4) and (5) then the distribution of income-power remains normal in every subsequent year t and the arithmetic mean A_t and the variance B_t of the normal distribution of z_t, the income-power in any subsequent year t, may be derived by repeated application of the difference equations

$$A_{t+1} = (1 - c_t)A_t + a_t \tag{A}$$
$$B_{t+1} = (1 - c_t)^2 B_t + \sigma_t^2 \tag{B}$$

provided we have rules for obtaining the values of the parameters a_t, c_t and σ_t^2 in each year.

This solution where the initial distribution was lognormal extends at once to the case where the initial distribution was a weighted arithmetic mean of any number of lognormal distributions. All we need do is to use the difference equations to find for each separate initial lognormal distribution the corresponding lognormal distribution in the later year, and then to take the same weighted average of these later lognormal distributions as in the initial year.

The behaviour of this model is obviously going to depend on the way that the parameter values a_t, c_t and σ_t^2 change. It is high time to consider the economic interpretation both of these parameters themselves and of what determines their values. From (4)

119

$$\mu_t(z_t) = a_t - c_t z_t \qquad (4)$$

and at any particular income-power level, z_t, this measures the average increase $(\triangle z_t)$ in income-power over the next year and

$$\mu_t(A_t) = a_t - c_t A_t = \triangle A_t \qquad (6)$$

is the overall arithmetic mean increase in income-power from the level A_t between year t and year (t+l) and thus represents the effects of the general factors causing change in income-power at all levels.

On the other hand c_t the regression coefficient of $-\triangle z_t$ on z_t measures the strength of the income-determined influences in reducing inequality, provided $c_t > O$, (or in increasing inequality if $c_t < O$). Finally σ_t^2 measures the strength of the income-independent influences in increasing inequality.

It is in considering how a_t, c_t and σ_t^2 are determined that the links between this kind of stochastic models of income distribution and other models based on sociological, neoclassical, Marxist or other macro-economic foundations begin to emerge.

The advantage of imposing the very special assumptions, (3) that $\triangle z_t$ is for given z_t normally distributed and (4) that μ_t is a linear function of income-power and (5) that σ_t^2 is independent of z_t, is that we need only consider the determination of a_t, c_t and σ_t^2 for each year. Provided we do investigate the effects of any hypothetical macroeconomic disturbance or change of policy on the values of these three parameters in each year, then within the simplifying assumptions of the model, we can deduce the whole effects of these hypothetical changes in every subsequent year.

Having thus obtained a preliminary sketch of the effect of our hypothetical changes under these artificial simplifying assumptions we can embark on a more careful investigation by computer simulation under less artificial assumptions.

The method in both cases is to consider a dynamic equilibrium or smooth development of the income-power distribution in the absence of disturbances and then to impose a disturbance, such as a change in fiscal policy, and observe the divergence of the modified development of income-power distribution from the unmodified dynamic equilibrium development.

On great advantage of the simple model based on the difference equations, (A) and (B),

$$A_{t+l} = (1 - c_t)A_t + a_t \qquad (A)$$
$$B_{t+l} = (1 - c_t)^2 B_t + \sigma_t^2 \qquad (B)$$

is that a_t, c_t and σ_t^2 can be made to depend on A_t and B_t themselves.

5. *Numerical examples of the effect of a policy change on the dynamic equilibrium of personal income distribution.* We may use the generalised Kalecki model outlined in the last section to illustrate both the concept of dynamic equilibrium development of the personal income distribution and the shift of such a dynamic equilibrium development due to a policy change. We will consider three examples of increasing degree of complexity.

First consider the very simple case where initially when t = O the distribution of income is lognormal so that the distribution of income-power z_O is normal. Suppose the mean of z_O is 0·5 and the variance of z_O is 0·25.

Suppose that the probability density function for Δz_t is of the special kind described in equations (3), (4) and (5), in the previous section 4, so that the distribution of z_t must remain normal for t = 1, 2, . . , etc. and the means A_t and variances B_t of the normal distributions of z_t must obey the difference equations (A) and (B) already derived as

$$A_{t+1} = (1 - c_t) A_t + a_t \tag{A}$$
$$B_{t+1} = (1 - c_t)^2 B_t + \sigma_t^2 \tag{B}$$

Suppose that c_t, σ_t^2 and a_t are given as

$$c_t = 0 \cdot 10 + \frac{1}{10(t+10)}$$
$$\sigma_t^2 = 0 \cdot 05 \tag{7}$$
$$a_t = c_t A_t + 0 \cdot 04$$

then since we know that the mean income-power is initially $A_O = 0 \cdot 5$ and the variance of income-power is initially $B_O = 0 \cdot 25$, we can use the equations (A) and (B) in the form

$$A_{t+1} = A_t + 0 \cdot 04$$
$$B_{t+1} = (0 \cdot 9 - \frac{1}{10(t+1)})^2 B_t + 0 \cdot 05 \tag{8}$$

to compile values of A_t and B_t given in the second and third columns of the following table.

Table 1   First Example

Values of A_t, B_t and ln. $(\overline{x}_t)$ for t = 0(1)10 and ∞.

t	A_t	B_t	$\ln(\overline{x}_t)$	t	A_t	B_t	$\ln(\overline{x}_t)$
0	0·500	0·2500	0·6250	6	0·740	0·2465	0·8632
1	0·540	0·2480	0·6640	7	0·780	0·2469	0·9034
2	0·580	0·2469	0·7035	8	0·820	0·2474	0·9437
3	0·620	0·2463	0·7432	9	0·860	0·2479	0·9840
4	0·660	0·2461	0·7831	10	0·900	0·2485	1·0242
5	0·700	0·2462	0·8231	∞	∞	0·2632	∞

By including the feedback term $c_t A_t$ in the formula (7) we have imposed the restraint that the annual increase of the mean income-power A_t is given by the remainder of the expression for a_t, which we have here chosen to be the constant 0·04, so that A_t simply increases at the constant rate 0·04 per annum, which implies that the geometric mean income grows at a constant rate of about 4·08 % per annum.

The distribution remains log-normal in each year and its variance B_t falls to a minimum at 0·2461 after four years and thereafter rises to 0·2485 at t = 10 and, for large t, must rise asymptotically toward the value $\frac{0·05}{0·19} = 0·2632$.

Since the distribution remains lognormal, the arithmetic mean income, $\overline{x}_t$, is given each year by

$$\ln.(\overline{x}_t) = A_t + 0·5 B_t \tag{9}$$

from which were calculated the entries in the fourth column of Table 1.

Since B_t has a varying annual increase, the growth-rate of $\bar{x}_t$ is by a slightly varying percentage. Had we wished to impose the constand percentage growth-rate (4·08 %) on the arithmetic mean income rather than on the geometric mean income we should have needed a further feedback term in the formula for a_t, thus modifying it to

$$a_t = c_t \left[A_t + (1 - \frac{1}{2} c_t)B_t\right] - \frac{1}{2} \sigma_t^2 + 0.04 \tag{10}$$

We should then have obtained the values shown in Table 2.

Table 2 Second Example

Values of $A_t, B_t, \ln(\bar{x}_t)$ and $\bar{x}_t$ for $t = 0(1)10$ and ∞

t	A_t	B_t	$\ln(\bar{x}_t)$	$\bar{x}_t$	t	A_t	B_t	$\ln(\bar{x}_t)$	$\bar{x}_t$
0	0·5000	0·2500	0·6250	1·8682	6	0·7418	0·2465	0·8650	2·3750
1	0·5410	0·2480	0·6650	1·9445	7	0·7816	0·2469	0·9050	2·4718
2	0·5816	0·2469	0·7050	2·0238	8	0·8213	0·2474	0·9450	2·5728
3	0·6219	0·2463	0·7450	2·1064	9	0·8611	0·2479	0·9850	2·6778
4	0·6620	0·2461	0·7850	2·1924	10	0·9008	0·2485	1·0250	2·7871
5	0·7019	0·2462	0·8250	2·2819	∞	∞	0·2632	∞	∞

Now suppose that a tax-policy is considered which is expected to increase the prospects of growth of low incomes at the expense of the prospects of growth of large incomes, whilst leaving the growth of the average income unaffected; suppose that these equalising effects can be approximated by a change of c_t from

$$c_t = 0.10 + \frac{1}{10(t+10)} \tag{7a}$$

to

$$c_t = 0.12 + \frac{1}{10(t+10)} \tag{7b}$$

then we can easily recalculate the values of A_t, B_t, $\ln(\bar{x}_t)$ and $\bar{x}_t$ as in the following table 3.

Table 3 Values of A_t, B_t, $\ln(\bar{x}_t)$ and $\bar{x}_t$ under progressive tax system under the conditions of second example.

t	A_t	B_t	$\ln(\bar{x}_t)$	$\bar{x}_t$	t	A_t	B_t	$\ln(\bar{x}_t)$	$\bar{x}_t$
0	0·5000	0·2500	0·6250	1·8682	6	0·7565	0·2171	0·8650	2·3750
1	0·5454	0·2392	0·6650	1·9445	7	0·7971	0·2157	0·9050	2·4719
2	0·5893	0·2314	0·7050	2·0238	8	0·8376	0·2148	0·9450	2·5728
3	0·6321	0·2259	0·7450	2·1064	9	0·8779	0·2143	0·9850	2·6778
4	0·6741	0·2219	0·7850	2·1924	10	0·9180	0·2139	1·0250	2·7871
5	0·7155	0·2190	0·8250	2·2819	∞	∞	0·2216	∞	∞

Since the distribution remains lognormal in every year this provides complete information about the distribution in each year specified. The arithmetic mean income, due to our assumption, is unaffected but the inequality parameter, B_t, is gradually reduced by the tax policy: by 0·0272 in the first five years, by a further 0·0074 in the second five years and eventually it will be reduced by a further 0·0069 : compared with the dynamic equilibrium without the progressive tax system as given in Table 2 above.

Chart 1

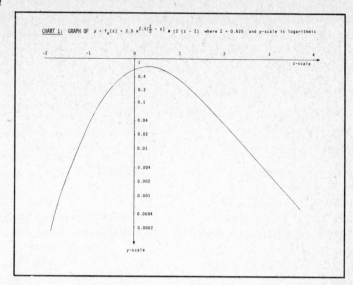

CHART 1: GRAPH OF $y = f_0(z) = 2.5 \, e^{2.5(\frac{Z}{2} - z)} \, \cdot \, (2 \, (z - Z)$ where $Z = 0.625$ and y-scale is logarithmic

The example which we have so far considered was artificially simplified by the assumption that in the base year, $t = 0$, the distribution of income-power was normal, i.e. that the distribution of income was lognormal. This assumption can be relaxed without making the analysis much more difficult. We may assume instead that the initial density function of income-power is of the form

$$\int_{-\infty}^{\infty} \int_{0}^{\infty} g(A,B) \, \varphi(x; A,B) \, dB \, dA \tag{11}$$

where $\varphi(x; A,B)$ denotes the normal density function of mean A and variance B and where $g(A,B)$ is any density function for A and B.

To illustrate the method we may consider the example where the original distribution of income-power, $z = \ln(x)$, (x = income) is

$$f_0(z) = \int_{0}^{\infty} 2 \cdot 5 \, e^{-2 \cdot 5A} \, \varphi(z; A, 0 \cdot 25) \, dA \tag{12}$$

which is a weighted average of normal distributions of variance, $0 \cdot 25$, and of means A which have a negative exponential distribution.

It is possible to evaluate this integral in terms of the normal distribution function as

$$f_0(z) = 2 \cdot 5 \, e^{1 \cdot 25Z - 2 \cdot 5z} \, \Phi[2(z - Z)] \tag{13}$$

where $Z = 0 \cdot 625$ and $\Phi(w)$ is the distribution function

$$\Phi(w) = \int_{-\infty}^{w} \frac{1}{\sqrt{(2\pi)}} \, e^{-u^2/2} \, du \tag{14}$$

This function is illustrated in Chart 1 which is plotted on a logarithmic scale. It corresponds to a distribution of income which asymptotically obeys Pareto's law with $\alpha = 2 \cdot 5$.

123

The original values of the mean and variance of the whole distribution $f_0(z)$ are given by

$$A_0 = \int_0^\infty 2 \cdot 5Ae^{-2 \cdot 5A}dA = 0 \cdot 4 \tag{15}$$

and by

$$V_0 = \int_0^\infty 2 \cdot 5(A-A_0)^2 e^{-2 \cdot 5A}dA + 0 \cdot 25 = 0 \cdot 41 \tag{16}$$

although the variance of each constituent normal distribution of z is $B_0 = 0 \cdot 25$.

It is possible to impose the restriction that the arithmetic mean income increases *approximately* at the constant percentage rate 4·08 % by inserting a further correcting feed-back term into the formula for a_t so that it becomes

$$a_t = 0 \cdot 015 + c_t[A_t + (1-0 \cdot 5c_t)B_t] \tag{17}$$
$$+ c_t[0 \cdot 16(1-0 \cdot 4\lambda_t) - 0 \cdot 08c_t]\lambda_t^2/(1-0 \cdot 4\lambda_t)^2$$

where $\lambda_0 = 1$, $\lambda_{t+1} = (1-c_t)\lambda_t$ for $t > 0$ and where we may retain from our earlier example

$$\sigma_t^2 = 0 \cdot 05 \quad \text{and} \quad c_t = 0 \cdot 10 + \frac{1}{10(t+10)} \tag{7}$$

The variance of each constituent normal distribution of income-power will obey

$$B_{t+1} = (1-c_t)^2B_t + 0 \cdot 05 \tag{8}$$

where originally $B_0 = 0 \cdot 25$.

This is exactly the same development as in our earlier example. Accordingly the numerical values of B_t will be those already given in Table 2.

The mean $A_{u,t}$ of a normal distribution of z which originally took the value u must be governed by

$$A_{u, t+1} = (1-c_t)A_{u, t} + a_t \tag{18}$$

Comparing this with

$$A_{t+1} = (1-c_t)A_t + a_t \tag{A}$$

we see that

$$A_{u, t+1} - A_{t+1} = (1-c_t)(A_{u, t} - A_t) \tag{19}$$

and so by repeated application

$$A_{u, t} - A_t = \lambda_t(u - 0 \cdot 4) \tag{20}$$

124

Using this equation it is possible to integrate the expression for $f_t(z)$, the distribution of z at later date, t, namely,

$$f_t(z) = \int_0^{\infty} 2 \cdot 5 e^{-2 \cdot 5u} \, \varphi(z_t, A_{u,\,t}, B_t) du \qquad (21)$$

to obtain

$$f_t(z) = [\frac{2 \cdot 5}{\lambda_t} e^{-3 \cdot 125(s_t/\lambda_t)^2}] e^{2 \cdot 5(Z_t - z)/\lambda_t} \Phi(\frac{z - Z_t}{s_t}) \qquad (22)$$

where $\quad Z_t = A_t - 0 \cdot 4\,\lambda_t + 2 \cdot 5(s_t^2/\lambda_t) \qquad (23)$

and where $\quad s_t^2 = B_t. \qquad (24)$

Since the values of A_t, B_t and λ_t are easy to tabulate, this means that the exact distribution $f_t(z)$ can be found for each year if required.

To investigate the effect of the same tax change as in the earlier example, we simply change the formula for c_t as before from

$$c_t = 0 \cdot 10 + \frac{1}{10(t+10)} \quad \text{to} \quad c_t = 0 \cdot 12 + \frac{1}{10(t+10)} \qquad (7a, 7b)$$

and recalculate the values of A_t, B_t and λ_t for each year. We can then observe the effects of the tax on the distribution in any particular year by tabulating the function $f_t(z)$ for each of the two cases

$$c_t = 0 \cdot 10 + \frac{1}{10(t+10)} \quad \text{and} \quad c_t = 0 \cdot 12 + \frac{1}{10(t+10)} \qquad (7a, 7b)$$

It is also possible to calculate the arithmetic mean income, $\bar{x}_t$, in any year, t, from the formula:

$$\begin{aligned} \ln(\bar{x}_t) &= Z_t - (5 - \lambda_t)(B_t/\lambda_t) - \ln(1 - 0 \cdot 4\lambda_t) \\ &= A_t + 0 \cdot 5B_t - 0 \cdot 4\lambda_t - \ln(1 - 0 \cdot 4\lambda_t) \end{aligned} \qquad (25)$$

where Z_t was defined above in (23).

The values of B_t in the two cases have already been given for the early years in Tables 2 and 3 above: the following Table 4 gives the values of A_t (the logarithm of the geometric mean incomce), λ_t, $\ln(\bar{x}_t)$ and $\bar{x}_t$ (the arithmetic mean income) in each year t = 1,2,3,4,5,6,8,10,15,20 and 25 in each of the two cases

$$c_t = 0 \cdot 10 + \frac{1}{10(t+10)} \quad \text{(standard)} \qquad (7a)$$

and

$$c_t = 0 \cdot 12 + \frac{1}{10(t+10)} \quad \text{(progressive)} \qquad (7b)$$

Table 4 Third Example

Vari-able Taxation Year t	A_t Standard	Progressive	λ_t Standard	Progressive	$\ln(\bar{x}_t)$ Standard	Progressive	$\bar{x}_t$ Standard	Progessive
0	0·4000	0·4000	1·0000	1·0000	0·6358	0·6358	1·8886	1·8886
1	0·4676	0·4763	0·8900	0·8700	0·6757	0·6756	1·9654	1·9653
2	0·5279	0·5418	0·7929	0·7577	0·7156	0·7155	2·0455	2·0452
3	0·5829	0·5999	0·7070	0·6605	0·7556	0·7555	2·1289	2·1286
4	0·6341	0·6530	0·6309	0·5761	0·7956	0·7954	2·2157	2·2154
5	0·6825	0·7025	0·5633	0·5029	0·8356	0·8354	2·3061	2·3058
6	0·7288	0·7494	0·5032	0·4392	0·8755	0·8754	2·4002	2·3998
8	0·8173	0·8381	0·4021	0·3354	0·9555	0·9554	2·6000	2·5997
10	0·9022	0·9228	0·3218	0·2566	1·0355	1·0354	2·8166	2·8162
15	1·1071	1·1269	0·1853	0·1319	1·2355	1·2354	3·4402	3·4397
20	1·3079	1·3274	0·1072	0·0682	1·4355	1·4354	4·2018	4·2013
25	1·5078	1·5272	0·0622	0·0353	1·6355	1·6354	5·1321	5·1314

Since the correction (17) is only *approximate* the entries in the two columns for $\ln(\bar{x}_t)$ do not exactly increase by 0·400 for each unit increase in t, nor do they remain exactly equal to each other. The approximation is however decidedly close and will suffice for drawing rough conclusions. The small difference between the

values of the arithmetic mean incomes in the two cases in later years have of course no economic significance whatsoever.

Table 5 and Chart 2 compare the effects of the progressive tax in this example in terms of their influence on the inequality index

$$i = 1 - (\bar{x}_g/\bar{x}_a)\lambda 1 - (e^{A_t}/\bar{x}_t)$$

where $\bar{x}_g$ and $\bar{x}_a$ denote the geometric mean and arithmetic mean incomes.

Table 5 Inequality Index: $i = 1 - (\bar{x}_g/\bar{x}_a)$.

Time t	Tax System Standard	Progressive	Time t	Tax System Standard	Progressive
0	0·210	0·210	8	0·129	0·111
1	0·188	0·181	10	0·125	0·106
2	0·171	0·159	15	0·120	0·103
3	0·159	0·144	20	0·120	0·102
4	0·149	0·133	25	0·120	0·103
5	0·142	0·124			
6	0·136	0·118	∞	0·123	0·105

Chart 2

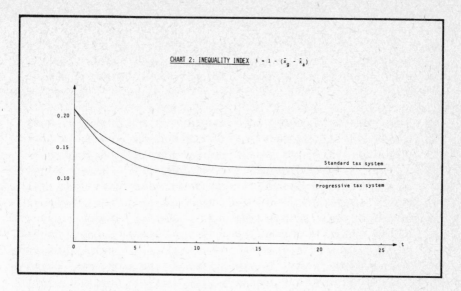

CHART 2: INEQUALITY INDEX $i = 1 - (\bar{x}_g - \bar{x}_a)$

Standard tax system

Progressive tax system

6. Reconciliation of stochastic models of personal income distribution with multifactor models of the determination of levels of earnings. If one were to compare the personal distribution of income from wealth with the personal distribution of wealth in an economy one would of course not find that the one was exactly proportional to the other since, due for example to frictions and differing prospects of capital gain, the yields on different items of property will not all be the same. Notwithstanding this, one would still find some similarity between the distribution of wealth multiplied by a normal annual yield and the distribution of income from that wealth.

Economists often generalise the concept of wealth to include human capital in the form of other qualifications for obtaining income, but it is not easy to place a market evaluation on these qualifications except where they were obtained for a fee as in the case of a course of training. But one can attempt to do so by studying the effectiveness of these qualifications in securing larger incomes for those who possess them. If one succeeded in putting notional values on a number of such qualifications for obtaining income then one might arrive at estimates of an extended concept of wealth for each individual which included such notional wealth as his human capital as well as ordinary material wealth. In this case one might hope to find some similarity between the distribution of personal income from whatever source and the distribution of wealth thus extended, and multiplied by a normal annual yield.

Some such notion is useful in rationalising the assumptions built into a stochastic model. It may be helpful to think of most causes of change of a persons income as operating through changes in his wealth, including not only material wealth but also his stock of human capital and other qualifications for earning income. One must always bear in mind the possibility of general changes in the percentage yield on wealth, but in so far as these affect yields on all types of wealth, material and human capital and other qualifications alike, they will not affect the proportionate distribution of income. Where they do affect relative yields this can be thought of as altering the distribution of income through a change in the relative effectiveness of different types of wealth as qualifications for obtaining income.

A stochastic theory analysing the dynamic changes in the distribution of income from all types of wealth is answering a different question from that tackled by multifactor theories of income determination. These latter theories pick out a set of specific qualifications for obtaining income such as race, sex, age, schooling, occupational training, location, health, I.Q. etc. and by means of some such technique as regression analyses estimate the marginal values of suitably defined units of each of them for obtaining income. This alone can no more explain the overall personal distribution of income than can a study of the dividend yields of different types of share explain the personal distribution of income from investments. Obviously one needs as well a theory of the distribution of the specific qualifications — and indeed of their joint distribution. Since there is likely to be considerable correlation between ownership of different qualifications this is probably too ambitious a demand: but at least one needs a theory of how the personal distribution of some measure of the total value of such qualifications is determined and modified. It is with questions of this nature that stochastic models are concerned.

Thus there is no contradiction between multifactor theories of income distribution which examine the relative values at the margin of different qualifications for obtaining income — and stochastic theories which should continue from that point and study the determination of the distribution of ownership of these qualifications.

As a particular instance of this there need be no contradiction between theories which attribute differences in earnings to contrasts in levels of education and stochastic theories of income distribution which consider the development of the overall frequency distribution of total income from all sources.

There is rather more difficulty in reconciling stochastic models of income distribution with models which relate the proportionate distribution of the total income« of a closed economy between »wages« and »profits« to other macroeconomic variables such as the proportion of investment to total income and as the savings propensities of the workers and of the capitalists or as the growth rate of the system — or even as the characteristics of some aggregate production function and the current level of capital per head. It seems at first sight decidedly difficult to find any point of contact between any of these theories and any stochastic model of personal income distribution. This difficulty is related to a weakness of any stochastic model which attempts to regard income from all sources as being homogeneous. If one regards earnings as being the income yielded on human or labour-capital, then there can be a significant change in the distribution of income without there being *any* change in the distribution of either material capital or human capital — if there is a change in the rate of profit on material capital at the expense of earnings — i.e. at the expense of the yield on labour-capital. One may regard it as a change in the relative market values of the two kinds of capital — i.e. of material capital and of human or labour capital. One can allow for this in the working of a stochastic model but one must do so by explicitly arrangeing for those macroeconomic factors which influence the rate of profit on capital to operate in the model directly on the parameters governing the expected rates of change of income-power at various levels of income-power. This is an example of feedback, since the various macroeconomic factors will themselves, as a rule, be influenced to some extent by the present personal distribution of income-power in the model: thus, present degree of inequality feeds back an influence on the prospects of change in income-power inequality and does so in such a way as to constrain the model to conform with whatever macro-economic theory of distribution between earnings and profits, the model builder may place his faith in.

A better solution for any stochastic model builder who also believed in the relevance of macroeconomic theories of distribution between earnings and profits would be to build two models — one related to personal income distribution amongst wage-earners and one related to personal income distribution amongst capitalists. This still leaves much of the complication in at least one of the two models, since the two classes overlap, in the sense that many workers have some income from property and many wealthy capitalists earn a substantial proportion of their total income.

High negative feedback also offers the means of reconciling a stochastic model of personal income distribution with those theories which attribute the form of the frequency distribution of earnings to the hierarchical structure of management and to the need for incentives to seek promotion and take responsibility. Lack of space forbids any adequate summary of such theories but the point is that if they are correct it would seem that whatever the qualifications which aspiring managers may have, provided there is not an overall shortage, the personal distribution of their salaries is determined by the available structure of management posts with their suitable relative salary levels, and the aspirants will have to fit into the slots available. Accordingly, any stochastic model of personal distribution of incomes is bound to be wrong if it is based on the kind of dynamic process which we have been describing and which is quite alien to the crystalline management structure which is the true determinant of the distribution of salaries.

This is one particularly clear example of the difficulty that personal distribution of some particular type of income might be completely fixed by technical, political or sociological determinants and that in this case any stochastic model of that distribution *must* be wrong. If the distribution were *completely* fixed, then one could simply set both the means and variances of the changes z_t in income-power equal to zero — so the difficulty would be resolved. But suppose that the personal distribution *could* vary but only within very narrow limits: changes z_t in income power must then be allowed; can the stochastic model avoid being wrong in this case?

The stochastic model can provide for this situation if it so designed that any increase of inequality must feed back into the parameters governing prospects of change of income power so quickly as to check that tendency — and the same must hold for any decrease of inequality. This can only be managed in such a way as to avoid antidamped cycles if the time-unit is taken to be very short — but in principle there is no difficulty in a mathematical model about making the time unit as short as may be needed for this. Thus there is no need in priciple for any contradiction between the stochastic model and the managerial structure model.

129

Appendix. *The long-run distribution of Income-power under constant conditions*

Under the assumptions of the simple type of stochastic model in section 3, if the various influences are held constant through time, a typical behaviour of the model is that although average income-power may increase steadily, adapting to macro-economic changes associated with rising real and money incomes, yet the distribution of income-power about that average will approach some equilibrium state in the very long run.

Suppose that $\bar{z}_t$ denotes the arithmetic mean income-power in year t and that $\mu_t(u)$ denotes the effect of the income-determined influences on income-power at level $\bar{z}_t + u$ in year t, whereas $\sigma_t^2(u)$ denotes the variance of the effect of income-independent effects on income-power at that same level, $\bar{z}_t + u$, then an approximate formula to give the long-run equilibrium distribution of income-power, u, in excess of $\bar{z}_t$ is

$$\varphi(u) = C\, e^{\psi(u)} \text{ where C is a constant} \tag{A.1}$$

and where $\mu_t(u) = \mu(u)$ and $\sigma_t^2(u) = \sigma^2(u)$, both independent of t. We have approximately

$$\frac{d\,\psi(u)}{du} = 2\,\mu(u)/\sigma^2(u) \tag{A.3}$$

The approximation will only be close for values of u for which the derivatives with respect to u of both functions, $\mu(u)$ and $\sigma^2(u)$, are small.

The working of this formula may be illustrated with the two specially simple cases:

   i. $\mu(u)$ is a negative constant and $\sigma^2(u)$ a positive constant, both independent of u for values of u in excess of some threshold u_0,

   ii. $\mu(u) = -cu$, where c is a positive constant independent of u, and $\sigma^2(u)$ is a positive constant independent of u for all values of u.

In case i., $\mu(u) = -\lambda$ and $\sigma^2(u) = \sigma^2$ for $u > u_0$ and so, for $u > u_0$, (A3) gives

$$\frac{d\psi}{du} = -2\lambda/\sigma^2 \text{ and so } \psi(u) = c - \alpha u \text{ where } \alpha = 2\lambda/\sigma^2 \tag{A4}$$

for $u > u_0$ and hence,

$$\varphi(u) = \text{Const. } e^{-\alpha u} \tag{A5}$$

This indicates that at high levels of income-power the equilibrium distribution about the mean income-power is approximately a Pareto distribution. (For a fuller discussion of this case see Champernowne (1973) Appendix 5.)

In case ii., $\mu(u) = -cu$ $(0 < c)$ and $\sigma^2(u) = \sigma^2$ $\tag{A 6}$

and we shall find that c must be fairly small if the approximation is to be at all close. (A 3) gives

$$\frac{d\psi}{du} = -2cu/\sigma^2 \text{ so that } \psi(u) = \text{Const.} -cu^2/\sigma^2 \tag{A7}$$

whence

$$\varphi(u) = \text{Constant. } e^{-cu^2/\sigma^2} \tag{A8}$$

indicating that in long-run equilibrium under these conditions income-power will be normally distributed about its mean with variance $\sigma^2/2c$.

130

In this particular case one can obtain the exact solution by a different approach and it is that the distribution of income-power will be normal about its mean with variance $\sigma^2/2(c-c^2)$. This shows that the approximation is good provided c is small but may be poor otherwise.

In more elaborate examples the goodness of the approximation is likely to depend on the smallness of the derivatives of the functions $\sigma^2(u)$ and $\mu(u)$ with respect to u.

For a fuller discussion of the case ii. see Kalecki (1945) and for discussion of the general case see Champernowne (1973).

References

Champernowne D.G., *The distribution of income between persons,* C.U.P. (1973)
Kalecki M., *On the Gibrat distribution* p. 161, Econometrica (1945).

Horst Albach, Thomas Fues and Bernd Geisen

Approaches to a Theory of Income Distribution in the Firm

I. Introduction

Since the beginning of the seventies the social role of the corporation has become a focus of public discussion in the Federal Republic of Germany. Criticism of the activities of the big corporations has increased and questions of social responsibility of the firm have come to the floor.

The discussion originated in the fact that more and more services were demanded of the various local, state and federal governments, and financing the activities in the public sector to render these services required an ever-increasing share of national income. Questions as to which burden could be levied on the corporations were asked and led to heated political discussions in Germany around the turn of the decade. It seems that a conviction is spreading now that the limits to further burdening the German corporations with taxes have been reached. It seems to have been recognized that investment in plant and equipment is not independent of the tax burden and that one cannot on the one hand have a reduction in the rate of unemployment and on the other a higher rate of corporation income taxes.

At the same time it was recognized that investment in plant and equipment in the private sector cannot be increased by only turning the taxation screw back. One has to take the whole picture of distribution of income within the firm into consideration. It is one of the problems of this discussion that it cannot be based on a sound theory of income distribution within the firm nor can it rely on statistical data at firm level. The present paper is an attempt to make a contribution in these two areas of theoretical and empirical research.

In what follows we will first define firm income based on published financial data (section II). Then we will show the development of the shares that the different groups participating in the firm received during the period from 1953 to 1974 and report on some preliminary results of empirical analysis of these data (section III).

II. Firm income and its derivation from published financial statements

1 Definition of firm income.

If we want to derive a sound basis for social audits which permit to quantify the services rendered by the company to its environment and the contribution to national income, it is necessary to derive a scheme for the computation of firm income.

One of the first to introduce the concept of »business income« into the field of business administration was Nicklisch. However, the main contribution to the theory and the computation of firm income is due to M. R. Lehmann (2).

However income is defined and in whatever context the term is used, be it on the level of a division, the whole company or be it on the level of a branch of industry, it is the intention to measure the contribution of these units of measurements to national income in a particular period (3).

2 Types of measuring firm income.

Firm income is defined as the income derived from the productive services of a company in a particular period. It can be measured in two different ways. One way is to compute business income from the side of its origin and the other is to measure it from the side of its distribution.

If we measure firm income from its origin we have to define income as total revenue minus costs of goods and services. If we base computation of firm income on its distribution we define firm income as the sum of income of employees of the company, payments to creditors and shareholders, payments to government and withholdings in the company itself.

The following table shows the basic computational schemes.

Table 1

Firm income based on origin:	Total revenue
	./. Costs of goods and services
	————————————
	= Firm income
Firm income based on distribution:	Income of employees
	+ Government
	+ Cost of capital invested:
	dividends on equity
	interest on liabilities
	+ Retained earnings
	————————————
	= Firm income

However, these computational components of firm income cannot be derived directly from the financial statements of the corporations. Thus it was necessary to make these concepts, which are used in economics to determine income and distribution, operational and to identify the various entries in the companies' profit and loss statements which add up to the components given in table 1.

2.1 Firm income computed from its origin.

Attempts to derive firm income from its origin based on published financial data meet with severe difficulties which stem from the fact that this concept in economics is a concept which tries to measure the periodic contribution of the firm to national income in real terms. However, the traditional profit and loss statement does not differentiate very clearly between entries that pertain to the particular period and nonperiodic figures.

According to the extent of the elimination of entries in the profit and loss statement which do not measure the result of the productive services in the period under consideration we can derive five different levels of income computation. These levels are given in figure 1.

Figure 1 Levels of Income Computation

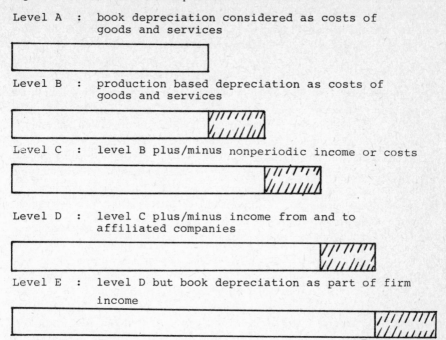

Level A : book depreciation considered as costs of goods and services

Level B : production based depreciation as costs of goods and services

Level C : level B plus/minus nonperiodic income or costs

Level D : level C plus/minus income from and to affiliated companies

Level E : level D but book depreciation as part of firm income

Figure 1 clearly indicates the different levels of firm income. Figure 1 helps to clarify which concepts of firm income are being measured by different approaches in the literature.

The different levels of firm income result from a different treatment of some entries in the profit and loss statement

     — depreciation
     — periodic breakup
     — unit of computation.

2.1.1 Depreciation.

In economics depreciation is treated as costs of goods and services and is measured as the part of capital stock in real terms consumed during that particular period in the production of national income. The reported book depreciation cannot be compared easily with this economic concept because of two reasons: depreciation is based on nominal value of fixed assets and not measured in real terms. In what follows we will have to base all computations on nominal values. No attempt will be made here to transform the reported financial data into real terms. The second reason is that book depreciation is based on accounting conventions which may not necessarily measure the productive services rendered by plant and equipment in the production process of that particular year. A misjudgement of the economic life-time of equipment as well as the standardization of depreciation rates may result in a gross distortion of production-based depreciation. Depreciation allowances for the purposes of taxation in addition cause book entries to deviate from what might be considered production-based depreciation allowances.

If we attempted to bring our computations as closely in line with economic concepts as possible, it is evident that we should try to measure production-oriented depreciation allowances. It is possible to derive such figures in nominal terms if we estimate the economic lifetime of plant and equipment. On the other hand it seems defendable to treat depreciation as income of the productive factor »capital invested«. This would then mean that depreciation forms part of that firm income which is considered the cake to be distributed among the various interest groups of the firm.

2.1.2 Periodic breakdown.

An analysis of the income shares over time can only lead to meaningful results if we can compute firm income for the particular period during which it is generated.

This means that those entries in the profit and loss statements which report nonperiodic income or cost should be eliminated. Such an approach would require the elimination of income from plant and equipment sold, income from a reduction in contingent liabilities, and losses from the sale of plant and equipment to mention just a few entries which are of considerable importance. These entries are actually part of firm income of previous periods which were not subjected to the process of income distribution because at that time they could not be considered part of income but had to be treated as costs of goods and services. If these entries are not considered part of current income as is done frequently in the literature, of course these entries then have to be eliminated and added to that period when they originated.

However, we would like to make the point that they have to be treated as current income. If in prior periods depreciation was fixed at too high a rate and therefore reduced distributable income, we find a corresponding profit from the sale of equipment in the period when the piece of equipment is sold. If this profit is eliminated from current income as a nonperiodic item, there is no chance to add it to the period of origin and then subject it to the process of distribution. These periods are gone. On the other hand it is hard to believe that negotiations on the shares of income to be distributed among the various participants with a claim on part of the firm's income would agree to eliminate a nonperiodic item from their income and thus induce the owners of the firm to try and influence their share of total longterm income by constantly underestimating total firm income by accounting conventions.

2.1.3 Unit of computation

The third problem of major importance is the question how the unit should be delineated for which firm income can be computed. Lehmann (4) is of the opinion that the individual plant should be considered as the entity for which income is computed. Kroenlein (5) on the other hand maintains that income should be computed for the individual firm if it is not affiliated with other firms or for the total group if the legal entity is an affiliated company of a larger group. A third author, Wedell (6), strongly urges to base computations of firm income on the legal entity because different interest groups have to address their claims to the legal entity and not to the group or the individual plant. Of course, if we base the computation of firm income on the legal entity concept, we meet with a number of conceptual difficulties if the company under consideration is an affiliated company. It might seem necessary then to deduct from reported income income received from subsidiaries and to add payments to other legal entities but here again we fell that we should not stick to the rigorous concept of income which derives from a functual theory of distribution but that we should rather base our analysis on an income which can be considered as the basis for the bargaining process within the firm. We contend that income received from subsidiaries is considered part of the distributable income of the firm or on the other hand payments to affiliated companies reduce this basis and are considered as part of the cake which can be distributed by those firms that receive these payments.

In the following table 2 (see page 138) we present a detailed scheme of computation of firm income based on its origin.

After having defined total distributable income based on its origin we now ask how this income is distributed among the groups with a stake in the company. It is then the task of distribution theory to determine the magnitude of the shares and to identify the causal factors behind the distribution of income.

It is customary in distribution theory to distinguish between functional and personal distribution on the one hand and between primary and secondary distribution on the other. Functional distribution theory analyses income according to its economic origin in the production process and tries to determine the shares that go to the different factors of production. Functional income therefore distinguishes between capital income and wage income. Personal income distribution theory on the other hand analyses income of households regardless of the functional sources from which it is derived (7).

The functional approach is the more adequate one in the analysis of the distribution of firm income. The bargaining process does not take individual income differences among the participants into consideration but tries to influence the relative shares of wages and capital income.

However, an analysis of the primary distribution of firm income between the two factors of production labour and capital would be insufficient because the bargaining process is not so much concerned with the gross shares but rather with the net shares that the factors of production gain. The share that government takes out of firm income has therefore to be taken into consideration. Figure 2 (see page 139) gives a scheme of the components which have to be taken into consideration when one tries to determine the effects of secondary distribution.

The primary distribution is concerned with the income distribution resulting from the market process. Therefore primary distribution deals with gross sums of income. However, if we want to analyse the role of government in the redistribution of income by taxation and transfer payments we have to analyse secondary distribution. Secondary distribution tries to analyse the net shares of income that go to capital and labour.

In the present context we define secondary distribution at the firm level. We do not take into consideration that shareholders have to pay income tax on their dividends and that interest payments received by creditors are subject to income

Table 2   Computation of Firm Income Based on its Origin

gross sales
± changes in inventory
+ other cost items entered in the balance sheet

= total value of productive services of the period
+ other ordinary revenue

= gross company contribution
- costs of goods and services without depreciation
  costs of raw material on hand
  costs of goods in process
  costs of finished goods bought
  depreciation on inventory
  other taxes
  additions to pretax reserves
  other expenses

= firm income of period before depreciation
- depreciation on plant and equipment and immaterial
  assets

= firm income of financial year
+ nonperiodic income
  income from the sale of equipment
  income from a reduction of inventory depreciation
  reserve
  income from a reduction of contingent liabilities
  other extraordinary income
- nonperiodic expenses
  losses from the sale of equipment
+ income derived from investments in associated companies
  income from affiliated companies
  income from other associated companies
  other dividends
  interest and royalties
  income from lossassumption of subsidiaries
- income and dividends paid to affiliated companies
  depreciation on financial assets
  losses assumed from subsidiary companies

= firm income

Figure 2 Distribution of Firm Income

Primary distribution

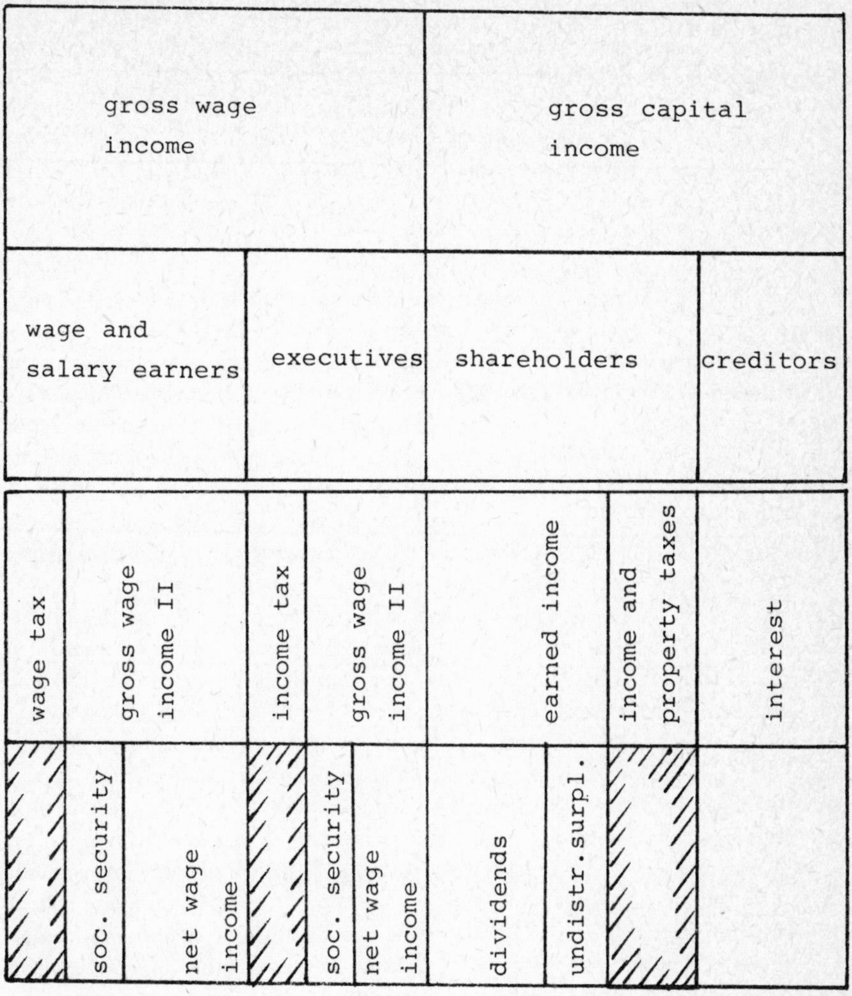

gross wage income				gross capital income			
wage and salary earners		executives		shareholders			creditors
wage tax	gross wage income II	income tax	gross wage income II	earned income	income and property taxes		interest
(soc. security / net wage income)	soc. security · net wage income	*(soc. security / net wage income)*	soc. security · net wage income	dividends · undistr. surpl.	*(income and property taxes)*		

Secondary distribution

tax in certain cases as well. Figure 2 is the basis for a concept of income distribution at firm level which tries to integrate primary and secondary distribution. Such an integration seems to be necessary for various reasons. Each secondary distribution is based on a particular primary distribution from which taxes and other contributions are deducted. Changes in primary distribution have therefore direct consequences for secondary distribution. On the other hand taxes and payments for social benefits influence primary income based on contract. Higher income taxes as well as the effect of rising income tax rates with a change to higher income brackets lead to higher demands of wage earners in primary distribution. It will become evident from the empirical analysis that the interdependence of primary and secondary distribution in the bargaining process has played a major role in the development of the relative shares and that the bargaining process was influenced by a very definite shift of the sources from which the governments derived their income in the form of taxes.

Table 3 (see page 141) gives a scheme of the computation of firm income based on its distribution. It is to be noted that in Germany the companies are held liable to withhold wage taxes from wages paid and transfer them to the IRS.

III. Empirical analysis of income distribution of German corporations

1 Preliminary remarks

In the empirical analysis that follows we want to describe frist how the shares of the various participating groups vary from period to period. At this stage of our analysis it has to be understood that a considerable amount of work had to be devoted to the collection of data and the description of the development of income distribution over time. Such a description, however, is based on certain hypotheses and can be used to derive others. The process of theory formation will be made clear in the course of the analysis.

It should be added that the analysis forms part of a broader analysis of empirical models of firm growth, and parts of the model which would have helped to clarify questions which arose in this context were not available yet.

The analysis is based on the data derived from the financial statements of a sample of 100 industrial corporations quoted at German stock exchanges. The sample is a random sample from the total number of all quoted stock corporations. Financial data were collected for the period from 1953 to 1974. The original sample was taken in 1961 and had over the subsequent 10 years a limited purpose. Therefore, only a limited number of all the entries in the balance sheets as well as in the profit and loss statements was collected and stored on magnetic tape. For the present analysis it was necessary to collect many different data and other data in more detail. The completion of the time series for all the financial data of the published report covers the period from 1960 to 1974. A complete collection of all the necessary data was possible for a subsection of 20 chemical companies for the period 1953 to 1974. We will indicate at each individual point of the analysis which data base was used.

2 Sketch of the results of the bargaining conflict 1953 to 1974.

An overall picture of primary as well as secondary distribution of firm income is given in table 4 (see page 142) for the sample of 100 industrial corporations.

Table 4 clearly indicates that wage earners receive the overwhelming part of firm income. It should be noted in particular that between 1968 and 1974 gross wage income rose by 6.81 percentage points from 75.85 % to 82.66 %, whereas prior to 1969, gross wage income remained fairly stable on the average and fluctuated with the business cycle. During recessionary periods the share of wage income is considerably higher than in the years prior and after these phases of business activity, and in the boom periods we note that the wage share is very clearly lower than the trend average. A notable break in the time series occurs in 1969. This can

Table 3   Computation of Firm Income Based on its Distribution

<u>Primary distribution</u>

employees

wages and salaries
+ social benefits
+ contributions to pension funds etc.
= gross wage income

capital owners

interest
+ profits before taxes
profits after taxes
taxes on income and property
equalization of burdens levy
= gross capital income

<u>Secondary distribution</u>

employees

wages and salaries
- wage tax
+ social benefits
+ contributions to pension funds etc.
= net wage income

capital owners

interest
+ dividends
+ undistributed surplus
= net capital income

government

taxes on income and property
+ equalization of burdens levy
+ wage tax
= government income

Table 4 Primary and Secondary Distribution of Firm Income

Year	Primary Distribution		Secondary Distribution		
	GWI (%)	GCI (%)	NWI (%)	NCI (%)	GI (%)
1953	74.29	25.69	66.96	8.80	24.22
'54	73.40	25.76	66.45	10.05	22.60
'55	73.74	26.30	66.20	8.39	25.45
'56	73.31	26.68	65.21	9.24	25.54
'57	71.40	28.64	63.15	10.53	26.36
'58	69.70	30.29	62.60	12.74	24.65
'59	69.77	30.21	62.52	13.44	24.02
'60	73.41	26.60	64.98	12.17	22.86
'61	74.07	25.93	64.94	12.37	22.69
'62	74.48	25.54	64.75	12.30	22.97
'63	75.57	24.44	65.25	11.52	23.24
'64	76.68	23.31	65.86	12.15	21.98
'65	75.92	24.09	65.47	13.00	21.54
'66	77.22	22.80	66.28	12.10	21.62
'67	77.98	22.48	66.81	12.80	20.85
'68	75.85	24.49	64.78	13.13	22.43
'69	78.22	21.80	66.55	12.09	21.38
'70	78.67	21.35	66.34	12.03	21.55
'71	80.47	19.53	67.55	11.04	21.41
'72	79.74	20.30	66.42	11.57	22.05
'73	81.09	18.91	67.18	10.68	22.14
'74	82.66	17.34	67.43	9.53	23.04

1953 – 59   20 chemical corporations
1960 – 74   100 industrial corporations
GWI — gross wage income
GCI — gross capital income
NWI — net wage income
NCI — net capital income
GI — government income

be attributed to the change in the power structure in the Federal Republic which resulted from the change of the political parties in power. However, we will try to present a deeper analysis of the underlying forces. It should be evident though that such a remarkable change in the relative shares that wage earners and capital owners receive cannot remain without effect on the investment volume of private business. One of the authors has analysed the effect of distribution of firm income on the volume of business investment in some more detail and has attributed the slump in business investment in the private sector to this change of relative income (8).

A deeper insight into the forces behind firm income distribution is obtained if we look at the secondary income distribution in table 4. We note that net wage income has increased from 1968 to 1974, but this increase amounts to only 2.6 percentage points as compared to the 6.81 percentage points in the case of gross wage income. And prior to that the net share of wages in relation to its 1974 level has been higher than the corresponding figures for the gross wage income. It is therefore evident from looking at the secondary distribution of firm income that the true recipient of the benefits of an increased intensity in the bargaining conflict has been government. Government has been able to keep its share of total firm income constant by taking an ever-increasing share out of gross wage income. The built-in progressive taxrate of the German wage tax system has allowed government to participate more than proportionally in the increase in gross wages that labour achieved during the period under consideratión and in particular during the period from 1969 to 1974.

Table 4 shows that with government income remaining constant in relation to total income, capital income decreased from a level of 13 % at the beginning of the sixties to 9.5 % in 1974. This downward trend is the direct effect of the rising trend in net wage income. However, table 4 does not give the full picture. A more detailed analysis is given in table 5 (see page 144). Table 5 shows that the share of total firm income that went to the shareholders decreased constantly from the early sixties to the mid-seventies whereas the creditors could double their share of total firm income. This is partly due to rising debt levels and partly due to rising interest rates. We will deal with this phenomenon in some more detail in a later section.

It is obvious that rising wages and increasing interest payments exerted a significant sqeeze on company profits. The decreasing profitability of the German corporations resulted in a decreasing share of corporation income taxes. It is therefore quite easily understandable that the corporation taxes in relation to total firm income should have decreased. However, as will be shown later, the decrease has been retarded considerably due to the fact that part of corporation taxes levied on the firm is not based on taxable income but rather on taxable property. Therefore we note two tendencies that result in a constant share of government in firm income: The first factor is the shift from corporation taxes to wage taxes. This shift is clearly evident from figure 3 (see page 145) below. While on the one hand corporation taxes in proportion to firm income decreased by 50 %, the share of wage taxes to firm income increased by almost 100 %. Figure 3 below shows the second effect: The relative share of corporation property taxes increased whereas the proportion of corporate income taxes to firm income showed a remarkable decline.

Table 5 Secondary Distribution of Firm Income

Year	GI		NCI		NWI
	WT (%)	CT (%)	creditors (%)	share-holders (%)	(%)
1953	7.33	16.89	3.66	5.14	66.96
'54	6.95	15.71	2.33	7.72	66.45
'55	7.54	17.91	2.56	5.83	66.20
'56	8.10	17.44	4.48	4.76	65.21
'57	8.25	18.11	4.23	6.30	63.15
'58	7.10	17.55	3.67	9.07	62.60
'59	7.25	16.77	2.96	10.48	62.52
'60	8.43	14.43	3.09	9.08	64.98
'61	9.13	13.56	3.51	8.86	64.94
'62	9.73	13.24	4.14	8.16	64.75
'63	10.32	12.92	3.59	7.93	65.25
'64	10.82	11.16	3.70	8.45	65.86
'65	10.45	11.09	4.07	8.93	65.47
'66	10.92	10.70	4.92	7.18	66.28
'67	11.17	9.68	5.15	7.65	66.81
'68	11.07	11.36	4.13	9.00	64.78
'69	11.67	9.71	4.52	7.57	66.55
'70	12.23	9.32	6.00	6.03	66.34
'71	12.92	8.49	5.48	5.56	67.55
'72	13.32	8.73	5.40	6.17	66.42
'73	13.91	8.23	6.33	4.35	67.18
'74	15.23	7.81	6.26	3.27	67.43

GI — government income
NCI — net capital income
NWI — net wage income
WT — wage tax
CT — corporation tax

Figure 3 Distribution of Firm Income

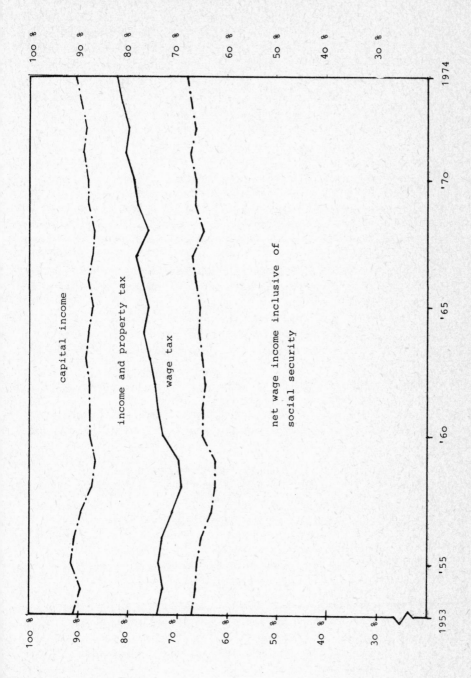

3 Causal analysis of the income shares.

The theory of income distribution has so far focussed its interest primarily on the macro-economic level. We do not have to go into detail here. There are, on the other hand very few contributions to a theory of income distribution at corporate level. The early writings by Gordon (9) and by Crum (10) seem to have found very few followers. Focus among business scientists has remained very strongly on corporate wage models. The absolute magnitude of wages was considered as given by macro-economic forces, and the analysis went on the assumption that the individual firm could not influence total wages paid. Therefore analyses of the determinants of income distribution within the firm are lacking. There are only very few exceptions to the fact that research in the distribution of firm income among wage owners and capitalists is highly deficient.

3.1 Explanation of wage income

We want to explain the determination of the share of gross wage income by a combination of marginal productivity theory, power theory, and bargaining theory. We therefore advance the hypothesis that gross wage income depends on the following factors:

1. Technical progress as an indicator of the longterm effects of changes in the production function which determines changes in the marginal productivity of the factors involved.

2. Developments in the currency exchange rate as an indication of the relative strength of German industry in the international markets.

3. Cyclical fluctuations as indicators of the changing power of employees in the distribution conflict.

4. The bargaining position of the employees.

5. The bargaining position of the employers.

We estimate the impact of these determinants on the formation of wage income by time series analysis, using the least squares method. We used the following variables.

BLQ1	...	Share of gross wage income to firm income
TF	...	Production volume per employee hour in the manufacturing industry
CAP	...	Degree of average capacity utilisation in the firms of the sample
EX	...	Exchange rate (DM/$)
POW	...	Degree of unionisation of the employees in industry
PR	...	Price index of industrial goods[1]

Measurement of the relative power of the bargaining position of the employees raises problems. We have used the degree of unionization as an indicator of the bargaining power and are well aware of the fact that there might be other indicators which might prove to be better proxies for the relative power of the employees' bargaining position.

Since we measure the effect of distribution conflicts, we can use prices as an indicator of the relative power of the employers' position. If in the negotiations the employers have to grant a distribution which does not meet their original expectations, the corporations can always try to correct the result of the negotiations by changes in pricing policy. Increases in prices do indicate to which degree corporations can shift increased prices for goods and services bought and wage increases in order to defend disadvantageous effects of wage negotiations.

Many different combinations of the determinants of wage income as well as various lag structures were tested. From these time series analyses we derive the following results:

1. The hypothesis that marginal productivity theory as measured by technical progress serves to explain the longterm effects of changing the scarcity of the factors of production seems to be valid. The signs of the regression coefficients of TF and of the lag variables TFL1 and TFL2 are positive in all regression analyses. We therefore conclude that technical progress changes distribution in favour of wage income in the long run. This result may of course also be the simple effect of an economic distribution policy which maintained that wage earners should not demand a higher rate of increase of gross wages than the rate of change in labour productivity. Higher wage increases would necessarily lead to higher inflation which in turn would weaken the bargaining position and at the same time have the effect that real wage increase would drop below the nominal wage increase.

Multiple correlation coefficients improve if the variable TF is substituted by the lag variables TFL1 and TFL2.

2. The coefficients of variable EX have a negative sign in all the regression equations. Thus we find that a revaluation of the deutschmark with respect to the dollar has an adverse effect on the profitability of the companies and thus indirectly causes a rise in the share of wage income. The statistical significance of this result is, however, not very convincing with respect to the 100 industrial corporations. We will show below that this variable is highly significant for the chemical industry.

3. The regression coefficients of the variable CAP, which measures changes in the relative power of the employees, show the expected negative values in all computations run. We therefore conclude that changes in the economic environment do have a clear impact on the relative power in the wage negotiations. In most cases the regression coefficients for the variable CAP are different from zero at a level of at least 95 %.

4. Price is not significant at the probability level of 95 %.

5. Also, the variable POW does not add to the explanatory force of the other variables. In almost all equations the regression coefficients of the variable POW are negative, but they are on the other hand not significant due to the high standard deviation in the sample. We therefore do not find empirical support for the hypothesis that a higher degree of unionization improves the strength of the bargaining position of the employees and hence leads to an improvement of the distribution situation of workers.

6. The following equation led to the best statistical fit:

$$BLQ1 = 76.75 + 0.0476 \text{ TEFL2} - 0.90 \text{ EX} - 0.0485 \text{ CAP}$$
$$(4.75) \quad (0.0073) \qquad\quad (0.74) \qquad (0.0251)$$

$$R^2 = 0.9518 \qquad\qquad DW = 2.87$$

The regression analysis shows very clearly the impact of capacity utilization on the wage rate. An improvement in the overall degree of capacity utilization leads to a lower wage income share whereas phases of economic depression improve the relative situation of the employees. This is, of course, due to the residual character of profit.

Productivity increases due to technical progress have clearly improved the long-term position of the employees. The rapid increase of technological knowledge during the years after World War II went clearly to the disadvantage of capital income. The rising trend of the wage share can therefore be attributed to technical progress. It seems important to note that in the regression analyses the lag structure of technical progress plays an important part. Changes in the production process through technological innovation have an immediate effect on the improvement of the share of capital income, as will be shown later, but after two periods the new structures of the technical production facilities deploy their full impact on the relative share of wage income. From the regression equation above we can therefore conclude that in the period under consideration, which showed a remarkable rate of growth in the economy, the longterm tendency of the share of wage income was determined by technical progress. On the other hand it seems that the short-run development of wage income was influenced very strongly by cyclical fluctuations. The unions do not have a significant effect on the distribution of firm income and at the same time the princing policy of the enterpreneurs had only small effects on the relative shares of income distribution, if there was any. More detailed information was available for the 20 chemical companies in the Bonn Sample. Therefore, we could estimate a regression function for net firm income of level A for these companies. Table 6 (see page 149) gives the date for this analysis.

The following regression function was estimated.

$$BLQ2 = 145.61 + 0.1005\ NPROD - 7.54\ EX - 0.2411\ CAP$$
$$(49.47)\quad (0.0305)\qquad\quad (3.88)\qquad\quad (0.0783)$$

$$-\ 0.3678\ PRL1 \qquad\qquad R^2 = 0.9160$$
$$(0.3150)\qquad\qquad\qquad DW = 2.23$$

BLQ2	...	Gross wage income for the chemical companies
NPROD	...	Index of industrial net production
PRL1	...	Index of industrial prices. lagged for one period
CAP	...	Degree of average capacity utilisation
EX	...	Exchange rate (DM/$)

We note that net industrial production which is an index of cyclical fluctuations is highly significant. On the other hand the influence of prices on gross wage income is not significant because the regression coefficient is not significant at the 95 % level as one notes from the regression equation.

The exchange rate has a significant influence on the distribution of firm income. This may be due to the fact that the chemical industry in Germany is highly export-oriented so that any change in the currency exchange rates which weakens its competitive position in the export markets causes a deterioration of company

Table 6 Gross Wage Income as a Percentage of Net Firm Income
(for 20 chemical companies)

Year	Lower[+] Limit	Mean Value	Upper[+] Limit	Coeff. of Variation
1953	62.34	69.04	75.73	0.19
'54	53.94	62.75	71.55	0.31
'55	60.12	66.37	72.61	0.20
'56	61.44	68.51	75.58	0.22
'57	58.36	63.97	69.57	0.19
'58	61.11	65.35	69.59	0.14
'59	60.33	64.75	69.18	0.15
'60	57.98	63.00	68.02	0.17
'61	59.95	65.94	71.93	0.20
'62	66.07	60.74	75.40	0.14
'63	63.36	69.20	75.04	0.18
'64	63.43	70.69	77.95	0.22
'65	64.15	70.20	76.25	0.19
'66	64.32	71.41	78.50	0.22
'67	66.30	73.13	79.96	0.20
'68	61.08	68.87	76.66	0.25
'69	63.90	71.69	79.47	0.24
'70	73.06	78.10	83.15	0.14
'71	71.89	78.64	85.39	0.19
'72	72.34	78.81	85.27	0.18
'73	72.28	79.39	86.50	0.19
'74	71.38	79.63	87.89	0.22

[+] Confidence intervals are given for a probability of error of 5 %.

profits. It is obvious from looking at the time series of BLQ2 that the high level of wage income between 1970 and 1974 coincides with a period of frequent increases of the exchange rate of the deutschmark.

The time series analysis shows the average impact of the economic factors on the distribution of firm income. It does not permit to estimate the influence of these variables on the various individual firms. We therefore ran cross-section analyses on individual firms' income for the 100 corporations in the Bonn Sample. The cross-section analysis was run for the year of 1974. The results are as follows:

1. We could not find an influence of company size on gross wage income.

2. Capital intensity of the firms on the other hand has a highly significant influence on gross wage income. This influence is significant at the 99 % level. The rising capital intensity improves the position of the capital owners. This seems very much in line with the intention of the entrepreneurs that they want to improve their profit position by substituting capital for labour and save labour cost. This, however, works only in comparison with the other companies. On the average workers have been able to finally take the advantages of rising capital intensity from the capital owners, however, as we have seen with a lag of two periods.

3. We have also estimated the impact of ownership on gross wage income. We went on the hypothesis that the more concentrated ownership in the corporation is in one or just a few hands, the more powerful is resistance against rising wages in the bargaining process. We found that a variable which takes into account the fact that more than 25 % of equity capital is held by three or fewer persons has an impact on gross wage income which is significant at the 95 % level. Other variables (which were entered as Kronecker variables) which measured a majority holding of 50 % and 75 % respectively did not prove significant. It is interesting to note that the regression coefficient on the significant Kronecker variable for 25 % ownership is positive. This means that contrary to our expectations concentration of ownership is connected with higher wage income shares.

3.2 The share of capital income.

We now address our attention to capital income. There are two sources of capital for the firm: creditors and shareholders. That part of capital income which goes to the creditors is entered in the profit and loss statement as interest paid. According to German accounting law, companies had to report the difference between interest paid and interest received only until the year of 1959. In 1959 a new law was passed which reformed the accounting law with regard to the profit and loss statement. Since then companies had to report interest received and interest paid separately.

The share of firm income which goes to the creditors has risen over the past 15 years. This rise is due to two factors: On the one hand the debt-equity-ratio has risen over time (12), on the other hand it is due to rising interest rates in Germany. If we divide total interest paid by the total liabilities of the company, then we get a rate of between two and four percent. This rate has gradually risen over time, but it is only in 1974 that this relation is greater than the cost of equity. If, however, one wants to determine the effective interest rate, one has to determine that part of liabilities which is interest earning. Since a large part of the liabilities invested in the company does not carry nominal interest rates, the effective interest rate on interest bearing loan capital is more than twice the rate which is derived by simply dividing interest paid by the total amount of loan capital invested. The effective interest rate has risen much more considerably over time than the rate of interest on total loan capital employed. Table 7 (see page 152) gives details of capital cost.

The reasons for the steady increase of interest paid lie on the one hand in the rising debt-equity-ratio and on the other in the inflationary developments in Germany. Correlation analysis shows that creditors have been able to adjust interest rates to inflationary developments by rising inflation premia as a consequence of rising inflation rates.

It was shown previously that the share of net capital income has decreased over time. Since on the other hand that part of net capital income that goes to creditors has risen over time, it is easily demonstrated that group of participants in the firm that has really suffered from the outcome of the bargaining process as well as from inflation has been the group of shareholders. We now turn to their share of firm income. An analysis of table 7 shows that the return on equity of the German corporations has decreased steadily. While the share of capital income that went to shareholders amounted to about 9 % at the beginning of the sixties, it was reduced to 3.27 % by 1974. The decrease was particularly marked between 1970 and 1974. Table 7 also shows that the firms try to maintain at least some minimum amount of withholdings so that dividend income decreases at an even faster rate than the shareholders' total income. However, during the last five years firms were not able to withhold enough earnings to finance investment. On the contrary in 1974 reserves had to be reduced in order to be able to pay dividends. The juxtaposition of the return on equity and of interest paid on liabilities clearly demonstrates that return on equity of German corporations is insufficient indeed. It is obvious from table 7 that the shareholders have suffered doubly from redistribution and inflation.

3.3 Government income.

Local and federal governments participate in firm income through taxes on income and property, through the equalization of burdens levy, and franchise taxes. The corporations have to withhold wage taxes from the wages earned by the employees and pay the sum total to the tax authorities.

Table 8 (see page 153) shows the different sources of government income within firm income. It is clearly evident from table 5 that a shift has taken place from corporation income tax to wage taxes as a source of government income.

A second shift has taken place within corporation taxes. Taxes levied on the corporations are partly based on corporation income and partly based on corporation property. Since the profitability of German corporations has gradually and constantly declined over the past 15 years and most notably during the last 5 years, the share of corporate income tax as a percentage of firm income has decreased constantly.

On the other hand the property taxes have increased their share of firm income because the property tax base increased due to rising capital intensity and due to rising prices because of inflation. Therefore we can say that property-based taxes

Table 7 Capital Cost (%)

Year	FKKS 1	FKKS 3	JUE/EK	JUE/GK·BK	DIV/GK·BK	DIV	RL
1953	2.02	4.78	1.65	5.99	5.43	7.34	− 2.20
'54	1.48	3.25	3.68	4.69	4.02	6.59	1.13
'55	1.63	3.61	5.48	4.30	3.57	7.12	− 1.29
'56	2.05	4.38	5.90	4.77	4.13	6.84	− 2.08
'57	2.05	4.95	6.56	5.55	4.37	7.71	− 1.41
'58	1.98	4.51	6.99	2.95	3.29	9.38	− 0.31
'59	1.83	5.34	8.20	2.50	2.21	9.73	0.75
'60	2.03	6.19	9.29	2.58	2.34	6.97	2.11
'61	2.21	7.15	8.65	2.27	2.68	6.78	2.08
'62	2.37	5.28	6.80	3.65	3.69	6.67	1.49
'63	2.24	5.93	8.99	4.44	3.41	6.40	1.53
'64	2.31	5.79	8.42	3.90	3.32	6.02	2.43
'65	2.34	5.71	8.81	5.13	3.88	6.06	2.87
'66	3.05	6.46	7.60	5.08	4.05	5.53	1.65
'67	3.10	6.87	6.44	3.57	2.99	5.22	2.43
'68	2.59	6.41	9.16	4.63	3.10	5.83	3.17
'69	2.70	6.25	7.65	3.58	2.75	6.16	1.41
'70	3.59	7.53	6.98	3.48	3.13	5.25	0.78
'71	3.32	7.70	5.74	3.27	2.77	4.67	0.89
'72	2.90	8.17	6.40	2.42	2.19	4.52	1.65
'73	3.57	8.80	3.84	2.00	2.51	4.11	0.24
'74	4.12	9.36	3.56	1.80	2.83	3.51	− 0.24

FKKS 1	−	Interest paid divided by total liablilities
FKKS 3	−	Interest paid divided by interest bearing liabilities
JUE/EK	−	Income earned divided by equity capital and surplus
JUE/GK·BK	−	Income earned divided by market value of total shares outstanding
DIV	−	Dividends divided by firm income
RL	−	Withholdings divided by firm income

152

Table 8 Government Income (%)

Year	WT	CT	Sum	CIT	CPT
1953	7.33	16.89	24.22	81.34	18.66
'54	6.95	15.71	22.60	80.44	19.56
'55	7.54	17.91	25.45	80.34	19.66
'56	8.10	17.44	25.54	83.73	16.27
'57	8.25	18.11	26.36	85.44	14.56
'58	7.10	19.55	24.65	83.48	16.52
'59	7.25	16.77	24.02	85.20	14.80
'60	8.43	14.43	22.86	83.83	16.17
'61	9.13	13.56	22.69	81.14	18.86
'62	9.73	13.24	22.97	82.98	17.02
'63	10.32	12.20	22.52	81.63	18.37
'64	10.82	11.16	21.98	80.52	19.48
'65	10.45	11.09	21.54	79.07	20.93
'66	10.92	10.70	21.62	76.08	23.92
'67	11.17	9.68	20.85	74.44	25.56
'68	11.07	11.36	22.43	73.93	26.07
'69	11.67	9.71	21.38	69.55	30.45
'70	12.23	9.32	21.55	72.52	27.48
'71	12.92	8.49	21.41	72.78	27.22
'72	13.32	8.73	22.05	70.64	29.36
'73	13.91	8.23	22.14	70.86	29.14
'74	15.23	7.81	23.04	71.04	28.96

WT — wage tax (%)
CT — corporation tax (%)
CIT — corporation income tax divided by corporation taxes (%)
CPT — corporation property tax divided by corporation taxes (%)

now constitute a part of firm income which can no longer be treated as a negligible item. Since property taxes of this magnitude favour procyclical investment and constitute a very heavy burden on the firms in periods of recession, demands to abolish property taxes completely have been raised (8).

It seems an important and urgent objective of distribution policy to improve the profitability of the corporations and to make equity financing more attractive to shareholders and outside investors. Otherwise there would be no inducement to increase private business investment. Stimulation of investment in the private sector, however, has now been recognized as one of the major tasks of an economic policy oriented towards growth and full employment. It remains to be seen whether the abolition of double-taxation of corporate income which has been effected in the corporation income tax reform (13) will prove to be a step in the right direction.

Notes

[1] The time series of TEF, POW, EX, PR were all taken from the Statistical Year Books of the Federal Republic of Germany. The regression analysis is run for the period of 1960 through 1973 because the time series of CAP which was derived from the data of the Bonn sample were only available for this period (11).

References

(1) Brockhoff, K., Ist die gesellschaftsorientierte Berichterstattung ein geeignetes Meßinstrument, um die Auswirkung gesellschaftlicher Veränderungen auf die Unternehmenspolitik zu messen?, in: *Die Bedeutung gesellschaftlicher Veränderung für die Willensbildung im Unternehmen*, ed. Horst Albach and Dieter Sadowski, Schriftenreihe des Vereins für Socialpolitik, N.F. Band 88, Berlin-München 1976, p. 837.

(2) Lehmann, M.R., Planvolles Rechnen in Betrieb und Gruppe. Ein Beitrag zur Wertschöpfungs- und Wirtschaftlichkeitsrechnung, 1937; Leistungsmessung durch Wertschöpfungsrechnung, Essen 1954.

(3) Köhler, H.W., *Einkommensverteilung im Unternehmen*, Düsseldorf 1961, p. 11.

(4) Lehmann, M.R., *Leistungsmessung durch Wertschöpfungsrechnung*, Essen 1954, p. 21.

(5) Kroenlein, G., *Die Wertschöpfung der Aktiengesellschaft und des Konzerns*, Berlin 1975, p. 38.

(6) Wedell, H., *Die Wertschöpfung als Maßgröße für die Leistungskraft eines Unternehmens*, in: *Der Betrieb*, 29 (1976), p. 210.

(7) Krelle, W., *Verteilungstheorie*, Wiesbaden 1962, p. 11.

(8) Albach, H., *Steuersystem und unternehmerische Investitionspolitik*, Wiesbaden 1970. Besteuerung und Investitionen, Paper presented to a conference of Verein Deutscher Maschinenbauanstalten in Bonn-Bad Godesberg on March 31, 1976 (forthcoming)

(9) Gordon, R.A., Enterprise profits and the modern corporation in: Fellner, W. and B.F. Haley, *Readings in the theory of income distribution*, Philadelphia-Toronto 1949, p. 558.

(10) Crum, W.L., Corporate earnings on invested capital, in: Fellner, W. and B.F. Haley, *Readings in the theory of income distribution*, Philadelphia-Toronto 1949, p. 571.

(11) Werhahn, M., Capacity-, Investment- and Manpower Demand Functions for growing and non-growing Firms, Schriftenreihe des Instituts für Gesellschafts- und Wirtschaftswissenschaften (Betriebswirtschaftliche Abteilung), Nr. 57, Bonn, 1976.

(12) Albach, H., The Development of the Capital Structure of German Companies, in: *Journal of Business Finance and Accounting*, Vol 2 (1975), No. 3, p. 281.

(13) Bundesrat, Drucksache 421/76 vom 11.06.76, Gesetzesbeschluß des Deutschen Bundestages — Körperschaftssteuerreformgesetz.

Carl Christian von Weizsäcker
A Small Contribution to the Theory of Wage Structure in Collective Bargaining

In this paper I try to contribute to the understanding of the wage structure in systems of collective bargaining. The contribution is very limited. It centers around the observation that collective wage contracts for an industry quite frequently take the form: The wage rate of each employee i is raised by the maximum of two numbers s and ay_i, where s is a fixed amount of money (in dollars, pounds, Deutsche Mark, franc or whatever applies) independent of i and where a is a fixed percentage (independent of i) and y_i is the employee's wage rate before the wage increase.

Such a type of wage contract seems to have acquired a certain plausibility among wage earners. It may therefore not be completely wrong, if we assume that unions restrict themselves to demand and settle for a collective wage contract of this type. Now, of course, unions and their members prefer a higher wage increase to a lower wage increase, whereas the opposite is true of employers. What is not so clear, is the preference of the union and its members for the structure of wage increases, given their total height. If not everybody gets the same wage rate, low wage earners would benefit from a flat wage rise without proportional component. High wage earners would prefer a proportional wage increase. What will the outcome be? I develop a model in which I assume the total sum of wage increases is given.

Let y be the wage rate and let f(y) be the density function representing the distribution of the workers according to their wage rate. Let z be the new income after the new settlement. Then the general class of wage increases considered here implies

$$z(y) = Max\ [y + s, (1+a)\, y]$$

The density function g(z) of the new incomes is

$$g(z) = f(z-s) \text{ for } z \leqslant \frac{s}{a} + s$$
$$g(z) = \frac{1}{1+a} f\left(\frac{z}{1+a}\right) \text{ for } z > \frac{s}{a} + s$$

The average income z after the wage contract is

$$\bar{z} = \int_0^\infty g(z)z\,dz = \int_0^{s\frac{1+a}{a}} g(z)z\,dz + \int_{s\frac{1+a}{a}}^\infty g(z)z\,dz =$$

$$= \int_0^{\frac{s}{a}} f(y)\,(y+s)\,dy + \int_{\frac{s}{a}}^{\infty} \frac{1}{1+a}\,f(y)\,(1+a)\,y\,(1+a)\,dy =$$

$$= \int_0^{\frac{s}{a}} f(y)\,dy + \int_0^{\frac{s}{a}} f(y)\,y\,dy + (1+a)\int_{\frac{s}{a}}^{\infty} f(y)\,y\,dy =$$

$$= sm(s,a) + a\int_{\frac{s}{a}}^{\infty} f(y)\,y\,dy + \overline{y}$$

where $m(s,a) = \int_0^{\frac{s}{a}} f(y)\,dy$ represents the proportion of people getting a flat rise and $\overline{y}$ is the former average income. Given the value of $\overline{y}$ and $\overline{z}$ and given the density function $f(y)$ the last equation implies a functional relation between s and a. Obviously, the higher a the lower is s.

Let us now look at the increase in the wage rate for a worker with a present wage rate y. He gets $x = \max\,[s, ay]$, which, taking into account the functional relation between s and a, can be written as a function of a

$$x(a) = \max\,[s(a),\, ay]$$

The extreme points with s = o or a = o are local maxima.

This is an interesting feature. The minimum is obtained at the point where a y = s (a) i.e. at the value which makes the person a borderline case between those who receive a flat rise and those who receive a proportional rise. Let us also note: if only small modifications of a given proposal s,a are under consideration, then those in the flat rise group under the proposal are interested to raise s, those in the proportional group are interested to raise a. Given that the relative strength of the two groups depends on the initial proposal, there will be pressure to move in the direction of the wishes of the stronger group under this proposal. But such a modification will increase the membership of the stronger group. The process will accelerate and end up at one of the extreme points. Which extreme point will be reached depends on the initial proposal. If, for example, the relative strength of the two groups is given by their numerical size, an initial proposal s,a such that more than 50 percent would receive a flat rise tends towards the extreme egalitarian solution, as long as people only consider small modifications of proposals.

But, of course, people could anticipate the move to the extremes and thus push into the direction of the extreme which is more favourable to them. If $\overline{z} - \overline{y}$ is given, the egalitarian extreme would be a = o, s = $\overline{z} - \overline{y}$. The proportional extreme would be a $= \frac{\bar{z} - \bar{y}}{y}$, s = o. A person with income y thus either receives $\bar{z} - \bar{y}$ or ay $= \frac{y}{y} (\bar{z} - \bar{y})$. He prefers the proportional solution, whenever $y > \bar{y}$. Taking again majority rule as a decision mechanism, the proportional choice will be made, if more than 50 percent receive a wage rate above the average, i.e. if the median lies above the average. It should be noted that both extreme solutions stabilize the relative position of average and median.

So far, our analysis yielded results which are not consistent with what we observe. In many cases a mixed solution is chosen. Let us try to understand this. It definitely refutes the majority voting hypothesis. Let us look at the relative preference of people among three outcomes: E = the egalitarian extreme, P = the proportional extreme, and M = a mixture of both. Somebody who receives a very high wage rate, has a gain function like this

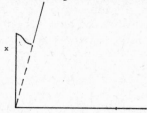

his preference is P > M > E. He, who receives a very low income, has a gain function like this

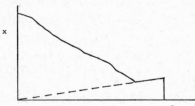

His gain function is E > M > P.

Somebody in the middle will least prefer the mixed solution. His preferences are

$$P > E > M \qquad \text{or} \qquad E > P > M$$

Given the strong conflict between the low income and high income of people, it may look plausible to say that the middle group is decisive. But then again an extreme solution should prevail, as a rule.

We have to proceed in a different manner. We should take note of the fact that all union members have a certain interest to maintain union solidarity. This is a value independent from the problem of distributing a given gain among the members. For the total gain will depend on this solidarity. This interest of the union members coincides with the interest of the union leadership to maximize union membership. Let me therefore try a tension minimising hypothesis. The union leaders try to propose a structure which minimizes tension. Tension is due to potential dissatisfaction with the result. Given the average increase $c = \bar{z} - \bar{y}$, potential dissatisfaction of a worker is measured by the square of the difference between the possible maximum and the actual gain for the individual. For a member with income $y < \bar{y}$ the possible maximum is s = c. For a member with income $y > \bar{y}$ the possible maximum is $c\frac{y}{y}$. For any given proposed combination s,a we thus obtain the following tension index for the individual

$$t = (c - s)^2 \qquad \text{for } y \leqslant \bar{y} \text{ and } y \leqslant \frac{s}{a}$$

$$t = (c - ay)^2 \qquad \text{for } y \leqslant \bar{y} \text{ and } y \geqslant \frac{s}{a}$$

$$t = (c\frac{y}{y} - s)^2 \qquad \text{for } y \geqslant \bar{y} \text{ and } y \leqslant \frac{s}{a}$$

$$t = (c\frac{y}{y} - ay)^2 \qquad \text{for } y \geqslant \bar{y} \text{ and } y \geqslant \frac{s}{a}$$

The tension integral $T = \int_0^\infty t(y)\, dy$ in the case of $\frac{s}{a} \leqslant \bar{y}$ is

$$T = \int_0^{\frac{s}{a}} f(y)\,(c-s)^2\, dy + \int_{\frac{s}{a}}^{\bar{y}} f(y)\,(c-ay)^2\, dy + \int_{\bar{y}}^\infty f(y)\,(c\frac{y}{y} - ay)^2\, dy$$

Assuming that the tension minimum problem has an interior solution, we can differentiate with respect to a and put the derivative equal to zero

$$\frac{dT}{da} = \frac{d\frac{s}{a}}{da}\,[\, f(\frac{s}{a})\,(c-s)^2 - f(\frac{s}{a})\,(c-a\frac{s}{a})^2\,] + \int_{\frac{s}{a}}^{\bar{y}} -2f(y)\,(c-ay)\, y\, dy$$

$$+ \int_{\bar{y}}^{\infty} -2f(y)\,(c\frac{y}{y} - ay)\, y\, dy = 0$$

The term in [   ] is obviously zero.

To evaluate the other terms, let us compute s' (a) from differentiating totally the constraint

$$s \int_0^{\frac{s}{a}} f(y)\, dy + a \int_{\frac{s}{a}}^\infty f(y)\, y\, dy = c$$

$$[s\, f(\frac{s}{a}) - a\frac{s}{a}\,]\, d\frac{s}{a} + ds \int_0^{\frac{s}{a}} f(y)\, dy + da \int_{\frac{s}{a}}^\infty f(y)\, y\, dy = 0$$

which implies

$$s'(a) = - \frac{\int_{\frac{s}{a}}^\infty f(y)\, y\, dy}{\int_0^{\frac{s}{a}} f(y)\, dy}$$

Let $m(a) = \int_0^{\frac{s}{a}} f(y)\, dy$. Let $\hat{y}\,(a) = \dfrac{\int_{\frac{s}{a}}^\infty f(y)\, y\, dy}{\int_{\frac{s}{a}}^\infty f(y)\, dy}$ = average income of

people with income above $\frac{s}{a}$. Then we can write

$$s'(a) = - \frac{1 - m(a)}{m(a)}\, \hat{y}\,(a)$$

Putting this into the minimum tension condition above and calling $\sqrt{t(y)} = \lambda(y)$ (the »loss« compared to the maximum) implies

158

$$\int_0^{\frac{s}{a}} f(y)\,\lambda(y)\,\frac{1-m(a)}{m(a)}\,\hat{y}\,(a)\,dy = \int_{\frac{s}{a}}^{\infty} f(y)\,y\,\lambda(y)\,dy$$

or

$$\hat{y}\,(a) \int_0^{\frac{s}{a}} f_1(y)\,\lambda\,(y)\,dy = \int_{\frac{s}{a}}^{\infty} f_2(y)\,y\,\lambda\,(y)\,dy$$

where $f_1(y) = \dfrac{f(y)}{m(a)}$ and $f_2(y) = \dfrac{f(y)}{\lambda - m(a)}$

are the densities in the intervals below resp. above $\frac{s}{a}$ blown up so as to add up to one within the intervals. Given the fact that

$$\hat{y}\,(a) = \int_{\frac{s}{a}}^{\infty} f_2(y)\,y\,dy$$

we can interpret the last equation roughly to mean: the average »loss« compared to the individual maximum, must be the same in the two groups: the group which gets a flat increase and the group which gets a proportional increase.

This implication of the tension minimization hypothesis can easily be tested. It is not likely that it will be literally fulfilled in a majority of cases. Life is more complicated than the models we are able to build. But the result of »balanced sacrifice« implied by our assumption could be used as a reference point. One could attempt to explain empirically observed deviations from the reference point by the specific circumstances prevailing in the special cases or by development of a more complex theory. What the reference point provides us with is a plausible point of comparison for actual data.

Hans-Juergen Krupp[*]
The Contribution of Microanalytic Simulation Models to the Theory of Income Distribution

1. Microanalytic Simulation Systems and the Theory of Income Distribution

The purpose of this paper is two-fold. First, it gives a progress report on a large microanalytic simulation project which is done at the Universities of Frankfurt/ Main and Mannheim. In 1971 the socio-political research group Frankfurt/Mannheim was founded. The members of the group have intended the development of a socio-political indicator and decision system for the Federal Republik of Germany. The project has been called SPES-Project[1].

The basic idea was to develop a system which gives information needed for an active social policy. Information on socio-structural trends and interdependencies is necessary for this purpose, as well as information on the consequences of actual measures of economic and social policy.

This task requires an analysis and discussion of the goals and objectives of an active social policy. A system of social indicators may serve as a framework for this purpose[2]. It permits, moreover, the control of social policy in an operational way. If the goal variables of social policy are formulated in an operational way, it is possible to measure the difference between intended and actual values. If policy instruments are chosen, it may be measured whether they are successful with respect to the goals.

The preparation of policy decisions requires the knowledge on the relation between policy instruments and goals. For this purpose a decision system is developed[3].

For purposes of social policy a high degree of disaggregation is needed. Especially when considering the situation of marginal groups in society, it can be shown that the analysis can not be restricted to aggregates. The decision system therefore is conceived as a microanalytic simulation system implemented on a computer. The system allows to make forecasts and to analyse the effects of hypothetical political instruments. The effects are measured in the system of social indicators which is incorporated into the decision system. Therefore the output of the decision system are values for the different social indicators which serve as goal variables.

[*] The author is Professor of Social Policy and President of the Johann Wolfgang Goethe-University in Frankfurt/Main. He is a member of the Socio-Political Research Group Frankfurt/Mannheim (Sozialpolitische Forschergruppe Frankfurt/Mannheim) which develops the system reported here. He wishes to thank his colleagues of this group who have contributed many ideas and discussions to it and so to this paper. He is especially grateful to Dr. Frank Klanberg who read the first draft of this paper and made very helpful comments.

The combination of an indicator- with a decision system raises a broad spectrum of problems which will not be dealt with in this paper. A short overview of the system is given in Section 4.

One of the variables which describe the economic and social situation of individuals and households is the income of individuals and households. The decision system therefore includes the generation of individual- and household income. The distribution of individual earnings, of household income and household income per head can be determined by using the concept of gross and disposable income. It is possible to make forecasts of the development of incomes and their distribution as well as to show the influence of policy instruments on these values.

The subsystem of the decision system which generates incomes can be regarded as an operational theory of income distribution. Hypotheses used in the simulation system are hypotheses which are also useful for the theory of income distribution. Therefore a microanalytic simulation system of this type constitutes an approach to the theory of income distribution too.

This leads to the second purpose of this paper. An assessment is made of the current state of the theory of income distribution with special emphasis on the requirements a meaningful theory of income distribution should fulfill and on the role microanalytic patterns and paradigms can play in the further development of the theory of income distribution.

2. Some Requirements for a Meaningful Theory of Income Distribution

The Social Indicator Movement has lead to a more extensive discussion of goal dimensions. This is valid for the problems of income distribution too. The goal system related to this field has to include quite different dimensions[4]. The most important ones are:

1. The adequacy of the income of a person with respect to his contributions in the production process.
2. The degree of equality of consumption possibilities
3. The level of poverty
4. The steadiness and security of incomes.

The first dimension requires the explanation of the income of individuals, the other the explanation of incomes of households. Some of these problems allow the restriction to a small number of social groups, others require a differentiation which shows the situation of fringe-groups too.

From this broader goal system the following requirements for the theory of income distribution can be deduced:

1. The theory must allow a relatively high degree of disaggregation. A unit of analysis has to be chosen which allows the formulation of goal-oriented questions. In any case, two units of analysis as in the two-group-systems are not sufficient. The usual two-group-scheme of the so-called functional distribution theory is not very useful because the groups are very heterogenous and because of the fact that all social groups have incomes from different functional sources. The minimum requirement would be a disaggregation that is related to the social status of the head of the household and the income level.

2. The income distribution theory must distinguish between the distribution of income of individuals and of households or spending units.

3. The theory of income distribution must include the information available up to now on the determinants of income. If we accept only the different explanations of income distribution presented at this Symposium, we have to include a large number of factors which determine the distribution of income. The minimum requirement is here the relation to the economic process on the one hand and on the other hand the inclusion of socio-economic characteristics of individuals and households. This means that a purely functional theory of the distribution of income is as inadequate as a theory of size distribution of income which neglects the macroeconomic conditions. Monocausal theories are not very helpful in this situation.

4. The broadening of the goal system reflects also the improved data situation. The use of computers in economics and statistics has allowed the construction of large microdata bases. Even if the situation may be regarded as unsatisfactory with respect to some questions, the statistical situation has improved considerably. The minimum requirement would be that the theory of income distribution uses the available information.

5. The income distribution theory should be flexible enough to answer changing questions. The process of social change leads to changing questions. It is not advisable to develop in each case single purpose theories.

A very simple formal framework may serve the definition of the minimum requirements of a theory of income distribution[5].

Generally, distributions can be described by distribution vectors where the elements represent the share that a unit or a group gets of the income. The sum of all elements of these vectors is 1. By using this concept it is possible to define the distribution of income over persons by the vector vy where the elements show the share which the different persons have in the overall income. Principally, the same approach can be used for groups. In this case an element of the vector represents the share of the group.

Distribution vectors of this type can also be defined for the different types of income. The vector v_f describes the distribution of the fth type of income or the income derived from the fth sector. The factor distribution vectors v_f can be regarded as columns of a distribution matrix VYF which shows how the different types of income are distributed over the persons. The functional distribution may be described by a distribution vector vY where the elements constitute the share of the different factors or types of incomes in the overall income.

Then it is valid by definition

$$vy = VYF \cdot vY.$$

The relation between functional and size distribution of income depends on the matrix VYF. It is an empirical question whether the vector vY can be used as a proxy for vy. This is merely then possible if the non-diagonal elements of VYF are equal to zero. This, however, is not the case as regards most industrialized countries.

If the income of households has to be considered too, it is necessary to find an algorithm A which generates the household distribution vector hy. This algorithm has to add up the shares of persons who belong to the same household and it has to rearrange the household vector.

162

In many cases the distribution per head has to be taken into account too. It can be derived in dividing the household distribution vector hy by the household size matrix QN which solely has diagonal elements that represent the number of persons in a household. The result is the household income per head

$$ky = (QN)^{-1}. hy.$$

It can be empirically shown that the distributions represented by vy, vY, hy and ky differ considerably. An income distribution theory related to the different distributional goals has to include all these vectors into the consideration.

3. Shortcomings of the Theory of Income Distribution

By using the requirements as developed above, the state of the art in the field of income distribution theory is not very satisfactory. It has been indicated that the requirements have increased considerably due to the goal discussion and the improved scientific and statistical possibilities. Therefore it may be unfair to judge the traditional theories of income distribution by these increased requirements. It must be stated, however, that the traditional theories of income distribution do not meet these requirements. The development of new approaches or new paradigms therefore is necessary.

The so-called functional distribution theory is still related to heterogenous groups and neglects the fact that incomes of the same people may originate from different sources. A differentiation of the personal base is not possible, i.e. individual and household income can not be distinguished. In the formal framework of the last section only the functional distribution vector vY can be explained. Trivial conclusions to the other distribution vectors are impossible. It may be asked whether this type of theory has social relevance at all.

Contrary to the above, theories of size distribution of income are usually related to a small number of socio-economic characteristics. A relation to macroeconomic processes usually is not possible. Most of these theories have a strong inclination toward a mono-causal argument. In some approaches, in the final analysis one single factor is used for the explanation of the variance of income.

In the formal framework of the last section, in most cases the distribution vector for one kind of income is analysed. This means that only one row of the distribution matrix VYF is explained. Neither the distribution of the sum of all incomes of an individual nor that of households can be clarified in this manner.

An explanation of the functional distribution vector vY is as necessary as that of the size distribution vectors for the different types of income. In this respect the approaches mentioned above contribute to a theory of the income distribution. Each constitutes a necessary, but not sufficient part of a theory of income distribution.

It is necessary to combine these different approaches. Especially useful are attempts to relate the size distribution of income to macroeconomic variables by combining personal and functional elements. These attempts still pose many problems, especially because of the difficulties of handling large theoretical systems. Therefore many of the factors which have been shown to be important in partial analyses are still neglected in these approaches.

In this situation it may be asked to what extent a micro-analytic simulation approach may be helpful for the development of a theory of income distribution.

It is not feasible to give a detailed description of a large socioeconomic system on a few pages. This is especially true if the reader has a different degree of experience with simulation methods, particularly with the microanalytic approach. The presentation of the system shall therefore be restricted to a systematic sketch of the whole system and to a flow-chart that shows the microanalytic part.

Figure 1 (see page 165) gives a systematic view on the whole system. It demonstrates how social welfare, operationalized in social indicators, is determined by non-controllable factors and policy instruments. The simulation system consists of two subsystems which are linked together. On the one hand macroeconomic models constitute the macroeconomic framework which secures the circular flow conditions. For most purposes the Bonn Model V (Krelle) is used[6].

The central part of the system is the microeconomic model which uses microanalytic simulations methods for individuals and households. It is built up in a modular way; the single modules can be seen in Figure 1. The block »Supply of Income and Demand of Private and Public Goods« is most important in the context of income distribution. This block contains three modules:

> Income Generation and Distribution
> Income Maintenance and Transfers
> The Uses of Income.

Figure 2 (see page 166) shows the technical structure of this system with an emphasis on the microeconomic model. The simulation is controlled on three main levels: The period loop allows the application of the system in different periods.

The interdependence loop permits feed-backs between the macroeconomic and the microeconomic system. It may be necessary to have an iteration run of the microeconomic model depending on the results of the macroeconomic model.

The household loop controls the different operations for the single household. The necessary information for these households is available on a start-file which is fed into the computer, household by household[7]. This information is then changed by the operators included in the modules of the transformation and interdependence circuit (left circuit in Figure 2). Some operators involve more than one household. Marriage, for example, brings together two persons who normally come from different households. In this case the necessary information is stored on a cross-reference-file. If the transformation and interdependence circuit is at least run through for all households, it is possible to applicate the necessary combinatory algorithm. For new households and for households which have been changed by this procedure the transformation circuit after combination has to be applied.

During the operations on the household level all information that is necessary to calculate the input variables for the macro-system and the social indicators is stored. After one period a result-file is available and may serve as a start-file for the next period, and for values of the relevant macro-variables and social indicators.

Figure 1 Sociopolitical Decision and Indicator System for the Federal Republic of Germany

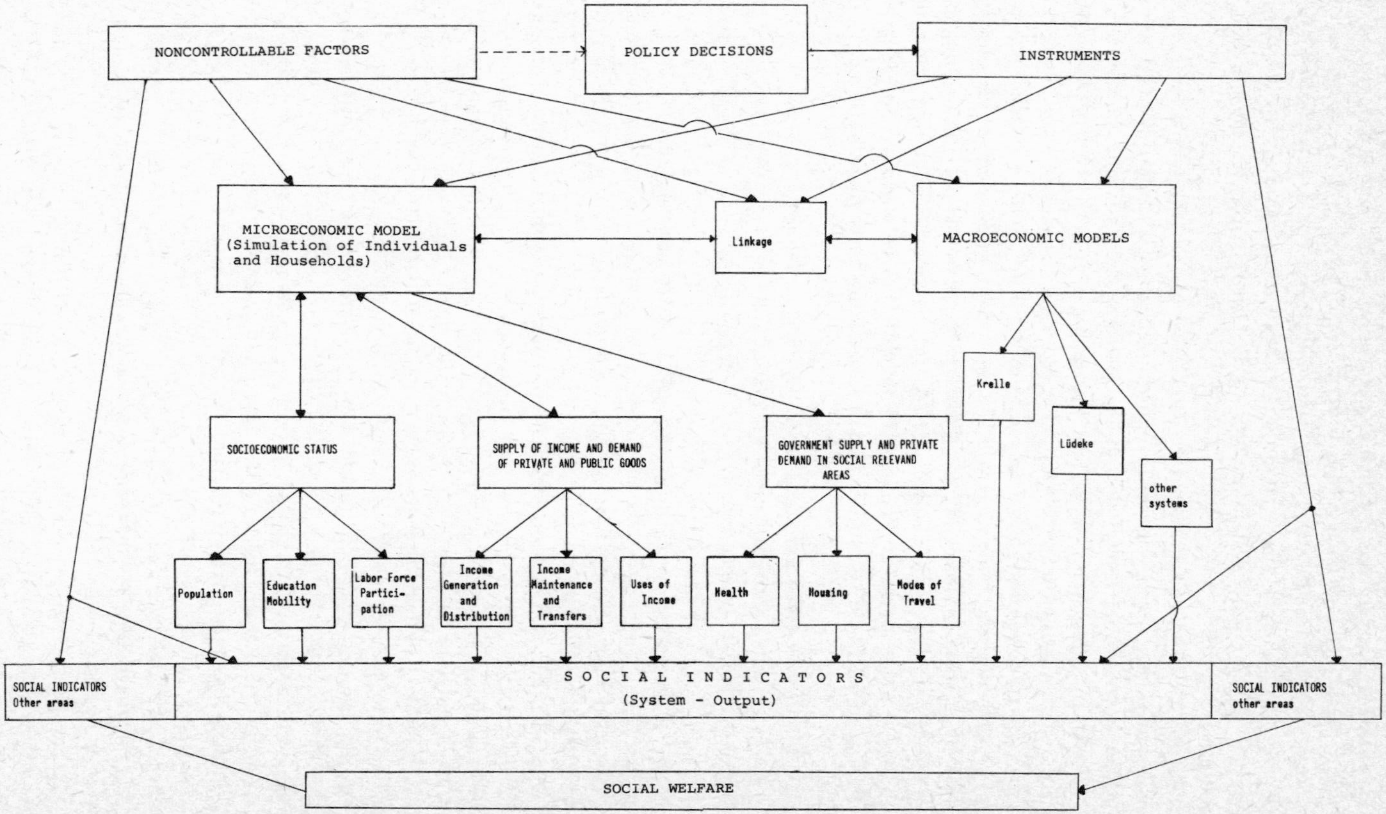

165

166

Figure 2 Structure of the Decision and Indicator-System

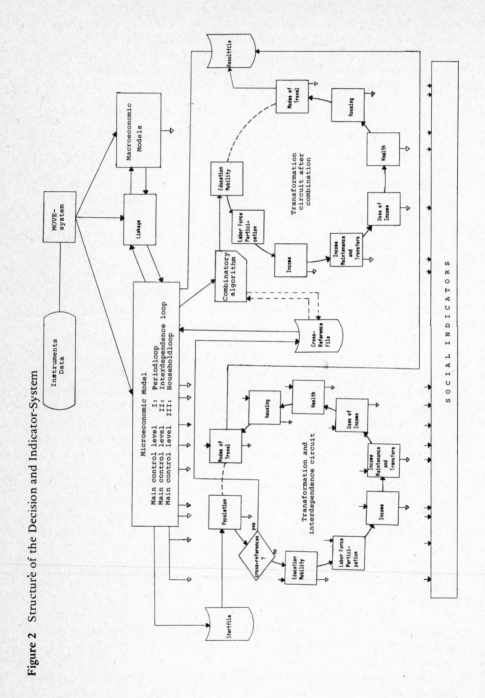

These few remarks may at least give an impression of the volume and the operating of the system. Most parts of the simulation system as described above are programmed and working. There still are technical restrictions in the linkage of the whole system. Therefore, up to now, partial analyses are prevailing.

Many of the hypotheses used are, however, very crude or on a weak empirical base. Therefore it may be useful to ask for the experience that has accumulated up to this point as regards this type of microanalytic simulation system. For this representation the discussion will be restricted to hypotheses that concern the distribution of income, e.g. to the income- and transfer modules.

5. Types of Hypotheses used for the Microanalytic Simulation of the Income Distribution

The most important hypotheses used in microanalytic simulation processes[8] that are related to the problems of income distribution can be grouped as follows:

1. The macro-hypothesis
2. The transition hypothesis
3. The correlation hypothesis
4. The causal hypothesis
5. The institutional hypothesis

The macro-hypothesis uses macro-information for the generation of a micro event. It is found very often, especially in the field of income distribution, as it allows the reliance on available macro-information to generate non-available micro-information. A very simple example is the use of different growth rates for different types of income. In the national accounts the growth rates of the macro-aggregates are given. It is possible to determine the size of the individual income by applying these different growth rates to the different components of the household income. If, as an example, the wage income increases at a lower rate as income from profit, the effect of this development on the size distribution of income may be shown. This example requires the hypothesis that the size distribution matrix VYF is constant, at least for a short period, and that changes in the size distribution of income are only due to changes in the functional distribution vector vY. It is not very likely that this hypothesis holds generally. If the household income is also taken into account, a further hypothesis on the constancy of working force participation of the different members of the household is necessary. Again this may be valid solely for the short-run. So it is very likely that this simple type of macro-hypothesis which relies mainly on the functional distribution is solely of limited importance.

The macro-hypothesis may also be used in more sophisticated manners. For wage income it is possible to distinguish between fixed and proportional increases. This would change the columns of the distribution matrix VYF related to the wage income. This may be especially useful if the result of collective bargaining agreements includes wage increases by a fixed amount as well as proportional increases.

A further improvement may be reached if different average wage increases for different social- or occupational groups are known. Thus, in many cases the different results of collective bargaining agreements for different groups are known. In using hypotheses on the wage drift, it might be possible to include this information as macro-hypothesis, too.

The set of hypotheses necessary to use the macro-hypothesis seems to be very restrictive. Nevertheless, the macro-hypothesis in many cases generates very useful results which are at least more reliable than the ones based on other approaches. The distributional impact of economic policy and of collective bargaining can be derived in this way in a more or less sufficient manner, at least for the short-run. Therefore the macro-hypothesis will remain a very powerful instrument of micro-analysis, at least within the years to come.

The transition hypothesis relates to a transition matrix approach. It is useful in the context of a cell concept where the cells are determined by a set of socio-economic characteristics. In this context it is necessary to explain, respectively to forecast, the transitions of individuals from one cell to another. The theoretical background may be a stochastic process that generates the transition.

A simple example can be taken from the field of education. The participation of an individual in the different stages of the educational system may be simulated by transition quotas which are governed by a stochastic process. A similar approach could be used to explain social mobility.

In this context Markoff-processes have been used very often. This leads, however, in many cases to considerable difficulties since the hypothesis that an event is independent of an individual's history, longer than one period, may be a wrong specification. This is, however, not a principle obstacle as it is possible to develop transition hypotheses which include the history of individuals too.

The transition hypothesis is typical of a cell concept. Even if one does not use a pure cell concept, it is possible to use this approach to alter different charac-teristics of the individual. The question changes slightly. One does not ask whether this individual will move into a different cell, but, on the contrary, one asks whether this individual will change a certain socio-economic characteristic.

If one leaves the pure stochastic interpretation of the transition hypothesis, one comes close to correlation hypotheses. This hypothesis uses information on the correlation between the generated variable and explanatory variables. This information usually is taken from cross-section surveys. Mostly the multiple linear regression approach is used for the estimation of coefficients. Variables which are measured on ordinal or nominal scales are usually introduced by defining a set of dummy variables. Beside multiple regression methods other multi-varied methods are applicable too.

Examples for this approach can be easily given. It is possible to use correlations among income, the different types of income, age, education, region, mobility, experience, race, sex, experience in the participation in the labour force, religion, and others for the determination of income or its components. If the income of the last period is known, it may be easier to restrict the analysis to the forecast of the change in the income.

One considerable advantage in using this type of hypothesis is the possible differentiation for purposes of microanalytic simulations. If the simulation is done on an individual level, i.e. the operations are performed for each unit, it is possible to determine the coefficients on a level of disaggregation which can be obtained for each function. If, for example, the wage income is to be de-termined, it is possible to form subgroups suitable for this purpose. The coefficients are then determined for these subgroups. If on the other hand the spending behaviour is to be generated, it is possible to choose a completely different grouping for this purpose. Generally, it is not surprising that this approach is widely used in microanalytic simulation systems.

The correlation hypothesis usually is related to one point in time or to one time-period. It therefore does not include causal information. It does not say anything about the relation between a cause and an effect.

The causal hypothesis relates causes and effects. It is that type of hypothesis which we usually call explanatory hypothesis. An event is explained by its causes. The wage income of an individual, for instance, could be explained by the individual or the collective bargaining process, the influence of supply and demand on the labour market, and similar causes.

There is no doubt that the use of causal hypotheses is most satisfactory on theoretical grounds. On the other hand, the difficulties related to the use of this type of hypothesis are considerable. A sequence of cross-sections which include the same population would be the necessary data base. This type of data is available in a few rare cases only. Usually it is solely related to the household sector. An information about both sides of the labour market, for example, in the necessary degree of disaggregation usually is not available. Therefore this type of hypothesis is very rarely used in microanalytic simulation approaches.

The last type of hypothesis is the institutional hypothesis. It uses institutional regulations like tax laws or social security laws for the generation of income or transfers. Examples may be given especially in the field of positive or negative transfers.

One of the most powerful properties of the microanalytic approach is the possibility to use institutional hypotheses. On the micro-level institutional regulations may be used in a very precise way. Whereas it is nearly impossible to use institutional regulations to establish a macro-relation, it is very easy to reproduce the single steps of institutional regulations on the micro-level.

The micro-data bases used mostly contain all the information necessary for this purpose. The results are very exact. If they are summed up, they come very close to the macro-aggregates.

These different types of hypotheses are used to a very large extent in microanalytic simulation approaches. Principally, all of them could be used, in practice, however, operational microanalytic simulation systems only use them partly.

Macro-hypotheses of the different types still are very widely used. The micro-data base necessary for microanalytic simulation usually stems from one or more cross-sectional samples. The number of available samples is restricted whereas on the other side macro-aggregates and marge-distributions are available to a larger extent. The macro-hypothesis allows to combine the structural information available in the cross-sections with the more actual information on the development that is included in macro-aggregates and marge-distributions. The use of macro-hypotheses may be regarded as a very simple technique. It still is a very powerful instrument.

If structural considerations will be included in the theory of income distribution, the use of correlation hypotheses is necessary and possible. Thus, microanalytic simulation systems related to problems of income generation include this type of hypothesis too. Usually the income of the last period is also introduced since the attempt to explain the income of an individual or household solely by its socio-economic characteristics has proved to be less successful. This is partly due to the fact that the part of the variance which is not »explained« by the independent variables remains very large.

The application of institutional hypotheses so far has been particularly successful. Especially the determination of positive and negative transfers has been solved by this type of hypothesis.

The transition hypothesis is not used very often, except in systems which are constructed by transition matrices that relate sets of cells. This approach, however, is restricted to special problems. The introduction of this concept into the normal microanalytic concept is still the exception.

The use of causal hypotheses is very rare as data problems can not easily be solved and since our knowledge as regards this type of hypothesis still is weak.

The use of microanalytic simulation methods in the theory of income distribution therefore is ambivalent. On the one hand, it is possible to generate income distributions and show in this way determinants of the distribution, on the other hand causal hypotheses in a very narrow sense are not available and thus are not used.

The explanatory and theoretical power of these different types of hypotheses varies greatly. A very narrow interpretation of theory would restrict ourselves to merely causel hypotheses. This would imply that the microanalytic approach could be built upon a few theoretical elements only.

This restriction, however, would be damaging to the development of theory to an unnecessary extent. The requirements for a complete theory of income distribution developed in section 2, are not met by any theoretical approach. The microanalytic simulation approach may not be a sufficient substitute. However, it can be an operational and pragmatic step to the further development of a theory of income distribution. At least right now there is no alternative as powerful as the one described visible.

Notes

[1] For a short review of the system see: Krupp (1973). A longer description is given in: Brennecke/Krupp (1976).

[2] The system of social indicators used in the SPES-Project is presented in Zapf (1977).

[3] Information on the decision system may be found in: Brennecke/Krupp (1976), Brennecke (1975), Brennecke (1976/2), Brennecke (1976/3), Galler (1976).

[4] Compare: Glatzer/Krupp (1975) and Chapter 2 of Krupp (1975) and the contribution of Glatzer in: Zapf (1977).

[5] The formal framework used here is developed generally in: Krupp (1968).

[6] A description of the latest version may be found in Krelle (1974). The first version of the model of Lüdeke may be found in: Lüdeke (1969).

[7] The SPES-Project uses for this purpose the integrated micro-data-file IMDAF 1969. The properties of this file are described in: Kortman/Krupp/Schmaus (1976).

[8] Overviews over microanalytic simulations systems and the methodological problems encountered in microanalytical model building are given by Orcutt (1976) and by Orcutt, Caldwell and Wertheimer II. References to prior work are listed therein. For further comments on the design of microanalytic simulation models, see also the discussion in the paper by Budd and Whiteman in this book.

References

(1) Brennecke, R.: *Die Konstruktion von sozioökonomischen Großsystemen — Verknüpfung von Modellen zur Analyse wirtschaftspolitischer Prozesse.* Campus Verlag, Frankfurt/ New York, 1975

(2) Brennecke, R.: *Anforderungen an die Datenverarbeitung bei der Entwicklung und Simulation mikroökonomischer Modelle.* In: S. Dickhoven (Hrsg.), Modellierungs-Software, Proceedings der GMD-Tagung: Status und Anforderungen auf dem Gebiet der Modell-Software; Gesellschaft für Mathematik und Datenverarbeitung mbH, Bonn, IPES-Bericht 76.102, Selbstverlag GMD, Oktober 1976, p. 179—202

(3) Brennecke, R.: *Implikationen der Modellverknüpfung für die Entwicklung eines Modellbanksystems.* In: S. Dickhoven (Hrsg.), Modellierungs-Software, Proceedings der GMD-Tagung: Status und Anforderungen auf dem Gebiet der Modell-Software; Gesellschaft für Methematik und Datenverarbeitung mbH, Bonn, IPES-Bericht 76.102, Selbstverlag GMD, Oktober 1976, p. 453—469

(4) Brennecke, R., and Krupp, H.-J.: Das Sozialpolitische Entscheidungs- und Indikatorensystem für die Bundesrepublik Deutschland — Genesis, Ziele, Struktur und Stand des Forschungsprojektes. In: H.-J. Hoffmann-Nowotny (Hrsg.), *Soziale Indikatoren — Internationale Beiträge zu einer neuen praxisorientierten Forschungsrichtung;* Verlag Huber, Frauenfeld und Stuttgart, 1976, p. 139—163

(5) Galler, H.-P.: Das MOVE-System: Der Stand der Entwicklung, Erfahrungen und Weiterentwicklungen. In: S. Dickhoven (Hrsg.), *Modellierungssoftware . . .,* op. cit., p. 343—366

(6) Glatzer, W., and Krupp, H.-J.: Soziale Indikatoren des Einkommens und seiner Verteilung für die Bundesrepublik Deutschland, in: Zapf, W. (Hrsg.), *Soziale Indikatoren — Konzepte und Forschungsansätze III,* Campus Verlag, Frankfurt 1975, p. 193—238

(7) Kortmann, K., Krupp, H.-J., and Schmaus, G.: Strukturen der Einkommensverteilung 1969. Erste Ergebnisse und Erfahrungen mit einem integrierten Mikrodatenfile für die Bundesrepublik Deutschland 1969. In: *WSI-Mitteilungen,* Heft 10, 1975, p. 539'— 552.

Kortmann, K., Krupp, H.-J., and Schmaus, G.: Integrierte Verteilungsrechnungen bedürfen der wissenschaftlichen Diskussion — Zum Vergleich der Verteilungsrechnungen des DIW und des SPES-Projekts (IMDAF 1969). In: *WSI-Mitteilungen,* Heft 8, 1976, p. 475—489.

(8) (Krupp, H.-J.: *Theorie der personellen Einkommensverteilung,* Duncker & Humblot, Berlin 1968

(9) Krupp, H.-J.: Sozialpolitisches Entscheidungs- und Indikatorensystem für die Bundesrepublik Deutschland (SPES) in: *Allgemeines Statistisches Archiv,* 57. Band, Heft 3/4, 1973, p. 380—387

(10) Krupp, H.-J.: *Möglichkeiten der Verbesserung der Einkommens- und Vermögensstatistik, Schriften der Kommission für wirtschaftlichen und sozialen Wandel,* Band 50, Verlag Otto Schwartz & Co., Göttingen 1975

(11) Krelle, W.: *Erfahrungen mit einem ökonometrischen Prognosemodell für die Bundesrepublik Deutschland. Mathematical Systems in Economics.* Band 12, Verlag Anton Hain, Meisenheim am Glan 1974

(12) Lüdeke, D.: *Ein ökonometrisches Vierteljahresmodell für die Bundesrepublik Deutschland,* J.C.B. Mohr (Paul Siebeck), Tübingen 1969.

(13) Orcutt, Guy H.: Methodological Problems in the Design of Large-Scale Socioeconomic Simulation Systems, in: *Anwendung von Simulationsverfahren in den Sozial- und Wirtschaftswissenschaften,* 3. Internationale Arbeitstagung Bad Homburg 1976, p. 219—247

(14) Orcutt, Guy H., Caldwell, S. and Wertheimer II, R.: *Policy Exploration through Micro-analytic Simulation*, The Urban Institute, Washingston. D.C., 1976

(15) Zapf, W. (Hrsg.), *Lebensbedingungen in der Bundesrepublik — Sozialer Wandel und Wohlfahrtsbedingungen 1950 — 1975*, Campus Verlag, Frankfurt 1977

C. Accounting for Inequality of Earnings:
The Human Capital Approach

George J. Borjas and Jacob Mincer*

The distribution of earnings profiles in longitudial data

I. Introduction

The availability of longitudinal microdata on earnings and on other aspects of personal histories provides a new range of opportunities to improve our understanding of the interpersonal structure of earnings.

Recent research on the determinants of earnings, especially the human capital approach, stresses the whole life-cycle earnings stream as the basic unit of analysis rather than a single period observation. Indeed, by emphasizing individual accumulation of earning power, the analysis directly focuses on the longitudinal dimension, albeit one that is rather abstract, since all economy-wide trends and fluctuations in prices and productivities must be removed from it.

In the cross-section studies of Census and other data, earnings of different individuals are analyzed as if they were pieced together around a single synthetic earnings profile, typical for all groups or distinguishable for groups classified by school education. The profiles so obtained slope upward through most of the working age, decelerating after some initial interval, and levelling off at a later stage[1].

In the human capital interpretation of the earnings profile, its level is proportional to (since it is a rental payment on) the accumulated stock of market skills, its rate of growth is a positive function of current investment in such skills or earning powers, and the deceleration reflects the declining rate of investment over the life cycle. It is understood that the term »investment« covers a broad range of activities such as schooling, occupational choice, job training and learning, job and geographic mobility, job search and acquisition of information, work effort, and so forth.

This interpretation is summarized in the following model[2] :

$$\ln Y_t = \ln E_o + r_s \sum_{i=0}^{s-1} k_i + r_p \sum_{j=0}^{t-1} k_j + \ln (1-k_t)$$

*This resrach was supported through the National Bureau of Economic Resrach by a grant from the National Science Foundation (Grant No. SOC71—03783 AO3). The opinions expressed herein are those of the authors and do not necessarily reflect the views of the National Science Foundation.

This report has not undergone the review accorded official NBER publications; in particular, it has not been submitted to the Board of Directors for approval. This paper reports on a part of ongoing research on the Determinants of Earnings, conducted at the National Bureau of Economic Research jointly with Ann Bartel.

where

y_t = earnings at working age t

E_0 = »original« earning capacity, or »endowment«

r_s = average rate of return to schooling

r_p = average rate of return to postschool investments

$k_t = \dfrac{C_t}{E_t}$, where C_t is the dollar investment expenditure and E_t is the earning capacity at working age t.

With simplifying assumptions $k_i = 1$ and $k_t = k_0 - \beta t$, we have:

$$\ln Y_t = \ln E_o + r_s s + r_p k_o t - \frac{r_p \beta}{2} t^2 + \ln (1-k_t)$$

and an approximate estimating equation is:

$$\ln Y_t = b_o + b_1 s + b_2 t + b_3 t^2 + u$$

where[3] :

$$b_o = \ln E_o - k_o$$

$$b_1 = r_s$$

$$b_2 = r_p k_o + \beta$$

$$b_3 = - \frac{r_p \beta}{2}$$

Note that β may also be expressed as $\dfrac{k_0}{T}$, where T is the investment period.

When applied to a cross-section, equation (3) may be augmented by information on personal, background, or regional characteristics of the individuals. We shall have a look at these personal characteristics later on, but will direct our attention first to the application of equation (3) both in time series and in the cross-section.

In this equation there are only two schematic variables, years of schooling and years of work experience. Perhaps surprisingly, these two crude but readily available variables contain relatively sizable explanatory power. This has been shown in Census and other cross-section microdata which cover complete ranges of schooling and of working ages[4] .

The coefficients of the variables in (3) represent rates of return and investment ratios, and the intercept $\ln E_0$ reflects endowment. These parameters obviously vary among individuals, but aside from schooling and working age no such variation is observable. Distributional analyses, therefore, miss a potentially important source of interpersonal variation in earnings.

We take advantage of our longitudinal data to explore individual variation in the parameters of individual earnings functions. (1) For this purpose we fit an earnings function to each of the individual histories in the sample. (2) We then try to ascertain the extent to which the estimated variation in individual parameters helps in explaining the cross-sectional variation in earnings. (3) We further inquire into the relation between the individual parameters and a vector of personal characteristics, as well as (4) into indirect (via variables and parameters) and direct effects of these characteristics on earnings.

of personal characteristics, as well as (4) into indirect (via variables and parameters) and direct effects of these characteristics on earnings.

The analysis was carried out on the Coleman-Rossi Life History data, a sample of males aged 30–39 in 1968 who were residing in households in the U.S. The data contains information on the starting and ending dates (month and calendar year), earnings and hours worked for every job the individual held from the time he first entered the labor force until the date of interview in January 1969. Thus we have a job history for the individual, and for every job we have at least two earnings points: initial and ending wages or salaries. Respondents also provided a lifetime family and educational history, as well as all the characteristics listed in our notes to Table 5 below.

The sample contains 1,589 men of whom 739 are black. Data requirements and omissions reduced our sample almost in half[5]. As the information was collected retrospectively, we caution ourselves and the readers that large memory errors may exist in such data[6].

II. Longitudinal Earnings Profiles

We estimated individual earnings functions [using equation (3)] for each of the 884 men in the usable sample. The data for the dependent variable are logarithms of price-deflated monthly earnings. Table 1 presents the average intercepts and coefficients of equation (3) together with their standard errors for all men, each of the two race groups, and four education groups. In the individual regressions schooling is a constant, so the intercept is $(b_0 + b_1 s)$ of eq. (3). The coefficient of t (working age, or experience) which is b_2 in eq. (3), we call β_1 and it equals $(r_p k_0 + \beta + g)$, where g is the economy-wide rate of growth of productivity per worker, assumed fixed over the period and net of the contribution of human capital. The coefficient of t^2 is b_3 of eq. (3), which we call β_2.

A similar set of regressions was performed using hourly wage rates rather than monthly earnings. The results were quite similar. We decided to continue our analysis with monthly earnings only, especially since we believe these to be more reliable than retrospective data on hours of work[7].

The standard errors in Table 1 are actually upper limits since each individual regression utilized more than one degree of freedom[8]. At any rate this statistic indicates that, on average, the longitudinal earnings profiles has an upward slope. This is true also when the economy-wide rate of growth g is subtracted from the coefficient at t. The annual rate of productivity growth was estimated to be 2.5 percent. It was found as the average rate of growth of wages of men age 25–35 at fixed levels of education for the period 1956–66[9]. Thus, in Table 1 the coefficient of t which includes g, for all men, is .077; excluding g it is .052. The coefficient of t^2 is −.0014 and the small standard error indicates a significant deceleration of earnings over the observed working life.

Given these coefficients it is possible to analyze the rate of growth of earnings at any working age by including and excluding g. Since $\frac{d \ln y_t}{dt} = \beta_1 - 2 \beta_2 t$, we find that two-thirds of the growth of earnings with working age is accounted for by individual progress and one-third by economy-wide progress at the start

177

of working life (when t = 1). The contribution to growth are reversed one and a half decades later (at t = 15) and they are about equal after a decade of work experience (at t = 10).

The important conclusion to be drawn from Table 1 is the concavity of the typical earnings profile revealed in these longitudinal data. This shape, heretofore observed only in cross-sections cannot, therefore, be viewed as an artifact of the cross-section. It characterizes both races in the sample and all education groups, with an apparent exception of the highest education group. However, a significant degree of concavity is evidently not apparent until after a decade of work experience, and the most educated group in this sample does not have more than a decade of work experience. Given the relatively narrow age range in the sample,

Table 1 Longitudinal Earnings Functions — Summary Statistics[a]

Variable	All Men	s < 12	s = 12	13 ≤ s ≤ 15	s ≥ 16
			A. Pooled Sample		
Constant	5.442	5.206	5.540	5.594	5.833
	(.597)	(.688)	(.448)	(.455)	(.358)
	[.020]	[.036]	[.030]	[.032]	[.037]
t	.077	.083	.068	.076	.075
	(.137)	(.142)	(.143)	(.130)	(.112)
	[.005]	[.007]	[.010]	[.009]	[.012]
t^2	-.0014	-.0021	-.0015	-.0013	.0013
	(.010)	(.008)	(.011)	(.010)	(.013)
	[.0003]	[.0004]	[.0007]	[.0007]	[.0013]
Number of Observations	884	373	220	198	93
			B. White Men		
Constant	5.518	5.260	5.565	5.577	5.836
	(.574)	(.714)	(.466)	(.471)	(.353)
	[.027]	[.061]	[.043]	[.042]	[.042]
t	.079	.079	.062	.091	.088
	(.135)	(.124)	(.158)	(.134)	(.114)
	[.006]	[.011]	[.015]	[.012	[.014]
t^2	-.0009	-.0015	-.0004	-.0018	.0010
	(.011)	(.007)	(.013)	(.011)	(.014)
	[.0005]	[.0006]	[.0012]	[.0010]	[.0017]
Number of Observations	446	136	116	124	70

(continued on next page)

Table 1 (concluded)

Variable	All Men	s < 12	s = 12	13 $\leq$ s $\leq$ 15	s $\geq$ 16
			C. **Black Men**		
Constant	5.365	5.174	5.512	5.623	5.825
	(.611)	(.672)	(.430)	(.431)	(.378)
	[.029]	[.044]	[.042]	[.050]	[.079]
t	.074	.084	.076	.050	.036
	(.139)	(.152)	(.124)	(.120)	(.098)
	[.007]	[.010]	[.012]	[.014]	[.020]
t^2	-.0019	-.0024	-.0028	-.0003	.0023
	(.009)	(.009)	(.008)	(.010)	(.012)
	[.0004]	[.0006]	[.0008]	[.0012]	[.0025]
Number of Observations	438	237	104	74	23

[a]The statistics are: Mean (Standard Deviation), [Standard Error].

work experience is inversely related to years of schooling. Therefore, the less schooled the group the more clearly discernible is the shape of its earnings profile[10].

There is, of course, a great deal of individual variation in the slopes and curvatures of this early segment (an average of 16 years) of the earnings profile. While the standard errors in Table 1 are small enough to lend significance to mean values, the standard deviations in the sample are larger than the means. This is perhaps not surprising since the individual profiles are fit to a few observed points only, so a great deal of instability can be expected. In addition, lack of reliability of the individual regression is attributable to a certain degree of arbitrariness in the timing of initial earnings: We defined initial as the first full time job after completion of schooling, but many persons worked before on a part- or full-time basis.

While Table 1 depicts the typical longitudinal earnings profile, Table 2 takes account of the individual variation around the average profile. It measures the importance of that variation in inducing a corresponding variation in earnings of individuals in the cross section.

Specifically, we observe the effect on R^2 of introducing the individual longitudinal parameters β_{1i} and β_{2i} into the earnings function (3) applied to the cross-section. In column (1) of each panel we show the usual cross-section regression for the 1968 survey data. It includes the variables schooling (s) and years of work experience (t and t^2). The parameters are some sort of average of individual parameters. In this sample these are rather unstable and the signs appear perverse, compared to previous studies based on much larger samples[11]. At any rate the

179

Table 2 Current Earnings Functions[a]

Variable	Coeff. (1)	t	Coeff. (2)	t	Coeff. (3)	t	Coeff. (4)	t
			A. Pooled Sample					
Constant	5.8378		5.4784		5.8635		5.4967	
s	.0504	(10.02)	.0524	(13.78)	.0502	(11.83)	.0526	(17.47)
t	-.0141	(-.82)			-.0153	(-1.04)		
t^2	.0006	(1.11)			.0005	(1.15)		
$\beta_1 \cdot t$			.3516	(17.27)			.3201	(19.79)
$\beta_2 \cdot t^2$			.4067	(17.40)			.3954	(21.35)
v					.4333	(18.84)	.4361	(22.88)
RACE	-.2181	(-8.10)	-.1487	(-6.32)	-.2014	(-8.86)	-.1363	(-7.31)
R^2	.220		.419		.445		.636	
			B. White Men					
Constant	5.6491		5.3931		5.6051		5.4347	
s	.0660	(7.93)	.0557	(9.44)	.0664	(9.43)	.0540	(11.72)
t	-.0219	(-.83)			-.0200	(-.89)		
t^2	.0011	(1.27)			.0010	(1.46)		
$\beta_1 \cdot t$			.4149	(13.79)			.3837	(16.30)
$\beta_2 \cdot t^2$			.4890	(14.02)			.4815	(17.70)
v					.4790	(13.23)	.4817	(16.89)
R^2	.141		.400		.385		.635	
	(1)		(2)		(3)		(4)	
			C. Black Men					
Constant	5.6995		5.4394		5.8419		5.4522	
s	.0368	(6.31)	.0464	(9.69)	.0364	(7.59)	.0480	(12.66)
t	.0009	(.04)			-.0089	(-.48)		
t^2	-.00003	(-.04)			.00004	(.07)		
$\beta_1 \cdot t$			.2707	(10.04)			.2410	(11.25)
$\beta_2 \cdot t^2$			.3804	(10.06)			.2959	(12.18)
v					.3944	(14.31)	.3894	(16.10)
R^2	.105		.276		.393		.547	

[a]Notation used: β_1 = Linear coefficient from longitudinal function
β_2 = Quadratic coefficient from longitudinal function
v = Earnings capacity measure

replacement of variables t_i and t_i^2 by estimated $(\beta_1 t)_i$ and $(\beta_2 t^2)_i$ in column 2, more than doubles the explanatory power of the cross-section regression[12].

This is not to say that we have managed to explain more, but simply that if the information underlying the slope and curvature parameters of individual earnings functions were available to analysts, an additional 20—25 percent of the relative variance of (monthly or weekly) earnings could be explained. The information in these parameters pertains to the unobserved individual variation in volumes of postschool investments and in their efficiencies.

III. Estimating Individual Investment Parameters

With very few degrees of freedom and less than a complete life-cycle available, the individual longitudinal earnings regressions are far from being reliable. But even if they were reliable, it is not, in general, possible to solve the estimated coefficients for the component investment parameters which are of interest: These are: the vectors of postschool investments indexed by k_{oi} (the initial investment ratio), the (average) rates of return to postschool investment (r_i), and individual »endowments« or »initial earning capacities«, $\ln E_{oi}$.

It is tempting, nevertheless, to use the concept of an »overtaking stage« in the life-cycle of postschool investment for a procedure which is somewhat better than guesswork.

The »overtaking stage« is the working age $\hat{t}$ at which observed earnings $y_{\hat{t}}$ reach equality with initial postschool capacity earnings E_s. Note that initial earnings $y_0 = E_s - C_0$, or $\ln y_0 = \ln E_s + \ln (1-k_0)$, so that $\ln y_0 < \ln E_s$. Later on $\ln y_t = \ln E_s + r \sum_{j=0}^{t-1} k_j + \ln (1-k_t)$. At some stage the growing positive second term on the right begins to outweigh the declining (in absolute value) negative third term. This happens at about $\frac{1}{r}$ years of experience[13]. The ratio of $y_{\hat{t}}$ to y_0 does, therefore, provide estimates of k_0. The overtaking stage differs among persons as does r_i, but we do not know the latter either. A guess about the average r_i, which judging from past studies, is probably not too far away from 10 percent, may serve the purpose.

Alternatively, we may locate an average overtaking period $\hat{t}$ by studying the correlation between schooling and earnings across all persons in the sample for sequential years of experience. Presumably the highest simple correlation is between schooling and earning capacity E_s, that is earnings unaffected by subsequent investments. A common overtaking stage would produce, therefore, a clear maximum correlation at $\hat{t}$. This need not happen in practice, if the central tendencies in r_i or in the rate of decline of investments (β_i) are not well defined. In that case, the »overtaking stage« may be quite diffuse. When »random shocks« and data errors are superimposed on such data, a monotonically declining pattern of correlations may be observed in them.

In cross-section Census data the correlation has been found to decline clearly and strongly only after a decade of experience.

In our sample the correlation does, indeed, increase from an initial .40 to .47 at 10—13 years of experience, and declines continuously thereafter. This pattern is due mainly to the correlations in the sample of white men which rise from .39 to .50, while a very weak but persistent decline is observed in the sample of black men. We use the tenth year of experience as the common »overtaking« period. We then estimate k_{oi} as the percent differential between initial earnings (y_0) and earnings one decade later ($y_{10} \cong E_s$), after deflation for the 2.5 percent annual rate of the productivity trend. The means and standard errors of k_0 by race and schooling group are shown in Table 3.

According to Table 3 the average »initial investment ratios« are about one-third of the initial earning capacity and they increase with schooling starting with

Table 3 Summary Statistics of k_0 and r^*

Variable	All Men	s < 12	s = 12	13 ≤ s ≤ 15	s ≥ 16
			A. Pooled Sample		
k_{oi}	.294	.312	.240	.286	.370
	(.553)	(.661)	(.454)	(.484)	(.398)
	[.019]	[.034]	[.031]	[.034]	[.041]
r_i	.070	.055	.073	.077	.105
	(.080)	(.083)	(.068)	(.078)	(.080)
	[.003]	[.004]	[.005]	[.006]	[.008]
			B. White Men		
k_{oi}	.350	.350	.290	.340	.444
	(.528)	(.640)	(.443)	(.524)	(.399)
	[.025]	[.055]	[.041]	[.047]	[.048]
r_i	.075	.058	.074	.077	.110
	(.079)	(.084)	(.067)	(.081)	(.073)
	[.004]	[.007]	[.006]	[.007]	[.009]
			C. Black Men		
k_{oi}	.250	.291	.168	.207	.162
	(.574)	(.674)	(.460)	(.397)	(.325)
	[.027]	[.044]	[.045]	[.046]	[.068]
r_i	.064	.054	.073	.078	.090
	(.080)	(.083)	(.070)	(.075)	(.097)
	[.004]	[.005]	[.007]	[.009]	[.020]

* The statistics are: Mean, (Standard Deviation), [Standard Error].

s = 12. The dispersion in k_{oi} across individuals is large and appears to be inversely related to education: Recall errors may be larger at lower levels of education, since work experience of persons with lesser schooling starts early and requires, therefore, a longer memory span.

The black sample shows smaller average k_0 in each schooling class, and the white-black differences appear to increase with schooling level. The implication that relative black-white differences in earnings grow over the life-cycle are confirmed in our data: Where the initial earnings differ by 5–8 percent in the various schooling groups, the percent differential increases several fold by the time 15 years of experience have elapsed.

The k_{0i} estimates enable us to attempt the estimation of the rates of return r_i. This successive step compounds the preceding errors and inaccuracies, but hoping that some fraction of the estimate is »true« we follow our curiosity. We use every individual longitudinal earnings function for this purpose[14].

Note that equation (3) can be written as:[15]

$$[\ln Y_t - \ln Y_o] - [\frac{k_o}{T} + g] \, t = r \, [k_o \, (1 - \frac{t}{2T}) \, t \,]$$

Using estimates k_{0i}, g, and trying several values[16] of T, we obtain individual r_i's by estimating (4) using the earnings data given by each individual's earnings profile. These estimates are shown in Table 3.

The »rate of return« coefficients increase with schooling level in both race groups. They are only slightly lower among black than among white men. Hence, the main reason for the flatter profiles of blacks is the lesser volume of job-related investments as measured by k_0[17].

The remaining parameter which the assumed overtaking point allows us to extract from the data is $\ln E_{oi}$, the »endowment« or »earning capacity« which exists apart from measured investments. In contrast to the parameters k_{0i} and r_i which affect *shapes* of earnings profiles, the endowment component is a shift factor which creates differences in *levels* of individual earnings profiles in addition to those created by differences in individual accumulations of investments. The cross-section distribution of earnings should therefore contain the endowment capacity E_{oi} as a persistent factor at various stages of experience. It can be estimated very roughly as the residual from the cross-section regression of earnings on schooling at the overtaking stage. The estimate is rough, because it assumes the same rate of return to schooling for all individuals and the same period of overtaking (i.e. the same rate of return to post school investments). Of course, differential rates of return to schooling, all the unmeasured components of investment, such as quality of schooling, aspects of work experience, efficiencies of various sorts, not to speak of errors and of transitory factors, all of these are impounded in the residual v. For all these reasons the residual variance overstates the variance of endowments. We estimate the residual v_i from the overtaking regression[18]:

$$\ln Y_{10} = \overline{\ln E_o} + r_s \, s_i + v_i$$

The residual variance of earnings at overtaking is large (74 percent for whites and 89 percent for blacks). For reasons discussed above, of which measurement error is not the least important, the residual variance $\sigma^2(v_i)$ overtakes the variance of endowments $\sigma^2(\ln E_{oi})$ perhaps significantly. In columns 3 and 4 of Table 2 we show the effects of v_i in the current (survey) cross-section of earnings.

Despite large errors in v_i as an estimate of $\ln E_{oi}$ indicated partly by the attenuated coefficient of v_i (it is much less than 1) the transplanted residual is a strong »explanatory« factor in current earnings. Whether fixed (column 3) or variable (column 4) experience coefficients are used, the introduction of v_i »explains« an additional 20—30 percent of the cross-section inequality in earnings.

An interesting conclusion based on Table 2 (column 4) ist that the understanding and measurement of factors underlying individual postschool-investments and their efficiency would contribute nearly as much as the understanding of the factors impounded in the residual category.

The fact shown in Table 4 that this conclusion does not survive the attempt to decompose the experience coefficients into parameters k_{oi} and r_i does not mean that it is wrong. The decomposition compounds the errors in k_{oi} and r_i, reducing their explanatory power in the cross-section earnings function, while v_i is unaffected. It is nevertheless of some interest to proceed with a step-wise introduction of the r_i, k_{oi}, and v_i parameter into the cross-section. If not entirely attenuated by error, at least their qualitative conformity to the human capital model can be observed.

The steps are shown in Table 4. In column 1 we have the standard function

$$1. \quad \ln Y_t = (\ln E_o - k_o) + r_s s + (rk_o + \beta) t - \frac{r\beta}{2} t^2$$

In column 2 we allow r_i in the coefficients of t to vary:

$$2. \quad \ln Y_t = (\ln E_o - k_o) + r_s s + k_o (r_i t) + \beta t - \frac{\beta}{2} (r_i t^2)$$

Note that the experience coefficients acquire »correct« signs after r_i has been included and that the coefficient of $(r_i t^2)$ is not far from half the size of the coefficient of t (in absolute value). Some increase in R^2 is also observed. In column 3 we allow k_o in the coefficient of t to vary:

$$3. \quad \ln Y_t = (\ln E_o - k_o) + r_s s + r (k_{oi} t) + \beta t - \frac{r\beta}{2} t^2$$

The signs of t and t^2 remain perverse (or non-significant) but $k_{oi} t$ is positive and strong. Indeed the effect of k_{oi} on R^2 appears stronger than that of r_i.

When both k_{oi} and r_i are introduced in column 4 including k_{oi} in the intercept, the explanatory power increases further, but the sign of k_{oi} (in the intercept) is positive instead of negative: The equation is:

$$4. \quad \ln Y_t = \ln E_o - k_{oi} + r_s s + (r_i k_{oi} t) + \beta t - \frac{\beta}{2} (r_i t^2)$$

Finally, v_i is added into the equation in column 5, so that:

$$5. \quad \ln Y_t = \overline{\ln E}_o - k_{oi} + r_s s + (r_i k_{oi} t) + \beta t - \frac{\beta}{2} (r_i t^2) + v_i$$

We then find that k_{oi} becomes negative and strong, and the other signs are mostly correct (in the sense of the model) as well[19].

Errors in the decomposed investment coefficients k_{oi} and r_i weaken their measured effects on earnings (compare Table 4 with Table 2). At the same time these errors cause an inflation of v_i, since v_i contains unmeasured components of k_{oi}, r_i, and s_i apart from true endowment. Consequently the contribution of v_i to R^2 is over 30 percent in Table 4, when it was over 20 percent in Table 2, while the experience coefficients appear to contribute less than 10 percent in Table 4, but were adding about 20 percent to R^2 in Table 2.

Table 4 Set of Current Earnings Functions

A. Pooled Sample

Variable	Coeff. (1)	t	Coeff. (2)	t	Coeff. (3)	t	Coeff. (4)	t	Coeff. (5)	t
Constant	5.8378		5.5597		5.7947		5.6084		5.7996	
s	.0504	(10.02)	.0482	(9.67)	.0530	(10.67)	.0537	(10.92)	.0522	(13.78)
k_{oi}			.0119	(2.98)			.0929	(3.17)	-.4253	(-13.75)
t	-.0141	(-.82)			-.0158	(-.92)	.0042	(1.23)	-.0054	(-2.01)
t^2	.0006	(1.11)			.0006	(1.12)				
v									.6926	(24.51)
$r_i t$			.2030	(4.41)						
$r_i t^2$			-.0093	(-3.72)			-.0002	(-.29)	.0006	(1.32)
$k_{oi} t$					.0061	(5.52)				
$r_i k_{oi} t$							.0389	(2.43)	.2227	(15.41)
RACE	-.2181	(-8.10)	-.2189	(-8.23)	-.2039	(-7.67)	-.1952	(-7.42)	-.2010	(-9.92)
R^2	.220		.242		.246		.267		.565	

(continued on next page)

Table 4 (continued)

Variable	Coeff. (1)	t	Coeff. (2)	t	Coeff. (3)	t	Coeff. (4)	t	Coeff. (5)	t
					B. White Men					
Constant	5.6491		5.3025		5.6866		5.3933		5.4749	
s	.0660	(7.93)	.0605	(7.30)	.0658	(8.03)	.0647	(7.97)	.0689	(11.46)
k_{oi}	-.0219	(-.83)	.0175	(2.72)	-.0304	(-1.17)	.0663	(1.45)	-.5425	(-11.68)
t	.0011	(1.27)			.0013	(1.53)	.0082	(1.45)	.0012	(.30)
t^2										
v									.8080	(19.09)
$r_i t$			.2452	(3.41)						
$r_i^2 t$			-.0109	(-2.75)			.0003	(.31)	.0025	(3.31)
$k_{oi} t$					.0071	(3.78)				
$r_i k_{oi} t$							.0674	(2.84)	.2593	(12.83)
R^2	.141		.171		.168		.197		561	

(continued on next page)

Table 4 (concluded)

C. Black Men

Variable	Coeff. (1)	t	Coeff. (2)	t	Coeff. (3)	t	Coeff. (4)	t	Coeff. (5)	t
Constant	5.6995		5.5868		5.6260		5.6317		5.8892	
s	.0368	(6.31)	.0365	(6.31)	.0409	(7.03)	.0419	(7.24)	.0376	(8.35)
k_{oi}			.0056	(1.15)	.0035	(.16)	.1376	(3.74)	-.3125	(-7.99)
t	-.0009	(.04)					.00001	(.00)	-.0121	(-3.74)
t^2	-.00003	(-.04)			-.0002	(-.23)				
v			.1423	(2.51)					.5996	(16.85)
$r_i t$			-.0069	(-2.26)						
$r_i t^2$							-.0008	(-1.20)	-.0010	(-1.97)
$k_{oi} t$					.0051	(3.98)				
$r_i k_{oi} t$							-.0063	(-.30)	.1703	(8.76)
R^2	.105		.120		.137		.159		.493	

As already remarked, the patterns of observed sizes and signs of the investment parameters are not inconsistent with the human capital interpretation. The coefficients of t and $r_i t^2$ (in column 2) are consistent with a linear investment decline described by coefficients β and $-\frac{\beta}{2}$ respectively. More basic is the strong negative effect of k_{oi} in step 5, an observation for which, short of econometric sins, it would be difficult to find alternative explanations.

IV. Individual Parameters, Personal Characteristics, and Earnings

The potential explanatory power of the usually unmeasured individual variation in endowment, in postschool investments, and in investment efficiencies (or abilities) was demonstrated in Tables 2 and 4. The Coleman-Rossi survey provides a great deal of information on personal and behavioral characteristics of respondents which may affect earnings indirectly by influencing the magnitudes of endowments, investments, and efficiency, or directly, that is net of these variables and parameters.

As a first step in exploring this matter we relate the individual parameters k_{oi}, r_i, v_i, and s_i to a vector of personal characteristics described in Table 5. One subset of these variables represents information on human capital investments; such as: education, work experience before completion of schooling, training on the job, and job mobility. A second set represents background characteristics: parental education, number of siblings, and whether or not both parents were present in the household at the age of 14.

Other variables such as age and marital status do not necessarily fit into these categories. One important variable which straddles the human capital and the background characteristics is »verbal ability« measured by a score on a test administered at the interview.

The regressions in Table 5 tell a striking story: At least in the white sample, schooling levels are easily and powerfully »explained« by the four family background variables by pre-graduation work experience, and by verbal ability (R^2 = .50 in the white sample, and .28 in the black sample). These variables have the expected effects: Father's and mother's education, previous experience, and verbal ability affect son's education positively; number of siblings and broken home negatively. Of course, the verbal ability may be an effect of schooling rather than a background variable[20]. Verbal ability is probably a mix of both: Without it R^2 falls to .28 and the coefficients of the background variables become attenuated. At any rate a range for R^2 from .28 to .50 represents very strong explanatory power.

In contrast, the k_o, r, and v parameters are barely affected by a dozen or so variables, even though some of them are statistically significant. We also regressed the longitudinal coefficients β_1 and β_2 (first shown in Tables 1 and 2) on the same battery of variables, again with little success. In the white sample R^2 was .04 and .08, respectively. The black sample, however, shows R^2 of .12 and .14 respectively. This finding is due mainly to the »training« (apprenticeship or other formal job training) variable which was not significant in the separated components k_{oi} and r_i.

188

One might argue that the reasons k_i, r_i and v_i, are not really explainable is because of the overwhelming amount of error attached to them.

If this were true, but personal characteristics that we used in Table 5 are nonetheless relevant to earnings even if only indirectly (and certainly if directly), they should show up as significant when entered in the earnings regression.

Table 5 Determinants Regressions[a]

Variable	Dependent = k_{oi}		Dependent = r_i		Dependent = v_i		Dependent = s	
	Coeff.	t	Coeff.	t	Coeff.	t	Coeff.	t
				A. Pooled Sample				
Constant	.1359		-.1974		-.3125		7.1909	
s	-.0083	(-.75)	.0018	(1.36)				
PREV	.0159	(1.03)	-.0001	(-.07)	.0088	(.81)	.1683	(3.72)
AGE1	-.0242	(-1.86)	-.0025	(-1.58)	-.0132	(-2.10)		
CALEN	.0091	(1.12)	.0049	(5.02)				
MARITAL	.1258	(1.85)	.0061	(.75)	.1076	(2.19)		
ABILITY	.0192	(1.53)	.0031	(2.04)	.0298	(3.49)	.6014	(14.63)
NJOBS	.0006	(.09)	.0001	(.16)	.0118	(2.54)		
TRAIN	.0281	(.99)	-.0014	(-.41)	.0034	(3.73)		
CURRENT	.0026	(.51)	.0021	(3.41)	.0131	(.16)		
SIBLINGS	.0161	(2.30)	.0008	(.98)	.0093	(1.86)	-.1333	(-5.22)
FATHER	.0108	(1.44)	-.0006	(-.71)	.0031	(.57)	.0722	(2.62)
MOTHER	-.0108	(-1.27)	.0006	(.63)	.0109	(1.77)	.1369	(4.42)
BROKEN	.1398	(2.77)	.0026	(.43)	.0771	(2.11)	-.7191	(-3.87)
RACE	-.1548	(-3.21)	-.0031	(-.54)	.0117	(.33)	-.1347	(-.77)
R^2	.042		.076		.053		.403	

(continued on next page)

189

Table 5 (continued)

Variable	Dependent = k_{oi} Coeff.	t	Dependent = r_i Coeff.	t	Dependent = v_i Coeff.	t	Dependent = s Coeff.	t
				B. White Men				
Constant	-.4609		-.1422		-.3468		7.0073	
s	.0270	(1.60)	.0045	(2.16)				
PREV	.0418	(1.92)	.0002	(.08)	.0365	(2.23)	.3167	(5.92)
AGE1	-.0503	(-2.96)	-.0043	(-2.01)	-.0159	(-1.76)		
CALEN	.0178	(1.62)	.0039	(2.89)				
MARITAL	.2293	(2.18)	.0093	(.71)	.0984	(1.23)		
ABILITY	.0290	(1.59)	.0048	(2.11)	.0345	(2.77)	.7041	(13.86)
NJOBS	.0037	(.46)	.0001	(.13)	.0066	(1.08)		
TRAIN	.0271	(.84)	-.0036	(-.89)	.0102	(.41)		
CURRENT	.0052	(.80)	.0017	(2.06)	.0139	(2.91)		
SIBLINGS	.0228	(2.05)	.0003	(.23)	.0170	(2.04)	-.1552	(-4.21)
FATHER	.0122	(1.28)	-.0004	(-.30)	.0038	(.53)	.0981	(3.09)
MOTHER	-.0119	(-1.07)	-.0004	(-.28)	.0139	(1.64)	.0511	(1.36)
BROKEN	.0928	(1.26)	-.0123	(-1.33)	.1159	(2.06)	-.1724	(-.69)
R^2	.055		.087		.087		.498	

Notes to Table 5

[a]Key:

PREV	=	years of experience prior to entry into the labor force
AGE1	=	age of entry into the labor force
CALEN	=	calendar year of entry into the labor force
MARITAL	=	1 if married currently; 0 otherwise
ABILITY	=	score on a verbal comprehension test given at the time of the interview
NJOBS	=	number of jobs held since entry into the labor force

Notes to Table 5 (contd.)
(continued on next page)

Table 5 (concluded)

Variable	Dependent = k_{oi} Coeff.	t	Dependent = r_i Coeff.	t	Dependent = v_i Coeff.	t	Dependent = s Coeff.	t
				C. **Black Men**				
Constant	.6880		-.2697		-.1738		7.3623	
s	-.0350	(-2.36)	-.0002	(-.12)				
PREV	-.0172	(-.77)	-.0003	(-.10)	-.0158	(-1.06)	.0033	(.04)
AGE1	-.0023	(-.11)	-.0007	(-.31)	-.0167	(-1.81)		
CALEN	-.0014	(-.12)	.0060	(4.23)				
MARITAL	.0628	(.70)	.0073	(.69)	.1016	(1.61)		
ABILITY	.0031	(.18)	.0010	(.47)	.0269	(2.26)	.4863	(7.65)
NJOBS	-.0074	(-.72)	.0001	(.09)	.0165	(2.32)		
TRAIN	.0391	(.72)	.0011	(.18)	.0042	(.11)		
CURRENT	-.0031	(-.40)	.0024	(2.70)	.0123	(2.36)		
SIBLINGS	.0114	(1.24)	.0012	(1.15)	.0057	(.89)	-.1291	(-3.68)
FATHER	.0022	(.18)	-.0015	(-1.07)	.0039	(.46)	.0348	(.76)
MOTHER	-.0099	(-.76)	.0014	(.96)	.0076	(.84)	.2198	(4.48)
BROKEN	.1718	(2.43)	.0139	(1.68)	.0470	(.95)	-1.0891	(-4.05)
R^2	.061		.093		.057		.277	

TRAIN	=	years of formal post-school training obtained
CURRENT	=	duration of current job
SIBLINGS	=	number of siblings in the family
FATHER	=	father's education
MOTHER	=	mother's education
BROKEN	=	1 if respondent lived in a broken family at age 14; 0 otherwise
RACE	=	1 if black; 0 otherwise

This we do in three steps shown in Table 6: First we add to schooling (s) and experience (t, t^2) the subset of personal characteristics which represent additional information on postschool human capital, including »verbal ability« and marital status among them. The results are shown in column 2. The second subset, of family background variables, is then added and shown in column 3. Finally, the estimated parameter k_i, r_i, and v_i are included in column 4.

Table 6 Personal Characteristics in Current Earnings Function

Variable	Coeff. (1)	t	Coeff. (2)	t	Coeff. (3)	t	Coeff. (4)	t
				A. Pooled Sample				
Constant	5.8378		5.4607		5.3275		5.5229	
s	.0504	(10.02)	.0291	(4.70)	.0271	(4.24)	.0385	(7.87)
t	-.0141	(-.82)	-.0033	(-.17)	-.0005	(-.03)	-.0032	(-.89)
t^2	.0006	(1.11)	.0002	(.32)	.0001	(.23)		
RACE	-.2181	(-8.10)	-.1556	(-5.68)	-.1500	(-5.39)	-.1677	(-7.78)
PREV			-.0014	(-.15)	-.0002	(-.02)	-.0048	(-.70)
AGE1			.0043	(1.77)	.0041	(.53)	.0068	(1.17)
MARITAL			.1070	(2.73)	.1124	(2.88)	.0764	(2.54)
ABILITY			.0489	(6.84)	.0472	(6.54)	.0255	(4.53)
NJOBS			.0073	(2.00)	.0080	(2.17)	.0009	(.31)
TRAIN			.0093	(.57)	.0091	(.56)	.0012	(.09)
CURRENT			.0105	(3.61)	.0108	(3.73)	.0027	(1.18)
SIBLINGS					.0040	(.98)	-.0001	(-.03)
FATHER					.0050	(1.15)	.0019	(.57)
MOTHER					.0083	(1.76)	.0030	(.78)
BROKEN					-.0157	(-.54)	-.0018	(-.52)
k_{oi}							-.4032	(-12.95)
$r_i t^2$							.0004	(.84)
$r_i k_{oi} t$							.2154	(14.93)
v							.6559	(22.73)
R^2	.220		.283		.290		.584	

(continued on next page)

Generally, the results are negative. The personal characteristics on the whole do not substitute for parameters k_{oi}, r_i, and v_i; nor do they have net direct effects on earnings when these parameters are included. Actually, the first subset of personal characteristics especially verbal ability, marital status, and job mobility (or tenure) do supplement the experience parameters— — R^2 does increase from the first to the second column of Table 6. However, there is no increase in R^2 due to family background variables at any stage, while k_{oi}, r_i, v_i and education remain very strong (column 4), as they are without the vector of personal characteristics (Table 4). Indeed, comparing the last column of Table 4 with the last column of Table 6 we see that the explanatory power of the earnings equation is

Table 6 (continued)

Variable	Coeff. (1)	t	Coeff. (2)	t	Coeff. (3)	t	Coeff. (4)	t
				B. White Men				
CONSTANT	5.6491		5.3074		5.1165		5.1197	
s	.0660	(7.93)	.0355	(3.21)	.0326	(2.83)	.0533	(6.15)
t	-.0219	(-.83)	.0080	(.26)	.0098	(.32)	.0073	(1.31)
t^2	.0011	(1.27)	.00002	(.03)	,.00004	(.04)		
PREV			.0275	(1.77)	.0282	(1.81)	-.0002	(-.02)
AGE1			-.0026	(-.22)	-.0003	(-.03)	.0129	(1.47)
MARITAL			.1107	(1.54)	.1053	(1.46)	.0564	(1.05)
ABILITY			.0586	(4.77)	.0554	(4.44)	.0187	(1.96)
NJOBS			.0051	(.93)	.0051	(.93)	-.0045	(-1.10)
TRAIN			.0196	(.89)	.0211	(.96)	.0021	(.13)
CURRENT			.0108	(2.45)	.0115	(2.60)	-.0005	(-.14)
SIBLINGS					.0057	(.74)	.0041	(.73)
FATHER					.0079	(1.21)	.0059	(1.22)
MOTHER					.0079	(1.04)	.0002	(.03)
BROKEN					.0392	(.78)	.0062	(.16)
k_{oi}							-.5325	(-11.11)
$r_i t^2$							.0023	(2.97)
$r_i k_{oi} t$							.2580	(12.44)
v							.7833	(17.49)
R^2	.141		.209		.219		.574	

(continued on next page)

raised barely at all (from $R^2 = .57$ to $R^2 = .58$) when all the additional variables shown in Table 6 augment the last regression in Table 4. Of these additional variables only »ability«, current job tenure, and marital status were marginally significant. But the introduction of the ability variable detracts from the education variable and does not provide an independent explanation.

We believe it is fair to conclude from Tables 5 and 6 that background, especially family characteristics of persons, affect their schooling attainment quite significantly, but have little if any effects on postschool investments, or an earnings, holding investment variables and parameters constant. Their indirect effects work

193

Table 6 (concluded)

Variable	Coeff. (1)	t	Coeff. (2)	t	Coeff. (3)	t	Coeff. (4)	t
				C. Black Men				
CONSTANT	5.6995		5.3345		5.2603		5.7753	
s	.0368	(6.31)	.0210	(3.06)	.0190	(2.68)	.0289	(5.31)
t	.0009	(.04)	.0054	(.23)	.0081	(.34)	-.0145	(-3.30)
t^2	-.00003	(-.04)	-.0003	(-.35)	-.0003	(-.45)		
PREV			-.0248	(-2.37)	-.0229	(-2.17)	-.0105	(-1.28)
AGE1			.0087	(.88)	.0070	(.71)	-.0010	(-.13)
MARITAL			.1056	(2.51)	.1118	(2.64)	.0873	(2.67)
ABILITY			.0413	(5.02)	.0411	(4.94)	.0243	(3.75)
NJOBS			.0091	(1.93)	.0110	(2.28)	.0059	(1.57)
TRAIN			-.0090	(-.35)	-.0094	(-.37)	.0001	(.00)
CURRENT			.0097	(2.67)	.0100	(2.76)	.0064	(2.24)
SIBLINGS					.0026	(.61)	-.0013	(-.39)
FATHER					.0014	(.24)	-.0020	(-.45)
MOTHER					.0096	(1.58)	.0063	(1.34)
BROKEN					-.0473	(-1.42)	-.0263	(-1.01)
k_{oi}							-.2855	(-7.27)
$r_i t^2$							-.0012	(-2.23)
$r_i k_{oi} t$							.1644	(8.46)
v							.5559	(15.47)
R^2	.105		.196		.207		.531	

almost wholly through educational attainment and almost not all through post-school investment behavior or efficiency.

The human capital model which served as a guide appears to have survived the reported experiments. There does remain a challenge of measuring behavior expressed by the variables k_o, r, and v, whose role in earnings is undiminished even after the application of so many rarely available personal characteristics to the earnings function.

V. Summary

1. In this paper we analyzed the distribution of earnings histories of 884 men aged 30–39 in 1968. On average, the longitudinal profiles of earnings covered

the first sixteen years of work experience. Deflated for price-level changes and for economy-wide growth, the profiles showed pronounced individual growth as well as individual differences in the growth of earnings. Typically, the profiles were concave with respect to experience, confirming the general shape suggested by cross-section data.

2. The distribution of individual earnings profiles shows a great deal of variation in levels, slopes, and curvatures of this initial part (about one-third) of the earnings profile. The individual variation in levels is interpreted in human capital terms as reflecting differential endowments at the time of entry into full-time work. Those endowments consist of schooling levels, of rates of return to schooling, and of capacity levels independent of (or predating) schooling. The variation in slopes and curvatures reflects differential volumes, timing, and profitability of »postschool investments«. These cover a broad range of activities such as occupational choice and progressions, job training and learning, job and geographic mobility, job search and acquisition of information, work effort, and the like. Since only variation in schooling and in years of work experience can be observed in cross-sections, analyses of the distribution of earnings miss a great deal of individual variation which we just described. In this paper we attempted to quantify this variation in a schematic fashion: (a) As variation in the coefficients (slopes, curvatures, and levels) of the earnings profiles, and (b) as variation in the parameters of the earnings function which represent postschool investment ratios, rates of return, and levels of endowment, aside from levels of schooling. The investment ratios and rates of return enter as multiplicative components of the coefficients of the earnings function and we attempted to decompose these coefficients in order to analyze the parameters.

We find that if slopes and curvatures of individual trajectories were available to analysts, an additional 20—25 percent of the relative variance of (monthly or weekly) earnings could be explained beyond the usual power provided by the cross-section earnings function approach. The decomposition of the slope and curvature coefficients into investment ratio and rate of return parameters provides a smaller increase in explanatory power because of errors introduced by the procedure. However, the estimated parameters are of reasonable magnitude and acquire the appropriate signs in the cross-section regressions.

We estimated individual capacities within schooling groups as the residual from the schooling regression« at the »overtaking stage« (at about ten years of experience). We then find that individuals with greater investment ratios grow more rapidly than others, and——holding capacity constant——have lower initial earnings. Finally, in terms of the potential explanatory power, variation in earning capacity is at least as important as variation in slopes and curvatures of earnings in the residual left over by the usual earnings function in which only years of schooling and years of experience are specified.

3. Our next step was to explore which of the many personal and background characteristics of individuals appear to be related, perhaps as determinants, to the slopes, curvatures, and human capital parameters implicit in the individual earnings profiles. The characteristics were (a) education, »verbal ability« measured at time of interview, work experience prior to completion of schooling, training on the job, job mobility status, age, and marital status; (b) parental education, number of siblings, and whether or not both parents were present in the house-

hold at the age of 14. Set (a) may be viewed as additional measures of the person's human capital stock, set (b) as his family background variables.

We found that, overall, the individual coefficients and parameters of the earnings profiles are very weakly, if at all, associated with the personal and background characteristics. Education, verbal ability, and job training appear to be of some significance, but family background has no effect at all on the postschool earnings trajectory. In contrast, education of the respondent is quite strongly explained by the family background variables and by verbal ability which is probably more an effect than a determinant of schooling. In human capital terminology, family background appears to affect schooling but not postschool investments.

4. It is possible that postschool investment parameters are in fact affected by the background variables, but we find no relation because our estimates of the human capital parameters (k, r, v) are largely in error. If so, the personal and background variables would show up as »direct« determinants of earnings, without or with the (k, r, v) parameters in the earnings function. The results of the test are negative: While verbal ability, marital status, and job mobility appear to supplement experience coefficients prior to inclusion of k, r, and v, the family background variables have no effect before or after the inclusion of k, r, and v.

In sum, while the role of postschool investment parameters in earnings remains strong even after all the available personal information is utilized additionally, the latter show little or no relation to the personal accumulation of postschool human capital. Nor, less surprisingly, do they show »direct« effects on earnings. The indirect effects which do exist are almost entirely achieved via family investment in schooling of children. It is surprising, however, that no relation can be traced between (preschool?) earning capacity (v) and family background in our sample.

The findings and surprises in this study will call for replication on longitudinal data which are current rather than retrospective before they can be generalized.

Notes

[1]   Declines are observed in annual earnings, but not in wage rates.
[2]   For a more complete exposition of the model and of the econometric specification see Mincer (1974), or a summary in Mincer (1976).
[3]   This is a single term Taylor expansion of the term $\ln (1-k_t)$. The degree of approximation seemed to make little difference in our empirical applications.
[4]   For references see the bibliography in Mincer (1976).
[5]   The sample was restricted to 884 males who reported at least three earnings points, who never held multiple jobs, and who provided all the necessary basic information.
[6]   We have the reassuring statement from James Coleman that a cross-check of the earnings and employment data with the Social Security file showed »rather good conformity«.
[7]   Evidently, the source of similarity is that very little variation over time was reported by individuals in their histories of hours of work.
[8]   The mean number of observations for each individual regression was 11.3. The standard deviation was 6.6
[9]   Estimated from U.S. Census data. For details see Mincer (1974), p. 79.
[10]   Weiss and Lillard (1976) find a concave longitudinal profile among Ph. D's in science. Their sample (NSF) covers one decade in a wide spectrum of ages.
[11]   The coefficients of t and t^2 acquire the proper signs in our own sample when experience is defined as total number of months ever worked (rather than time elapsed since the start of a full-time job after completion of schooling), and when earnings (in logs) are averaged over several years.

[12] We postpone the discussion of variable v in columns 3 and 4 of Table 2.

[13] The proof is on p. 17, Mincer (1974).

[14] In principle, the idea can serve as a start of an iteration procedure. We do not go beyond the first step.

[15] To obtain equation (4) it is necessary to assume that $\beta = k_o/T$, where T is the length of the working life cycle.

[16] $T = 40$ appeared to fit best.

[17] To the extent that these are firm-specific, they are jointly determined by employers and workers. The greater job turnover and shorter job tenure of blacks is consistent with this interpretation.

[18] We also included calendar year of entry into the labor force in the equation in order to standardize for productivity growth in the economy.

[19] In the white sample the size of the coefficient k_o is $-.5$, of v_i is $+.8$ and of $(r_i k_{oi} t)$ is .26. Under certain zero correlation assumptions the deviation of these coefficients from unity represents a measure of the importance of error in the data or concepts.

[20] The regression of verbal ability on schooling and family background yields an $r^2 = .43$, on schooling alone $R^2 = .31$.

References

(1) Mincer, Jacob, *Schooling, Experience, and Earnings,* New York: National Bureau of Economic Research, 1974.

(2) »Progress in Human Capital Analyses of the Distribution of Earnings«, in *Personal Income Distributions,* ed. by A.B. Atkinson for the Royal Economic Society, Weidenfeld and Nicolson, London, 1976.

(3) Weiss, Yoram and Lillard, Lee A. »*Experience, Vintage and Time Effects in the Growth of Earnings: American Scientists, 1960—70«.* NBER, Working Paper No. 138.

Robert E. B. Lucas*
Variances in returns to human capital

I. The Problem

An individual's market income is dependent both upon factor services supplied and upon rewards to such services, so that income inequality is truly generated by the joint distribution of factor endowments and prices. In the context of the size distribution of income, interpersonal variations in accumulations of human capital, together with the population average rewards to such accumulations, have received considerable empirical attention over the last two decades. However, such studies seem to have entirely neglected the variations in returns to human capital across individuals.

The present paper therefore undertakes an empirical investigation of the variances in rates of return to schooling and experience for U.S. white males. A satisfactory approach to this problem unfortunately demands the use of some rather complex estimation techniques which, presumably, partially explains the prior lack of attention granted to this fundamental aspect of the size distribution of incomes.

The basic model adopted here, being well-known from much previous work on human capital, is outlined in brief in the following section. Section III outlines the estimation techniques employed, and IV discusses the measurement of variables and sample limitations imposed. The resulting estimates are presented in the subsequent section, and a series of inferences about the nature of the underlying human capital model are drawn at this juncture. VI then undertakes an exercise in accounting for inequality, employing the estimated parameters of the distribution of rewards to human capital and sample parameters of the distribution in endowments. The closing section mentions some possible directions for future research in this vein and finally summarizes the principal findings.

II. The Basic Model

A basic earnings equation in terms of human capital may be simply derived in the following manner[1]. Define an internal rate of return for person i, r_i, which equates the present values of two mutually exclusive streams of earnings:

> $Y_i(t)$ being earnings at time t, given that i elects to attend school for the first s_i years;
> $X_i(t)$ being earnings at time t, given that i never attends school.

---

*Resarch for this paper is partially supported by a grant from Boston University.

Thus, r_i is given by:

$$\int_{t=0}^{T_i} Y_i(t) \, e^{-r_i t} \, dt \equiv \int_{t=0}^{T_i} X_i(t)^{-r_i t} \, dt, \qquad (1)$$

where T_i is the life-horizon for person i upon entering school.

Under the following assumptions:

A. i. $Y_i(t) = 0$ during schooling, and foregone earnings represent
the only private cost of schooling[2];
ii. $X_i(t) = X_i(0)$ all t;

(1) may be solved to provide:

$$\ln Y_i(t) = \ln X_i(0) + r_i s_i. \qquad (2)$$

This simple schooling model may be extended to encompass post-school, on-the-job training in the following form:

$$\ln Y_i(t) = \ln X_i(0) + r_i s_i + \rho_i \int_{t=0}^{T_i - s_i} k_i(\tau) d\tau, \qquad (3)$$

where $k_i(\tau)$ is the fraction of time spent in on-the-job training by person i at time τ after leaving school, ρ_i is the rate of return to such on-the-job experience for i.

Ben-Porath (1967) suggests that optimization on behalf of individuals is likely to render k_i a declining function of τ. Assuming then for simplicity[3]:

$$k_i(\tau) = k_i(0) - \frac{k_i(0)\tau}{T_i - s_i}, \qquad \text{for } \tau > s_i, \qquad (A.iii)$$

(3) becomes:

$$\ln Y_i(t) = \ln X_i(0) + r_i s_i + \rho_i k_i(0) \tau_i - \frac{\rho_i k_i(0)}{2(T_i - s_i)} \tau_i^2 + \varepsilon_i \qquad (4)$$

where ε_i is a stochastic term introduced in general recognition of the approximate nature of the assumptions A.i $-$ A.iii.

The equation (4) is by now a fairly standard specification for a human capital earnings equation and is the underlying form adopted here.

III. Estimation Techniques

In addressing the empirical issue of estimating equation (4) it is commonly possible to construct from micro data files measures of Y_i, s_i and τ_i. (4) may then be rewritten in terms of observed and unobserved elements as[4]:

$$y_i = \sum_j z_{ij} \beta_{ij}$$

(5)

$$y_i = \ln Y_i(t)$$

$$z_{i1} = 1, \ z_{i2} = s_i, \ z_{i3} = \tau_i, \ z_{i4} = \tau_i^2$$

$$\beta_{i1} = \ln X_i(0) + \varepsilon_i$$

$$\beta_{i2} = r_i$$

$$\beta_{i3} = \rho_i k_i(0)$$

$$\beta_{i4} = \frac{-\rho_i k_i(0)}{2(T_i - s_i)}$$

As a linear regression equation, (5) belongs to the class of equations known equivalently as random coefficient regression equations or regression equations of the second kind[5]. In essence, the elements β_{ij} may best be treated as random since (as Becker (1967) suggests) they are likely to depend upon such unobserved demographic data as ability, family wealth, taste, discriminatory characteristics and luck[6].

(5) may, of course, be rewritten:

$$y_i = \sum_j z_{ij} \beta_j + u_i$$

(6)

$$u_i = \sum_j z_{ij} (\beta_{ij} - \beta_j)$$

Estimation of (6) by ordinary least squares, generates estimates:

$$\hat{\beta} = (Z'Z)^{-1} Z'y$$

(7)

$$Z = \| z_{ij} \|, \ y = \| y_i \|.$$

$\hat{\beta}$ are unbiased estimates of the $E(\beta_{ij}) = \beta_j$, if $E(u_i) = 0$.

200

However, since u_i are basically heteroskedastic $\hat{\beta}$ are not the best estimators[7]. Our concern here is to estimate the $a_j = E(\beta_{ij} - \beta_j)^2$, which terms are usually dismissed to the variance of disturbances u_i. The procedure here employed for this estimation was apparently initiated by Theil and Mennes (1959), then extended and modified by Hildreth and Houck (1968). Let v be the vector of residuals from the regression (7).

Then:
$$v = y - Z \hat{\beta} = Mu \tag{8}$$

where
$$M = (I - Z (Z'Z)^{-1} Z')$$
and
$$u = \| u_i \|$$

Hence:
$$E(v\, v') = M\, E(u\, u')M'. \tag{9}$$

It is natural to suppose in a cross-section of this type that the u_i are uncorrelated across individuals. In addition, however, we shall impose at this sate the assumption:

$$E(u_i)^2 = \sum_j z_{ij}^2\, a_j \tag{A.iv.}$$

In essence, this key assumption may be viewed as comprising two parts. As noted above, the common practice of estimating $\hat{\beta}$ by (7) already assumes $E(z_{ij}(\beta_{ij} - \beta_j))$ = 0 if $\hat{\beta}$ are to be unbiased estimators. In addition, A.iv. imposes zero correlation between the β_{ij} for a given i, so that $E(\beta_{ij} - \beta_j) (\beta_{ij'} - \beta_{j'}) = 0$. It must be emphasized that neither component of A.iv. is new to the human capital literature being explicitly employed by Chiswick and Mincer (1972), p. 539.

It now follows that:

$$E(\dot{v}) = \dot{M} \dot{Z} \alpha \tag{10}$$

where $\dot{v}$, $\dot{M}$ and $\dot{Z}$ are v, M and Z with each element replaced by its own square, and $a = \| a_j \|$. Defining $w = \dot{v} - E(\dot{v})$ and $G = \dot{M}\dot{Z}$ and rearranging provides:

$$\dot{v} = G\alpha + w \tag{11}$$

One might then consider performing ordinary least squares on α. However, as Hildreth and Houck (1968) note, such estimators may take negative values with positive probability. In general, it seems desirable to take account of the prior information that a_j are variances and hence non-negative. Hildreth and Houck thus suggest a constrained estimator which is efficient in minimizing $w'w$, so their estimator a^* is the solution to the quadratic programming problem[8]:

$$\underset{\alpha}{\text{Min}}\ (\dot{v} - G\alpha)'\ (\dot{v} - G\alpha) \tag{12}$$

$$\text{s.t.}\ \alpha \geq 0.$$

This estimator is adopted here to examine the variances in the coefficients of (5). Computationally, this is far from trivial for the large data base employed below, which does not permit direct matrix operations on Z. The matrix G'G is in fact here computed cumulatively, and then problem (12) is solved by use of the computer algorithm programmed by Ravindran (1972)[9].

IV. Data

The date for this study are taken from a twelve percent random drawing of white headed households from the U.S. 1970 census 1 in 100 sample. From this basic file are selected those adult white males up to 70 years old, not in school or the military, who worked for pay in the year prior to the survey.

For each such person, the variables in (5) are measured in the following manner:

y_i — natural logarithm of weekly earnings, computed as annual earnings over midpoint of the reported weeks worked interval. If weekly earnings equal zero, y_i is set equal to zero[10].

s_i — grades of school complete with elementary = 1 and the upper open-ended interval set = 21.

τ_i — age in years minus grades of school attended minus n,
where n = 8 if $0 < s_i < 13$
9 if $13 < s_i < 16$
10 if $16 < s_i$.[11]

Since τ_i^2 is also included, observations with τ_i computed as < 0 are dropped from the sample.[12]

The number of observations for the following regressions is 40,890.

V. Results

The estimates obtained for $\hat{\beta}$ are reported in table 1 (see page ●●●), with estimated t-statistics in parentheses, although the latter are known to be biased by the presence of heteroskedasticity. Comments on these results may be foregone in this report, similar equations having been extensively examined elsewhere[13]. Rather, it is the values of α^* given in table 1 which are of primary interest here[14], and the remainder of this section offers a few comments on the implications of these estimates for human capital theory.

1. Perhaps the most striking feature of these results is the zero value estimated for the first element of α. Since:

$$\alpha_1 = E(\beta_{i1} - \beta_1)^2 = \sigma_x^2 + \sigma_\epsilon^2, \tag{13}$$

where σ_x = variance $(\ln x_i(0))$

σ_ϵ = variance (ϵ_i)

this result suggests that $\sigma_x^2 = \sigma_\epsilon^2 = 0$.[15] The latter equality, (combined with the ordinary least squares assumption that $E(\epsilon_i) = 0$), lends support to the argument that assumptions A.i − A.iii. are quite credible.

Table 1 Estimates of $\hat{\beta}$ and a^*

	$\hat{\beta}$ [t-statistic]	a^*	$\dfrac{\sqrt{a^*}}{\hat{\beta}}$
1 Intercept	3·591 [140·43]	0·0	0·0
2 Schooling	0·0802 [46·93]	0·0032	0·709
3 Experience	0·0481 [37·01]	$5·84 \times 10^{-4}$	0·503
4 Experience ^{2}	$-9·18 \times 10^{-4}$ [35·40]	$1·19 \times 10^{-7}$	0·375

That σ_x^2 is estimated to be zero also tends to substantiate a further common assumption not made above, namely that $\ln X_i(0) = \ln X(0)$ for all i. The economic interpretation of this result is indeed intriguing, indicating that the projected earnings of all white males is essentially identical upon school entrance. In other words, effects of variations in pre-school family environment and inherited abilities upon earnings apparently tend to be confined to indirect paths through influences on schooling, experience and their rewards.

2. The absolute magnitudes of the remaining elements of a are, of course, rather small, as should be anticipated given the nature of β. In order to gain some impression of relative magnitudes however, table 1 presents the values of $\sqrt{a^*}/\beta$. Thus, the coefficient of variation for rates of return to schooling is estimated to be approximately seventy per cent. Indeed, the very substantial degree of inferred relative spread in rates of return to both schooling and experience prompts the next three observations.

3. In the earlier literature on returns to human capital, it is frequently assumed that $r_i = r$ for all i.[16] Clearly, the above results run counter to this simplification.

4. The disparities in individuals' average returns to human capital investments (r_i) generally point also to large inequalities in marginal returns. Hence, in terms of the loanable funds framework developed by Becker (1967), there apparently exist rather wide interpersonal shifts in the supply curve of funds for investment in human capital, or in the demand curve for such funds, or both.

5. In the context of aggregate production functions, it is a great convenience empirically to speak of aggregated factor inputs. If different individuals' investments in human capital could simply be summed to form a single factor of production sold at a common price on a competitive market, then the assumption that $r_i = r$ for all i would truly be tenable. The above rejection of this notion consequently indicates that at least this simple form of aggregation is not justified for investments in either schooling or on-the-job training by white males[17].

6. In section III it is noted that the distribution of u_i is basically heteroskedastic. It is thus natural to consider some form of generalized least squares estimation for β. Hildreth and Houck (1968) suggest the following estimator:

$$\beta^* = (Z' \; \Omega^{-1} \; Z)^{-1} \; Z' \; \Omega^{-1} \; y, \tag{14}$$

where the diagonal elements of Ω are given by Za^*. The results of applying these estimators to the above regression are given in table 2, with estimated t-statistics again in parentheses.

Table 2 Estimates of β^*

	β^* [t-statistic]
1 Intercept	3·272 [152·36]
2 Schooling	0·0975 [62·92]
3 Experience	0·0580 [42·13]
4 Experience^2	−0·00107 [34·16]

Comparing β^* with $\hat{\beta}$, it is clear that the weighted least squares estimators generate greater estimated values for the rate of return coefficients. Thus, both β_2^* and β_3^* exceed their $\hat{\beta}$ counterparts by more than twenty per cent.

VI. Accounting for Inequality

The results presented in the foregoing section included a zero estimated variance for the intercept term in the earnings equation (5). The converse of this result is, of course, that the entire variance of log earnings for white males is attributable to the joint distribution of schooling, experience and the returns to each. In order to acquire some sense of the relative contributions of the parameters of this joint distribution to the dispersion of earnings, the latter is here decomposed to account for the sources of inequality.

Taking variances in (4), using A.iv., one obtains[18]:

$$\sigma_y^2 = \alpha_1 + \sum_{j=2}^{4} \{\alpha_j (z_j^2 + \sigma_{z_j}^2) + \sum_{j'=2}^{4} \beta_j \beta_{j'} \sigma_{z_j z_{j'}} \}, \quad (15)$$

where σ_y^2 = variance (y_i)

$\sigma_{z_j}^2$ = variance (z_{ij})

$\sigma_{z_j z_j'}$ = covariance $(z_{ij}, z_{ij'})$

The various components of the sum on the right in (15) may then be evaluated, using sample values for z_j, $\sigma_{z_j}^2$ and $\sigma_{z_j z_j'}$, and employing the estimated values in α^* and β^*. Table 3 presents the results of this »analysis of variance.«

Table 3   Accounting for Inequality.

	$\alpha_j z_j^2$	$\alpha_j \sigma_{z_j}^2$	$\beta_j \beta_{j'} \sigma_{z_j z_{j'}}$		
			Schooling	Experience	Experience²
Schooling	0·411	0·037	0·108	-0·112	0·110
Experience	0·295	0·118	-0·112	0·681	-0·608
Experience²	0·060	0·062	0·110	-0·608	0·590
$\sum_j$	0·982		0·158		
σ_{y*}^2	1·140				

Clearly, the terms in the variance of returns together contribute (0.982) far more to earnings inequality than does the net contribution (0.158) of terms in the average returns to human capital. To ignore the consequences of the a terms in the study of the size distribution of income would then, of course, miss a great deal of the role of human capital in accounting for inequality.

Of course, part of the reason for this contrast in net contributions of a and β terms is that the latter can be negative and off-set other contributions, whereas all a components are necessarily non-negative. The largest single positive components in this decomposition of income inequality arise from the products of average returns to experience and experience squared with their respective variances (.681 and .590). However, the equally large negative covariance term in experience and experience squared leaves on balance a negligible contribution to overall inequality. Clearly, the remaining large single components arise from the variance in returns to schooling and experience terms. Taking the product of these a terms with both mean and variance in endowment elements, $a_j(z_j^2 + \sigma_{z_j}^2)$, one finds a roughly equal contribution to earnings inequality from these two sources.

In total, this accounting for inequality generates a value for the estimated variance in earnings, σ_y^2*, equal to 1.140. This may be compared to the sample variance in y of 1.209. The fact that σ_y^2* is some 94 % of the sample variance suggests that on balance the assumption A. iv is not too misleading. Nonetheless, this does not deny that individual off-setting components, ignored under these assumptions, may be very substantial.

Finally, it should be noted that one cannot proceed immediately from table 3 to statements about the consequences for earnings inequality of changing the distribution of schooling and experience. In general, as the latter shift, the structure of returns to these elements also changes. Although estimates of the kind presented in this paper represent a fundamental first step toward such predictive capability, a single equation model cannot suffice both for estimating the returns to human capital and for studying how such rewards vary with changes in quantities[19].

VII. Summary and Closing Remarks

The principal findings of this study are as follows:

1. The entire variance in logarithm of weekly earnings of U.S. white males is accounted for by the joint distribution of schooling, experience and their returns.

2. There exists a very substantial degree of relative inequality in returns to both schooling and experience amongst U.S. white males. This result is at odds with at least some of the earlier human capital models, and also denies the possibility of simply adding up investments in human capital to form an aggregate input in production function analysis.

3. Pre-school family environment and inherited ability have no direct effect on white males earnings, their effects being channelled through extent of schooling and experience and returns to each. Let me emphasize, however, that this by no means denies a substantial role for environmental or genetic traits in influencing earnings.

4. The more efficient, generalized least squares estimators adopted in this paper generate estimated rates of return to schooling and experience some twenty per cent higher than the previously adopted ordinary least squares.

5. In accounting for income equality, the terms in the variance of returns clearly dominate the net contribution of the terms in average returns.

6. Under the assumptions of our model, the means, variances and covariances of schooling, experience and experience squared, suitably combined with the

average returns and variance in returns to each, account for ninety four per cent of variance in white males earnings.

In terms of future research, it would clearly be of interest to move in the direction of examining how the distribution of returns shifts as the distribution of investments in human capital moves. Also, it is in principle possible to relax at least a part of our assumption A. iv. and thus consider estimating the entire covariance matrix of returns to human capital investments.

Moreover, in broader terms, this paper apparently represents one of the very first attempts to apply random coefficient estimators to large scale household survey data. Since this broad class of models is almost always appropriate in such studies, with reactions varying from individual to individual, the present demonstration of practicability of these techniques should serve to encourage investigation of their implications beyond the human capital framework.

Notes

[1] See Mincer (1974)
[2] A somewhat weaker assumption would suffice here; that any earnings during school years just off-set direct costs.
[3] This particular form is probably the most widely adopted in existing empirical work. See Mincer (1974).
[4] The term β_{13} is sometimes referred to as the adjusted rate of return to experience. See Chiswick (1974).
[5] For a history of the literature on this subject, see Swamy (1971). I am most grateful to J. Heckman for drawing my attention to this book.
[6] Thus, see Hildreth and Houck (1968), p. 584 or Fisk (1967) p. 266.
[7] See Hildreth and Houck (1968).
[8] This is not however the best estimator of a, Froelich (1973) suggests a two-step estimation, employing a^* to reestimate β and reiterating (12).
[9] I am most grateful to W. Dent for correspondence concerning this algorithm.
[10] On the latter, cf. Welch (1973). It is probably preferable to use hourly rather than weekly wage, but suitable measures of hours worked are not reported on the census; see Lindsay (1971). Persons with business plus farm income in excess of $\$1,000$ are excluded from the working sample, it being difficult to distinguish labor from capital components, and two-thirds of any such income for remaining persons is added to annual earnings; see Hall (1973). The above measure follows conventional practice in omitting psychic wages, but see Lucas (1977).
[11] cf. Hanoch (1967).
[12] cf. Welch (1973). Approximately 1.1 per cent of the sample generated $\tau_i < 0$.
[13] See, for example, Mincer (1974).
[14] Unfortunately, no satisfactory test-statistics have yet been developed for the Hildreth-Houck quadratic programming estimator.
[15] Note that this assumes the covariance $\sigma_{x\epsilon} = 0$, or at least that any such negative component in (13) does not just off-set positive values for σ_x^2, σ_ϵ^2.
[16] For references, see Mincer (1970).
[17] On this general aggregation problem, see Griliches (1970).
[18] See Goodman (1960). For a recent application, see Chiswick and Mincer (1972).
[19] See Lucas (1977, b)

References

Becker, G.S., »Human Capital and the Personal Distribution of Income,« *W.S. Woytinsky Lecture No. 1*, (Ann Arbor; Univ. of Michigan), 1967.

Ben-Porath, Y., »The Production of Human Capital and the Life-Cycle of Earnings,« *Journal of Political Economy*, Vol. 75, August 1967, pp. 352−365.

Chiswick, B.R., *Income Inequality*, (New York; NBER, Columbia Univ. Press), 1974

Chiswick, B.R., and J. Mincer, »Time Series Changes in Personal Income Inequality in the U.S. from 1939 with Projections to 1985,« *Journal of Political Economy*, vol. 80, supplement, May/June 1972, pp. S34−S66.

Fisk, P.R., »Models of the Second Kind in Regression Analysis,« *Journal of the Royal Statistical Society*, vol. 29, Series B, No. 2, 1967, pp. 266−281.

Froehlich, B.R., »Some Estimators for a Random Coefficient Regression Model,« *Journal of the American Statistical Association*, vol. 68, June 1973, pp. 329−335.

Goodman, L., »On the Exact Variance of Products,« *Journal of the American Statistical Association*, vol. 55, December 1960, pp. 708−713.

Griliches, Z., »Notes on the Role of Education in Production Functions,« in *Education, Income and Human Capital*, W.L. Hansen (ed.), (N.Y.; NBER, Columbia Univ. Press), 1970.

Hall, R.E., »Wages, Income and Hours of Work in the U.S. Labor Force,« in *Income Maintenance and Labor Supply*, G.C. Cain and H.W. Watts (eds.), (Chicago; Rand McNally), 1973.

Hanoch, G., »An Economic Analysis of Earnings and Schooling,« *Journal of Human Resources*, vol. 2, summer 1967, pp. 310−329.

Hildreth, C. and J.P. Houck, »Some Estimators for a Linear Model with Random Coefficients,« *Journal of the American Statistical Association*, vol. 63, June 1968, pp. 584−595.

Lindsay, C.M., »Measuring Human Capital Returns,« *Journal of Political Economy*, vol. 79, Nov./Dec. 1971, pp. 1195−1215.

Lucas, R.E.B., »Hedonic Wage Equations and Psychic Wages in the Returns to Schooling,« American Economic Review, Vol. 67, September 1977.

Lucas, R.E.B., »Is there a Human Capital Approach to Income Inequality?«, *Journal of Human Resources,* Vol. 12, Summer 1977, pp. 387−396.

Mincer, J., »The Distribution of Labor Incomes: A Survey,« *Journal of Economic Literature*, vol. 8, March 1970, pp. 1−26.

Mincer, J., *Schooling, Experience and Earnings*, (New York; NBER, Columbia Univ. Press), 1974.

Ravindran, A., »Algorithm 431: A Computer Routine for Quadratic and Linear Programming Problems,« *Communications of the Association of Computer Machinery*, vol. 15, September 1972, pp. 818−820.

Swamy, P.A.V.B., *Statistical Inference in Random Coefficient Regression Models*, (Berlin; Springer-Verlag), 1971.

Theil, H. and L.B.M. Mennes, *Multiplicative Randomness in Time Series Regression Analysis*, Mimeographed Report No. 5901 of the Econometric Institute of the Netherlands School of Economics, 1959.

Welch, F., »Black-White Differences in Returns to Schooling,« *American Economic Review*, vol. 63, Dec. 1973, pp. 893−907.

Zvi Griliches
Earnings of Very Young Men*

This paper has three purposes: (1) to replicate earlier results (Griliches, 1976) on newer data; (2) to discuss the distribution of earnings as against that of wage rates (covered in the earlier paper); and, (3) to outline a model for the analysis of time series on individuals, to be pursued further in subsequent papers.

I In recent years I have been analyzing the data collected by the National Longitudinal Survey of Young Men in some detail (cf. Griliches 1976, 1977 and Chamberlain and Griliches, 1975). In this survey, a random sample of about 5,000 young men was interviewed in 1966, followed up annually through 1971, and bi-annually thereafter[1]. At the moment only the 1966 through 1970 Surveys are publicly available[2]. Besides the usual economic and demographic variables, a test of the »knowledge of the world of work« was administered at the time of the initial interview (1966) and IQ test scores were collected from the high schools of the respondents. I have interpreted the first test (KWW) as a test of »late« ability and the second (IQ) as a test of »early« ability. Unfortunately, the latter tests are unavailable for about a third of the sample, including all those who did not continue school beyond the 9th grade.

From our point of view, the basic difficulty with this sample is its extreme youth. As of 1969 (the data base used in the earlier papers) close to half of the total sample were still in school. Moreover, those who were out of school and working were only about 22 years old, on average, and had only an average of four years of work experience.

With the availability of the 1970 Survey of these same Young Men, their average age rises by a whole year (to 23) and their average work experience to 4.5 years. It is thus of some interest to see if the conclusions of the earlier papers still hold as these Young Men age (if only slightly).

Table 1 presents the characteristics of 1970 samples: one unweighted and comparable to that reported in the earlier paper (Griliches, 1976) the other limited to a subsample with good income data and weighted to reflect the sampling scheme of the survey. Table 2 presents the regression results for 1970 with the logarithm of the wage rate (LW) as the dependent variable. They are essentially similar to those reported earlier: given our large sample size, the introduction of ability measures (KWW or IQ) is statistically significant, but does not really contribute much to reducing the unexplained variation in wage rates. The change in R^2 is .01 or less. When the early ability measure (IQ) is introduced, the change in the schooling coefficient is about .006. Whether that is a large number or not depends on the base used for comparison. Holding age constant this is

Table 1: Characteristics of Various Sub-samples of Not-Enrolled in School Young Men in 1970 from the National Longitudinal Survey. Means, Proportions, and (Standard Deviations).

Variable	Unweighted N=2136	Good IQ N=1395	Weighted Fuller time workers N=1735
Age	23.0 (3.3)	23.4 (3.1)	23.8 (3.0)
SC	11.0 (2.5)	12.7 (2.0)	12.3 (2.5)
EXP	4.5 (3.3)	4.3 (2.9)	5.0 (3.1)
IQ	99.0* (15.3)	99.0 (15.3)	100.8* (14.0)
DIQ	.35	0	.27
KWW	33.2 (8.9)	35.6 (7.8)	35.6 (8.1)
LWW			3.89 (.197)
LHWU			3.76 (.134)
LW	5.70 (.440)	5.80 (.413)	5.81 (.412)
LY			8.80 (.530)
FOMY 14	5080 (1943)	5220 (1810)	5181 (1786)
BLACK	.262	.166	.102
RNS	.396	.312	.324
SMSA	.624	.650	.632
MRT	.61	.64	.72
UNION	.17	.19	.20
HEALTH	.08	.09	.08

* Good IQ portion only

Table 2: Not Enrolled NLS Young Men in 1970 — Wage Equations (LW Dependent)

Equation No.	Coefficients (t—ratios) of SC	KWW	IQ	Other Variables in Equations	R² (SEE)
A N = 2 1 3 6					
1.	0.041 (12.99)			AGE, RN	.373 (.349)
2.	0.028 (7.77)	0.0081 (6.95)		AGE, RN	.387 (.345)
3.	0.073 (21.71)			Cubic in Exper, AFEXP, RN	.3976 (.342)
4.	0.058 (13.88)	0.0073 (6.31)		Cubic in Exper,AFEXP, RN	.408 (.339)
5.	0.059 (14.35)	0.0074 (6.39)		XBT, AFEXP, RN	.402 (.341)
6.	0.068 (18.04)		0.0020 (3.02)	XBT, AFEXP, RN, DIQ	.395 (.343)
7.	0.071 (21.71)			XBT, AFEXP, RN, CS	.431 (.332)
8.	0.065 (17.40)		0.0020 (3.20)	XBT, AFEXP, RN, CS, DIQ	.435 (.331)
9.	0.065 (16.00)		0.0017 (2.51)	XBT, AFEXP, RN, BKG, DIQ	.399 (.342)
B Good IQ subsample N=1395					
1.	.078 (16.1)			RN, XBT, AFEXP	0.313 (.343)
2.	.063 (10.8)	.0071 (4.80)		RN, XBT, AFEXP	0.324 (.341)
3.	.072 (13.4)		.0019 (2.66)	RN, XBT, AFEXP	0.316 (.343)
4.	.069 (12.8)		.0017 (2.26)	RN, XBT, AFEXP, CS BLACK	0.361 (.332)
5.	.063 (11.3)		.0015 (2.04)	RN, XBT, AFEXP, CS, BKG	0.367 (.331)

Notes to Table 1:

Age — in years in 1970

SC — years of school completed

EXP — work experience as of 1970, in years

IQ — score on IQ type tests, collected from the high school last attended by the respondent

DIQ — IQ missing

KWW — Score on the »Knowledge of the World of Work« test, administered in 1966

LWW — Logarithm of weeks worked during the previous year

LHWU — Logarithm of usual hours worked per week on current or last job

LW — Logarithm of the wage rate per hour (in cents) on the current or last job

LY — Logarithm of respondent's earnings from all jobs and self-employment during the previous year

FOMY 14 — Occupation of father or head of household when respondent was 14, scaled by the median earnings of all U.S. males in this occupation in 1959.

BLACK — respondent black

RNS — Region now South

SMSA — Currently in SMSA

MRT — Married, whether living together or seperated

UNION — Member of union in 1969 *and* 1970 job same as 1969

HEALTH — Health in 70 limits work

Fuller time workers subsample: Excludes those with earnings less than $ 1,000, less than 30 weeks worked, less than 30 hours per week worked usually, and those with less than one-half year of work experience. Weighted inversely to the probability of being included in the sample.

Notes to Table 2:

RN — Region Now consists of SMSA, RNS, and BRNS (Black and Region Now South)

AFEXP — Years served in the armed forces

CS — Current situation; consists of UNION, MRT, and HEALTH

· BKG — Background; consists of FOMY 14 (father's occupation when 14, scaled by 1959 median occupational income), FED (father's education), MED (mother's education), SIBLINGS (number of), TOGETHER (father and mother living together with R when 14), CULTURE (an index, 0–3, indicating the presence of newspapers, books, or library cards at home), and dummy variables for missing observations on FOMY 14, FED, and MED.

See the Notes to Table 1 for definitions of the other variables.

close to 15 percent of the original schooling coefficient (.041). Holding the more relevant concept of work experience constant the same .006 change accounts for less than 10 percent of the original schooling coefficient (.071 or .077). Using the late ability (KWW) measure, the change in the schooling coefficient is about twice as large. But that is not the appropriate variable to hold constant, since it is clear that it itself is affected by schooling (at least as of the 1966 test date). Allowing for such an effect (the indirect effect of schooling on LW via KWW) narrows down the difference between these two estimates greatly.

The »early ability« regressions give a schooling coefficient of about .07 and an IQ coefficient of .002, implying that a one standard deviation increase in schooling (holding work experience constant) would increase the wage rate by about 18 percent while a similar one standard deviation increase in IQ would only result in 3 percent increase in wage rates. Since it is harder presumably to change IQ than schooling, schooling does appear to remain a major avenue for reducing *systematic* wage differences between various groups in the society[3].

A similar story can be told about the various family background variables. While they are important determinants of who gets how much schooling, their major effect is via schooling. Given our large samples, adding them to the other variables results in some significant coefficients but leads to very littly improvement on fit: the standard error of estimate goes down by only .001 (regressions A.5 vs A.9 or B.4 vs B.5).

Column 1 of Table 3 presents details on one of the better fitting equations (B.4). Several items are worth noting: the overall black coefficient is small and not significant but being black in the South (BRNS) is still quite costly (−.17). Among the more important variables is being married (+.13) or being a member of a union (+.16). Work experience is quite important. Given our functional form (XBT = exponent −.1 experience), its effect declines slowly (an additional year of experience increases wages by 6, 4, 2 and 1 percent after 1, 5, 10, or 20 years of earlier work experience respectively).

Since an additional year of schooling costs our young men 0.7 years of work experience on average, the net rate of return to schooling (ignoring returns from more employment per year) rises from about zero at the date of entry into the labor force to about .05 after twenty years of work experience[4].

II The results discussed above focus on wage rates as the »rental price« of human capital, evading thereby the necessity to deal with issues of labor force participation and leisure-labor choices. But much of the return to schooling and possibly much of the discrimination of blacks depends on the access to good jobs, jobs with a higher intensity of work and a lower experience of unemployment. Looking solely at wage rates misses some of this and may result in a misleading account of the total returns to schooling, ability, or family background.

Ideally one would estimate a complete model, explaining jointly both the wage rate received by an individual and his supply of labor (over the year and within a week). Such an endeavor (Hanoch, 1975; Heckman, 1976) is beyond the scope of this paper. Instead I will present several semi-reduced form estimates, trying to account for the contribution of schooling both via weeks and hours worked and via the wage rate received per hour. Unfortunately, the quality of the data will not allow us to distinguish clearly between these various effects.

Table 3: Detailed Results for Selected Wage and Earnings Functions: Not Enrolled NLS Young Men, 1970

Coefficient of (and t–ratio)	LW dependent		LY dependent – weighted: N=1735		
	Unweighted[1] N=1395	Unweighted[2] N=1735	1	2[3]	3[3]
SC	.069 (12.8)	.068 (16.7)	.086 (17.0)	.082 (16.0)	.027 (6.2)
XBT	−.659 (10.7)	−.673 (12.4)	−1.25 (18.6)	−1.17 (17.4)	−.252 (8.3)
AFEXP	.040 (1.7)	.019 (.8)	.006 (.2)	.001 (.0)	−.012 (.5)
IQ	.0017 (2.3)	.0018 (2.5)	.0011 (1.3)	.0010 (1.1)	−.0002 (.3)
BLACK	−.046 (1.2)	−.062 (1.3)	−.128 (2.2)	−.112 (2.0)	−.050 (1.1)
BRNS	−.167 (3.4)	−.138 (2.5)	−.105 (1.5)	−.113 (1.6)	−.000 (.0)
RNS	−.057 (2.5)	−.094 (5.0)	−.088 (3.7)	−.098 (4.2)	−.029 (1.5)
SMSA	.151 (7.7)	.159 (9.6)	.145 (7.1)	.154 (7.5)	.047 (2.8)
MRT	.128 (5.8)	.135 (6.4)	.244 (10.0)	.231 (9.6)	.116 (5.9)
UNION	.163 (7.0)	.145 (7.2)	.168 (6.7)	.162 (6.6)	.061 (3.1)
HEALTH	−.058 (1.8)	−.071 (2.0)	−.071 (2.0)	−.061 (1.8)	−.008 (.3)
LHWU				.296 (3.4)	.797 (11.1)
LWW				.652 (6.5)	.635 (7.9)
LW					.779 (31.6)
R^2	.361	.395	.433	.453	.654
SEE	.332	.322	.401	.394	.314

1. Good IQ subsample
2. Fuller income subsample. This and the subsequent regressions include a dummy variable (DIQ) for observations with imputed (originally missing) IQ values.
3. In addition to DIQ includes also a dummy variable for observations which reported more than 60 usual work hours per week, which were reduced to 60 for computing LHWU.

Table 4 presents first the reduced and semi-reduced form equation estimates for the major variables of interest (SC, EXP, LW, LWW, LHWU, and LY), while Table 5 repeats the major equations of Table 2, but now using LY (the logarithm of total earnings in the previous year from all jobs and self-employment) as the dependent variable[5].

Turning to Table 5 first, we see that in this age range, the effects of IQ on earnings are even smaller than its effects on wage rates. The change in the schooling cofficient with the introduction of IQ is about the same as in Table 2, about .007, though the estimated »percentage ability bias« is now much smaller, because of the higher base. The estimated schooling coefficients are somewhat higher than those in Table 2, presumably because they capture some of the schooling associated effects of differences in intensity of work and overtime, not already reflected in the weeks worked variable.

More interesting contrasts can be found in Table 4, which presents most of the ingredients for a complete model of status achievement. The first column shows the obvious relation of completed schooling to family background and

Table 4: Recursive Equations: 1970 Not Enrolled NLS Young Men, N = 1735

Independent Variables	Dependent Variable					LY		
	SC	EXP	LW 1	LW 2	LWW[1]	1	2	3
FOMY14*	.114 (3.0)	−.047 (2.2)	.023 (4.3)	.022 (4.1)	−.003 (2.1)	.019 (2.8)	.021 (3.0)	.022 (3.4)
FED	.105 (5.6)	−.046 (3.4)	−.004 (1.2)	−.006 (1.7)	.000 (.3)	−.004 (.8)	−.002 (.6)	−.003 (.8)
MED	.128 (6.5)	.029 (2.1)	.009 (2.5)	.004 (1.1)	.000 (.4)	.010 (2.2)	.005 (1.1)	.005 (1.1)
SIBLINGS	−.046 (4.7)	−.020 (1.4)	−.004 (1.1)	−.000 (.0)	.000 (.3)	−.005 (1.0)	−.001 (.2)	−.001 (.03)
CULTURE	.490 (8.2)	.058 (1.4)	.008 (.7)	−.010 (.9)	−.008 (2.6)	−.009 (.7)	−.026 (1.9)	−.018 (1.3)
BLACK	.627 (2.4)	−.472 (2.5)	−.012 (.2)	−.014 (.3)	−.027 (1.9)	−.099 (1.6)	−.082 (1.4)	−.065 (1.1)
IQ	.048 (12.3)	−.001 (.2)	.0030 (4.1)	.0016 (2.2)	.0002 (1.1)	.0016 (1.8)	.0008 (.9)	.0006 (.7)
SC		−.729 (42.4)		.061 (9.7)	.003 (2.6)		.078 (9.9)	.067 (8.5)
XBT				−.709 (6.6)			−1.336 (9.9)	−1.134 (8.4)
LWW								.800 (7.6)
Other variables in equation	Missing data dummies. RN, Age, Age Sq.	Same	Same	Same plus AFEXP	Same	Same	Same plus AFEXP	Same plus AFEXP
R²	.469	.824	.330	.365	.041	.351	.391	.411
SEE	1.84	1.31	.339	.330	.096	.430	.416	.410

* In $ 1,000

Table 5: Earnings Equations (LY Dependent)
Not Enrolled NLS Young Men, N = 1735, weighted.

Equation No.	Coefficients (t—ratios) of			Other Variables in Equation	R^2 (SEE)
	SC	IQ	BLACK		
1.	.099 (21.1)		−.112 (1.9)	RN, XBT, AFEXP	.376 .420
2.	.093 (17.7)	.0010 (1.1)	−.0096 (1.6)	Same plus DIQ	.379 .419
3.	.094 (19.9)		−.097 (1.7)	Same, plus LWW	.394 .414
4.	.087 (16.7)	.0008 (.9)	−.083 (1.4)	Same plus LWW and DIQ	.397 .413
5.	.082 (16.2)	.0010 (1.1)	−.116 (2.1)	RN, XBT, AFEXP, LWW, CS	.447 .396

IQ. Two things are worth noting, however: 1) only about half of the observed variance in completed schooling is explained by a rather long list of family background variables or IQ. Either these variables are not very good measures of such vague concepts as »parental status« or »ability«, or there are other major forces determining the distribution of schooling which we haven't identified yet. 2) For given parental background and test scores, young blacks were actually completing *more* schooling in the late 1960's than their white counterparts.

The experience equation (in the second column of Table 4) indicates that an additional year of schooling postpones work experience by about .7 years on average. Other things equal, youths with well-to-do fathers seem to have accumulated less work.experience. Blacks also seem to acquire less work experience and rather significantly so. The wage equations have been discussed already in the earlier section. It is worth noting however, that most of the family background effect and about half of the IQ effect on LW is transmitted via schooling. Only Father's Occupational Income (FOMY 14) remains statistically significant in both the LW and LY equations, when schooling and experience are accounted for. The effect is not very large (one standard deviation of parental status being equivalent to the effect of about .7 years of the son's schooling) and may be related to unaccounted for differences in school quality.

The number of weeks worked (and similarly for hours worked per week, not shown here) appears to be unrelated to most of the variables examined in this study. There is a faint indication that those with more schooling work a bit more per year and that both blacks and youths from well-to-do homes, work slightly less.

The earnings equations (summarized in the last three columns of Table 4), together with the weeks worked equation, indicate that family background and

IQ affect earnings via their effect on the supply of effort (or unemployment experience). The only exception, really, is the effect of being black. While not very significant statistically, it is on the order of 10 percent and appears to persist even after we have accounted for employment intensity as best as we can. This can be seen also in the last equation of Table 3, which also held the wage rate constant. If the timing of the variables were right, that equation should be an identity and none of the other variables (besides LWW, LHWU, and LW) should be significant. But LHWU stands for »usual« hours per week, not average annual, and LW stands for the wage rate on the current or last job, and is not the average annual wage rate. Thus, there must be significant errors in these variables (at least relative to their intended effect on LY). Nevertheless, the lack of fit is surprising. About a third of the reported earnings variance still remains unexplained.

The fact that being black, or being married, or having higher schooling has still a significant effect on earnings in 1970, net of the wage rate and weeks and hours worked, must imply a differential wage rate growth for some of these people in 1970, or a systematic discrepancy between »usual« and actual hours, and/or a differential access to overtime. To check out such leads further will require us to use the time series nature of these data more explicitly. This would allow us also to look further into the reasons for the observed lack of fit at the individual level. Currently, we are left with a standard deviation of the unexplained residuals of .3 or about 35 percent. That is quite large. It wouldn't loom as large, however, if the correlation over time in these residuals were very low. That's unlikey, but we don't really know yet how »permanent« such unexplained income or wage differences really are. The next section is intended to lay the groundwork for an attack on this problem.

III Very little has been done yet to utilize the time series nature of these observations (for exceptions, cf. Brown, 1976, and Lazear, 1974). There are several questions that can be asked here: (1) Can one define and detect some concept of »permanent income« so early in the career of these young men? (2) Are the theories of »on-the-job training« supported by such data? (3) Or more generally, what are the time series properties of wages and earnings at the individual level? Are they consistent with the »level« models reported on in this and earlier papers?

The first and perhaps simplest question to ask is do the equations estimated earlier survive first-differencing? Since only a few of the variables in these equations are likely to be changing over time, this comes down to asking are wage and earnings changes well explained by changes (and previous levels) in work experience and by reported changes in health. Next, one should ask whether the unexplained wage and earnings changes persist from year to year. Also, are they related to initial age, schooling or ability levels? If yes, this would imply that the coefficients of these variables in the level equations may be changing over time.

Since on-the-job training is actually unobservable it may be only weakly and fortuitously related to work experience as conventionally measured. Assuming that individuals optimize with respect to the range of on-the-job training opportunities, the resultant wage trajectories should reflect this type of behavior. To illustrate such an approach, I shall borrow a very simple model from Rosen (1973), which can be written as

$$x_{it} = a_i + \gamma x_{it-1}$$

where x_{it} is the permanent change in the earnings of individual i during the time period t, a_i is a *negative* constant related to the unobserved initial human capital (or ability) level and γ is related to the discount rate used in the optimization process $[\gamma = (1+r)^2]^6$. We can observe only actual earnings, not permanent ones, and they are affected by random and time independent transitory components v_t. Then, in terms of the *change* in observable earnings or wage rates ($y_{it} = x_{it} + v_{it} - v_{it-1}$),

$$y_{it} = a_i + \gamma y_{it-1} + v_t - v_{t-1} - \gamma(v_{t-1} - v_{t-2})$$

where the v's are transitory errors in the earnings levels, implying a negative correlation for the residuals in the earnings change equation. The estimation problem here is twofold: first, the a_i's are unobservable and, second, the y's are subject to correlated measurement error. If we have a long enough time series on individuals this presents little problem. We can difference out the a_i's (i.e. use within individuals estimates) and use y_{t-3} as an instrumental variable, since the $(v_t - v_{t-1}) - \gamma(v_{t-1} - v_{t-2})$ transitory errors are moving averages which are uncorrelated three terms apart[7]. This could be implemented on the NLS data set, since it contains five years of data for a subset of young men and hence four consecutive income changes.

Alternatively, for a given experience category (say all those who had less than a year of experience in 1966) one could write the set of »reduced form« equations (solving out y_{t-1}) as

$$y_3 = \gamma^3 x_0 + (1+\gamma+\gamma^2)a + v_3 - v_2$$
$$y_2 = \gamma^2 x_0 + (1+\gamma)\quad a + v_2 - v_1$$
$$y_1 = \gamma x_0 + \qquad\quad a + v_1 - v_0$$
$$y_0 = x_0 + \qquad\qquad\quad v_0 - v_{-1}$$

The variance-covariance matrix of the observable wage or earnings changes is then

$$\text{Eyy}^| = \text{Var}(y) = \gamma_1 \gamma^|_1 \sigma^2_{x_0} + \gamma_2 \gamma^|_2 \sigma^2_a + \begin{bmatrix} 2 & -1 & 0 & 0 \\ & 2 & -1 & 0 \\ & & 2 & -1 \\ & & & 2 \end{bmatrix} \sigma^2_v$$

Where $\gamma^|_1 = (\gamma^3, \gamma^2, \gamma, 1)$, $\gamma^|_2 = (1+\gamma+\gamma^2, 1+\gamma, 0)$, and we have assumed that a and x_0 are independently distributed. Relaxing the last assumption would add a $2\gamma_1\gamma_2\sigma_{x_0a}$ term. There are only 4(γ, $\sigma^2_{x_0}$, σ^2_a, σ^2_v) or 5 (adding σ_{x_0a}) unknown parameters to be estimated on the basis of 10 observed moments. This model is highly non-linear but should be susceptible to estimation. Similar moment matrices could be constructed for different experience categories and the results pooled using the estimated precision matrices to weight the various samples. Before we go that far, however, we should use simpler methods to determine what is going on in these data and whether they are at all consistent with this type of model.

Notes

* I am indebted to the NIE (Grant No. NE–6–00–3–020) and NSF (Grant No. SOC73–05374–A01) for financial support and to Bronwyn Hall and Stephen Messner for research assistance.

[1] See Griliches (1976) and Parnes et al (1964—1974) for more details on these data. They are based on a national sample of the civilian non-institutional population of males who where 14 to 24 years old in 1966. Blacks were oversampled in a 3 to 1 ratio. The original sample consisted of 5,225 individuals of whom 3,734 were white. By 1970 about 24 percent of the original sample was lost, 12 percent of it only temporarily (to the army).

[2] The 1971 and 1973 surveys were released in late 1976.

[3] These results do not allow for errors in the ability measures or in reported schooling. This topic is explored at some length in my earlier papers where it is shown that when an allowance is made for errors in *both* IQ and schooling, the contrasts presented in the text are even stronger.

[4] This is a very rough estimate since it extrapolates far beyond the range of our sample.

[5] These regressions (as distinct from those presented in Table 2) are weighted by the sample weights of the respective observations in the Survey. This minimizes somewhat the overemphasis on blacks and the South in the unweighted sample, but doesn't have much of an effect otherwise.

[6] The following passage is a revision of the argument first presented in Griliches (1974), p. 46.

[7] Actually, we have a version of the Balestra-Nerlove (1966) problem here and a more complicated estimation procedure may be called for.

References

(1) Brown, Charles, 1976. »A Model of Opitmal Human Capital Accumulation and the Wages of Young High School Graduates«, *Journal of Political Economy,* 84(2), 299—316.

(2) Balestra, P. and M. Nerlove, 1966. »Pooling Cross Section and Time Series Data in the Estimation of a Dynamic Model: The Demand for Natural Gas«, *Econometrica,* 34, 585—612.

(3) Chamberlain, G. and Z. Griliches, 1975. »Unobservables with a Variance-Components Structure: Ability, Schooling and the Economic Success of Brothers«, *International Economic Review,* Vol. 16 (2), 422—449.

(4) Griliches, Z., 1974. »Errors in Variables and Other Unobservables«, *Econometrica,* Vol. 42 (6), 971—998.
Griliches, Z., 1976. »Wages of Very Young Men«, *Journal of Political Economy,* 84 (4, Part II), 69—86.
Griliches, Z., 1977. »Estimating the Returns to Schooling: Some Econometric Problems«, *Econometrica,* 45 (1), 1—22.

(5) Lazear, E., 1976. »Age, Experience, and Wage Growth«, *American Economic Review,* Vol. 66 (4), 548—558.

(6) Parnes, H.S., et al, 1970—73. *Career Thresholds,* Vols. 1—4, Center for Human Resource Research, Ohio State University, Columbus, Ohio.

(7) Rosen, S., 1973. »Income Generating Functions and Capital Accumulation«, HIER Discussion Paper No. 306, Cambridge, MA.

P. Taubman, J. Behrman and T. Wales *

The Roles of Genetics and Environment in the Distribution of Earnings

Much research on the distribution of earnings is based on a model in which each individual receives compensation equal to his marginal product, adjusted for investments in on-the-job training[1]. The natural question to ask is why marginal products differ across individuals. In general people argue that marginal product depends on skills which are »produced« by combining innate or genetic endowments with various inputs provided by, for example, family, friends, schools and the workplace. Meade, for instance, uses this framework. Advocates of the human capital model, such as Becker and Mincer, also use the same framework, though their interest is often in determining the optimal amount to invest in schooling or child care and the effects of these investments on compensation.

In this paper we will be concerned with two issues. The first is obtaining unbiased or consistent estimates of the effects on compensation of schooling and other variables for which we have measures. The second is partitioning the variance of earnings into that arising from the family and that outside the family. We will also try to break up the family effect into genetic endowments and family environment. As the reader will discover, we are able to estimate a lower bound to the total family effects and an upper bound to the genetic effects.

There are several cautions the reader should keep in mind. First, since the sample used is not a random drawing of the population, it is possible that our results do not generalize to the U.S. population. Moreover, our results are based on white males born between 1917 and 1927. It is possible that the mean and variance of some important but unmeasured variables such as »family environment« are different for other cohorts[2].

The results in this paper are obtained by using data on twins with a variety of techniques. We will first introduce our model and indicate why twins can be used

* This paper draws heavily on a previous paper by the same authors. Taubman is given first billing here because he did the rewriting. We would like to thank the Medical Follow-up Agency for making the data available and for conducting the surveys and Dr. Norman, Dr. Hrubec, Mr. Simon and Miss Hanamura for their assistance. Professors Chamberlain, Goldberger, Griliches and Jencks have provided many helpful suggestions and corrected numerous errors. Barbara Atrostic and Shah Fardoust supplied able research assistance. The research in this paper was supported by NSF Grant SOC73–05543.

to solve these problems. We will then introduce the techniques to be used. Subsequently, we present and discuss the sample and present our results.

1. The Model

While ultimately we will estimate a model which will contain equations for schooling, initial occupation, occupation in 1967 and earnings in 1973, most of our interest will focus on the earnings equation, which we will discuss in some detail here.

As noted earlier, we will assume that a person receives a real wage rate equal to his marginal produce which is dependent upon his skills.

$$(1) \qquad w_i = MP_i = f(K_{1i}...K_{Mi})$$

In this equation a person has M skills which can influence his marginal product. These M skills may include many different types, such as intelligence, knowledge, memory, physical strength, dexterity, motivation, confidence, leadership and dependability.

As is the case with most, if not all, samples, we have little information on skills such as those given above. Thus following the example of other studies we assume that each skill is produced by combining the R various innate or genetic endowments with T various environmental factors.

$$(2) \qquad K_d = g_d(G_r, N_t) \qquad \begin{aligned} d &= 1 \ldots M \\ r &= 1 \ldots R \\ t &= 1 \ldots T \end{aligned}$$

For simplicity we will assume that each skill production function is log linear[3]. The N_t will include but not be limited to such elements as schooling, family income and number of siblings—— variables we can either measure directly or construct proxies. But most of the N and nearly all the Gs will not be measured. Suppose for expositional ease that everyone is the same age and that the only measured element of the N_T is schooling. Then we can substitute the skill production function for each of the M skills and obtain an earnings equation such as

$$(4) \qquad \ln w = a + bS + cG + dN + u$$

where G is an overall genetic index and N is an index which includes all *unmeasured* environmental effects except random events which are included in u.

Similarly, we can find an equation for hours worked which depends on w, S, G and N. We can then use the identity that $Y = wH$ to obtain an equation like (4) but with ln Y as the dependent variable. In this paper we will estimate this equation for earnings but for reasons that will become clearer below, we also need to estimate a model with additional dependent variables and with additional genetic and evironmental indices.

The general model we wish to estimate is given in Table 1. For simplicity in presentation we have assumed that there are no exogenous measured genetic or environmental variables. The model is easily modified to include such measures. The left-hand part of the table contains so-called structural equations, which may be thought of as solutions of supply and demand equations, while the right-hand side contains reduced-form equations[4].

Table 1 Model

Structural Equations	Reduced Form
1) $Y_1 = S = aG + bN + u$	$Y_1 = S = aG + bN + u$
2) $Y_2 = OC_i = c'G + d'N + eG_1 + fN_1 + gS + u_1$	$Y_2 = OC_i = cG + dN + eG_1 + fN_1 + gu + u_1$
3) $Y_3 = OC_{67} = h'G + j'N + k'G_1 + mG_2 + n'N_1 + pN_2 + qOC_i + rS + u_2$	$Y_3 = OC_{67} = hG + jN + kG_1 + mG_2 + nN_1 + pN_2 + qu_1 + ru + u_2$
4) $Y_4 = \ln Y_{73} = s'G + t'N + v'G_1 + w'G_2 + xG_3 + y'N_1 + z'N_2 + \alpha N_3 + \beta OC_{67} + \gamma S + u_3$	$Y_4 = \ln Y_{73} = sG + tN + vG_1 + wG_2 + xG_3 + yN_1 + zN_2 + \alpha N_3 + \delta u + \lambda u_1 + \beta u_2 + u_3$

where
$c = c' + ag$ $k = k' + qe$ $y = y' + \beta n + \gamma b$

$d = d' + bg$ $n = n' + qf$ $z = z' + \beta p$

$h = h' + ra + qc$ $s = s' + \beta h + \gamma a$ $\delta = \gamma + \beta r$

$j = j' + rb + qd$ $t = t' + \beta j + \gamma b$ $\lambda = \beta q$

                  $v = v' + \beta k$

                  $w = w' + \beta m$

S = years of schooling
OC_i = Status (Duncan Scale) on initial occupation
OC_{67} = Status (Duncan Scale) on occupation in 1967
$\ln Y_{73}$ = natural log of 1973 earnings

To allow for different Gs and Ns affecting Y_1 through Y_4, we include four genetic and four environmental indices ($G...G_3$, $N...N_3$). Since an index can be written as $\Sigma_j b_j X_j$, we can construct each index such that all the X_j appear in each of the four genetic indices, but their weights, which may be zero, differ. It is easy to demonstrate that at most four separate indices are needed for our four equation model and that it is to a certain extent arbitrary which indices are included in which equation. The same statements hold for the environmental indices.

As noted earlier, in our earnings equation we assume that schooling, family and other environments and genetic endowments are combined to produce skills which determine a person's marginal product. Occupational status is included in the equation, partly to capture the level of general and specific training given in various occupations, partly to capture trade-offs for occupational nonpecuniary costs and rewards and partly to capture windfall gains and losses for unexpected shifts in equilibrium wages for various occupations[5].

In some studies, occupational status is used as a proxy for annual or lifetime earnings. Since we have the status measures earlier in the earnings life cycle, our model is consistent with that view. We think, however, that a somewhat broader view in which people choose occupations to maximize their expected utility whose arguments include the wage and nonpecuniary payments from an occupation is appropriate[6].

The years of schooling equation also incorporates supply and demand considerations. Becker has shown how family environment and innate abilities will affect the individual's demand for schooling. On the supply side, schools often select or reject students on the basis of ability.

These equations include four genetic and four environmental indices, all of which are not measured. In the next section we will indicate why data on twins can be used to control for and estimate the effects of these unmeasured variables.

2. Twins, Genetics and Environments

By genetic endowments (G), we mean the innate capabilities that are based on a person's genes, half of which are contained in the egg and the other half in the sperm[7]. Environment (N) includes all other determinants of skills, including prenatal development. The level of some elements in an environment can be chosen by an individual or his parents, while others may not be subject to choice.

Twin Types

Males and females normally have 23 pairs of chromosomes. The genes are located on the chromosomes. In the population each gene may come in one form such as A or in many varieties A, B..., Z. In an individual location there are two genes (one contributed by each parent) which may be the same or different, e.g., AA or AB. We will assume that each skill or trait is influenced by many genes, some of which have more than one variety. Only a randomly determined member of each parents' gene pair or chromosome is contained in egg or sperm, each of which is a gamete of one parent. But once the egg is fertilized, i.e., the two gametes combine, the two genes are merged to form the individual's gene pool.

There are two types of twins—— monozygotic (MZ) and dizygotic (DZ). The MZs, often known as »identical«, are the result of the splitting of an already fertilized egg, while the DZs, or »fraternal« twins, are the result of two different eggs fertilized by two different sperm. Thus, DZ pairs do not have the same genetic composition although they will be more alike than randomly drawn individuals. The MZ pairs, however, have the same genetic makeup because each piece of the split fertilized egg contains all and only the genetic information of the original fertilized egg (barring mutations)[8].

3. Controlling for Genetic Endowments and Family Environment

In previous studies of the effects of education on earnings, it has not been possible to control completely for the other determinants of earnings that might be correlated with schooling. With twins, however, it is possible to eliminate genetic differences for the identical twins and common background for both types by studying the within pair differences in earnings.

To compare the estimates obtained when using individuals and within pair differences, let us order individuals within each pair randomly, e.g. alphabetically, and denote the within pair difference by Δ. We can write a within pair equation corresponding to (4) as

4a) $\qquad \Delta \ln Y = a\Delta S + b\Delta G + c\Delta N + \Delta u$

We can estimate both 4 and 4a and compare both OLS estimates of a^9. Denote the estimate from equation 4 as a_1 and that from 4a as a_2. Using standard methods, it can be shown that

5) $\qquad plim\ (\hat{a}_1) = a + \dfrac{plim\ cov(S, bG + cN + u)}{plim\ var\ (S)}$

6) $\qquad plim\ (\hat{a}_2) = a + \dfrac{plim\ cov\ (\Delta S,\ b\Delta G + c\Delta N + \Delta u)}{plim\ var\ (\Delta S)}$

As is well known, 5 yields biased estimates if plim cov $(S, bG + cN + u)$ is nonzero, which is generally thought to be the case for the earnings, schooling model.

For MZ twins ΔG is zero. Making the usual assumption that Δu is uncorrelated with ΔS, plim $\hat{a}_2$ will be unbiased provided either c is zero or ΔN is uncorrelated with ΔS. The first condition means that the differences in MZ brothers' environments have no direct effect on earnings, though they may affect schooling. The second condition means that the differences in environment that determine earnings are not correlated with schooling. The latter condition may prevail if N consists of adult environment such as on-the-job training. If the bias in $\hat{a}_1$ arises only because of genetics or common environment, $\hat{a}_2$ will be a consistent estimate.

For DZ pairs, ΔG is not zero and $\hat{a}_2$ will not be consistent if plim cov(ΔS, $b\Delta G$) is not zero. It is interesting to note that the bias in $\hat{a}_2$ can be larger than that for $\hat{a}_1$ because both the numerator and the denominator in the plim expression change when we go from levels to within pair differences. It is possible to determine if genetics should be controlled for by testing the null hypothesis that the MZ and DZ within equations are the same. This test includes in its maintained hypothesis that plim cov (ΔS, $c\Delta N$) is zero. If this is not true, it might explain why the two within equations were different. Fortunately, this latter possibility can be examined within the context of the latent variable models described below.

4. Variance Components Model

In this section we will describe a variance components model that is often used to analyze twin data. We will perform this analysis on an equation which, with an appropriate rescaling, can be expressed as

(7) $\qquad Y = G + N$

We can write the variance for individuals as

(8) $\qquad \sigma^2 = \sigma_G^2 + \sigma_N^2 + 2\sigma_{GN}$

Now denote an MZ brother by an asterisk. We can then calculate cross sib covariances as

(9) $\quad \sigma_{YY^*} = \sigma_{GG^*} + \sigma_{NN^*} + 2\sigma_{NG^*}$

Since for MZ twins $G^* = G$, we can rewrite this as

(10) $\quad \sigma_{YY^*} = \sigma_G^2 + \sigma_{NN^*} + 2\sigma_{NG}$

we can thus calculate that

(11) $\quad \sigma_Y^2 - \sigma_{YY^*} = \sigma_N^2 - \sigma_{NN^*} = (1-\rho^*)\sigma_N^2$ where $\rho^* = \sigma_{NN^*}/\sigma_N^2$

Thus the expected value of the difference between the individual and MZ cross sib covariance is the additive effect on Y of noncommon environment. Common environment presumably arises because of treatment in the family, neighborhood, school and elsewhere. Since the neighborhood and school are chosen by the family, it does not seem unreasonable to assume that the family influence is quite considerable in these common environmental effects. However, $\sigma_Y^2 - \sigma_{YY^*}$ is an upper bound for nonfamily environment since parents may treat twins differently in relevant respects, an issue to which we will return shortly.

If we denote a DZ brother by a prime, we can also calculate

(12) $\quad \sigma_{YY}{}' = \sigma_{GG}{}' + \sigma_{NN}{}' + 2\sigma_{NG}{}'$

Since for DZ twins, G does not equal $G{}'$, other assumptions have to be made for us to be able to estimate other parameters. For example, $\sigma_{GG}{}' = 1/2\, \sigma_G^2$ if all genetic effects are additive, if there is random mating, and if there are no sex linkages of genes. Also, $\sigma_{NN}{}' = \rho{}'\sigma_N^2$. Next, assume that $\rho^* = \rho{}' = \rho$. Finally, assume that $N = \rho N' + v$ and $E(G', v) = 0$, so that $\sigma_{GN'} = \rho\sigma_{GN}$. As we will stress in a moment, each of these assumptions are questionable, but even if they are true, the model still contains four parameters—— $\sigma_G^2, \sigma_N^2, \sigma_{NG}$, and ρ—— but only three observed statistics—— $\overset{\triangle}{\sigma_Y}, \sigma_{YY^*}$, and $\sigma_{YY}{}'$. Thus this model is underidentified.

Now let us consider these assumptions, beginning with those that yield $\sigma_{GG}{}' = 1/2\, \sigma_G^2$. Various studies have indicated that on some traits, there is nonrandom or assortive mating of parents. As long as people choose to mate on the basis of the observed traits, there will be correlation of their genes. Existing studies have shown positive assortative mating for measures of IQ and schooling and negative assortative mating for measures of personality such as extroversion. Nonadditive genetic effects encompass both dominant, recessive genes and the effect of one gene depending on the level of another gene. Examples of both types of nonadditive effects exist in the genetics literature.

The assumption that $\rho^* = \rho'$ has been questioned by a number of people. Evidence exists as in Koch that MZ twins are more likely to be dressed alike or treated alike in any on day than DZ twins. However, it has been argued that different observed parental treatment may indicate either that the parents of the DZ twins responded to the different genetically-based needs of the brothers or that it is because of their genes that the brothers selected different items from parental offerings[10]. Thus the observed differences in treatment are, in this view, due to genetic differences[11]. Moreover, concentrating on the day-to-day treatment of twins or on dressing alike may be less appropriate than the year or childhood-long average treatment and quality of clothes. In addition, it is possible that the dimensions of family environment that are important are values and attitudes inculcated by the same examples or good or bad nutrition offered jointly to both brothers.

However, some people still argue that σ_G^2 is zero and that $\sigma_{YY*} > \sigma_{YY'}$ only because $\rho^* > \rho'$. This view is difficult to accept since there are diseases that are caused by known genetic problems and result in mental retardation (if not treated) or are debilitating with respect to energy levels. Nevertheless, the general proposition that $\rho^* > \rho'$ may still be valid.

The assumption that $E(G',v)=0$ can be interpreted as one DZ brother's non-common environment being uncorrelated with his sib's genes. While this assumption may not be valid, it is not patently absurd. But note that this restriction has not been imposed on the MZ pairs.

5. Latent Variables and Indicators

A »latent« variable is defined as an unobserved variable which affects two or more observed variables, called »indicators«[12]. Under certain conditions, it is possible to estimate the effect of the latent variable. Chamberlain and Griliches have used the variance components model with brothers and have estimated family effects. They are not able to decompose family effects into genetic and environmental components.

Recently Behrman, Taubman and Wales have shown how maximum likelihood estimators can be developed for the model given in Table 1. Essentially, they augment a standard latent variable model with the variance component model (presented in the previous section) but modified so that for DZs $\sigma_{GG'}/\sigma_G^2$ and $\sigma_{GN'}$ are treated as parameters to be estimated.

Behrman, Taubman and Wales —— with heavy reliance on a paper by Chamberlain—— indicate what parameters in this model are identified under what conditions. In general the model given in Table 1 is underidentified. In the empirical section, we will estimate various models which impose different restrictions to identify or overidentify the model.

6. The Sample

In this study we will use the NAS-NRC twin sample, which is described in more detail in Taubman. Briefly, however, for this study we have a maximum of 2,478 *pairs* where each brother answered a questionnaire mailed in 1974[13]. The twins had to be born between 1917 and 1927, be white, have served at some point in the military and be alive in 1974. These last restrictions suggest an underrepresentation of people with low intelligence or education, or with poor mental and physical health as compared to the corresponding white male cohort. Even compared to a population of veterans, the respondents to our questionnaire have more earnings and education[14]. Regression estimates from stratified samples with nonpopulation weights still yield unbiased coefficients over the same sample space[15].

Table 2 Some Summary Statistics for Individuals in the NAS-NRC Sample (calculated separately for MZ's and DZ's)

	MZ's		DZ's	
	Mean	Variance	Mean	Variance
1973 annual earnings	18.4[a]	150[b]	18.1[a]	166[b]
ln 1973 annual earnings	9.67[a]	.28	9.64[a]	.32
1967 or 1972 occupational score[d]	50.4	472	49.8	445
Years of schooling	13.5	9.1	13.3	9.8
Initial full time civilian occupation[c,d]	36.7	610.	35.0	590,
Age	51.0	8.4	51.2	8.8
Mother's education years	10.0	9.6	9.7	11.9
Father's education years	9.3	12.6	9.1	14.8
Father's occupational status[d]	29.6	532	28.6	503
% Catholic	26	19	23	18
% Jewish	4	4	5	5
% Other non-Protestant	2	2	3	3
Number of siblings alive 1940	2.6	4.9	3.0	5.6
Number of older siblings alive 1940	1.6	3.3	2.1	3.7
Number of pairs	1019		907	

Note: Calculations are for those for whom earnings are non-zero for both brothers. For other variables, if one brother answered and the other did not, non-respondent is set equal to his brother. If both did not answer, both are set at mean or put in »other category«. For mother and father data, if brothers' answers differ, mean of responses is used.

[a] Thousands of $ [b] Millions of $
[c] As recalled in 1974.   [d] Duncan Score

The means and variance of earnings, schooling and several other variables by twin types are given in Table 2. Our DZ twins come from families in which the parents have a bit less education and occupational status, and in which the number of siblings and older siblings are somewhat greater. These last two differences are statistically significant[16]. The religious distributions are also very similar for MZs and DZs, which is a bit surprising since we expected Catholics to have more children at older ages and thus to be a larger portion of the DZ pairs.

The means of schooling, initial and later occupational status and earnings are nearly the same across twin type although the variances differ by up to 10%[17].

The conclusion that MZ and DZs are random drawings from the same population is further strengthened by a comparison of the simple correlations given in Table 3[18]. The left-hand portion of that table treats both brothers as individuals and the results are close for MZs and DZs. The right-hand portion consists of cross sib correlations, defined for example as $\sigma_{SY}{}^{l}/\sigma_S\sigma_Y$ where $\sigma_{SY}{}^{l}$ is the covariance of one brother's years of schooling and his sib's ln of earnings. The cross sib correlations are uniformly lower than the comparable ones for individuals. The DZ cross sib correlations are uniformly lower than the comparable MZ ones.

Table 3 Individual and Cross-Sib Correlations

	Individuals				Cross–Sib			
	S	OC_i	OC_{67}	ln Y	S	OC_i	OC_{67}	ln Y
MZs								
S	1	.53	.54	.44	.76	.47	.44	.40
OC_i		1	.45	.35		.53	.35	.32
OC_{67}			1	.35			.43	.27
ln Y				1				.54
DZs								
S	1	53	51	44	.54	.37	.29	.29
OC_i		1	.43	.36		.33	.22	.22
OC_{67}			1	.35			.20	.19
ln Y				1				.30

Note: Correlations for individuals calculated as $\dfrac{\sigma_{xy}}{\sigma_x\sigma_y}$

Correlations for sibs calculated as $\dfrac{\sigma_{xy}{}^{l}}{\sigma_x\sigma_y}$

Note: Calculated for both brothers having nonzero earnings 1973. For other variables, missing observations are replaced with brother's values, or if both are missing, with the mean. Less than 20 people did not report years of schooling. About 500 people did not report initial occupation. About 800 people did not report 1967 occupation. A comparison of cross sib correlations for OC_{67} based only on people who reported indicates slightly smaller figures for MZs and DZs with the difference between the two cross sib correlations practically unchanged.

7. Regression Results

In this section we will present a variety of regressions for the log of 1973 earnings. The various questions we will explore include: What are the effects of education and related variables? What are the effects of various proxies for family environment and gentic endowments? To what extent do the variables affect earnings through education? How adequate are these available proxies for controlling genetic endowments and family environment?

Table 4 contains reduced form and so-called structural equations for $\ln y_{73}$ estimated for all individuals with nonzero earnings. In equation 1 the only independent variable is years of schooling, which has a highly significant coefficient of .08. (Probably because the men are about 50 years old, this coefficient is unchanged if age is included.) It is encouraging to note that essentially the same results are obtained in random samples such as the Census[19]. Equation 2 includes an occupational status variable. The education coefficient is reduced because part of the effects of education are entry into a higher paying occupation. If we include the indirect effect of education via OC_{67}, the total effect of education on earnings remains at .08.

Now consider the reduced form equation 3. The variables in this equation are proxies for home environment, (except for age, which measures cohort effects and experience, and marital status, which is supposed to correct for differences in labor/leisure choices). We find, as have others, higher earnings for those whose parents are more educated or whose father worked in a higher status occupation. We also find, as have others, that those who come from larger families earn significantly less[20]. Also, those who are Jewish earn about 40 % more than Pro-

Table 4 Structural and Reduced Form Equations Estimated for Individuals by OLS From runs 2/10/76

	S	OC_1	OC_{67}	Age	Raised Rural	Married 1974	Cath	Jew	Born South	#Sibs alive 1940	ED_F	ED_M	OC_F	Constant	$\bar{R}^2$
Years of Schooling															
(E-1) ED				-.05 (3.5)	-.41 (4.3)	.23 (1.9)	-.24 (2.3)	1.61 (7.8)	-.01 (..1)	-.20 (10.2)	.12 (8.1)	.10 (6.4)	.017 (9.4)	13.82 (17.7)	.19
Initial Occupation															
(OCI-1) OC_1	.42 (40.8)													-2.01 (14.7)	.28
(OCI-2) OC_1				.0092 (.7)	-.31 (4.0)	.08 (.8)	.11 (1.3)	1.22 (7.2)	.46 (4.8)	-.14 (8.7)	.086 (7.0)	.066 (4.9)	.0095 (6.3)	1.66 (2.6)	.12
(OCI-3) OC_1	.37 (33.2)			.028 (2.6)	-.15 (2.2)	-.0030 (.03)	.20 (2.6)	.62 (4.1)	.46 (5.4)	-.064 (4.4)	.041 (3.6)	.027 (2.2)	.0030 (2.2)	-3.49 (5.9)	.30
1967 Occupation															
(OC67-1) OC_{67}	.36 (40.0)													.134 (1.1)	.27
(OC67-2) OC_{67}	.29 (27.2)	.19 (14.6)												.50 (9.0)	.31
(OC67-3) OC_{67}				-.021 (1.9)	-.61 (8.8)	.15 (1.8)	-.10 (1.3)	.77 (5.2)	.30 (3.6)	-.075 (5.4)	.040 (3.5)	.043 (3.2)	.011 (8.1)	5.16 (9.9)	.10
(OC67-4) OC_{67}	.28 (25.0)	.18 (13.7)		-.006 (.7)	-.45 (7.4)	.077 (1.1)	-.030 (.5)	.23 (1.8)	.23 (3.2)	.004 (.3)	.0086 (.8)	-.010 (.9)	-.004 (3.4)	1.10 (2.1)	.32
$\ln Y_{73}$															
(Y1) $\ln Y_{73}$	.080 (32.4)													8.58 (262.5)	.20
(Y2) $\ln Y_{73}$		.067 (23.6)	.039 (9.5)											8.55 (262.8)	.22
(Y3) $\ln Y_{73}$				-.011 (4.1)	-.054 (3.0)	0.14 (6.6)	.032 (1.6)	.43 (11.2)	.007 (.32)	-.021 (6.0)	.014 (5.2)	.012 (4.0)	.0018 (5.3)	9.8 (67.5)	.108
(Y4) $\ln Y_{73}$	.059 (19.5)			.035 (8.8)	.0079 (3.1)	-.008 (.5)	.13 (6.3)	.05 (2.6)	.29 (8.3)	-.0080 (.4)	-.0082 (2.4)	.0082 (3.0)	.0050 (1.6) .0004 (1.3)	8.84 (63.5)	.25

Note: OC_{67} and OC_i divided by 10 and are scaled from 0 to 10.

Note: OC_{67} and OC_i divided by 10 and are scaled from 0 to 10.

Table 4 a: Structural Equations
Within Pair, MZ and DZ Separately, OLS

	MZ							DZ						
	ΔED	ΔOC_i	ΔOC_{67}	Married$_1$	Married$_2$	Constant	R^2	ΔED	ΔOC_i	ΔOC_{67}	Married$_1$	Married$_2$	Constant	R^2
OC$_i$														
(OCI-1)	.210 (5.9)			-.126 (.6)	.047 (.2)	.061 (.3)	.03	.28 (9.5)			-.15 (.6)	.24 (1.0)	.10 (.4)	.09
(OC2-2)	.209 (5.9)					.13 (82.5)	.03	.28 (9.5)					-.023 (31.3)	.09
OC$_{67}$														
(OC67-1)	.26 (8.4)	.15 (5.8)		-.15 (.9)	.12 (.7)	.013 (.08)	.11	.29 (11.3)	.14 (5.5)		-.14 (.7)	-.42 (2.2)	.43 (1.9)	.19
(OC67-2)	.26 (8.4)	.15 (5.8)				-.009 (2.7)	.11	.29 (11.3)	.14 (5.4)				-.04 (48.3)	.19
(OC67-3)	.29 (9.5)					-.027 (33.4)	.08	.33 (13.4)					-.05 (259.5)	.16
(Y-1)	.017 (2.2)		.026 (4.1)	-.10 (2.4)	.13 (3.0)	-.02 (.4)	.04	.048 (6.0)		.038 (3.8)	.063 (1.0)	-.109 (1.9)	.035 (.5)	.09
(Y-2)	.019 (2.4)		.025 (3.9)			.0005 (.7)	.03	.048 (6.0)		.038 (3.9)			-.002 (4.8)	.08
(Y-3)	.026 (3.5)			.124 (2.9)	-.095 (2.2)	-.020 (.4)	.02	.059 (8.3)			.052 (.9)	-.12 (2.0)	.057 (.8)	.07
(Y-4)	.027 (3.6)					.0030 (9.2)	.01	.059 (8.2)					-.00094 (5.2)	.07

Variable Definitions

S	is years of schooling, reported in 1974
OC_i	is initial full time civilian occupation, reported in 1974, scaled on the Duncan Score
OC_{67}	is current occupation, reported mostly in 1967 but later for some of the sample, scaled on the Duncan Score
$\ln Y_{73}$	is the natural log of annual earnings in 1973, reported in 1974
Age	is 1974 minus birth date, taken from birth certificates
Raised Rural	is a dummy variable equal to 1 if raised in rural districts, reported in 1967
Married 1974	is a dummy variable equal to 1 if married in 1974, reported in 1974
Catholic	is a dummy variable equal to 1 if raised in Catholic religion, reported in 1974
Jewish	is a dummy variable equal to 1 if raised in Jewish religion, reported in 1974
Born South	is a dummy variable equal to 1 if born in the Census defined region of the South, taken from birth certificates
# Sibs alive in 1940	is number of sibs alive in 1940, reported in 1974
ED_F	is years of schooling of father, reported in 1974
ED_M	is years of schooling of mother, reported in 1974
OC_F	is father's occupation, Duncan Score, reported in 1967

testants[21]. Those married earn more while those who were raised in rural environments and are older earn less. Being born in the south has no effect on earnings.

These variables, which include all those generally used as proxies for family environment and genetics with the exception of family income and IQ, explain about 10 % of the variance in the log of earnings.

In equation 4, we have included all the variables. The education coefficient has declined to .06 but if we include the indirect effects via occupation, education has a coefficient of .07 or about 85 % of the estimate in equation 1. While this suggests that controlling for family environment and genetics is not of major importance, we present contrary evidence below.

The changes in the coefficients on the proxies from equation 3 to 4 indicate the extent to which the effects of these variables are indirect (or channeled through schooling and occupation) and direct. Note first that all the coefficients in (3) that were significant remain so in (4), except raised rural, mother's education and father's occupation. The coefficients on all variables are closer to zero in (4) than (3), except Catholic, which has negative indirect effects via both schooling and 1967 occupation. Father's occupational status changes sign once the total effect is divided up into direct effects and indirect effects via schooling.

In the above equations we have used various proxies to control for family environment and genetic endowments. The proxies used include those generally available in Census data and in most other studies except perhaps IQ and family income. We can, however, control for genetic endowments and/or common environment using twins. (Common environment will only equal family environment if the family treats both members of a twin set the same in all relevant dimensions.) The results are given in Table 4a.

In the DZ within equations in which we control for common environment, the estimate of the total effect of education declines to .06. In the MZ within equation, in which we control for common environment and genetic endowments, the total effect of education declines to less than .03. We have used an analysis of covariance (Chow test) to test the null hypothesis that the MZ and DZ within equations are the same. For both the equation with and without OC_{67}, this null hypothesis is rejected at the 5 % level.

The implied bias of 2/3 between the individual and MZ within equation probably is an upper bound because the variance of measurement error to variance in true years of schooling is almost surely greater in the within equations. But as indicated in Taubman, Fall 1976, the bias will remain large for likely magnitudes of measurement error.

Even ignoring measurement error, the MZ within equations may not be free of bias because whatever factors that influenced identical twins to obtain different amounts of schooling may also have direct effects on earnings. We will examine this issue below in the latent variable section.

8. Latent Variables

Behrman, Taubman and Wales have used a latent variable cum variance components technique to estimate the model in Table 1. Because of problems in identification, it is not possible to estimate the full model set out in that table. Instead they estimated various subsets. On important subset consisted of a core model with four genetic and one environmental indices and a variety of alternatives. Another core consisted of a model in which there were four environmental indices and in which there is a common ρ_{MZ} (σ_{NN*}/σ_N^2) that differs from a common ρ_{DZ} ($\sigma_{NN}|/\sigma_N^2$).

The »best« fitting of the first core model is given in Table 6. The coefficients in the structural equation for lnY_{73} are nearly identical to those in 4a[22]. (The coefficients on S and OC_i in the other structural equations are very similar to those in the MZ within eqautions in Behrman, Taubman and Wales.) The other coefficients in the structural and reduced form equations are on the unobserved genetic and environmental indices. The model is structured to allow for different genetic indices affecting the four dependent variables. Three of the four genetic

Table 6 For Indicator Model (23 Paramters)
Reduced From Equations

	G	N	G_1	G_2	G_3	u	u_1	u_2	u_3
S	2.090 (20.5)	1.710 (13.7)				1			
OC_1	.847 (7.0)	1.043 (8.2)	1.143 (17.1)			.197 (5.7)	1		
OC_{67}	.814 (7.3)	.658 (5.4)	.361 (4.8)	.794 (13.0)		.290 (5.7)	.149 (8.8)	1	
lnY_{73}	.210 (7.8)	.150 (5.1)	.102 (5.6)	.016 (.6)	.300 (23.1)	.024 (3.1)	.0045 (3.6)	.030 (3.2)	1

Structural Equations

	G	N	G_1	G_2	G_3	u	u_1	u_2	u_3	S	OC_1	OC_{67}	lnY_{73}
S	2.090 (20.5)	1.710 (13.7)				1							
OC_1	.436 (2.7)	.706 (5.7)	1.143 (17.2)				1			.197 (5.7)			
OC_{67}	.144 (.9)	.058 (.5)	.192 (2.0)	.794 (13.0)				1		.261 (5.7)	.149 (8.8)		
lnY_{73}	.155 (4.2)	.105 (3.8)	.091 (5.0)	−.0078 (.3)	.300 (23.1)				1	.015 (1.9)		.030 (3.2)	

Restrictions and other Parameter estimates

Normalizations and Restrictions:

$\sigma_G^2 = \sigma_{G_1}^2 = \sigma_{G_2}^2 = \sigma_{G_3}^2 = \sigma_N^2 = 1;$

$\sigma_{N_1}^2 = \sigma_{N_2}^2 = \sigma_{N_3}^2 = 0$

$\rho = \rho* = 1,$

$\sigma_{NG} = \sigma_{NG'} = \sigma_{G_1N} = \sigma_{GG_1} = \sigma_{G_1N'} = 0,$

random mating.

$\sigma_u^2 = 2.18 \quad (22.6)$

$\sigma_{u_1}^2 = 2.80 \quad (25.2)$

$\sigma_{u_2}^2 = 2.49 \quad (26.2)$

$\sigma_{u_3}^2 = .13 \quad (24.0)$

Functional value = 13 435.44

	G	N	G_1	G_2	G_3	u	u_1	u_2	u_3	S	OC_1	OC_{67}
Reduced Forms												
S	1.85 (15.9)	1.98 (17.5)				1						
OC_1	.68 (5.5)	1.16 (11.7)	1.16 (18.5)			.21 (6.0)	1					
OC_{67}	.69 (6.3)	.78 (8.4)	.37 (5.1)	.82 (13.8)		.29 (8.9)	.14 (5.4)	1				
lnY	.17 (5.9)	.19 (7.7)	.098 (6.0)	.019 (.8)	.31 (26.2)	.026 (3.4)	.0044 (3.5)	.031 (4.7)	1			
Structural Equations												
S	1.85 (15.9)	1.98 (17.5)				1						
OC_1	.30 (1.9)	.75 (5.7)	1.16 (18.5)				1			.21 (6.0)		
OC_{67}	.113 (.1)	.090 (1.0)	.20 (2.3)	.82 (13.8)				1		.26 (7.9)	.14 (5.4)	
lnY	.12 (3.3)	.13 (5.2)	.087 (5.2)	-.0068 (.3)	.31 (26.1)				1	.016 (2.3)		.031 (4.7)

Restrictions and Other Parameter Estimates

Estimates

AM Coef = .34 (6.1)

$$\text{Restriction} \begin{cases} \sigma_G^2 = \sigma_{G_1}^2 = \sigma_{G_2}^2 = \sigma_{G_3}^2 = \sigma_N^2 = 1 \\ \rho_{MZ} = \rho_{DZ} = 1, \ \sigma_{NG} = \sigma_{NG'} = 0 \end{cases}$$

$$\sigma_{N_1}^2 = \sigma_{N_2}^2 = \sigma_{N_3}^2 = 0$$

$\sigma_u^2 = 2.17$ (22.6)

$\sigma_{u_1}^2 = 2.75$ (24.4)

$\sigma_{u_2}^2 = 2.45$ (25.1)

$\sigma_{u_3}^2 = .127$ (23.1)

Functional Value = 13431.87
Parameters = 24

indices have significant direct and total effects on lnY_{73}. Thus some genetic endowments that affect earnings also appear to have common effects on schooling and occupational status, but G_3 only affects earnings. Common environment also has a significant and large effect on earnings and the other dependent variables.

We also estimate that $\sigma_{GG'}/\sigma_G^2$, which is restricted to be the same for all four genetic indices, to be .34. If there were to be random mating and no dominant/recessive genes the coefficient would be .5. Either negative assortive mating or dominant/recessive genes could cause the estimate to be less than $1/2$. A breakdown of the sources of variance of earnings and the other dependent variables implied by the results in Table 6 is given in Table 7. Genetics accounts for about 35 % of the variance in occupational status and 45 % of the variance in 1973 earnings. Common environment (N) accounts for 41 % of the variance in schooling, 22 % in initial occupation and 12 % of 1967 occupation and 1973 earnings. The remainders, which are attributable to specific environment, account for 25 to 55 % of the total.

Of the genetic effects, most of the total (direct plus indirect) impacts are attributable to the index introduced in an equation for a particular indicator, e.g., G_2 for Y_2. However, the first genetic index has noticeable effects on all four indicators while the second accounts for 3 % of the variance in OC_{67} and Y_{73}.

The results in Tables 6 and 7 are based on a model in which we restrict $\rho_{MZ} = \rho_{DZ} = 1$ and $\sigma_{GN} = \sigma_{GN}{}^{|} = 0$. When we tested this version against one in which $\rho_{MZ} = \rho_{DZ} \neq 1$, twice the difference in the ln of likelihood function was only about .5 which is far from significant. (The estimate of ρ was .9.) It is worth emphasizing that if ρ is less than one, then there are differences in noncommon environment which (if not controlled for) would yield a bias in the MZ within equation.

As indicated in Behrman, Taubman and Wales, as the model is structured, it is not possible to identify separate estimates for ρ_{MZ} and ρ_{DZ}. It is possible to restrict ρ_{DZ} to be a fixed fraction of ρ_{MZ} but for any nonzero fraction, the log of the likelihood function is the same as when $\rho = .9$. When $\rho_{DZ} < \rho_{MZ}$, the coefficients on G decline and those on N increase. Table 7a presents the allocation of variance when $\rho_{DZ} = .8\, \rho_{MZ}$.

When $\rho = 1$ we can, in principal, estimate $\sigma_{NG} = \sigma_{NG}{}^{|}$. However, in our sample the likelihood function has a very shallow gradient and we cannot converge to

Table 7 Sources of Variance of Schooling, Initial and Later Occupational Status and Earnings (Assuming $\sigma_{NG} = \sigma_{NG}{}^{|} = 0$)

	Schooling	Initial Occupation	1967 Occupation	1973 Earnings
σ^2_G	36 %	8 %	11 %	10%
$\sigma^2_{G_1}$		23%	3 %	3%
$\sigma^2_{G_2}$			15	0.01 %
$\sigma^2_{G_3}$				32
$\Sigma\sigma^2_G$	36	31	29	45
σ^2_N	41	22	13	12
σ^2_u	23	02	04	0.5%
σ^2_{u1}		46	01	0.02%
σ^2_{u2}			53	0.8
σ^2_{u3}				42

Source table 6a AM = .35, $\rho_{MZ} = \rho_{DZ} = 1$

Table 7a Sources of Variances of Schooling, Initial and Later Occupations and Earnings (Assuming $\sigma_{NG} = \sigma_{NG}| = .6$)

	Schooling	Initial Occupation	1967 Occupation	1973 Earnings
σ^2_G	36%	08	11	10
$\sigma^2_{G_1}$		23	03	03
$\sigma^2_{G_2}$			15	0..01
$\sigma^2_{G_3}$				32
$\Sigma\sigma^2_G$	36	31	29	45
σ_{NG}	26	11	07	08
σ^2_N	14	11	05	04
σ^2_u	23	02	04	0.04%
$\sigma^2_{u_1}$		46	01	0.01%
$\sigma^2_{u_2}$			55	0.4%
$\sigma^2_{u_3}$				42

Note: $\rho_{MZ} = \rho_{DZ} = 1$

Source Table 5f in Behrman et altera: Coefficient on $\sigma_{GG'}$ terms for DZ = .35
$$\sigma_{GN} = \sigma_{GN}| = .6$$

any particular set of estimates. When $\sigma_{GN} = \sigma_{NG}|$ is not restricted to zero, the coefficients on N vary greatly but the others are unchanged. The results are shown in Table 7a. An allocation of the σ_{GN} term between G and N effects will be arbitrary, but any such allocation would, if anything, increase the genetic contribution.

The estimates of the genetic contribution are affected by our assumption about assortive mating and dominance. As can be inferred from Table 6b, estimates of the effects of the first G index would be about 25 % greater if we assumed that there was random mating and additive genetic effects.

The estimates would not change greatly if we were to use the variants in which we had only three genetic indices or in which we add a second environmental index with a ρ of 1. If in our basic model we do not restrict ρ to 1, we transfer part of the specific environmental affect from the errors uncorrelated over equations to the N term which is correlated over equations. Other than such a change, this model's results would be unchanged from above.

The other version of the model we have estimated is one in which initially there are four environmental indices. In this model we need not restrict ρ_{MZ} to be

Table 7b Analysis of Variance

Percent of Total Arising from	$\rho_{DZ} = .8\rho_{MZ}$			
	S	OC_i	OC_{67}	lnY_{73}
σ^2_G	25%	02%	08%	09%
$\sigma^2_{G_1}$		19	03	04
$\sigma^2_{G_2}$			14	0.07
$\sigma^2_{G_2}$				30.
$\Sigma\sigma^2_G$	25	21	25	43
σ^2_N	56	33	17	14
σ^2_u	18	0.2	03	0.04
$\sigma^2_{u_1}$		45	01	0.02
$\sigma^2_{u_2}$			54	0.7
$\sigma^2_{u_3}$				43

Source Table 5 in Behrman et altera

equal to ρ_{DZ}; however, we can only estimate one ρ_{MZ} and one ρ_{DZ}. Thus we chose to restrict ρ_{MZ} and ρ_{DZ} to be the same across environmental indices, though ρ_{MZ} is not restricted to ρ_{DZ}. The results are shown in Table 6c. Note first that the coefficients on S and the other observed independent variables are approximately the same as in the earlier run[23]. The estimates of the effects of noncommon environment are approximately those in Table 6. This pure environmental model differs from the genetics and environment model embodied in 6 in only two respects. First, it attributes all the noncommon environment effects to common environment. Second, it fits the data noticeably worse, i.e., the difference in the function value is about 16[24]. Thus the pure environment model yields approximately the same answers on all questions except the partition of the variance due to the family.

Perhaps the best way to summarize this section is to say that all our various models (except the pure environmental one) suggest that genetic endowments, common environment and specific environment all contribute to schooling and labor market success. Common environment appears more important for schooling and early occupation, while genetics is more important for earnings and schooling.

9. Conclusions

Before summarizing our results, we wish to emphasize that the results may not generalize because the distribution of genetics and of environment can vary over cohort, because the slope coefficients between the omitted and observed variables may vary by cohorts and because of response bias. While we soon hope to be able to say something about response bias, the other important issues will require new data sources.

Our findings include the following. First, there appears to be a substantial bias on the coefficient on education in the equation for earnings around age 50 if genetics and family environment are not controlled for. Second, it appears that parental education, father's occupational status, religion, region of birth and number of siblings do not adequately proxy for genetics and family environment. Third, education in this sample accounts for 4 % or less of the variance of the ln of earnings around age 50 once genetic endowments and family environment are accounted for (and we make a reasonable allowance for measurement error).

The latent variable, variance components models strongly confirm the above findings and let us examine several new issues. For example, the MZ within equations let us control for genetic endowments and common environment, but do not let us control for noncommon environment. It certainly is possible that whatever induces one MZ brother to obtain different schooling than his twin will also affect his earnings. Using the latent variable we have tested this possibility. We do not reject the null hypothesis that noncommon environment need not be controlled for.

We can obtain a lower bound to the combined effects of common environment and genetics on the variance of the ln of earnings. This lower bound is about 47 % for the ln of earnings. These family effects on earnings include but are not limited to factors which help determine schooling and occupational status.

If we make other restrictions, we are able to estimate additional parameters of interest. In particular, if we assume that ρ, the correlation in brother's environments, is the same for MZs and DZs, we can estimate the separate contributions of genetics and family environment. With this restriction we obtain a point estimate for genetics of about 45 % of the variance of earnings. If ρ_{DZ} is less than ρ_{MZ}, genetics will account for a smaller proportion of the variance.

It is possible to estimate a model with only environmental variables. This model does not fit the data as well as one with genetic variables.

Our results would suggest that a society as laissez-faire as the one our sample was raised in would give rise to a substantial amount of inequality that would be passed on from one generation to the next (assuming relative prices on various skills do not vary). Moreover, if our preferred estimates on the contributions of genetics and family environment are approximately correct, a policy of equality of opportunity which eliminates differences in family environment will not eliminate most of the family's contribution to the welfare of their offspring.

Notes

[1] In this paper we normalize the price level to be one.

[2] For example, family income, which presumably is a component of family environment, is generally thought to be less unequally distributed after 1945 than, say, in 1929.

[3] Since G and N are mostly unobserved and can be rescaled, this is not such a strong assumption.

[4] The term »structural« is somewhat of a misnomer. The earnings equation, for example, can be considered to be a hedonic price index in which prices for individual skills are the ones that equilibrate supply and demand curves for that skill. Alternatively, the coefficients of the right-hand side variables in this equation can be thought of as efficiency units weights for the inputs which are necessary for the production of skills. However, within the framework of our model we find it convenient to distinguish between the »structural« equations, which incorporate both observable and unobservable variables, and the »reduced form« equations, which are in terms only of the unobservable variables.

[5] The occupational status index utilized has its limitations in representing these phenomenon. Nevertheless, it would seem to bear a definite relation at least to the first two of them. The degree of specific training and the extent of some nonpecuniary rewards (status, not having to punch a clock), for example, probably are positively correlated with the occupational index. Occupation-specific dummy variables, nevertheless, would permit a more compelling representation of such phenomenon.

[6] See, for example, Haspel and Taubman.

[7] We are ignoring mutations, which occur very rarely, i.e., about once in 100,000 or less. For discussion of the biological and statistical aspects of genes, see Cavalli-Sforza and Bodmer (1971).

[8] For a more complete discussion of the biological aspects, see Cavalli-Sforza and Bodmer (1971).

[9] The linear additive functional form assumption is crucial for the within pair equations to be appropriate. As discussed in Taubman (1976), we do not reject this hypothesis in favor of one which adds an interaction term between G and N.

[10] There is some evidence supporting this view in Scarr-Salapatek.

[11] However, differences in treatment or in environment lead to the difference in outcome.

[12] Econometricians' interest in this area dates from Zellner's pioneering study. Goldberger provides an extremely useful summary.

[13] We eliminate pairs if either does not have earnings, whose derivation is described in Taubman (1976). About 100 pairs whose zygosity is unknown are not used in this analysis.

[14] The average 1973 earnings and education in our sample are $ 18,000 and 13 years. In the population as a whole, the corresponding figures for white veterans of the same cohort are about $ 15,500 and 12 years. About 1/4 of the differential can be eliminated if we reweight by parental education and region of birth so as to produce the average of white males born during the period 1917 − 1927 on these variables.

[15] However, since less than 5 % of the sample have less than a ninth grade education, our results may not be appropriate for those with low education.

[16] In our statistical analysis, it is necessary to distinguish between MZ and DZ twins. For the most part, the twins' zygosity is determined by their answers to: »As children, were you and your twin alike as 'two peas in a pod' or of only ordinary resemblance?« This simple question assigns pairs accurately almost 95 % of the time. See Taubman (1976), Appendix A, for details.

[17] For samples of this size, the 5 % level of significance in an F test is about 1.2.

[18] See also the comparison below of our regression results with those based on Census data.

[19] See Mincer.

[20] See, for example, Olneck or Lindert.

[21] See, for example, Taubman, who found similar results to those in equation 4 in a sample based on the same cohort.

[22] This correspondence is not so surprising once it is realized that this model makes the same assumptions as in the MZ within estimates and that contribution of the MZ twins to the estimate is the same as that used in the MZ within equations. The DZ contribution, however, adjusts the information used in the DZ within equations by an estimate of the contribution of the genetic elements contained therein.

[23] The t statistics have declined in comparison with Table 6 but are comparable to those obtained when we rerun the model in 6 but with $\rho_{MZ} = \rho_{DZ} \neq 1$.

[24] When a single genetic index is added to the model, the function value improves by about 5, but we have difficulty converging to one answer.

References

Becker, G., *Human Capital,* Columbia University Press, 1974.

Behrman, J., P. Taubman and T. Wales, »Controlling for and Measuring the Effects of Genetics and Family Environment in Equations for Schooling and Labor Market Success«, University of Pennsylvania mimeo, 1976.

Cavalli-Sforza, L. and W. Bodmer, *The Genetics of Human Populations,* W.H. Freeman & Co., 1971.

Chamberlain, G., »Identification in Variance Components Models«, Harvard University mimeo, 1976.

Chamberlain, G. and Z. Griliches, »Unobservables with a Variance Components Structure: Ability, Schooling, and the Economic Success of Brothers«, IER, 1975.

Goldberger, A., »Structural Equation Models: An Overview«, in *Structural Equation Models in the Social Sciences,* edited by A. Goldberger and O. Duncan, Seminar Press, 1973.

Haspel, A. and P. Taubman, »The Choice of Occupations: Some Empirical Evidence«, SUNY-Buffalo, 1975.

Koch, H.L., *Twins and Twin Relations,* Chicago University Press, 1966.

Lindert, Peter H., »Sibling Position and Achievement«, forthcoming in JHR.

Meade, J., »The Inheritance of Inequality: Some Biological, Demographic, Social and Economic Factors«, *Proceedings of the British Academy,* 1973.

Mincer, J., *Schooling, Experience and Earnings,* Columbia University Press, 1968.

Olneck, M., »The Determinants of Educational Attainment and Adult Status Among Brothers: The Kalamazoo Study«, University of Wisconsin mimeo, 1976.

Scarr-Salapetek, S., »Twin Method: Defense of a Critical Assumption«, University of Minnesota mimeo, 1976.

Stauffer, S. et al., *The American Soldier,* Vol. 4, Princeton University Press, 1975.

Taubman, P., »The Determinants of Earnings: Genetics, Family and Other Environments«, AER, December, 1976.

Taubman, P., »Earnings, Education, Genetics and Environment«, *Journal of Human Resources,* Fall, 1976.

Taubman, P., *Sources of Inequality of Earnings,* North-Holland, 1975.

Zellner, A., »Estimation of a Regression Relationship Containing Unobservables«, IER, 1970.

R.B. Freeman
The Effect of the Increased Relative Supply
of College Graduates on Skill Differences
and Employment Opportunities

Whether the reduction in inequality found for the last century can be resumed after the stagnant period from 1950 to 1970. . . depends on the »race« between demand for third-level manpower due to technological development and the supply of it due to increased schooling.[1]

Jan Tinbergen

Income differentials among workers with different skills, while not the dominant factor in the distribution of income, contribute significantly to income inequality. As much as one-third of the variation in the logarithm of usual hourly earnings among 30 – 50 year old men in the U.S. in the early 1970s, for example, can be attributed to differences in pay by occupation[2]. Whereas within-group different-ials have, almost by definition, no clearcut economic meaning, differences among well-defined skill groups can be readily interpreted in terms of supply and demand forces and have pronounced social significance. In the U.S. in the first half of the twentieth century skill differences by occupation, measured by the ratio of the income of more to less skilled workers (Ober) or the variation of income among occupations (Keat), declined in the U.S., with much of the narrowing concent-rated during periods of war. In the 1950s and 1960s, by contrast, no clearcut pattern of change emerged: some studies of occupational wages found a modest widening in the structure, others reported stability or slight narrowing; educat-ional income ratios were either stable or rising; while certain highly skilled wor-kers, such as scientists or educators, enjoyed sizeable relative income gains[3]. Human capital theorists pondered the reasons for the maintenance of sizeable returns to schooling in the face of expanded higher education (Griliches).

The post-world-war II stability or widening of skill margins appears to have come to an end, at least for the higher educated, in the early 1970s as the supply of college-trained workers increased at unprecedented rates. Between 1967 and 1973 the number of bachelor's graduates grew by 46 %; the ratio of college to high school male workers, which was stable in the early 1960s, rose from .38 to .46; by 1974 24 % of male workers aged 25 – 29 had some college training compared to 17 % a decade earlier[4]. The conjunction of large demographic cohorts and increased propensity to enroll shifted the balance in Tinbergen's race toward supply forces, with substantial effects on the job market (Freeman, 1975, 1976).

240

While the period of change is too short for a definitive evaluation of its secular significance, the market turnabout is sufficiently sizeable to merit detailed analysis.

In this paper I examine the impact of the increased relative supply of »third level« manpower in the U.S. on income and employment and seek to determine whether the observed changes in skill margins and employment patterns can be attributed to the substantial influx of supply as opposed to cyclic or transitory forces. The paper diverges from traditional studies of skill margins and supply in several ways: it focuses on the premium received by the most highly trained, college graduates and professionals rather than, as in traditional wage structure studies, on skill margins among manual workers; it analyses time series changes in a single country, rather than the usual cross-country differences in relative numbers and wages; and it investigates quantity as well as salary adjustments to the increased supply of college graduates. The paper deals primarily with male workers, leaving detailed analysis of the market for highly educated females for the future.

There are three basic findings:

1. After widening in the 1950s and 1960s the premium received by »third level« manpower in the U.S. was substantially reduced in the 1970s, when the supply of graduates grew rapidly. The income advantage of young college men relative to high school men, in particular, eroded speedily, as did that for starting doctorate personnel.

2. The reduced college premium appears to be due to the rapid growth in the supply of college graduates, which caused a (possibly temporary) switch in the leadership of Tinbergen's »race«. It cannot be attributed to cyclic factors, as the evidence shows that skill structures widen rather than narrow in loose labor markets like those of the 1970—75 period.

3. The increased supply of college graduates caused substantial »quantity adjustments« in the employment structure, with employers substituting more for less educated personnel in white collar jobs, potentially in response to the narrower education margin. One important consequence of the growing number of college workers was a reduction in the proportion employed in traditional »college-level« jobs.

Evidence of change

Table 1 (see page 242) summarizes available data on the income differential between college-trained and professional workers and less educated or skilled men. The table covers the period from 1969, when the market for highly educated appears to have reached its post-world-war II peak, to 1974, when it was substantially depressed. Columns 1 — 2 record income ratios for all male workers; column 3 gives percentage changes in the ratios while columns 4 — 6 deal with year-round full-time employees, thereby getting a closer fix on wage rates.

The table reveals a sizeable decline in the relative position of the highly educated during the period under study, especially among the young. From 1969 to 1974 the income of 4 year college graduates relative to that of high school graduates dropped from 1.50 to 1.38 while the ratio for year-round full-time personnel was

Table 1 College to High School Income Ratios for Male Workers 1969 — 1974

Income Ratios	All Workers			Yeat-Round Full-Time Workers		
	1969	1974	%Δ	1969	1974	%Δ
1. College Grad./ High School Grad 25—34 years old	1,50	1.38	−8.0	1.53	1.35	−11.8
2. College Grad./ High Schol Grad, 25—34 years old	1.33	1.15	−13.5	1.39	1.16	−16.5
3. College Grad. 5+/ High School 25+	1.71	1.56	−8.8	1.72	1.55	−9.9
4. College Grad. 5+/High School 25—34	1.39	1.31	−5.8	1.51	1.38	−8.6
5. College Starting Salaries[a]/ Average Annual Earnings[b]	1.24	1.09	−12.1	−	−	−
6. Doctorate Starting Salaries[c]/Average Annual Earnings	2.18	1.78	−18.3	−	−	−
7. Professional/All Male Workers	1.55	1.48	−4.6	1.37	1.31	−4.4
8. Teachers, Secondary School/All Male Workers	1.30	1.14	−12.3	1.10	0.98	−10.9

[a]Estimated as weighted average of starting salaries from Endicott series using as weights .35 (engineering), .05 (accounting), .20 (business administration) .40 (sales).

[b]1974 is approximate. Calculated from percentage change in average hourly earnings from 1973 to 1974.

[c]Unweighted average of 8 Ph. D. fields

Source: U.S. Bureau of the Census, Current Population Reports, Series P-60 *Consumer Income* No. 75, p. 101, Table 47, p. 110, Table 49. No. 101, p. 116, Table 58, p. 131, Table 64.

College Placement Council, *Men's Salary Survey* (Bethlehem, Penn.), 1968 — 69, 1973 — 74).

F. W. Endicott, The Endicott Report: *Trends in Employment of College Graduates*, Northwestern University, 1948 — 74.

U.S. Department of Commerce, *Survey of Current Business*, national income editions off even more, by 11.8 % (line 1). In the 25 − 34 year old group (line 2), an even greater decline in relative incomes is observed: from 1.33 (1969) to 1.15 (1974) for all workers and from 1.39 to 1.16 for full-time year-round personnel. Comparisons of the income of graduates with 5 or more years of college relative to that of high school workers in lines 3 and 4 tell a similar story: sizeable narrowing in the income advantage of the better educated. Evidence from surveys of starting college workers and Ph.D.'s schows an even more striking pattern of decline among those just beginning their careers (lines 5 − 6). In 1969 starting bachelors men earned 24 % more than the average worker; in 1974 9 % more. The advantage of beginning Ph.D.'s fell by 18 %. More detailed analysis of the CPS data tapes confirm the concentration of the decline among the young graduates who constituted the margin of expansion in supply (Freeman, 1977).

An analogous but less pronounced drop in the relative income of professional workers also appears to have characterized the skill structure in the 1970s, though different professions fared quite differently (Freeman, 1976). According to the data in lines 7 and 8, professionals as a group experienced a modest drop in relative income while those working as elementary and high school teachers lost considerable ground[5].

Turning from income to employment, Table 2 presents evidence on the occupational employment of college graduates in 1969 and 1975. The data reveal a marked decline in the probability that a college graduates would be employed as a professional in the period; among men, the proportion in the professions dropped by 11 % in the six year interval; among women, an even more drastic decline is found, of 14 %. While there is some increase in the proportion of college men working as managers, the table shows the largest increases in employment in lower-level white-collar and in blue-collar and other jobs. Between 1969 and 1975 the proportion of male graduates working in nonwhite collar jobs increased by 49 %; the proportion who were salesmen rose by 24 %. Among women, there is a marked movement into sales and clerical jobs.

Table 2 Proportions of College Graduates Employed in Major Occupations, 1967 − 1975[a]

	College Men			College Women		
	1969	1975	%Δ	1969	1975	%Δ
Professional	60.9	54.4	−10.7	81.1	69.8	−13.9
Managers	22.3	23.6	5.8	3.7	7.1	91.9
Salesmen	6.6	8.2	24.2	1.2	3.2	166.7
Clerical	3.9	4.4	12.8	11.0	15.5	40.9
Other	6.3	9.4	49.2	3.0	4.4	46.7

Source: U.S. Department of Labor, *Educational Attainment of Workers*, March, 1969, 1975 (Special Labor Force Report 125, Table I, p. A−28) and unnumbered preliminary report for March 1975, Table 5, p. 6.

[a]College graduates with 4 or more years of college.

Additional data on the occupational position of young college workers — who, it can be argued, are more likely to be adversely affected by the substantial increase in the supply of graduates as they have yet to attain »permanent« jobs in enterprises — show greater deterioration in the job structure. First, the jobs held by young college graduates appear to have worsened at an extraordinary rate in the early 1970s. In the graduating class of 1972, for example, only 46 % of the male bachelors recipients obtained professional jobs compared to 71 % of similar graduates in the class of 1958. Among women, a similar pattern is observed: just 65 % in professional jobs in 1972 compared to 81 % in 1958 (Freeman, 1976, p. 20). Second, tabulations of the March 1969 and 1974 CPS data tapes show a similar picture: a drop in the proportion of 25 to 34 year old 4 year white male graduates working as professionals from 51 % in 1969 to 43 % in 1974. Over the same period the proportion employed as salesmen rose from 10.6 to 13.8 percent and perhaps most striking, the fraction employed as craftsmen rose from 4.6 % to 7.6 %. Third, among new Ph.D.'s, the fraction reporting that they were »seeking appointments but had no specific prospects« upon receipt of their degree increased, according to data tapes from the National Academy of Sciences, from 5 % in 1966 to 16 % in 1975[6].

In short, the evidence on the employment position of college-trained workers, as well as on their relative income, shows a significant change in the period under study, in marked contrast to previous post-war experience. Price adjustments, in the form of drops in relative earnings, and quantity adjustments, in the form of changes in the probability of attaining various types of occupations, both appear to have been important in the market, with the young being particularly affected[7]. To what extent do the observed developments represent normal short-term or cyclic ups-and-downs? Can it be attributed to the increased relative supply of more educated workers, in the context of a demand-supply model?

Decomposition of Change

As a first step in answering these questions, I have attempted to decompose the observed changes in income ratios into their cyclic, past trend, and 1970s turnabout components by regressing the ratios on three variables:

TIME, a trend variable over the entire post-world-war II period, which will measure past long term changes in income ratios. Since the highly educated made at least some relative gains in the period, TIME is expected to obtain a positive or at least nonnegative coefficient in the regressions.

CYCLE, the cyclic state of the economy, which will be measured by the deviation of real gross national product from its trend level. While most economists believe that skill margins widen in loose labor markets, the a priori case for this pattern is not clearcut. While, on the one hand, it seems plausible that production workers, who tend to be less educated, experience greater cyclic ups-and-downs than college graduates (presumably because of less specific job training and lower hiring costs), the concentration of the decline in the college income premium among the young could be explained as a cyclic phenomenon. Demand for young college graduates might be more cyclic than that for young high school graduates precisely because of the specific training of older college men. If older college men have relatively more specific training than older high school men, the brunt of cyclic declines would be borne to a greater extent by young college than high school workers. On the other hand, formal seniority systems in blue collar job markets would be expected to produce the reverse pattern. Extant empirical evidence, focused exclusively on skill margins among manual workers provides only weak evidence on these points (Reder, p. 269).

T70, a trend variable which began in 1970 when the market for the highly educated was asserted to have begun to narrow. Since the regressions contain two time variables, T70 represents the deviation of the 1970s trend from longer run changes. To estimate the actual change in the period, the coefficients on TIME and T70 must be added together.

The resultant regressions are given in Table 3 (see page 246)[8]. Lines 1 − 5 deal with the relative income of college graduates; line 6 with the differential between young (25 − 34 year old) and older (45 − 54) college men; while lines 7 − 10 present estimates for professionals versus all male workers, craftsmen, and factory operatives. Because the Census did not publish data for those with 4 years of college in 1956, lines 1 and 3 present estimates using data on those with 4 or more years, although the results are potentially contaminated by the growth of graduate education; in lines 2 and 4, the 1956 incomes of four graduates has been estimated from the incomes of those with 4 or more years (as indicated in table 2) and used in the regressions.

The major result of the table is that in each regression the T70 variable obtains a significant large negative coefficient, which highlights the divergence of the seventies' pattern from past trend and normal cyclic developments. The coefficient exceeds that on TIME substantially so that on net the 1970s were a period of sharp decline in the premium received by third-level personnel. The downward trend in income ratios is larger, by a considerable amount, for educational than for occupational groupings, presumably in part because at least some of the reduced advantage of degrees has taken the form of declines in the occupational standing of graduates (as will be seen in section 3).

The coefficients on T70 also tend to show greater declines in the relative income of young than all college men. In line 3, for example, the estimated seventies divergence in the relative income of 25 − 34 year old college men from past trend is −3.9 % per year compared to −1.9 % per year for all college men in line 1. This is consistent with the »active labor market hypothesis« that market changes show up more quickly and have greater impacts on new entrants than on experienced personnel (for a discussion of the hypothesis, see Freeman (1976, Chapter 1; also Reder, pp. 272 − 76).

The divergent experience of younger and older college workers is examined further in line 6, which records the results of regressing the ratio of the income of 25 − 34 year old to 45 − 54 year old college men on the cyclic, trend, and T70 variables. If, as seems reasonable, older and younger graduates are imperfect substitutes in production, the 1970s influx of young college workers compared to rough stability in the number of older graduates, could be expected to »twist« the age-income profile against the young. The significant large coefficient on T70 in this regression supports this expectation. Age-income profiles appear to be responsive to sizes of cohorts, as well as to investments in human capital.

Table 3 Regression Estimates of the Effects of Cyclic and Time Factors on the Relative Wages of Male »Third Level« Workers 1947 — 1974[a]

Relative Incomes by Group	constant	CYCLE	TIME	T70	R^2
1. College Grad (4 or 4+ yrs.)/ High School 1956–1974[b]	.40	−.34 (.30)	.003 (.003)	−.016 (.008)	.35
2. College Grad (4 yrs.)/ High School 1956–1974[c,d]	.30	−.26 (.26)	.005 (.002)	−.022 (.007)	.48
3. College Grad (4 or 4+ yrs.)/ High Dchool. 25–34 yr. olds 1956–1974[a]	.16	−1.14 (.30)	.006 (.003)	−.033 (.008)	.71
4. College Grad (4yrs.)/ 25–34, 1956–1974[c,d]	.16	−.47 (.28)	.006 (.002)	−.038 (.018)	.75
5. College Starting Salaries/ Annual Compensation, All Workers	−.03	−.57 (.16)	.012 (.001)	−.047 (.005)	.90
6. College Workers (4 or 4+) 25–34/College Workers, 45–54	−.69	−.50 (.76)	.011 (.002)	−.040 (.01)	.75
7. Professionals/All Workers[e] 1974–1947	.50	−.17 (.11)	.003 (.001)	−.009 (.004)	.57
8. Professionals/All, full-time[e] yr-round full-time 1955–1975	.44	−.16 (.13)	.004 (.001)	−.018 (.004)	.58
9. Professional/Craftsmen yr-round full-time 1955–1974	.12	−.04 (.17)	.008 (.001)	−.020 (.005)	.71
10. Professional/Operatives yr-round full-time 1955–1974	.26	−,15 (.24)	.009 (.002)	−.021 (.007)	.62

[a]Numbers in parenthesis are standard errors. All variables are in log form.

[b]CYCLE estimated from regression of real GNP (RGNP) on time:
RGNP = 8.02 + .037 TIME R^2 = .989
           (.008)

[c]Omitted years 1957, 1959, 1960, 1962 due to lack of data. Estimated 1965 by applying percentage change in median incomes to means given in Census bulletin

[d]Estimated college income in 1956 by regressing income for 4 year graduates on income for graduates with 4 or more years and using equation to extrapolate due to lack of data for 4 year graduates in 1956.

[e]All worker incomes are unweighted average of incomes of 10 occupational groups.

Source: Incomes in lines 1 — 4, 6 from U.S. Bureau of the Census, *Current Population Reports,* Series P—60, Consumer Income, No. 92, table 1, p. 17, ungrouped data spliced for consistency with grouped data using 1967 overlap and Series P—60 Consumer Income Nos. 97 and 101. Line 5, F.W. Endicott, *The Endicott Report,* estimated as described in Table 1 and U.S. Department of Commerce, *Survey of Current Business,* national income editions. Lines 7 — 10, Consumer Income, Series P—60 various editions, from table on Employment Status and Occupation (Table 59 in No. 101)

In each of the regressions, the past trend coefficient is modestly positive, indicative of the general upward trend in the relative income of the highly educated, which puzzled previous analysts. The positive TIME coefficient in lines 1 − 4 is due, it should be noted, largely to the small income premium received by college men in 1956, prior to Sputnik, the first year when the Current Population Survey provided data on income by education. As college-high school income ratios from the 1950 Census also show a modest premium for 1949, as does the starting salary average earning series used in line 5, I believe that this result is correct. Omission of 1956 from the sample does not, in any case, alter the estimated negative coefficient on T70.

Turning to the cyclic pattern of change, the regressions accord a negative effect to CYCLE in all cases[9], with the largest coefficients obtained for the young (lines 2,4 versus lines 1,3). Since CYCLE is measured as the deviation of real GNP from its trend, this implies that economic booms reduce the income advantage of the highly educated while recessions enhance their position. The relative income of college graduates, of young compared to older graduates, and of professionals moves countercyclicly, which makes it difficult to explain the 1969−74 narrowing of the premium by cyclic patterns.

Table 4 turns from the income changes to the deterioration in the employment prospects of graduates. It records comparable regressions to those in the previous table with four »quantity« dependent variables: the proportion of male employees who are professionals (line 1); the proportion who are professionals or managers (line 2); the ratio of male professionals and managers per college graduate (line 3); and the percentage of male graduates in professional and managerial jobs (line 4).

Table 4 Regression Estimates of the Effects of Cyclic and Time Factors on the Employment Position of Male »Third Level« Workers, 1947 − 1974

	Constant	cycle 1[a]	TIME	T70	R^2
1. Professional share of jobs,male	−2.86	−.45	.041	−.059	.977
		(.29)	(.001)	(.009)	
2. Professional and Managerial share of empolyment, male	−1.73	−.56	.020	−.027	.991
		(.09)	(.0004)	(.003)	
3. Professional and Managerial share per college graduate, Males	1.00	−.31	−.014	−.024	.982
		(.11)	(.001)	(.004)	
4. Percentage of Male Graduates in Professional and Managerial Jobs[b], 1961−1974	−.29	.27	.003	−.032	.799
		(.41)	(.008)	(.010)	

Notes:

[a]The residual from regression of real GNP − 8.02 + .037 TIME
                                                    (.008)
R^2 = .989 for the period 1947 − 1974

[b]Omitted 1960−61, 1963 due to absence of data.

Source: GNP, U.S. Department of Labor *Manpower Report of the President 1975*, Tables G−3, p. 340. College Graduates, *Manpower Report* Table B−9, pp. 264−5 with 1972−74 adjusted by addition of percentage difference in 1972 between 16+ and 18+ for comparisons with earlier data. Professional and Managerial Jobs from *Manpower Report 1975*, Table A−15, p. 225 and *Manpower Report of the President 1962*, Table A−7.

247

The estimated coefficients on the CYCLE, TIME, and T70 variables confirm the main results obtained for relative incomes: that there was a distinct post-1969 deterioration in the position of college graduates that cannot be attributed to normal cyclic or past trend developments. In each calculation, the T70 coefficient is significantly negative. The cyclic coefficients also are negative, save in line 4, where the years covered is quite limited. The coefficients on TIME show an upward trend in the professional or professional/managerial share of the work force but a downward trend in professional/managerial employment per graduate (line 3). Despite the more rapid increase in graduates than in number of male professionals, and managers, however, the percentage of graduates obtaining jobs in those occupations did *not* drop until after 1969 (line 4). Prior to 1969, college workers increased their share of professional and managerial employment »at the expense« of the less educated. After 1969, such substitution was not sufficient to maintain the probability of getting these jobs at previous levels.

We conclude that the turnaround in the college market was not the result of normal cyclic patterns nor the culmination of previous trend developments and turn to the question of the impact of the increase in the relative supply of third-level manpower on the changes under study.

Analytic models

The impact of the change in supply on relative incomes will be estimated with a recursive salary adjustment equation in which the ratio of the supply of college to other workers is taken as given, predetermined by past decisions regarding education, so that with market clearing the standard demand or elasticity of substitution equation becomes a wage determination equation

(1) $RW = -1/\sigma\,(C-H) + 1/\sigma\,DEM$

where RW = log of ratio of wages

$C-H$ = log of college to other workers, with C being the log of the number of college workers and H the log of the number in the comparison group

DEM = index of demand shifts for graduates relative to other workers

σ = elasticity of substitution between graduate and nongraduate labor.

The coefficient on the relative supply term will be interpreted as an estimate of the inverse of the elasticity of substitution between the two groups of workers. The use of time series data to estimate this parameter has advantages and disadvantages compared to the commonly employed cross-section data. The main disadvantage is that long run adjustments in the economic structure, in choice of technology, and industrial composition in response to relative supplies are unlikely to be picked up in the time series, but will have a major impact on the cross-section differences. The prime advantage is that the time series data deal directly with the question of concern in a manner that the cross-sections do not. Unmeasured structural differences in societies will contaminate the cross-section but

248

not the time series results. To deal with the problem of adjustments over time in some calculation I add lagged salary terms to obtain a better estimate of long run adjustments.

The effect of changes in relative supply on the employment position of graduates requires a more complex analysis. Increases in the supply of graduates can be expected to effect the employment structure adversely in two different ways. First, supply induced declines in relative wages are likely to lead employers to substitute graduates for the less educated *within* occupations. Since such substitution will be difficult in occupations dominated by college workers, demand and employment can be expected to increase most in occupations where graduates have traditionally been least represented (see equations (6) − (7) below). Second, in a world of general disequilibrium, where prices do not clear markets immediately, there are also likely to be problems in »absorbing« new graduates in the traditional professions. If salaries do not adjust sufficiently rapidly, desirable jobs will be »rationed« among applicants, with the result that many will be »pushed« into nontraditional occupations. In this case, it is the greater availability and reduced hiring cost of graduates, as well as their relatively lower pay, which will induce employers to substitute them into lower level white collar and even blue collar jobs.

I analyze both of these quantity adjustments with a simple variant of the standard marginal productivity demand model[10]. The prime element of the analysis is an *intra-occupational* demand function, which relates the ratio of college to noncollege workers in an occupation to the technical requirements of the work and relative wages. Technical requirements are represented by a parameter T_i, which is a positive monotonic index of the »necessity« (productivity advantage) of college training in the ith occupation. Wages operate through an *intra*-occupational elasticity of substitution σ_i, which measures the substitutability of graduate and nongraduate labor. This elasticity is less than infinite due to the range of tasks in an occupation, some of which can be performed by the less educated, and the costs of various »quality-quantity« combinations which can be used to complete the tasks[11]. At any given ratio of the wages of graduates to nongraduates, assumed the same for all occupations[12], the ratio of graduate (C_i) to nongraduate (H_i) labor will be determined by

(2) $\qquad C_i - H_i = -\sigma_i RW + T_i$

where all variables are in logarithmic form. T_i will be large in occupations requiring training, so that $C_i - H_i$ approaches infinity; it will be small in occupations where graduates are roughly as productive as nongraduates so that $C_i - H_i \approx 0$ when $RW_i > 0$; it will be positive but less than infinite in other occupations, where graduates and nongraduates tend to be employed in reasonable numbers.

Because relative employment of graduates in an occupation is also likely to depend on the »size« of the occupation[13], the full demand equation will have a nonhomothetic component as well, with a parameter Φ showing the relation between size and relative proportions:

(3) $\qquad C_i - H_i = -\sigma_i RW + T_i + \Phi E_i.$

where E_i is a measure of the size of the occupation, its share of total employment, in log form.

Equation (3) can be transformed into a relation between the ratio, in log form, of college (C) to nongraduate (H) workers in the overall economy and relative employment in the occupation by using the aggregate elasticity of substitution (σ). Differentiating (3) and replace $R\dot{W}$ by $-(C-H)/\sigma$ from (1) yields

(4) $\qquad \dot{C}_i - \dot{H}_i = (\sigma_i/\sigma)\,(\dot{C} - \dot{H}) + \Phi\dot{E}_i$

Since σ is the average elasticity of substitution, equation (4) shows that changes in relative supply increase the ratio of college to nongraduate workers in occupations with above average substitution possibilities and reduce the ratio in occupations with below average substitution parameters. By eliminating the wage term, (4) reveals the direct impact of changes in overall supply patterns on occupational employment. Nonprice incentives such as lower hiring costs and greater availability operating in the same direction as prices *will be reflected in the parameters of (4)* but not of (3). In this sense (4) is a more general representation of the intra-occupational adjustment, capturing both the price and quantity incentives described earlier. It can be estimated from readily available time series data by regressing ratios of graduates to nongraduates by occupation on the economy-wide ratio and the relative size of the occupation, assuming that T_i is fixed.

Finally, equation (4) can be rewritten to show the effect of changes in the supply of college graduates and in the total size of an occupation on the probability of employment in that field. Normalize total employment at one so that

(5) $\qquad \psi\dot{C} + (1-\psi)\dot{H} = 0$, where ψ is the share of graduates in the entire work force ($\psi = C/C+H$) and note that

(5)' $\qquad \dot{E}_i = a\dot{C}_i + (1-a)\dot{H}_i$, where a is the share of graduates in occupation i ($a = C_i/E_i$). Substitute (5) and (5)' into (4) to obtain

(6) $\qquad \dot{C}_i = [(1-a)\,\sigma_i/\sigma]\,\dot{C}/(1-\psi) + [\Phi(1-a)+1]\dot{E}_i$

$\qquad\qquad = a_i\dot{C} + b_i\dot{E}_i$ where $a_i = \dfrac{(1-a)\sigma_i/\sigma}{(1-\psi)}$ and $b_i = [\Phi(1-a)+1]$

Subtract $\dot{C}$ from both sides to obtain the proportion of graduates employed in i:

(7) $\qquad \dot{C}_i - \dot{C} = (a_i-1)\,\dot{C} + b_i\,\dot{E}_i$

In (7) the probability of employment in occupation i is enhanced by increases in relative supply when $a_i - 1 > 0$, i.e. when $(1-a)\sigma_i > (1-\psi)\sigma_i$ which is likely in occupations with a small share of graduates and where the elasticity of substitution exceeds the average. In occupations dominated by graduates, such as the professions on the other hand a_i is likely to be less than one. While the parameter b_i is likely to be positive, it can be negative when Φ is sufficiently below zero, implying a market »twist« in demand against graduates as the occupations grows.

The analysis thus far has dealt with only two types of workers, graduates and nongraduates, but it can be readily extended — along familiar lines — to the case of three or more classes of workers. With three types of workers, say college graduates, high school graduates, and other workers, equation (7) would require addition of a term for either of the other two groups, which could have positive or negative effects, depending on whether college and high school (other) workers were complementary or substitutes in the occupation.

Estimates of supply effects

Estimates of the effect of supply and the other variables of the model of equation (1) and (7) are given in tables 5 and 6 (see page 252 and 253). Table 5 uses time series data to determine the impact of supply changes on the salary of starting college graduates relative to other workers (lines 1−2), the ratio of the income of 25 − 34 year old graduates to high school graduates (lines 3,4) and the ratio of the income of all college to all high school men (line 5). The dependent variables measure the salaries of these groups relative to the specified comparison series in log form. The relative supply variable (SUPPLY) differs among the equations so as to obtain the most comparable groups; as »demand« variables, I simply use TIME and the CYCLE indicator.

The resultant estimates present a clear and reasonably consistent picture of the impact of relative supplies on relative incomes. In each case SUPPLY has a negative coefficient which is significantly different from zero in all cases except line 5. As most of the impact of the increased influx of new graduates is likely to show up among younger workers, the relatively weak result for all graduates in that line is not unreasonable.

The estimates suggest an elasticity of substitution of graduate with other labor on the order of 2 − 3. In lines 3 to 5 the coefficients on the supply variables are around 1/2, indicating an elasticity of substitution of about 2.00. In line 1, the coefficient is smaller, indicative of a surprisingly large elasticity of substitution between starting college graduates and other workers. However, addition of the lagged salary term in line 2 produces a more moderate result. Estimating the long run σ by dividing −.14 by 1 minus the parameter on the lagged relative wage [RW(−1)] term in the context of the lagged adjustment model yields an estimated long term coefficient of 0.36, which is similar to those in lines 3 − 5. These estimates are much below those obtained by Bowles, but similar to the estimates of Tinbergen and Layard and Fallon in cross-country analyses. Most importantly in terms of this essay, the estimates have a magnitude that is consistent with an increased supply explanation of the bulk of the decline in the premium to education.

Table 6 presents comparable estimates of the impact of the changed supply of college graduates on the proportion obtaining jobs in five major occupational areas. In this table, I regress the log of the proportion of college workers in occupations on the college and high school shares of the work force and the proportion of total employment in the occupation. The two relative supply variables expand the model of (7) into a three factor variant. High school graduates have been differentiated from other nongraduates because they are an important subgroup, with potentially greater substitutability for graduates than the less educated. The share of total employment in the occupation is a more direct measure of the demand factors likely to affect the probability that persons with a given level of schooling will obtain a job in the area than the TIME and CYCLE factors used earlier and is thus chosen as the relevant demand or scale factor[14].

251

Table 5 Regression Estimates of the Impact of the Increased Relative Supply of Graduates on Relative Incomes [a]

	constant	CYCLE[b]	TIME	SUPPLY[c]	RW(−1)	R^2
1. College Starting Salary Average Annual Compensation 1950–1973	−1.14	−.24 (.21)	.013 (.001)	−.20 (.03)		.86
2. College Starting Salary Average Annual Compensation 1950–1973	−.75	.11 (.18)	.006 (.002)	−.14 (.03)	.61 (.15)	.93
3. Income of 25–34 year old Graduates (4 or more years) Over High School Graduates 1956–1974[d]	−.19	−1.18 (.41)	.005 (.003)	−.47 (.18)		.72
4. Income of 24–34 years old Graduates (4 years of college) 1956–1974[d]	−.21	−.52 (.46)	.004 (.004)	−.52 (.20)		.47
5. Income of All Male Graduates (4 or more years) Over High School Graduates 1956–1974[d]	−.05	−.37 (.38)	.004 (.005)	−.45 (.41)		.16

[a]Numbers in parentheses are standard errors. All variables in log form.

[b]CYCLE as defined in Table 5.

[c]Supply defined as Male bachelors graduates / Civilian Labor Force in lines 1 − 2
      College graduate (4 or more) aged 25 − 34 relative to high school graduates aged 25 − 34 in lines 3 − 4
      All male graduates (4 or more) relative to high school graduates in line 5

[d]Omitted 1957, 1959, 1960, 1962 due to lack of data

Source: Income as in Table 5. B.A. graduates, U.S. Office of Education *Earned Degrees Conferred* civilian labor force, U.S. Bureau of Labor Statistics, *Handbook of Labor Statistics 1974*
      Education Attainment, U.S. Bureau of Labor Statistics, *Educational Attainment of Workers*, March 1974, Table A, pA−9 and earlier volumes of the series, with 1975 from unnumbered March 1975 preliminary report.

The estimates show that changes in the supply of college graduates had a major impact on the proportion of graduates working as professionals and on the proportion employed as salesmen and non-white collar workers but only a modest effect on the proportion employed as managers or clerical workers. Professional employment »opportunities« are significantly reduced by increases in the supply of college graduates, while the fraction in sales and non-white collar work is raised. The relative number of workers with high school training also has some

Table 6 Estimates of the Effect of the Supply of College and High School Graduates on Proportions Employed by Occupation, 1952 − 1975[a]

Gruops and Dependent Varable	constant	College share of all male workers	High school share of all male workers	Occupation share of all male workers	R^2
College Graduates					
1. Professional	−.24	−.57 (.05)	−.19 (.11)	.80 (.07)	.96
2. Managers	−.96	.18 (.25)	.41 (.40)	−.14 (.28)	.78
3. Salesmen	2.35	.59 (.35)	−1.22 (.47)	1.80 (.43)	.81
4. Clericals	−2.79	.13 (.43)	−1.38 (.69)	.60 (.50)	.82
5. Non White Collar	2.79	1.82 (.82)	−1.49 (.76)	6.83 (1.37)	.83

[a]All variables in log form. The dependent variable is the proportion of college graduates in the occupation in log form. Numbers in parentheses are standard errors. 1953–56, 1958, 1960–61, and 1963 omitted due to lack of data.

Source: U.S. Bureau of Labor Statistics, *Educational Attainment of Workers*, (various editions) U.S. Bureau of the Census, *Current Population Reports*, Series P−50, Nos. 49 and 78.

effect on the distribution of college graduates, with high school workers reducing employment of college workers by sizeable amounts in the lower-level white collar jobs and non-white collar positions but having little impact in the professions or in managerial jobs. Finally, the occupation share coefficient in the table reveals very different effects of changes in the share on employment of graduates, ranging from an implausible but insignificant −.14 for management to 6.83 for nonwhite collar work[15]. The causes of these differences, which presumably depend in large part on which of the more detailed occupations in the major categories are growing or declining, goes beyond the purview of the current study. What is important for present purposes is that the calculations in table 6 suggest that the increased supply of graduates has significantly affected the job structure of the college work force, reducing the proportion employed as professionals in the period of expansion of supply under study.

Conclusion

This study has found that there was a narrowing in educational income differentials, in the income advantage of professionals, particularly teachers over other workers, and a worsening in the job structure of college personnel in the 1970s, with young workers being most severely effected by the changes. The study has presented evidence that the changes cannot be attributed to normal cyclic ups-and-downs because the relative position of the educated tends to increase countercyclicly, rising in recessions and falling in booms, but rather appears due to the increased supply of third level manpower.

The question which remains is whether the 1970s narrowing educational premia represents a renewal of long term downward trends in skill margins or whether it is a more temporary phenomenon. For new entrants, forecasts in *The Over-educated American* (chapter 3) suggest a reversal of the downturn in the 1980s when the supply of young college graduates is expected to decrease. It is not clear, however, if the graduates of the 1970s will benefit from the reduced number of degree recipients: this depends on elasticities of substitution among cohorts about which little information is available. For graduates taken as a whole, supply will continue to rise, which should depress their economic position, barring a marked upturn in demand. At least some of the deterioration in the relative income and occupational position of the college-trained is likely to be maintained.

Notes

[1] J. Tinbergen, »Substitution of Graduate by Other Laborers« *Kyklos* 27 (1974) p. 224. I have transposed the sentence to make it easier to read in the present context.

[2] Based on analysis of variance of May 1973—75 Current Population Reports data on usual weekly earnings for men aged 30—50, with 352 occupational categories. Gary Chamberlain provided me with this computation.

[3] See M. Segal, »Occupational Wage Differentials in Major Cities During the 1950s« in M. Perlman (ed.) *Human Resources in the Urban Economy*, Johns Hopkins Press, which contains references to other studies in the period.

[4] The data on degrees are from U.S. Bureau of the Census, *Statistical Abstract* 1973, p. 137 and unpublished Table 105 from U.S. Office of Education. The data on ratio of workers with college and high school are taken from U.S. Bureau of Labor Statistics, *Educational Attainment* (various editions).

[5] Data from U.S. Bureau of Labor Statistics, *Handbook of Labor Statistics 1975*, table 105, p. 261 and table 109, pp. 274 — 282 tell a similar story about relative income changes. and toolroom and 5 custodial occupations.

[6] These computations give *different* figures than those published by the National Academy because my tabulations exclude persons responding as »other« from the category while the published figures include them.

[7] There are also important adjustments in the position of less educated workers, which I have *not* analyzed here. In particular, while the relative and possibly absolute income of the less educated is marred by increases in the relative number of college workers the prospects that those workers will obtain college-level jobs is decreased.

[8] Comparable decompositions using the rate of unemployment or the difference between potential and actual GNP as the cyclic measure yield essentially the same results. The deviation of GNP from its trend is correlated at better than .95 with those cyclic indicators. In short time series, there is, however, one possible problem with the »deviations methodology«: if the post-1969 period were to involve a distinct cyclic pattern the T70 variable could capture some of the cyclic effect. This is unlikely to occur in the data covered, since we have, in general, 20+ years of post war experience and the post-1969 period includes both cyclic ups and downs.

[9] The smallest coefficient is in line 9, which contrasts professionals to craftsmen, whose skills may also make them relatively less sensitive to the cycle.

[10] Since the model concentrates on demand factors and ignores unemployment or other measures of rationing, it is not a complete model of the adjustment process.

[11] That is, the work performed in an occupation is postulated to have a production function $F(Q,N)$ where Q = high quality workers and N = lower quality workers. In the function, substituting less for more qualified personnel is not costless.

[12] Differences in the ratios which remain stable over time will be »embodied« in the σ_1 coefficient. As long as *changes* in ratios are similar across equations, the analysis will be fruitful. cient. As long as *changes* in ratios are similar across equations, the analysis will be fruitful. Preliminary tests of changes in the college premium among occupations shows rough similarity over the period covered.

[13] Nonhomogeneity in the demand functions is likely for several reasons. First, changes in the overall size of one-digit occupations can be expected to involve changes in the distribution of more detailed occupations, which have different educational mixes. Second, the occupations may, in some cases, already employ a sufficiently large number of persons with particular levels of schooling that increases in employment »must« come from those with other levels. Put differently, the relative supply prices (adjusted for ability) by education class may be such that growth involves shifts in composition, which are most easily modeled as nonhomogeneous scale terms on the demand side. Third, the types of tasks performed may also alter with growth, as for example when technicians are promoted into »engineering« jobs and do less-skilled engineering tasks in periods of increases in demand. While it would be desirable to study the causes of scale effects in the analysis, for present purposes what matters is that nonhomogeneous scale effects are less restrictive and plausible than homogeneous effects.

[14] This assumes that the share is *not* affected by changes in the wages of different education groups in occupations and thus neglects the impact of reduced college wages on the occupational structure. It would not be difficult to amend the analysis to allow for this possibility. Since a large number of college graduates is likely to reduce the relative price of college-intensive occupations and thereby raise their share of the workforce, allowing for cross-occupation, as well as intra-occupation, effects would *lessen* the impact of the share terms on the probability of getting various types of jobs.

[15] The enormous coefficient on occupation shown in line 5 does not appear to be an error. It reflects the differences in the scale of the proportion of college workers in nonwhite collar jobs (about 10 %) and in their share of all jobs (about 50 %). The implied change in numbers of graduates per new nonwhite collar employee is reasonable.

References

Bowles, S. *Planning Educational Systems for Economic Growth,* Cambridge, Mass.

Freeman, R. *The Overeducated American,* Academic Press, 1976.

Freeman R. »Overinvestment in College Training?« *Journal of Human Resources,* Summer 1975.

Freeman, R. »The Decline in the Economic Rewards of College,« *Review of Economics and Statistics,* February 1977.

Freeman, R. »Employment Opportunities as an Economic Variable« unpublished paper, 1977.

Griliches, Z. »Notes on the Role of Education in Production Functions and Growth Accounting,« in *Education, Income and Human Capital,* W.L. Hansen (ed.), New York: N.B.E.R.

Keat, P. »Long-Run Changes in the Occupational Wage Structure, 1900 — 1956« *Journal of Political Economy,* Dec. 1960.

Layard, R, and P. Fallon, »Capital-Skill Complementarity: Income Distribution and Output Accounting« *Journal of Political Economy* 83: June 1975, pp. 279 — 302.

Ober, H. »Occupational Wage Differentials 1907 — 1947« *Monthly Labor Review* 67, August 1948, 127 — 134.

Reder, M. »Wage Differentials: Theory and Measurement« in National Bureau of Economic Research, *Aspects of Labor Economics,* Princeton, 1962.

Segal, M. »Occupational Wage Differentials in Major Cities During the 1950's« in *Human Resources in the Urban Economy,* M. Perlman (ed.) Johns Hopkins Press.

Tinbergen, J. »Substitution of Graduate by Other Labor«, *Kyklos* 27, 217 — 226.

D. Income Inequality in its Political Environment

Gustav F. Papanek
Economic Growth, Income Distribution, and the Political Process in Less Developed Countries

The extensive literature of the last five years dealing with income distribution in the less developed countries[1] (LDC) has been pre-occupied with the proposition advanced by Kuznets in 1955, that in the process of development income distribution first become less, then more equal. There has also been some analysis of changes in the absolute income of the poor as average income rises. In addition, substantial effort has been devoted to the effect of redistribution on growth and to the redistributive impact of various policies and programs. The relationship of redistributive policies and politics has largely been neglected, as has the effect of growth *rates* on income distribution and the absolute income of the poor.

Secular Relationship of Development and Income Distribution

W.R. Cline in his excellent survey summarizes the theoretical arguments for an inverted U-shaped curve of income distribution as development proceeds: Kuznets' argument when he originally advanced the hypothesis, that it is due to the more rapid accumulation of assets by the rich than the poor and to urbanization[2], the contention of others that it is due to the development of a dual economy, and so on. Empirical support for the hypothesis has been presented by several analysts, primarily based on cross-country data[3]. As a result the hypothesis has been generally accepted, even though there is little information on time trends in particular countries and that primarily for the developed world.

The most exhaustive study of income distribution for less developed countries, the book by Chenery et al., has sketchy data for growth over a decade or two in thirteen countries. These do not support the inverted-U hypothesis, but the time period is really too short for a relationship that is supposed to describe secular change. The evidence from cross-country data also is not conclusive. To use cross-country data to analyze temporal changes is, of course, always risky. The cross-country data on income distribution are biased first by the fact that the middle income group of countries, with per capita incomes of $ 200 − 700, includes a number of resource-rich countries with a socio-economic system sometimes described as neo-colonial or »internal colonialism«: a small enclave where »foreigners« and a few indigenous people benefit from mineral (or other) exports, while most of the population lives in a largely subsistence traditional sector. The »foreigners« may be citizens of the country, but ethnically different from the poor majority. Extreme examples are the highly dualistic economies of South Africa and Rhodesia, quite atypical for less developed countries. That such countries are not egalitarian provides little evidence for the contention that better integrated, more homogenous countries will also have an unequal income distribution when the latter reach the same level of per capita income. That Rhodesia's income was quite unequal when per capita income reached $ 200 does not really suggest that the income of, say, Pakistan or India, will become much less equally distributed when their per capita income increases from $ 100 to $ 200.

The influence on the results of the raw-material-rich, dualistic, neocolonial economies is shown by Table 1. With all countries from one study[4] included, the typical inverted-U distribution is clear; with seven neocolonial/dualistic countries[5] (and one duplication) excluded the evidence is not very conclusive.

Table 1 Per Capita Income and Income Distribution

% of National Income to:

Per capita income	N	Lowest 60 %	Middle 40 % to 80 %	Top 5 %
$145 or below	14	28 %	28 %	28 %
$146 to $300	21	21	25	24
Above $300	15	28	32	28
Excluding all neo-colonial, dualistic and duplication				
$145 or below	13	26 %	26 %	28 %
$146 to $300	10	24	28	28
Above $300	13	29	32	25

Source: Adelman-Morris (*op. cit.*) for income distribution; IBRD »World Tables« for per capita income.

A later cross-country analysis again provides somewhat mixed evidence (Table 2.) From that one can conclude the following:

i. There is no clear evidence that there is an increase in equality as per capita income goes beyond $ 850.

ii. The very poor countries, less than $ 150 in the late 1960s in most cases are quite egalitarian. This stands to reason. In countries with an average per capita income of $ 100, if the lowest 20 % had less than 4 % of total income, quite typical for countries with higher incomes, the average income of the poor would be less than $ 20 a year, probably not enough to live on, even if nearly all income goes for carbohydrates[6].

iii. There is no convincing evidence that once countries move out of the class of the really poor (around $ 150 per capita), income distribution continues to

Table 2 Income Levels and Income Distribution (numbers of countries)

	High	Moderate	Low	Total
	----------------inequality----------------------			
Average per capita income				
Up to $ 150	1	5	5	11
$ 150 – $229	9	3	3	15
$ 300 – $ 750	10	6	5 (3)	21
$ 850 or above	3	8	8 (5)	19
($ 1,800 +)	(1)	(6)	(4)	11

Source: Chenery et al., *op cit.* (Figures in parentheses exclude Eastern European countries)

deteriorate. On the contrary, if one takes the data in Table 2 seriously, income distribution tends to be better in the $ 300 – 750 group than in the $ 150 – 229 group.

In short, cross-country data do not permit the kind of firm conclusion that has been widely accepted about the inverted-U shaped pattern of income distribution. The two tails of the U seems to exist, or rather the really poor countries are inevitably reasonably egalitarian and the very rich countries are also egalitarian. Equal incomes among countries above $ 850 per capita may be due to the economic reasons usually cited, but may also be caused by the fact that the developed countries include the Western democracies where the poor majority influence the political process and the countries of Eastern Europe, where inequality in private asset holding is not an important factor. There appear to be three clusters of countries –– the egalitarian very poor and the egalitarian rich and the less egalitarian group from $ 150 to $ 850 –– not a relatively continuous curve.

Moreover, at all levels of per capita income, some countries are quite egalitarian and some have quite unequal distributions of income. In other words, there is nothing inevitable about changes in income distribution as average income rises. Economic structure and government policy appear to be more significant than per capita income in determining income distribution.

So much for a re-examination of data assembled so far. A somewhat different approach leads to further doubts on the existence of the inverted U-shaped distribution. Drawing on World Bank data[7], Graph 1 shows for 61 countries a comparison of income per capita and the Gini coefficient. No pattern appears evident. Regression equation (1) has the right signs, but the coefficients are low and not significant. Ahluwalia obtained significant results when he used different statistics for inequality (share of different groups), and a dummy for Eastern European countries. However, the use of the Gini coefficient as index of inequality, but using the same data and specifications as his, although without dummy, leads to no significant result. Clearly the relationship between income distribution and income per capita is not a robust one.

		Constant	Log per capita GNP	(Log per capita GNP)^2	
(1)	Gini =	– 1.06	0.14	– 0.016	R^2 = 0.059
					F = 1.8
	(t statistic)	(–0.85)	(0.34)	(–0.51)	N = 61

261

Graph 1 Income and Income Equality — A Cross Section Analysis

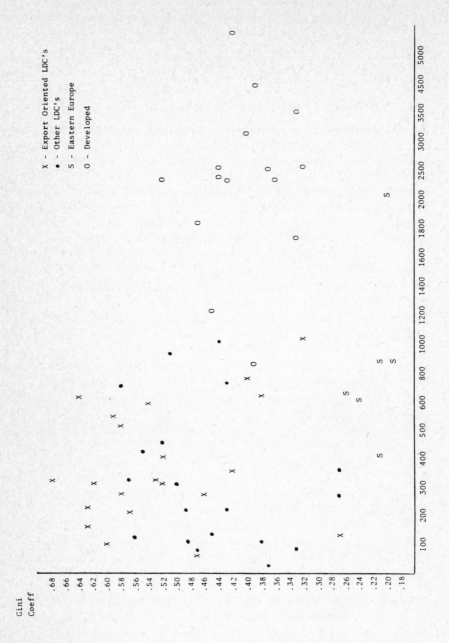

Source: See Footnote 7.

Examination of the scatter diagram suggests there are four clusters of countries, with different characteristics. The inverted-U shape derived from cross-country analysis may, to a considerable extent, be a statistical artifact, the result of forcing these four clusters with different characteristics to fit a relatively smooth curve.

First, there are the 14 developed market economy countries, with high incomes and an egalitarian income distribution, which show no evidence of any trend towards equality as per capita income increases (regression 2). Then there are

		Constant	Log per capita GNP	(Log per capita GNP)^2	
(2)	Gini =	6.45	−1.81	0.11	$R^2 = 0.04$
					$F = 0.2$
	(t)	(0.43)	(−0.47)	(0.45)	$N = 14$

the six East European countries, with a lower income (median $ 800 against $ 2,300) and an income distribution more equal than the other developed countries (Gini .24 against .40). The East European countries also show no trend within the group. In fact, since the East European cluster is lower in both income and Gini coefficient than the rest of the developed world, that part of the graph is the oppostie of the inverted-U hypothesis: the right hand tail rises again when it should be declining. Moreover the countries with per capita incomes above $ 1,000, which include all developed countries, plus one Eastern European and one less developed (LDC) show no trend when per capita income and Gini are compared.

The third group are the highly dualistic, raw material exporting, countries. They have higher incomes and more unequal incomes than the other LDC. Rents and quasi-rents tend to accrue to private owners of mines or oilfields or to the officials who administer them for the state. Production is capital intensive and there is therefore a strong incentive and considerable ability to increase the income of the professionals, managers and the handful of workers involved in the mining, oil, or planation sectors. Typically the workers for the national oil monopoly or the copper mines receive pay double or more that for comparable occupations elsewhere in the economy.

Within this group of raw material exporting, dualistic economies, are also found the handful of countries with an internal colonial structure: e.g., the handful of whites in Rhodesia receive several times the compensation of the majority of blacks, in the mines as elsewhere. This tends to exacerbate the characteristics of the groups. For this group as well there is no significant relationship within the group between income per capita and income distribution.

The last group are other LDC, not primarily raw-material export oriented, again with no significant relationship between per capita income and inequality. The following equation with the Gini coefficient as dependent variable and income per capita as the explanatory variable shows:

   i. no significant slope for any of the four groups
   ii. significantly different intercepts,

indicating that the Gini coefficient differs among the groups, but within the groups there is no significant relationship between income per capita and income distribution.

Somewhat different specifications produce similar results. For instance, with the slope dummys in log form the R-square rises to 0.63 and the t-statistic for »other LDC« becomes 1.2, while the t-statistic for all other country groups is 0.5 or less (DW: 2.3). Or if the income per capita squared for all countries is introduced as

(3)	Dummys for intercepts of following groups	Estimated Coefficient	Standard Error	T Statistic	
	Primary export oriented	0.53	0.037	14.1	
	Other LDC	0.43	0.033	13.1	
	Eastern Europe	0.24	0.073	3.3	
	Developed	0.42	0.059	7.1	
	Slope dummys for following groups				
	Primary export oriented	0.00003	0.00008	0.3	$R^2 = 0.55$
	Other LDC	0.00008	0.00007	1.1	DW = 2.2
	Eastern Europe	0.00002	0.00007	−0.3	N = 61
	Developed	0.00001	0.00002	−0.3	

another term the t-statistic for all groups drops further, the new term is completely without significance and nothing else changes. Similarly, nothing chages, if income per capita squared and all other slope dummys are logged. Of course, all of these attempts could be misspecified in a more fundamental way, but minor changes in the specifications do not change the results.

There is one interesting relationship however. For the LDC as a group, the more important raw material exports are in GNP, the more unequal the income distribution. Plausible explanations were offered earlier.

		Constant	Log per capita GNP	Log exports as % GNP	
(4)	Gini =	−0.78	0.05	0.14	$R^2 = 0.21$
	(t)	(−2.6)	(1.1)	(2.7)	F = 4.9
					N = 40

		Per capita GNP	Exports as % GNP		
(5)	Gini =	0.41	0.0	0.30	$R^2 = 0.17$
	(t)	(11.1)	(0.9)	(2.5)	F = 3.8
					N = 40

Finally, disaggregating countries into groups according to per capita income, none of the groups shows any very significant relationship with the Gini coefficient. If there is indeed rising inequality as per capita income rises, one would expect to find this in sub-samples for countries with per capita income up to $ 350 or to $ 500, but t-statistics are around 0.5. For the poorest LDC —— per capita incomes to $ 700 —— that are not raw material exporters, rising inequality and rising incomes appear to be slightly, but not very significantly correlated (regression 6).

The tendency for inequality to increase would be more evident but for the inclusion of Taiwan and Korea in the subsample: economic structure (labor-intensive industry) and strategy (e.g.: land reform) can more than compensate for the effect on income distribution of the normal changes in structure brought by development.

		Constant	Income per capita	
(6)	Gini =	0.09	0.00022	R = 0.14
	(t)	(8.8)	(1.5)	N = 16

In short, the conclusions reached on the basis of this more detailed analysis are:

i. There is no convincing support from cross-country analysis for the hypothesis that an n-shaped or inverted U-shaped realtionship exists between per capita income and income distribution.

ii. Instead there are probably four groups of countries with differences in average per capita income and inequality, which may permit in cross-country analysis an inverted U form to be imposed on the data.

iii. Within these four groups —— the developed, Eastern European, raw-material exporters and other LDC —— no clear relationship is observable between per capita income and income distribution.

iv. There is some tendency for inequality to increase as countries move from an essentially agricultural, subsistence economy with a per capita income around $ 100, to a more differentiated economic structure with incomes around $ 150 – 200. But there is no very good evidence that inequality continues to increase thereafter in less developed countries.

v. For the LDC, inequality is correlated with dependence on raw material exports.

The point of all this is to suggest that the pre-occupation with the conflict between the development process and equity is probably unwarranted; inequality does not necessarily, or even usually, increase as LDC become wealthier. A few countries with an internal neo-colonial system show up in cross-country analysis with high income and high inequality among the less developed. They help constitute the top of the inverted U. But one must obviously be careful about drawing conclusions for more integrated LDC from the experience of such countries. Most important is the fact that at all levels of per capita income there are highly egalitarian countries. The strategy of development pursued and the resulting economic structure, have far more influence on income distribution than per capita income. The Kuznets hypothesis does not justify the abandonment by policy makers of the goal of greater income equality as countries become wealthier.

The Secular Relationship of Development and the Absolute Income of the Poor

The contention that development initially leads to a worsening of income distribution has been carried a step futher by some analysts, who contend that it even results in a decline in the absolute income of the poor. The principal advocates of this position are Adelman and Morris[8], but it has been widely accepted and quoted. If true, it would be a dramatic and pessimistic conclusion, which leads Adelman and Morris to suggest »It takes at least a generation for the poorest 60 % to recover the loss in absolute income associated with the typical spurt in growth.«[9]

However, the Adelman-Morris conclusion is based both on the dubious assumption that inequality increases with per capita income, discussed earlier, and, apparently, on a fallacy: that with development the deterioration in the share of the lower income groups is instantaneous while the increase in average per capita income proceeds at only 3 % a year. Naturally on these assumptions the absolute income of the lower income group declines. But there is no logical basis for assuming that when growth begins the share of the poor drops instantaneously to a lower level, while the increase in average income is a gradual process. Even if the assumption is accepted that the share of the poor declines as a result of development, their absolute income will rise as long as the rate of decline in their share is not more rapid than the rate of growth in per capita income.

The cross-section evidence also runs counter to the Adelman-Morris thesis: as development proceeds and average per capita income increases, the absolute income of the lower income groups rises as well. Even using the Adelman-Morris cross-country data, the original source of the conclusions on deterioration in absolute income of the poor, it is clear that in fact the absolute income of poor groups increases.

Table 3 Average Income of Poorest Groups at Different Levels of Development

Income Ranges	Average income	Share of lowest 60 %	20 %	Average absolute income of lowest 60 %	20 %
$ 145 or less	$ 94	28 %	6 %	$ 44	$ 28
$ 146 − $ 300	194	21	4	68	38
$ 300 or more	502	28	4	234	100

Source: Calculated from Adelman-Morris, 1972. (N = 44)
Lowest 20 % from M.S. Ahluwalia, *op. cit.*

In other words, as per capita income moves from roughly $ 100 to $ 200, the poorest 60 % have an average increase of over 50 % in absolute income, and even the poorest 20 % have experienced an increase of one-third. As per capita income increases further, the absolute income of the poor shows an even more dramatic increase.

The Chenery et al. study confirms these conclusions: in (4) countries with GNP per capita above $ 400, only 1.5 % of the population had an estimated income below a minimum poverty level of $ 50 a year. For (6) countries with per capita GNP of $ 150 − 400, the figure below the poverty line is 21 %, and for those (5) below $ 150 it is 45 %. As the authors point out, there are some exceptions to the general rule that raising average incomes means a lower proportion of the very poor. Korea and Zambia, with per capita incomes around $ 200, have a smaller percentage of very poor than Peru, Colombia and Brazil, with per capita incomes about 25 % higher. But the general cross-country pattern is for absolute poverty to diminish as per capita income rises.

Ahluwalia, in his more detailed study, concludes that »estimated cross-country elasticity of the average incomes of the poor with respect to per capita GNP of the economy is 0.76 for the lowest 20 percent, 0.85 for the lowest 40 percent and 0.89 for the lowest 60 percent.«[10]

So much for the cross-country data. Again time series data on changes in absolute income in less developed countries exist only for relatively brief periods. However, they too confirm that absolute income of the poor rises, even if their relative share declines, as the economy develops.

For instance, Peru's rate of growth was just below 6 % from 1950 to 1966. The country was often criticized for an unequal income distribution and a government dominated by an insensitive oligarchy. According to a study by Webb[11] income distribution deteriorated, adding support to the contention that reasonably rapid economic growth is not sufficient to avoid growing inequity. But Webb also estimates that 75 − 85 % of the population experienced improvement in real income. A fairly rapid rate of growth meant economic improvement for the overwhelming majority of the poor, even in a rather dualistic economy and even before the beginning of a government committed to redistributive policies.

In Colombia, workers in industry, construction and commerce, and domestics had increases in real wages over a decade or fifteen years that ranged from 20 % to 65 %. The real wage of unskilled constructionworkers (in Bogota) also increases over 60 % from the early 1950's to the early 1960's and rose by another 5 % to the late 1960's[12].

In short, to the extent that available time series and cross-country data permit any conclusion, it is that with significant growth in average per capita income the absolute income of the lower income groups also rises. If one is concerned with the absolute income of the poor, no conflict between growth and equity seems to arise.

The Rate of Growth and Income Distribution

The effect on income distribution of the basic choice of capitalist or socialist strategy and the effect over time of development have often been confused with the effect of the *rate* of growth. They are obviously not the same. Once a country has started to develop and has decided to adopt a basically private enterprise or mixed economy, what is the short-run impact of different growth rates?

The policies and programs adopted to achieve higher growth are clearly important to the outcome. Steps that reduce consumption of the wealthy and that eliminate windfall profits are generally favorable for both a high rate of growth and for greater equity. On the other hand, steps that shift income to the rich *may* increase the rate of savings, and therefore of growth, but at the cost of equity.

On a priori grounds one can therefore not reach any conclusions about the effect of the growth rate on equity. The empirical evidence is unfortunately quite limited and mixed.

Chenery et al. have data for 18 countries comparing growth rates and the share of the poorest 40 %. The sample is small but it appears that in the rapidly growing countries income distribution improved in most cases, while among the slow growers as many showed deterioration as improvement. If anything, this suggests that a rapid rate of growth is good for equity. (The results would not change if Bulgaria and Yugoslavia were removed from the comparison.)

267

Table 4 The Growth Rate and Income Distribution (share of poorest 40 %)

| | Growth rate of GNP | | | |
| | 6 % or above | | Below 6 % | |
	All countries	LDC	All countries	LDC
Improved or unchanged equality	6	4	1	1
Reduced equality	5	5	6	4

Source: Calculated from Chenery *et al.*

Ahluwalia shows no correlation between high growth rates and inequality in his cross-country sample. At least there is no evidence in his study that more rapid rates of growth lead to more unequal income distribution. The final bit of data comes from a comparison of the rather similar economies of India and Pakistan. In the 1960's the per capita growth rate in Pakistan (3.1 %) was about double that of India (1.6 %). In rapidly growing Pakistan the Gini coefficient declined in the 1960's from .387 (in 63/64) to .330 (in 70/71) while in slowly growing India, it rose from .343 (in 53 −57) to .478 (in 67/68)[13] . While such data are not very robust, they at least suggest that rapid growth was not unfavorable to greater equity.

The Rate of Growth and the Absolute Income of the Poor

If income distribution is not affected by the rate of growth, then the absolute income of the poor should rise more quickly the higher the rate of growth. If rapid growth actually leads to an improvement in income distribution then the absolute income of the poor would benefit even more from rapid growth. There is independent evidence on the effect of the growth rate on the income of some groups among the poor majority.

As noted earlier, the per capita rate of growth of Pakistan was nearly double that of India in the 1960's. In the 1950's the situation was reversed, with India's per capita income growing slowly (1.8 %) but Pakistan's practically stagnant (.3 %). In the early 1960's the growth rate in both India and Pakistan was especially high. A third Asian country, Indonesia, had stagnant or declining per capita incomes until 1965, and a rapid rate of growth (about 5 %) from 1967 to 1972. In all three countries there was a high degree of correlation between changes in real wages and in per capita income. When the economy stagnated real wages fell, in some cases quite drastically; when the economy grew rapidly, real wages rose, in some cases very dramatically. The changes in both directions were moderate for industrial workers, who are not rich but are certainly not among the really poor. But the effects on the rural poor —— landless laborers in East Pakistan, now Bangladesh, and plantation workers in Indonesia —— was even greater. They lost most during periods of stagnation, gained most during periods of growth.

Table 5 Changes in Real Wages

	1950's	*early 1960's*
India	− 4 to + 8 %	+ 13 %
Pakistan	− 15 to + 3 %	+ 10 to + 35 %
Indonesia (1952 − 65)	− 60 %	+ 75 % to 200 % (1965−72)

Source: Calculated by the author, see *Ibid* and »Real Wages in Indonesia«
(mimeographed draft)

Evidence from these countries is especially persuasive because similar economies are being compared, so that the ceteris paribus clause is quite well observed. The comparison is between periods of stagnation and more rapid growth in all three countries and between more and less rapid growth in the early 1960's in two quite comparable countries (India and Pakistan). In effect there are four different comaprisons, three over time in the same country, and one for two similar countires, with consistent results.

Four cases do not unequivocal conclusions make, and the data are for wage earners rather than the lowest income groups, but they do provide additional evidence, consistent with that provided earlier in the paper.

The Relationship with the Political Process

The same three countries also provide some interesting insights into the relationship between growth, income distribution and the political process. Pakistan's disintegration as a state in 1971 was an occasion for drawing conclusions about the linkage between economic development strategies and political consequences. In somewhat oversimplified form they can be stated as follows:

i. In a mixed economy with heavy reliance on private enterprise, policies and programs to achieve a high rate of economic growth result in a deterioration of income distribution and no improvement in the absolute income of the poor.

ii. With the rich becoming obviously richer and the poor experiencing no improvement, political and social tensions are bound to rise, resulting in serious political difficulties for the government in power.

This position was stated in rather clear form in a book on Pakistan by K. Griffin and A.R. Khan, »Until recently Pakistan was widely acclaimed for its rapid growth of output per head. It was less widely recognised abroad, however, that this growth was accompanied by an increase in the number of poor people and a decline in their standard of living . . . this policy has been carried to such an extreme that the standard of living of the majority of the population has declined . . . the fact of growing inequality, have led to intense political controversy, to attempts by East Pakistan to achieve regional autonomy and, finally, to the declaration of an independent Bangladesh.«[14]

A superficial look at the experience of India and Indonesia, as well as Pakistan, supports these conclusions. The 1960's for Pakistan and the period 1967 − 1973 for Indonesia were periods of rapid growth under the aegis of governments that made growth their major objective and claim for political support. Criticism of government policy in both countries centered on neglect of the poor and increasing concentration of income, wealth and power. The period of rapid growth ended with riots and antigovernment agitation —— beginning in 1968 in Pakistan, 1973/74 in Indonesia —— which had economic grievances as a major focus and justification. In India, on the other hand, the Congress Party, which had been in power for twenty-five years of virtual economic stagnation, registered its great electoral triumph at the same time that Pakistan was disintegrating. Indonesia and Pakistan during their periods of stagnation seem to have experienced few political disturbances based on economic grievances.

On the face of it, one can therefore make a plausible case that emphasis on growth led to political problems.

However, the data provided above do not support the causal sequence: rapid growth leads to worsening inequality and deterioration or stagnation in the income of the poor, which in turn leads to political problems. Evidence for the middle link is missing: rapid growth does not lead to greater inequality and it does produce more rapid improvement in the absolute income of some groups of the poor. Therefore, alternative explanations need to be found for the political difficulties of the countries with a rapid rate of economic growth. There is some evidence in support of the following hypotheses:

a. All three countries have economies that are vulnerable to short-term economic shocks, especially as the result of poor weather. At the time of such shocks there is likely to be a drastic decline in the income of some important groups among the poor majority, unless deliberate policy steps are taken to avoid this effect.

Preliminary evidence indicates that, indeed, there was a drastic short-term decline in real wages and in the income of several groups just prior to political problems in both Pakistan and Indonesia. (In India as well, the food riots of the early 1970's seem to have occurred at such a time.)

Table 6 Short-Term Changes in Real Wages

	1972 − I/1968	1973 − I/1972
Indonesia	+ 54 to + 77 %	− 14 to − 51 %
	1964/1959	1966/1964
Pakistan	+ 20 to 35 %	− 15 to − 23 %

The political consequences of such a drastic, short-term decline in income may be especially severe if:

i. the decline follows on a period of rapid increase in income, which has raised hopes, and

ii. the decline in the income of the poor occurs at a time of undiminished conspicuous consumption by the rich.

Again both conditions seem to have held in Indonesia and Pakistan. One of the best indices of conspicuous consumption was passenger cars, used by the rich, and motorcycles, used by the upper middle-class and the sons of the rich. The increase in transportation facilities for the rich is especially dramatic when compared to changes in the number of buses used by the urban poor and lower middle class.

Table 7 Motor Vehicles — Indonesia

	Passenger Cars	Buses	Motorcycles
1963 — 66	+ 25 %	− 13 %	+ 44 %
1966 — 70	+ 34 %	+ 20 %	+ 56 %
1970 — 74	+ 41 %	+ 29 %	+ 115 %

b. Almost regardless of rates of growth and likely income distribution, the majority in these countries are and will remain poor for decades to come. They often live on hopes, the expectation that things will get better. It may therefore matter a great deal whether they see the government as being concerned with their lot, trying to improve their position, and curbing the extravagances of the rich, or as interested only in the well-being of the wealthy.

The governments of both Pakistan and Indonesia took steps in 1966 and 1972 respectively that could be interpreted as showing a lack of concern with the poor, while the Indian government consistently for 20 years had acted in a variety of ways to express its concern with poverty. (This was also true for Indonesia during the Soekarno regime.)

c. The continuing poverty of the majority may become a serious political issue only in contrast to the obvious consumption of the rich. If disparities in income are not ranslated into equally great disparities in consumption, because the rich save a substantial proportion, the poorer groups may hardly be aware of income disparities. Conspicuous consumption was obvious and growing in Pakistan in the mid-1960's, in Indonesia around 1970, but was severely curbed during periods of slow growth in Pakistan, Indonesia and India.

d. A variety of specific economic and related factors may also have contributed to developments in one or more of the three countries, including:

i. The effect of foreign competition on the economic well-being of politically important groups in Indonesia.

ii. The exclusion from economic (as well as political) benefits and power of an important elite group in Pakistan (the Bengalis of East Pakistan). This is somewhat different than the disparities in income and growth rates between East and West Pakistan, often cited as important.

iii. The access to economic rewards through the political process in India, but not in Pakistan.

In short, changes in income distribution as measured by overall economic indices, such as Gini coefficients, may have been less important in affecting the political process than the impact of short-term fluctuations and of specific policies on particular groups of the poor, the extent of conspicuous consumption and the impact of the image projected by the government.

On the other hand, the image projected by the Indian government and that of Soekarno's Indonesia was not without its cost. Some of the policies and programs designed to demonstrate a concern with the poor had economic consequences which partly explain the economic stagnation in both countries. Slow growth in turn meant fewer resources available to society and government, resources necessary if performance in meeting the economic needs of politically important groups was not to fall far short of promise. In both countries policies

271

that were poor economics but good politics in the short run resulted in longer-term economic, and therefore political, problems.

Conclusions

In many cases the conclusions of this paper run counter to the current conventional wisdom on the relationships of growth, income distribution and the political process. The evidence provided for these conclusions has been reasonably extensive in some cases, sketchy in others. The latter reflect the current state of work on these aspects. Stated without the usual qualifications they are:

1. There is no support for a relationship between long-term development (that is, a rise in per capita income) and income distribution which resembles an inverted U. At all levels of per capita income there are egalitarian economies. Therefore there is no necessary, or even likely, conflict between secular growth and equality of income distribution.

2. If income distribution generally does not deteriorate as per capita income rises, then growth tends to increase the absolute income of the poor. There is good independent evidence that over time the absolute income of the poor increases with development.

3. There is no evidence that a higher rate of growth in a mixed or predominantly capitalist economy results in a less equal distribution of income. There is some evidence to the contrary, but it is not very strong. The relationship is obviously affected by the policies pursued to achieve a high rate of growth.

4. Therefore a high rate of growth is favorable for a rapid rise in the absolute income of the poor.

5. Nevertheless, rapid growth may lead to political problems for the government in power if:

  a. short term economic setbacks, inevitable for many LDC, temporarily but sharply lower the real income of politically important groups of the poor;

  b. such setbacks occur after the hopes of these groups have been raised by rapid improvement;

  c. they are accompanied by continuing conspicuous consumption by the rich;

  d. in general the government gives the impression that it is little concerned with the poor and gives little ground to hope for improvement in their lot which, regardless of growth rate and almost regardless of feasible changes in income distribution, is bound to remain difficult.

In all respects discussed there appears to be no conflict between the objectives of growth and equality. One likely area of conflict was not discussed:[15] the choice of development strategy. Variants of socialist economies, among the less developed countries, if they involve massive direct government intervention in the economy for the sake of equality, or for other reasons, appear generally to have a more equal distribution of income, but a lower rate of growth. But, in the typical mixed/private enterprise economy, growth and equality may not be conflicting objectives.

Notes

[1] Covered in a comprehensive survey article by William R. Cline, (»Distribution and Development«, *Journal of Devleopment Economics,* February 1975.) Some of the material, reporting on earlier work on the same subject, was presented at the Seventh Rehovot Conference, September 1973 (G.F. Papanek, »Growth, Income Distribution and Politics in Less Developed Countries«, (mimeographed) and was excerpted/summarized in Y. Ramati, (ed.), *Economic Growth in Developing Countries,* Praeger, 1975.

[2] S. Kuznets, »Economic Growth and Income Inequality«, *American Economic Review,* No. 1, 1955.

[3] e.g.: H. Chenery, M.S. Ahluwalia, C.L.G. Bell, J.H. Duloy, R. Jolly, *Redistribution With Growth* (Oxford University Press, 1974); I. Adelman and C.R. Morris, *Economic Growth and Social Equity in Developing Countries* (Stanford University Press, 1973); M.S. Ahluwalia, »Inequality, Poverty and Development«, IBRD (mimeographed 1976).

[4] Adelman & Morris, *op. cit.*

[5] Dualistic: South Africa, Rhodesia, Libya in 1962, Trinidad in 1965, Iraq in 1956, Peru in 1961 and Gabon in 1960. In most or all of these countries, the rich were generally from a different ethnic, and often racial, group than the poor. Duplication: Chad and Niger are shown with essentially identical income distributions in the statistics.

[6] One kg. of rice cost between U.S. $ 0.10 and 0.20 in Asia, so 300 kg., the amount widely assumed to be required, costs $ 30 – 60. Children eat less, other carbohydrates cost less per kg. On the other hand, expenditures can not be limited wholly to carbohydrates, so $ 20 is probably inadequate to survive.

[7] Gini from Shail Jain, »Size Distribution of Income«, The World Bank, 1975. »Raw Material Exporters« are defined as countries whose primary goods exports were 20 % of GNP or more, from G.F. Papanek, S.C. Jakubiak, E. Levine, »Statistical Appendix to: AID, Foreign Private Investment, Savings and Growth in Less Developed Countries«, (mimeographed, Harvard University); per capita income from M.S. Ahluwalia, *op. cit.*

[8] cf: I. Adelman, »Planning for Social Equity«, in H.C. Bos, H. Linneman & P. deWolff (eds.), *Economic Structure and Development* (North Holland, 1973), pp. 184 – 185; I. Adelman, C.T. Morris & S. Robinson, »Policies for Equitable Growth«, Paper for the Conference on Economic Development and Income Distribution, University of Colorado, 1976 is the latest restatement. The initial presentation, widely quoted and used, was in Adelman-Morris, *op. cit.*

[9] *Op. cit.* p. 179

[10] Cline *(op. cit.)* also reaches the conclusion that Adelman and Morris are in error.

[11] Richard C. Webb, »Trends in Real Income in Peru, 1950 – 1966« and »Government and the Distribution of Income in Peru Since 1961«, (mimeographed, undated) Princeton

[12] A. Berry, »Some Determinants of Changing Income Distribution in Colombia: 1930 – 1970«, Economic Growth Center, Yale University (mimeographed), March 22.

[13] Growth data from G.F. Papanek, »India and Pakistan: the Effects of Development Stragegy on Growth, Efficiency, Equity and Politics« (mimeographed draft); income distribution from Jain, *op. cit.*

[14] K. Griffin and Azizur Rahman Khan, (eds.), *Growth and Inequality in Pakistan* (London: MacMillan, 1972) p. 204.

[15] Covered in Papanek, 1973, *op. cit.*

Oldrich Kýn*
**Education, Sex and Income Inequality
in Soviet-type Socialism**

There is no doubt that the social, political and economic transformation of East
European countries after the Communist takeover has led to considerable changes
in their income distributions. It is also quite apparent that these changes significantly diminished[1], but did not fully eliminate, the economic inequality among
various population groups.

The purpose of this paper is to study empirically two aspects of income distribution in Poland and Czechoslovakia, namely the inequality resulting from
different levels of education and from differentials in incomes of men and women.
Other aspects of income distribution will be mentioned briefly to allow for an
overall comparison of the reality of income distribution with the normative
statements of Marxian economic theory.

The Normative View of Marxian Theory on Income Distribution Under Socialism

The original Marxian view on distributive justice is very far from crude egali-
tarianism. Marx and Engels never argued for absolutely equal incomes of all
people, although they did believe that the capitalist distribution of income is too
unequal and unjust and must therefore be replaced by a new socialist or communist form of distribution. The best known reference for Marx's own view on
income distribution under socialism and communism can be found in his »Critique of the Gotha Programme,« where he states that under socialism, which he
defined as a lower stage of communist society, people should be rewarded according to their work or »contribution to society,« while in the second stage or »full
communism« people should be rewarded according to their needs. Neither of
these principles requires a full equality of incomes.

The Marxian principle »equal amount of product for equal amount of labor«
must necessarily produce quite considerable income differentials[2] especially if
it is interpreted in the context of the labor theory of value. The »contribution to
society« must be measured in some way, if it is to be a basis for the distribution
of income, and for Marxists it would be natural to measure it — at least in the case

* I am indebted to Ludmila Kýnová and Ruth Polak for research assistance and editorial help
on the final version of the paper.

of the so-called productive workers — by the value created by labor. But according to the labor theory of value the amount of value created depends on the skill of the worker and on the complexity of his labor. More complex labor is supposed to create more value in the same interval of time than simple labor[3]. The socialist principle of distribution therefore implies that a person with higher skills should receive a higher wage than a less skilled worker. As long as higher skills are obtained by individual effort, schooling or experience, such income differentials may be »deserved«. But income inequality under socialism may also result from variation in inborn physical and mental abilities. »One man is superior to another physically or mentally and so supplies more labor in the same time or can labor for longer time.«[4] Socialist equality is therefore only the equality of the right to income and not the equality of income. »It recognizes no class differences, because everyone is only a worker like everyone else; but it tacitly recognizes unequal individual endowments and thus productive capacity as natural privileges.«[5]

The principle »from everybody according to his abilities to everybody according to his needs« which was designed by Marx for the second stage of communism does not imply full income equality either. As long as people remain physically and intellectually different, they will continue to have different needs so that unequal incomes would be retained even under »full communism«. In the section called »Private Property and Communism« of his »Economic and philosophical Manuscripts« Marx distinguished two forms of communism:

The first one, which he called a »crude communism« seems to be a simplistic and spontaneous reaction of the formerly oppressed and under-privileged against the rich and powerful. Marx argued that »crude communism« called for »equality of wages« only because it was an expression of »envy and the desire to reduce everything to a common level«.[6] Obviously Marx did not like this kind of crude communism because »it aims to destroy everything which is incapable of being possessed by everyone,« because »it wishes to eliminate talent etc. by force« and because it »negates the personality of man in every sphere[7]. He even compared the crudely egalitarian view on income distribution with a similar crudely communist attitude toward women: »This tendency is expressed in an animal form, marriage is contrasted with the community of women ... just as women are to pass from marriage to universal prostitution, so the whole world of wealth is to pass from the relation of exclusive marriage with the private owner to the relation of universal prostitution with the community«.[8]

In constrast to crude egalitarian communism, Marx developed his vision of true communism which is to be more than a simple negation of private property; it is to be »a positive abolition« which »assimilates all the wealth of previous development«. True communism should, of course, bring distributive justice, but Marx's vision goes far beyond that, it is to be a society where man becomes a true human being, free not only from all forms of external, (i.e. economic, political, cultural, etc.) oppression and manipulation, but also free from internal self-oppression and self-manipulation. »Communism is the abolition ... of human self-alienation, and the real appropriation of human nature through and for man«.[9] As Erich Fromm stresses: »For Marx the aim of socialism was the emancipation of man and the emancipation of man was the same as his self-realization ... The aim of socialism was the development of the individual personality.« Or in Marx's words: »The suppression of private property is therefore the complete emancipation of all the human qualities and senses.«[10]

These extensive quotations are intended to demonstrate that although Marx was very critical of the injustices and inequalities of the capitalist income distribution, his view of socialist and communist income distribution did not imply an egalitarian leveling off all incomes. Marx never specified exactly which income inequalities should be eliminated and which should remain, but it may not be difficult to draw some inferences from his views. Generally, Marx would probably argue that all types of income inequality based on artifical, man-made stratification of society into classes, racial or ethnic groups as well as inequalities resulting from the usurpation and exercise of political and social power and from the specific forms of the operation of the capitalist market economy, should be eliminated. On the other hand, the income differentials which are based on natural differences in physical and mental abilities, in acquired skills and knowledge, and possibly also differentials resulting from personal preferences (e.g. between work and leisure) would remain.

It seems clear that Marx would not opt for income equality if it were to limit personal freedom and the full development of individual potential or if it sacrificed talents to barrack-type uniformity. Also, ascetic self deprivation would not be acceptable as a tool for eliminating inequality, because it would almost surely have to be achieved by ideological mass manipulation, rather than by a truly voluntary manifestation of personal preferences.

There are three basic reasons why Marxists justify income inequality:

1. Personal differences in the quantity of work measured either by its duration or by energy expenditures which each individual contributes to society. These differences may result from different physical endowments of individuals i.e. from biological or genetic factors, as well as from differences in attitudes toward work and preferences between work and leisure, i.e. primarily from cultural or »social environment« factors.

2. Personal differences in the quality or complexity of work. These may result from different mental endowments of individuals, which may be due both to biological or genetic factors as well as differences in skills and knowledge acquired by experience or education.

3. Differences in the costs of reproducing labor power of a particular kind. According to the Marxian theory, labor which creates value is divided into two parts, necessary and surplus labor. Necessary labor is used to cover the reproduction costs of labor power and as such should be the main determinant of wages. This is relevant especially for income differentials of workers with different levels of education. It is more costly to reproduce more educated labor power, therefore wages and salaries of people with more years of schooling should be higher. However, the fact, that a considerable part of the cost of education in socialist countries is paid by the government rather than by individuals, may weaken this line of reasoning.

It may seem surprising, but probably fair to conclude, that the Marxian normative view on income distribution under socialism, although based on totally different theoretical and ideological postulates, leads to conclusions very similar to those reached in human capital theory.

Let us now turn to those sources of income inequality, which according to Marxian theory should *not* exist in socialism.

1. Probably most objectionable to Marxists is income inequality based on unequal distribution of wealth. First, Marxists regard the income from owning property as a truly undeserved, exploitative return. Second, for functional reasons Marxists believe that under socialism private property should not exist. Third, they object to private property as a source of income because it tends to maintain or increase income inequality. Wealthier people have access to better schools and to jobs which bring them higher incomes, and people with higher incomes accumulate wealth faster than those with lower incomes.

2. It seems that Marxists would object to income inequality which results from the power structure of society. The communist party apparatchik, government official or central planner may deserve higher incomes than average workers if their jobs require more experience and higher level of education, but they should not earn more simply because they belong to the upper layers of the power hierarchy.

3. Marxists should also find objectionable income inequality based purely on sex, race or ethnicity. Such income differentials are discriminatory, and have nothing to do with a person's contribution to society.

4. Finally Marxists would probably object to income differentials resulting from persistent disequilibrium between supply and demand in the labor market. According to the original Marxist view all parts of a socialist economy should be rationally planned *ex ante* so that supply and demand for individual categories of labor should always be in equilibrium.

Empirical Evidence

It would be beyond the scope of this paper to attempt an exhaustive study of all aspects of income distribution. In any case, such a task could not be accomplished because the original source data on personal income in Poland and Czechoslovakia are not available to Western scholars. The only source of information available to us are data already processed by simple statistical routines, i.e. averages, frequency tables or cross-tabulations. For these reasons we shall concentrate our attention only on a few selected aspects of economic inequality, while other aspects may be mentioned only cassually, if at all.

Although we have almost no data on the distribution of personal wealth in Poland and Czechoslovakia, we may quite safely conclude that this source of income inequality has been almost totally eliminated. This does not mean that wealth is distributed equally — we know that considerable inequalities in this area still persist — it simply means that most of the privately owned property is »unproductive« and as such cannot generate income. There are a few exceptions, such as private farming in Poland for instance, or interest paid on personal savings, but private farmers are not very rich, and the interest rate on personal savings is only nominal.

Poland and Czechoslovakia also seem to have very few problems with income inequality based on race and ethnicity, and this is of course mostly due to the fact that both countries are in this respect relatively homogeneous. There are some indications that Czechoslovakia's policy of assimilating the gypsy population has not been very effective, but unfortunately no data on the current situation of the gypsies are available.

Somewhat more serious is the discrepancy which still exists between incomes of Czechs and Slovaks. This is an outcome of the historically lower level of economic development in Slovakia, rather then of a deliberate discrimination of Slovaks. Actually the preferential treatment of Slovakia, especially in the allocation of investment, has led to an apparent closing of the gap between the two nationalities.

For example, a comparison of average monthly wages in the two Republics[11] shows that in 1955 Czech wages were 6.1 % higher than Slovak wages, in 1960 — 3.4 %, in 1970 — 1.9 %, and by 1974 only 1.2 % higher.

However, the comparison of average monthly wages may lead to an underestimation of income inequality between Czechs and Slovaks. The micro-census data (family budgets) indicate, that the per capita income in Slovakia is still almost 20 per cent lower than in Bohemia and Moravia.

Table 1 Distribution of Czechoslovak Households According to Net Money Income per Capita (%)

Income Bracket	1970 Czech Republic	1970 Slovak Republic	1973 Czech Republic	1973 Slovak Republic
-7201	12.5	23.3	6.6	15.2
7201-9600	15.2	19.8	12.6	17.9
9601-12000	18.8	20.4	16.9	18.9
12000-14400	17.8	14.8	17.9	17.7
14401-16800	12.9	9.0	14.6	12.2
16801-19700	9.0	5.3	10.5	7.6
19201-	13.8	7.4	20.9	10.5
	100.0	100.0	100.0	100.0
Mean annual per capita income in Kčs	12,936	10,701	14,463	12,102

Source: *Statistical Yearbooks of CSSR*, 1972 pp. 475—476 and 1975 pp. 479—480.

There have been two remarkable tendencies in the intersectoral income distribution in postwar Czechoslovakia:

1. Income differentials among broad sectors of the economy have been diminished and the ranking of sectors has changed considerably (see Table 2, page 279).

Table 2 Sectoral Monthly Average Wages in Czechoslovakia

	Average wages in Kčs		Ranking of Sectors	
	1948	1970	1948	1970
Education and Culture	1022	1832	1	4
Health and Welfare	990	1776	2	7
Transportation	896	2239	3	1
Trade	840	1654	4	8
Construction	829	2195	5	2
Industry	759	1967	6	3
Agriculture	657	1806	7	5
Communication	656	1786	8	6

Source: J. Adam, *Wage, Price and Taxation Policy in Czechoslovakia 1948–1970*, Berlin, 1974.

2. Income differentials among branches of industry has not diminished and their ranking remained almost unchanged (see Table 3).

Table 3 Average Wages of Blue Collar Workers in Selected Branches of Czechoslovak Industry

	1950	1970	1950	1970
Electric power	1038	2109	3	3
Fuels	1093	2668	2	1
Ferrous metalurgy	1126	2251	1	2
Machine building	940	1936	4	4
Chemicals	894	1893	5	5
Wood working	836	1747	7	7
Glass, porcelain and ceramics	755	1661	8	8
Textile	609	1485	9	9
Food	880	1816	6	6

Source: *Statistical Yearbooks of CSSR*, 1966, p. 210, and 1972, p. 250.

3. Another interesting feature of income distribution in Czechoslovakia is the drastic change which has occurred among the relative incomes of three basic categories of workers in industry (see Table 4, page 280).

Table 4 Average Wages of Main Categories of Workers in Czechoslovak Industry

	1948	1960	1970
(1) Blue collar workers	734	1406	1902
(2) Engineering-technical personnel	1214	1868	2569
(3) Administrative staff	914	1225	1626
Ratio 2÷1 in %	165	133	135
Ratio 3÷1 in %	125	87	86

Source: J. Adam, *op.cit.*, p. 83.

There is very little direct statistical information about the relation between the level of education and incomes in Czechoslovakia. Data in Tables 2 and 4 seem to indicate that income differentials between more and less educated people have diminished, and in some cases the relation has been reversed. For example the average monthly earnings in Czechoslovakia in 1965 of a skilled coal-miner was 3521 Kcs, that of a lathe operator 2422, a doctor 2243, a locksmith 2010, a grammar school teacher 1907, a bricklayer 1865, and a hospital nurse 1178 [12].

Similarly, the cumulative income at age 60 in Czechoslovakia in the early 1960's (in thousands Kcs) was 1125 for an assembler, 989 for an engineer, 949 for a farmer, 900 for a technician, 888 for a lawyer, 771 for an economist, and 692 for an unskilled worker [13].

Probably the most striking feature of income distribution in Czechoslovakia is the persistent discrepancy between the wages and salaries of men and women. Notwithstanding the facts that (1) Marxist ideology clearly condemns discrimination of women, (2) Czechoslovak law gives them the legal right to the same wages as men, (3) the excess demand for labor and governmental policies of assistance to working women (eg. pregnancy leaves, subsidized day care centers etc.) has led to a very high level of women's participation in the labor force (47.8 % in 1974), and (4) equal educational opportunities are available to men and women, women nevertheless receive on average only two-thirds of the average income of men.

Table 5 Average Monthly Income of Men and Women in Czechoslovakia

May of the Respective Year in Kčs					
	socialist sector			industry	
	1959	1968	1970	1959	196
1) men	1596	2106	2338	1689	214
2) women	1046	1400	1565	1054	135
Ratio 2÷1 in %	65.5	66.5	66.9	62.4	63.

Source: J. Adam, *op.cit.*, p. 87.

In the breakdown of wages by industries (Table 6) we see that the overall discrepancy between the incomes of men and women can be explained partly by the fact that the women's participation ratio is higher in sectors with lower wages, and partly by the fact that in each sector the wages of women are lower than the wages of men.

Table 6 Monthly Average Wages in Sectors of Czechoslovak Economy May 1963 in Kcs

	Average Wages		Women's Wage as % of Men's Wage	Women's Participation Ratio
	Men	Women		
Construction	1787	1161	65.0	12.0
Railways	1778	1218	68.5	18.2
Bus transportation	1757	1198	68.2	14.4
Industry	1903	1192	62.6	36.4
Administration	1867	1218	65.2	45.7
Education and Culture	1759	1236	70.3	65.4
Forestry	1584	1061	67.0	33.0
Communication	1589	1179	74.2	47.2
State farms	1449	1123	77.3	40.9
Health and welfare	1824	1123	61.6	74.2
Retail trade	1565	1150	73.5	71.5
Municipal service	1463	1042	71.2	47.6
Public catering	1437	1076	74.9	67.8

Source: J. Adam, *op.cit.*, p. 89.

Several facts are noticeable: First, there is a clear negative correlation between the women's participation ratio and the level of wages among sectors. Second, the sectoral differences in women's wages are much smaller than the differences in men's wages. The standard deviation of the women's wage is only 63.8 Kcs while the standard deviation of men's wage is 166.5 Kcs. Third, the sectors with the highest women's participation level (health, education and trade) are those which have lost most in terms of relative wages (see Table 2), whereas the sectors with the lowest women's participation are those which have gained. Fourth, the above also holds for differentials among branches of industry. It can be shown that the branches with the highest women's participation level are those where the wages are lowest (e.g. textile, food), while the women's participation level in the branches with highest wages (e.g. metallurgy and coal-mining) is very low. These facts imply that in spite of a considerable increase in women's participation in the labor force, which was also accompanied by an increased level of education and training, the gap between wages and salaries of males and females has not diminished. Can this be explained rationally from the principles of socialist income distribution? Most likely not!

It may be argued, that the increased school enrollments and the increased employment of women are relatively recent pehnomena, so that their average level of education and work experience is still lower than the levels of education and experience of men. This may be true, but are the differences in education and experience large enough to explain the entire gap between incomes of men and women, so that pure sex discrimination can be ruled out? To answer this question we need data which would allow us to estimate simultaneously the role of education, experience and sex in the determination of personal incomes. Unfortunately, this kind of data cannot be obtained for Czechoslovakia. However, Polish statistics[14] contain the following two types of data, which can be used for our purpose:

1. The number of fully employed persons in the socialist sector of Polish economy in a 4-way breakdown according to 22 administrative regions (wojewòdztw), 13 economic sectors, 5 level of education, and sex.

2. Four categories of wage funds and the total number of employees in a 2-way breakdown according to 22 administrative regions (wojewòdztw) and 13 economic sectors.

Both sets of data are available for the years 1970 and 1971. The second set of data allows us to calculate average wages for each sector of each region for both years, by simply dividing the wage fund by the number of employees in the respective cells of the cross-tabulation. Two types of average wages will be used in the following regressions as left-hand variables.

W1 ... average wages of type 1 include only payments from the so called «personal wage fund«.

W2 ... average wages of type 2 include (in addition to W1) all other payments to individuals from the so called »nonpersonal wage funds«, and other funds of enterprises. This would include bonuses, honoraria, per diems, reimbursement of travel cost, etc.

The first data set was used to calculate the shares of individual educational levels, as well as the women's participation ratio in each sector of each region, for both years.

The following variables were thus obtained

UN ... share of employees with university education

SP ... share of employees with secondary professional education

SG ... share of employees with secondary general education

EP ... share of employees with elementary education and professional (vocational) training

WOM .. women's participation ratio

Our main task now will be to check whether, and how much of, the sectoral and regional variation of average wages can be explained by the above-defined five explanatory variables. We shall therefore attempt to estimate the following regression equation

$$W = \beta_0 + \beta_1 UN + \beta_2 SP + \beta_3 SG + \beta_4 EP + \beta_5 WOM + \epsilon$$

In the actual run several alternatively defined dummy variables and a special corrective variable which was designed to capture the impact of differences in the definition of total employment in the two sets of data were also included. The coefficients of this corrective variable as well as those of the dummy variables and the constants were in almost all cases significant, but they are not very interesting and will therefore not be reported.

The first regressions (see Table 7, page 284) were run for each region separately across sectors. To increase the number of observations, data for the two years were pooled and a dummy variable for 1971 was included in the regressions. The total number of observations was 22 for each of the five cities, and 26 for each of the remaining regions so that the residual number of degrees of freedom is relatively small: 15 for cities and 19 for the other regions. Although the regressions were run for both types of wage variables, only those for W1 are reported, because W2 gave the same kind of results.

The results of Table 7 show:

a. A relatively high share (.7 − .9) of sectoral differences of average wages in each region are explained by the explanatory variables of the model.

b. Consistently, the most significant explanatory variable is the women's participation ratio. The negative coefficients of WOM indicate that the average wage is 100 − 200 zlotys lower for each percent of women employed in the sector. From this type of regression however, we cannot conclude whether the lower average wage is due to the fact that women have lower wages than men, or to the fact that wages, including the wages of men, are generally lower in sectors with higher women participation. Probably both are true.

c. The majority of coefficients of educational variables are positive, but they vary quite a lot and are frequently insignificant. The only safe conclusion from these regressions seems to be that the average wages in sectors are positively correlated with the percentage of employees with a higher than elementary education. It cannot be conclusively established, however, that a secondary education will yield higher wages than an elementary education with vocational training, or that a university education always results in a higher income than a secondary education.

The second set of regressions (see Table 8, page 285) was run for each sector separately and across regions. Again, data for both years were pooled, and a dummy variable for 1971 was included in the equation. In each of the 13 sectoral regressions there were 44 observations so that the residual number of degrees of freedom was 36. This time, results for the left hand variable W2 are reported; the regressions with W1 on the left hand side gave very similar results. Although the regression equation in this case contains the same types of variables as the first case, the meaning of the regression coefficients is not indentical. For example the coefficient of WOM will no longer contain the effect of the fact that in sectors with higher women's participation, wages of men may be lower. It may seem at first glance, that the regressions should give better results because they include more homogenous units. This however, is not necessarily true, because the results may be biased by the fact that in regions with a higher general level of wages (i.e. in cities) is concentrated a higher proportion of managerial, clerical and research staff.

The results in Table 8 do actually present a somewhat different picture than the results in Table 7. With the sole exception of industry, the coefficients of WOM are small, insignificant and sometimes have positive signs. The estimated coefficients of the educational variables also seem to be unreliable − they frequently take on strange values and signs, and are very rarely significant. Only UN (the university education variable) has consistently positive, very high and rather significant coefficients.

Table 7

	Left-hand variable: W1 Region	UN	SP	SG	EP	WOM	R^2	F	Mean Wage
1.	Warszawa (city)	314 (4.62)	437 (2.32)	225 (2.90)	296 (2.08)	-304 (-6.13)	.866	12.88	35.111
2.	Krakow (city)	169 (2.77)	427 (2.94)	-.27 (-.00)	213 (1.46)	-232 (-6.47)	.818	8.97	32,138
3.	Lodz (city)	162 (2.08)	71 (.61)	61 (1.17)	49 (.27)	-150 (-5.91)	.827	9.58	31,088
4.	Poznan (city)	186 (2.98)	163 (.77)	88 (1.12)	126 (1.20)	-180 (-6.19)	.832	9.87	32,336
5.	Wroclaw (city)	153 (2.60)	302 (1.86)	78 (.86)	118 (.89)	-218 (-5.92)	.832	9.93	32,307
6.	Bialostok	74 (1.50)	146 (3.08)	80 (2.24)	204 (2.60)	-132 (-6.35)	.842	13.71	27,072
7.	Bydgosc	307 (6.83)	131 (2.47)	155 (3.37)	266 (3.43)	-159 (-6.76)	.880	18.86	28,150
8.	Gdansk	242 (7.00)	114 (1.28)	124 (2.57)	303 (3.50)	-192 (-7.54)	.933	35.81	30,267
9.	Katowice	314 (2.47)	190 (1.35)	169 (1.63)	419 (2.80)	-245 (-6.05)	.833	12.79	31,347
10.	Kielec	231 (5.13)	57 (.97)	57 (.99)	130 (.91)	-115 (-3.97)	.829	12.49	27,528
11.	Koszalinsk	219 (6.09)	128 (3.39)	146 (4.01)	345 (4.30)	-151 (-7.45)	.906	24.89	27.804
12.	Krakow	-28 (-.30)	170 (2.00)	12 (.19)	217 (1.76)	-136 (-3.99)	.759	8.09	27.965
13.	Lubelsk	237 (4.04)	37 (.59)	41 (.87)	117 (1.07)	-132 (-4.83)	.850	14.84	27,570
14.	Lodz (region)	200 (3.24)	47 (.62)	52 (.70)	183 (.94)	-62 (-1.60)	.659	4.96	27,079
15.	Olsztyn	221 (5.41)	163 (3.41)	184 (4.46)	376 (4.03)	-151 (-6.54)	.806	10.70	27.374
16.	Opolsk	192 (4.72)	184 (5.76)	187 (7.63)	310 (8.35)	-193 (-17.50)	.970	84.00	28,940
17.	Poznan (region)	456 (4.43)	252 (4.04)	266 (4.04)	648 (4.71)	-158 (-5.20)	.759	8.11	27.321

Table 7 (cont.)

	Region	UN	SP	SG	EP	WOM	R^2	F	Mean Wage
18.	Rzesow	286 (5.81)	234 (3.49)	123 (3.04)	298 (3.63)	-200 (-7.16)	.910	25.91	28,097
19.	Szcecin	230 (3.19)	267 (2.42)	191 (3.36)	538 (4.91)	-188 (-5.94)	.791	9.73	29,670
20.	Warszawa (region)	357 (5.40)	152 (2.55)	117 (2.15)	443 (3.43)	-139 (-4.69)	.848	14.37	27.886
21.	Wroclan (region)	-169 (-.77)	206 (2.33)	169 (2.40)	352 (2.79)	-147 (-4.14)	.646	4.68	27,609
22.	Zielena Gora	83 (.73)	14 (-.22)	23 (.37)	22 (.17)	-82 (-3.08)	.680	5.48	28,186

Table 8

Left hand variable: W2

	Sector	UN	SP	SG	EP	WOM	R^2	F	Mean Wage
1.	Industry	5564 (10.73)	-1291 (-4.21)	-2407 (-3.80)	-590 (-6.30)	-514 (-7.50)	.843	27.61	34,009
2.	Construction	1014 (3.57)	-457 (-2.24)	336 (.61)	391 (4.41)	236 (1.57)	.852	29.52	37,672
3.	Agriculture	372 (2.31)	-1 (-.02)	35 (.07)	59 (.05)	59 (1.64)	.776	12.88	30,707
4.	Forestry	850 (1.48)	-653 (-2.49)	-1237 (-2.01)	725 (2.82)	88 (.43)	.546	4.47	23,073
5.	Transport and Communication	1358 (1.60)	114 (.26)	-317 (-.88)	76 (.51)	40 (.35)	.539	6.02	32,187
6.	Trade	650 (4.77)	-7 (-.08)	74 (.48)	-66 (-1.11)	11 (.20)	.769	17.13	31,276
7.	Housing and Communal Services	2048 (8.89)	-150 (-.96)	-806 (2.49)	-229 (-2.65)	2 (.15)	.792	19.58	29,799
8.	Science	294 (2.78)	385 (3.32)	42 (.15)	5 (.03)	-105 (-1.18)	.611	8.07	41,913
9.	Education	176 (1.73)	-89 (-1.08)	286 (1.48)	22 (.14)	-108 (-1.43)	.932	70.57	30,292
10.	Culture and Arts	674 (4.06)	-175 (-.61)	170 (.47)	180 (.29)	-199 (-.70)	.697	11.82	41,239
11.	Health and Sport	444 (8.40)	-89 (-2.98)	-237 (-2.25)	-168 (-2.28)	74 (1.89)	.922	60.91	27,455
12.	Finance and Insurance	524 (5.35)	-33 (-.57)	-8 (-.09)	22 (.13)	146 (2.25)	.805	21.19	38,605
13.	Administration	371 (5.19)	-78 (-.37)	-83 (-.80)	-208 (-.71)	-139 (-1.54)	.874	35.65	33,457

Table 9 reports results of regressions which were run on pooled regional and sectoral data. Because pooling guaranteed a sufficient number of observations (276), it was possible to run the regression for each year separately. Two sets of dummy variables were introduced to control for the effects of regional and sectoral differences in the wage levels, therefore the coefficients reported in the table should in the clearest possible way represent the contributions of different levels of education, and pure sexual discrimination to the wage level. It is interesting to see, that university education seems to have quite a sizable and clearly significant positive impact on wages. Secondary professional education also has a positive, but significantly lower effect than university education. Elementary professional education apparently contributes not much less than secondary professional education to wages, while secondary general education has no recognizable effect on the level of wages. Finally, the large negative and significant coefficients of WOM indicate that women who have the same level of education as men are paid less.

Table 9

Year	WT	UN	SP	SG	EP	WOM	R^2	F
1970	W1	232 (7.48)	123 (4.92)	-33 (-.68)	79 (1.94)	-126 (-5.28)	.898	53.22
1971	W1	283 (8.73)	143 (5.62)	-45 (-.88)	103 (2.46)	-66 (-3.59)	.897	52.66
1970	W2	350 (9.32)	149 (4.92)	91 (1.54)	34 (.69)	-194 (-6.70)	.918	67.56
1971	W2	450 (10.06)	156 (4.46)	47 (.68)	115 (2.00)	-85 (-3.36)	.905	57.36

A summary review of the contribution of individual factors to the explained variation in average wages is given in analysis of covariance tables (Tables 10, page 287 and Table 11, page 287), which were constructed from the regressions of Table 9. (year 1970 only). The sets of variables were added successively in a hierarchical manner, which may overstate the explanatory power of those which entered earlier and understate the explanatory power of those which entered later. Nevertheless even the last entering factor (regions) appears to be highly significant.

It is interesting that education (when entered first) explains 40 − 45 percent of variation in both W1 and W2 and that sex alone (after controlling for five educational categories) explains an additional 16 percent of variation in W1, but only 7 percent of variation in W2. After controlling for education and sex, and correcting for the discrepancy in data, sectoral differences in average wage account for about 15 percent of variation in W1 and 25 percent of variation in W2. Finally, 7 to 8 percent of variation in both W1 and W2 is attributable to remaining regional differences in average wages.

Table 10 Analysis of Covariance Table for W1 and 1970

Source of variation	df	Sum of Squares	Mean Square	F statistic
Education	4	2.2030 E9	550.75 E6	232.94
Sex	1	.8591 E9	859.1 E6	363.35
Education and sex	5	3.0621 E9	612.42 E6	249.02
Corrective variable	1	.6609 E9	660.09 E6	279.52
Sectors	12	.81098 E9	67.58 E6	28.58
Regions	21	.373068 E9	17.76 E6	7.51
Sub total	39	4.90705 E9	125.82 E6	53.22
Residual	236	.55799 E9	2.364 E6	
Total	275	5.465 E9	19.87 E6	

Table 11 Analysis of Covariance Table for W2 and 1970

Source of variation	df	Sum of Squares	Mean Square	F statistic
Education	4	4.6789 E9	1169.6 E6	337.74
Sex	1	.7142 E9	714.2 E6	206.24
Education and sex	5	5.3926 E9	1078.5 E6	311.43
Corrective variable	1	.6551 E9	655.1 E6	189.17
Sectors	12	2.4619 E9	205.2 E6	59.25
Regions	21	.6152 E9	29.3 E6	8.46
Sub total	39	9.1248 E9	233.9 E6	67.562
Residual	236	.81737 E9	3.463 E6	
Total	275	9.942 E9	36.15 E6	

Conclusions

This study attempted to identify some of the primary factors which determine personal income distribution under Soviet-type socialism, and to compare the reality of the distribution with the normative statements of Marxian economic theory. The statistical evidence was based on scattered (and not always consistent) data for Czechoslovakia and Poland.

In conformity with Marxian theory, we find that income inequality has diminished an that wealth has ceased to be an important source of income differentials (this conclusion is based on evidence presented elsewhere). We also find that income inequality based on ethnic and regional differences has been diminishing since World War II, although some differences in personal incomes among Czechs and Slovaks, and among regions (wojewòdztwa) in Poland, still persist.

It was shown in the first part of this paper that income differentials based on education (human capital) are considered by Marxists to be healthy and necessary for socialism. The evidence from Czechoslovakia seems to indicate that the role of education as a source of income differentials has diminished, and in some cases was reversed. The evidence from Poland, however, shows that education — primarily university education — is an important source of income differentials.

The empirical data demonstrate that considerable sectoral differences exist both in Czechoslovakia and Poland. This can hardly be justified in light of the Marxian normative theory of income distribution. However, the most striking conclusion is the fact that pure sex discrimination still remains as a major source of income inequality under Soviet-type socialism. This phenomenon is in clear contradiction with the normative Marxian view on income distribution.

Notes

[1] The Gini coefficients calculated recently by F. Paukert (ILO 1973), S. Jain (World Bank 1976), J. Sláma (this volume) and Peter Wiles (*Distribution of Income: East and West*, North Holland Publishing House 1974) show that socialist countries of Eastern Europe have considerably smaller differences in personal incomes than other countries.

[2] »The first phase of communism, cannot yet provide justice and equality: differences, and unjust differences in wealth will still persist . . . the mere conversion of the means of production into the common property of the whole of society . . . *does not remove* the defects of distribution and the inequality . . . which *continues to prevail* so long as products are divided 'according to the amount of labor performed'.« (Lenin: *State and Revolution*, chapter V, paragraph 3, quoted from Lenin: *On Politics and Revolution*, New York 1968, pp. 222, 223).

[3] »Skilled labor counts only as simple labor itensified, or rather, as multiplied simple labor, a given quantity of skilled labor being considered equal to a greater quanity of simple labor.« (K. Marx: *Capital* vol I, chapter I quoted from R.C. Tucker: *Marx-Engels Reader*, New York 1972, p. 206).

[4] K. Marx: Critique of the Gotha Program, part I quoted from R.C. Tucker, *op.cit.* p. 387.

[5] K. Marx: Critique of the Gotha Program, part I quoted from R.C. Tucker, *op.cit.* p. 387.

[6] K. Marx: Economic and Philosophical Manuscripts quoted from E. Fromm: Marx's *Concept of Man*, New York 1974, p. 125.

[7] K. Marx: Economic and Philosophical Manuscripts quoted from E. Fromm *op.cit.* pp. 124, 125.

[8] K. Marx: Economic and Philosophical Manuscripts quoted from E. Fromm *op.cit.* p. 125.

[9] K. Marx: Economic and Philosophical Manuscripts quoted from E. Fromm *op.cit.* p. 127.

[10] K. Marx: Economic and Philosophical Manuscripts quoted from E. Fromm *op.cit.* p. 132.

[11] Average monthly wages in the socialist sector of the Czechoslovak economy

	(in Kcs)			
	1955	1960	1970	1974
Czech Republic	1201	1375	1946	2243
Slovak Republic	1132	1330	1910	2203

Source: *Statistical Yearbook of CSSR* 1966, p. 115 and 1975, p. 141.

[12] Earnings in other selected professions in Czechoslovakia 1965

Profession	Average monthly earnings in Kcs
Leading manager in engineering industry	4 692
Chief doctor of a regional hospital	3 381
Scientific worker (graduate)	3 022
Locomotive driver	2 363
Foreman in heavy engineering	2 149
Lawyer (graduate)	1 937
Labourer (5th wage class)	1 757
Dairywoman	1 632
Elementar school teacher	1 288
Shop assistant	1 011
Charwoman	940
Nursery nurse	802

Source: Jaroslav Krejci, *Social Change and Stratification in Postwar Czechoslovakia,* London 1972, p. 72.

[13] J. Adam, *op.cit.* p. 86.

[14] Zatrudnienie w gospodarce narodowej 1970, Statystyka Polski Nr 95;
Zatrudnienie w gospodarce narodowej 1971, Statystyka Polski Nr 123;
Zatrudnienie i płace według wojewodztw 1971, Statystyka Polski Nr 125.

Michael Wagner
Income distribution in small countries:
Some evidence from Austria*

I. Introduction: data problems

1. The analysis of the distribution of Austrian personal income is handicapped by the pecularities of Austrian statistics on personal income. The *tax statistics* split personal income into two classes:
- »wages«, including wages and salaries (which employees receive net of tax and social security contributions);
- »non-wage income«, including profits, interest, and professional fees (which are taxed on the basis of an annual self-assessment).

An integration of both sets of statistics is a precarious matter since the tax statistics up to 1974 assigned individuals as the units for wage income but households as units for non-wage income. In general, the wage income data are much more reliable than those on non-wage income, because underreporting is much more difficult if taxes are deducted at source.

In addition to tax statistics, data for wage income are available from *social insurance statistics*. These data exclude the employees of the civil service and contain very little information about the upper tail of the size distribution. All persons who earn more than the contribution ceiling make up one large class in the social insurance statistics. This class contains sometimes the three upper deciles of the personal wage income distribution.

Another source of income data is provided by the *expenditure surveys* carried out by the Austrian Central Statistical Office. These data need heavy adjustment as they are inconsistent as they stand; e.g. nearly all persons report less income than expenditures.

In addition, there exist data on the *wage structure in manufacturing industries* differentiated by branch, qualification and payment system. These data are collected in two ways. One set of data consists of a sample of all Austrian manufacturing industries, but this sample is heavily biased since it is not adjusted for differential response rates. The other set of data is an unbiased sample, but is only collected for Vienna.

* I am indebted to the participants of the conference for stimulating comments. Messrs. G. Chaloupek, F. Klanberg, B. Okner and H. Suppanz gave valuable criticism on an earlier draft. Remaining shortcomings are the sole responsiblity of the author. I am indebted to the Austrian Central Statistical Office and to the Bundeskanzleramt for giving me access to unpublished data. Assistance by Mrs. I. Horak, Mrs. G. Raunicher and Mr. M. Hauser is gratefully acknowledged. The research is supported by a grant from the »Jubiläumsfonds der Österreichischen Nationalbank«.

2. The low quality of the data — regardless of whether they are official records or survey results — has discouraged systematic research on personal income distribution[1]. Up to now, there exists no well established body of empirical research on the distribution of personal income in Austria, though some pioneer studies have been carried out (e.g. *Weissel* 1969). The Austrian *Institute for Advanced Studies* only recently has started a project which attempts to evaluate and integrate the existing data on personal income. This will be the starting point for an analysis of the influences of different variables — occupational structure, the tax system, public expenditures, macroeconomic fluctuations — on the distribution of personal income.

The following survey will concentrate mainly on two topics: (a) the size distribution of wage and non-wage income, and (b) differences in age-income profiles by sex, occupation and region.

II. The size distribution of personal income

1. The distribution of Austrian personal income reflects the economic and social development of a once privileged area of a large empire. Though there is still the historical legacy of an unbalanced economic structure, Austria has experienced in the last decades a remarkable growth in average income. A *substantial change in the composition of the labour force* accompanied this extraordinary growth of national income: The female participation rate has increased and so has the number of foreign workers. At the same time the average standard of qualification has been considerably raised. Table 1 indicates some of these changes.

The total size distribution of personal income has been little affected by all these changes in the composition of the labour force. Any factor which would have been expected to elicit a new distribution of income appears to have been met by compensatory forces. This holds especially true for the distribution of personal wage income (including salaries and wages). The confirmed changes in the occupational structure, the rising level of qualification, the regional relocation of the labour force have had next to no impact on the size distribution of wage income.

2. *Trade union policy* in Austria plays an important part in the homeostatic process generating the size distribution of personal wage income. The impact of trade union policy on wage distribution can clearly be identified because wage policy is harmonized by the strong influence exercised by the federal headquarters of the union on its industrial branches (*Suppanz-Robinson 1972*).

Any substantial change in the principles guiding wage policy of the federal trade union leads to a significant — short term — change in the size distribution of wage income[2]. Such a switch in the trade unions philosophy of »fair wage bargains« occured in the mid-fifties. The unions abolished their former guiding principle of narrowing occupational differentials. A new policy of proportional wage raise was adopted. The result of this switch in wage policy was a considerable increase in inequality during the second half of the fifties. This is reflected by a rise in the Gini-coefficient for the distribution of pre-tax wage income from 0,28 (in 1953) to 0,33 (in 1957) and up to 0,34 (in 1964).

Table 1 Composition and qualification of the labour force. Austria. 1951 - 1971

Occupation	Share of total labour force 1971	Rate of Change of employed persons 1)		Share of qualified labour 2) 1971	Share of foreign workers (in percent) 1971
		1951-1961	1961-1971		
Agriculture & Forestry	13,77	-30,0	-35,8	11,8	6,0
Manufacturing..	34,85	+ 4,2	- 4,5	48,0	8,6
Trade (whole sale, retail)..	8,97	+35,8	+20,6	61,2	2,5
Transport	6,28	+ 4,3	+12,3	48,4	1,7
Service	10,24	+10,9	+10,8	28,4	6,7
Specially skilled technical labourers	2,75	+32,6	+60,8	87,0	2,9
Clerks	14,66	+24,7	+25,2	71,8	1,3
Health, Art Teaching	5,96	+ 8,0	+30,1	80,4	3,7
Total	100,00 % (=3.303.000 persons)				5,6

1) Percentage growth of employed persons within an industry, adjusted for changes of the total labour force.
2) Percentage of persons with more than minimum compulsory schooling.

Source: Austrian Institute of Economic Research *Monatsberichte* 2/1976

The influence of the trade union conception of »fair« wage policy on the size distribution of wage income is again of current interest, since the federal unions have once more — as in the early fifties — adopted a policy of narrowing wage differentials[3]: Lower income groups within a branch get higher than average percentage wage raises. This policy will certainly show its impact on wage distribution in the late seventies.

3. The following figures indicate some features of *inequality in wage income:* In 1970 the Austrian top percentile earned 4 % and the top decile 22,4 % of total post-tax wage income. Whereas the average income of the top decile exceeded that of all employees by more than two times, the bottom decile earned only less than 19 % of the post-tax average income. Tables 2, 3 and chart 1 give more detailed informations about the size distribution of wage income and the changes it has undergone in the last two decades.

Table 2 Distribution of pre-tax personal wage income. Austria. 1953, 1964, 1970.

percentage of taxed persons	percentage share in total income		
	1953	1964	1970
bottom decile	1.7	1.6	1.8
2nd "	4.1	3.9	3.6
3rd "	6.2	5.9	5.9
4th "	7.9	7.4	7.3
5th "	9.1	8.5	8.5
6th "	10.1	9.7	9.8
7th "	11.1	11.5	11.0
8th "	12.7	12.1	12.7
9th "	14.5	15.0	15.0
top decile	22.6	24.4	24.4
all taxed persons	100.0	100.0	100.0
top 5 %	13.8	15.2	15.1
top 1 %	4.6	4.5	4.9

Source: Austrian Central Statistical Office, *Lohnsteuerstatistik 1953, 1964, 1970.*

Table 3 Distribution of post-tax personal wage income. Austria. 1953, 1964, 1970.

percentage of taxed persons	percentage share in total income		
	1953	1964	1970
bottom decile	1.8	1.7	1.9
2nd "	4.4	4.1	3.9
3rd "	6.5	6.2	6.2
4th "	8.1	7.6	7.7
5th "	9.4	8.8	8.8
6th "	10.3	10.0	10.1
7th "	11.3	11.7	11.3
8th "	12.8	12.3	12.8
9th "	14.5	15.0	14.9
top decile	20.9	22.6	22.4
all taxed persons	100.0	100.0	100.0
top 5 %	12.3	13.6	13.3
top 1 %	3.7	3.8	4.0

Source: Austrian Central Statistical Office, *Lohnsteuerstatistik 1953, 1964, 1970.*

Chart 1 Lorenz curves for pre-tax personal wage income. Austria. 1953, 1970.

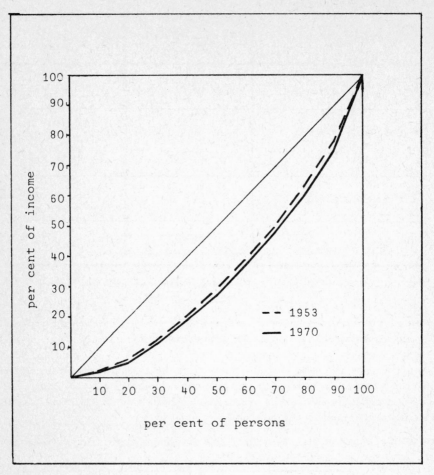

Source: Table 2.

A further comparison of the distributions of wage income in 1953 and 1970 is provided by table 4 which makes use of four different measures of inequality: The Gini-coefficient; Atkinson's measure with e = 0.5, indicating the sensitivity with respect to inequality *(Atkinson, 1970);* the ratio between the geometric and arithmetic mean as discussed in *Champernowne, 1974;* Theil's measure *(Theil, 1967).*

Each of the four measures indicate a higher degree of inequality for the 1970 distribution as compared to the 1953 distribution[4]. This confirms the impression one gets when looking at the corresponding Lorenz curves. With exception of the lowest decile, the Lorenz curve for 1953 lies entirely above the Lorenz curve for 1970. An inequality measure would have to be hypersensitive with respect to the lower tail of the distribution to rank the 1953 distribution as beeing more unequal than the 1970 distribution.

Table 4 Inequality measures for the distribution of pre-tax wage income. Austria. 1953, 1970.

	1953	1970
Gini	**0,28**	0,34
Atkinson e = 0,5	0,09	0,10
Champernowne	0,19	0,20
Theil	0,13	0,16

Source: Austrian Statistic Office, *Lohnsteuerstatistik 1953, 1970.*

4. From 1970 to 1975 inequality in wage income has *not* diminished. The relative positions of some of the less privileged groups have even deteriorated:
– the manual workers have lost relative to white collar employees;
– women have lost relative to men;
– the employees in the lower deciles – with the exception of the bottom decile – have lost relative to the employees in the upper deciles.

These trends are indicated by table 5 which is based on social insurance statistics excluding the employees of the civil service.

Table 5 Growth of personal wage income by occupation (civil service excluded), sex, and deciles. Austria. 1970 - 1975.

Upper bound of decile	Index value of wage income at decile boundaries in 1975 (1970 = 100)					
	Blue collar workers			White collar workers		
	male	female	total	male	female	total
1st	138,6	183,9	164,6	173,0	182,9	159,9
2nd	168,3	172,7	163,9	179,7	163,5	166,7
3rd	174,9	170,8	171,7	179,5	168,2	172,0
4th	176,3	171,3	174,7	179,5	172,4	173,2
5th	177,6	173,1	176,5	178,4	173,1	174,5
6th	178,3	174,7	177,5	178,0	173,2	175,5
7th	178,6	176,0	178,6	(x)	173,1	175,6
8th	178,4	176,4	179,0	(x)	178,0	(x)
9th	(x)	176,2	178,5	(x)	180,1	(x)

x) Data are not available because this decile is above the contribution ceiling.

Source: Hauptverband der Sozialversicherungsträger, *Lohnstufenstatistik.*

5. *Non-wage income* (including profits, interest and professional fees) is, naturally, distributed more unequally than wages and salaries. In 1970 the top percentile earned 20 % of total pre-tax non-wage income. The share of the top
decile was 47 % pre-tax and 38 % net of tax. The average income of the top
percentile was 15 times as high as the mean total income. The bottom decile
earned on the average less than 20 % of the total average income. The high degree
of inequality of distribution of non-wage income is reflected by a Gini-coefficient of 0,538 (pre-tax) for the 1970 distribution. A detailed account is given
in table 6.

Table 6 Distribution of post-tax personal non-wage income. Austria. 1953, 1970.

percentage of taxed persons	percentage share in total income	
	1953	1970
bottom decile	3.1	1.9
2nd "	4.3	3.3
3rd "	4.5	4.3
4th "	5.9	5.2
5th "	6.3	6.0
6th "	7.5	7.0
7th "	9.0	8.4
8th "	10.9	10.9
9th "	14.1	14.8
top decile	34.4	38.2
all taxed persons	100.0	100.0
top 5 %	27.7	28.0
top 1 %	12.3	15.1

Source: Austrian Central Statistical Office, *Einkommensteuerstatistik 1953, 1970.*

Table 6 reveals an increase in inequality, though the extent of the increase is
slightly overstated when one compares the figures for the two years 1953 and
1970 due to substantially different trade cycle positions in both years (1953
was the beginning of an upswing — 3,9 % annual growth of real GNP — while
1970 was an absolute peak with 7,8 %).

Chart 2 Lorenz curves for post-tax household non-wage income. Austria. 1953, 1970.

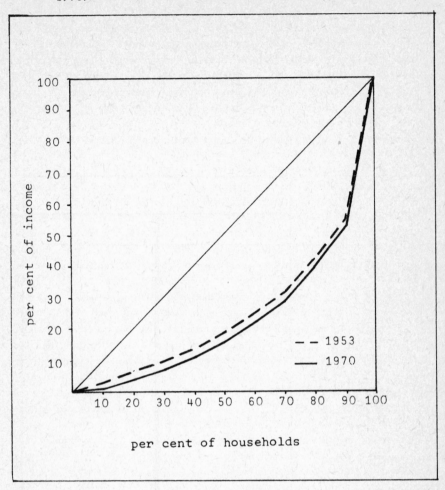

Source: Table 6.

III. Age earnings profiles

The quality of the Austrian data on age-earnings profiles is inadequate to implement a human capital analysis. Nevertheless, the available cross-sectional data shed some light on an important aspect of economic inequality. It is not necessary to assume that the cross-sectional data for 1971 are representative of a stable system of lifecycles, to conclude that even the static picture reveals a high degree of social and economic inequality. The determinants of this inequality are manifold. Certainly, some of them can be studied within a human capital framework which is described by Mincer *(1976, 136)* as an analysis of individual choice between alternative investments in human capital. Such a choice is always subject to constraints as »parental wealth, access to educational and market opportunities«. Now, the Austrian data seem to me to be shaped more by such constraints than by the parameters of the objective function of the individuals.

1. A considerable part of the Austrian working force, more than twenty percent, is on the public pay roll. In the payment system of the civil service *seniority* plays the major part as determinant for earnings. The emerging age-income profile is a straight ascending one, (it is not strictly concave). This is due to the combination of a biennial wage rise and an automatic promotion within the hierarchy of the public agency. Any attempt to explain this »public« age-earnings profile with the help of a human capital approach must necessarily fail. It is not the market place that evaluates the stock of human capital an individual has accumulated, but the traditional notion of seniority — in civil service now well established for more than threehundred years — dictates how the civil servant is to be compensated. In general, one can say that seniority by age is very important, while efficiency by »skill« is only of subsidiary significance.

A comparison of the *seniority-earnings profiles* in the civil service and in private manufacturing industry leads to a result one would expect. The private industry seniority-earnings profile is concave with a flat tail. The »private« seniority-earnings profile starts from a level which is one quarter to one third above the »public« profile. Both profiles intersect after 25 to 30 years of seniority. Chart 3 gives a fuller account of the relative importance of seniority in Austria.

The difference in the life cycle of wage incomes between civil service and private industries are even manified by different old age pensions schemes. The civil servant gets a much higher percentage of his pre-retirement income than the private industrial employee. Thus, the upper tail of the life cycle compensates the civil servant for low pay in the beginning and slow promotion, leaving him probably even better off than the private employee in the end.

2. However, such an averaging out over the life cycle[5] between civil service and private industries cannot be observed generally. On the contrary, those socio-economic groups which start from a lower income position usually have smaller chances to increase their income over the life cycle. This holds true especially for women and lower manual workers. Both groups — which coincide partially — start with low qualifications. They enter their jobs in positions where only little chance for promotion exists. For lower manual workers the only way to increase income is either to work harder — in the case of piece-rates — or to work overtime. Even these two chances are smaller for less qualified than they are for highly qualified blue collar workers.

This economic inequality is mirrored in the data of the 1971 Income Survey carried out by the Austrian Central Statistical Office: The cross-sectional earnings-profiles reflect unmistakably the *differing social positions of men and women.* Of all working *women* in the age-group of 20 to 30, more than 80 % earn less than the median value of all employees[5]. This number does not decline very much during the life cycle. The share of women below the median of all wage earners never declines below 70 %. In contrast, only 60 % of *men* in the age group 20 to 30 earn less then the median of all wage earners. This share declines to 38 % (group 40 to 50) and rises again for the group 50 to 60 to 42 %. A detailed account is given in table 7. This table is built on two of five income classes, which where used as income brackets in the income survey (= Mikrozensus

Chart 3 Seniority profiles of white collar employees; civil service and manufacturing industry. Austria. 1970.

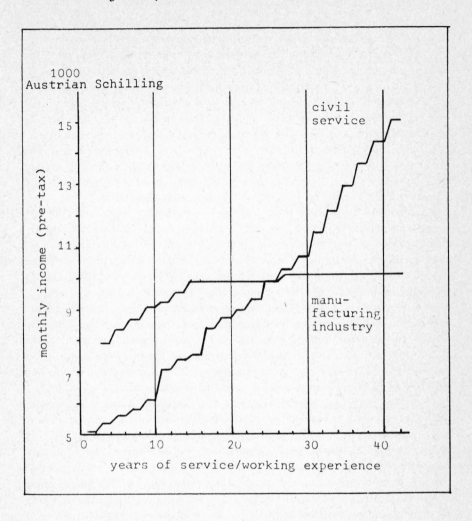

Source: Bundeskanzleramt. Bundeskammer der gewerblichen Wirtschaft.

1971/2). Each income class — with exception of class V — covers an intervall of
2000 Austrian Schilling (= AS). Class I covers AS 0 - 2000, class II covers AS
2000 - 4000; etc. The top class V is defined as »more than AS 8000,—«. The
classes refer to personal post-tax monthly income.

The following tables will pay special attention to the first two income brackets,
since the upper bound of the second class (= AS 4000) roughly equals the median
of all Austrian wage earners. This median for the distribution of personal post-
tax monthly income of all Austrian wage earners — shortly *aggregated median*
— will be used in the discussion of the age-earnings profiles of subsamples.

299

Table 7 Distribution of personal income by age and sex. Austria. 1971.

Age	Percentage of age group in income class I+II[x]	
	male	female
20–30	60	82
30–40	43	86
40–50	38	73
50–60	42	72

x) less than 4.000,– Austrian Schilling monthly personal income (post-tax).

Source: Austrian Central Statistical Office, Mikrozensus 1971/2.

The differences in the age-earnings profiles[6] become even more apparent when the two main determinants — sex and occupation — are varied simultaneously. The most privileged group are *male white collar workers.* They start in the age group 20 to 30 with a group median which is equal to the median of all wage earners. But for the group 30 to 40 the »aggregated« median falls in the lower group quartile. Only 20 % of male white collar workers in the age group 50 to 60 earn less then the median of all wage earners.

From female white collar workers the situation is worse. In the age group 20 to 30 the upper »group« quartile equals the median of all wage earners. It takes the female employees as a group all their life finally to reach a position in which their »group« median equals the »aggregated« median. The most under-privileged group are *female blue collar workers:* For all age groups, more than 90 % of female blue collar workers earn less than the median of all wage earners.

On the other hand *male blue collar workers* are better off. They start (20 to 30 age group) with a share of 67 % below the median of all wage earners. Then the factors of physical strength (in case of piece-rates) and overtime push the share for the age group 30 to 40 down to the average. However, the advance of age implies a decline of income. In the end the male blue collar workers are again worse off with 69 % of them being below the »aggregated« median.

An interesting comparison to note is that between female white collar workers and male blue collar workers. Though the women start off in a worse position, they experience a steady increase of income, so that for the age group 50 to 60 the share of income below the »aggregated« median is higher for the male blue collar labourers than for the female white collar employees. This is due to the differences in the social organization of work: White collar work gives more chances for additional qualifications, which are better rewarded since there usually exists a larger internal labour market for white collar work than for blue collar work.

Table 8 and chart 4 give a more detailed account of the above.

Table 8 Distribution of post-tax wage income by age, occupation and sex. Austria. 1971.

	Percentage of age group in income class I+II[x]					
	White Collar Workers			Blue Collar Workers		
Age	Male	Female	Total	Male	Female	Total
20-30	48	78	64	67	91	73
30-40	25	68	41	53	94	64
40-50	18	58	35	58	91	69
50-60	20	57	35	69	92	78

x) Class I + II = up to 4.000,– Austrian Schilling monthly personal income (post-tax).

Source: Austrian Central Statistical Office, Mikrozensus 1971/2.

Chart 4 Age-earnings profiles for male, female, white, blue collar employees. Austria. 1971.

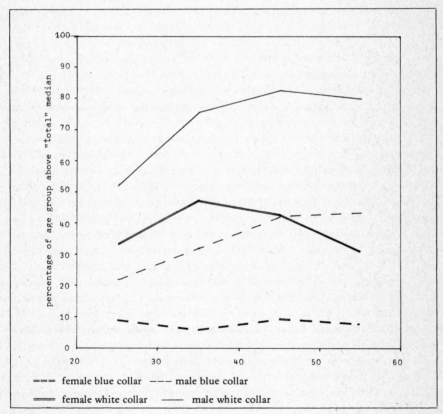

Source: Table 8.

3. The heterogeneity of age-earnings profiles for different socio-economic groups is reflected in *regional differences in earnings profiles.* In general, larger communities offer more chances to employees to experience an ascending part of an earnings profile. This is indicated by the following table 9:

Table 9 Percentages of employees in lower income class by age groups and size of the community; Austria; 1971

Age group	Number of persons in income class I + II[x)]		
	Austria	communities with less than 20.000 persons	communities from 20.000 to 250.000 persons
20 - 30	68	74	64
30 - 40	53	59	45
40 - 50	50	56	42

x) Class I + II = up to 4.000,— Austrian Schilling monthly personal income (post-tax).

Source: Austrian Central Statistical Office, Mikrozensus 1971/2.

The regional differences in the life cycle are, of course, mainly due to the location of opportunities for white and blue collar work, for highly qualified and less qualified labour. The location of farming, of service, and of manufacturing industries determine the typical regional age-earnings profile as well as the general level of personal wage income[7].

4. An aggregation over all the heterogenous types of age-earnings profiles, leads to a concave profile. The cross section of Austrian wage income in 1971 is composed of »ascending age groups« (up to 40) and of »years of stagnation and decline« (after 40). The youngest employees (up to 20) are nearly all concentrated in income class I, the lowest income group (the upper bound of which roughly amounts to half of the median of the total population), partly because they could not have experienced much promotion, partly because they have entered their life of labour with little qualification. The next age group (up to 30) is characterized by the effects of promotion and the influx of highly qualified white collar workers. The labour force between 30 and 40 is still in its »ascending« part of the age-earnings profile, since none of its groups is subject to a decline of income, but some of its groups are at the height of their profile. The years of stagnation and decline start with 40. The ascending life cycles just balance out the descending ones. Table 10 gives a more detailed account of the age-earnings profile of the Austrian labour force as a whole.

5. Lastly, it may be of interest to give an overall review of the *effect of retirement on the distribution of income.* Bearing inequality in mind the retired people cannot be neglected. After all, the proportion (in Austria) between the active working force and the already retired persons is roughly two to one.

Table 10 Distribution of post-tax wage income by age. Austria. 1971.

Age	Income class*			
	I+II	III	IV	V
-20	99	1	0	0
20-30	74	22	3	1
30-40	57	33	7	3
40-50	54	34	7	5
50-60	58	29	8	5
60-65	52	26	10	12
65-	62	21	7	10

x) Range of income classes (monthly personal income, post-tax):

I . . .   less than   2.000,– Austrian Schilling
II . . . 2.000,– –   4.000,–   ”   ”
III . . . 4.000,– –   6.000,–   ”   ”
IV . . . 6.000,– –   8.000,–   ”   ”
V . . . more than   8.000,–   ”   ”

Source: Austrian Central Statistical Office, Mikrozensus 1971/2.

The distribution of income of old people is shaped by the Austrian Social Insurance pension system. Every employee who has retired from full-time work receives a pension, (widows receive a special »widows-pension«). The pension depends mainly on the average gross earnings just before retirement and on the number of years for which the compulsory contributions to the Social Insurance had been paid, i.e. years of regular employment.

The Social Insurance pension system partly ·replicates the inequality due to occupational differentials. Those social groups who have been underprivileged all their life remain after retirement in an inferior position which may be below the poverty line in some cases. This is evident in the case of women who have been employed in low qualified jobs and who have not worked regularly; they receive only the minimum basic rate of pension which is too little for a decent standard of living. The position of low pension groups is further aggrevated by the fact that they usually have had little chance to accumulate either savings or consumer durables.

A more detailed account of the distribution of income among the retired is provided by table 11.

303

Table 11 Distribution of post-tax income of retired persons by pre-retirement occupations. Austria. 1971.

"Occupation" before retirement	Percentage of "occupational" group in income class[3]					
	I	II	III	IV	V	total[1]
Blue collar	48,9	45,0	1,3	0,1	0,1	100
White collar	20,4	51,0	16,0	2,4	1,2	100
Civil Service	3,7	47,7	29,1	6,0	4,0	100
not employed[2]	64,6	22,8	2,1	0,2	0,0	100

1 The rows do not add up to 100 % as they are not adjusted for »non-response«, which makes up four to ten per cent of each row.
2 Consisting mainly of persons receiving a widow's pension.
3 See Table 10 for the range of the five income classes.

Source: Austrian Central Statistical Office, Mikrozensus 1971/2.

Table 11 confirms the observation that women and the poorly qualified are in the final analysis the victims of a social insurance system which links its payments to pre-retirement contributions. Two thirds of all widows receive pensions which are near or below the poverty-line, whereas only less than 4 % of all civil servants have to share this fate. A similar conclusion about the inferior position of women may be drawn from the fact that more than two third of all blue collar-pensions in the lowest income class are received by women. This indicates that the Austrian Social Insurance needs substantial improvements to achieve the aims set by itself: to help the elderly people to fight successfully against the spectre of poverty.

Notes

1 In a recent OECD-study on Income Distribution (*Sawyer 1976*) Austria is excluded from the comparison with other OECD-countries because of data problems.
2 Sometimes it is difficult to decide whether the philosophy behind trade union policy is a reaction to restore the longterm size distribution of incomes which may have been disturbed by other factors, or whether the principless guiding trade union policy are »exogenously« determined.
3 This switch in trade union policy was due to political pressure caused by the rise of inflation rates in the early seventies.
4 The number of taxed wage earners was roughly the same in 1953 and 1971. Therefore the result — e.g. of Theil's measure — is not biased by a change in the size of the population.
5 The influx into civil service and private industry could be explained within a framework of optimal decision (depending on the individuals' assignment of utilities to different life-cycle consumption patterns offered by civil service and private industry).

[6] It should be noted that this is a comparison of aggregated age-earnings profiles. The age-earnings profiles of the individuals may deviate substantially from the profile of the aggregate. Nevertheless, the profiles of the aggregate indicate some restrictions. It is true that not necessarily 90 % of the female blue collar workers earn less than the »aggregate« median all their lives, though in each age group only 10 % earn more than this median. But the chance to experience an ascendance above the »aggregated« median is obviously under a severe restriction by the aggregate percentage below the »age« median.

[7] The Austrian economy follows a distinctive pattern of concentration of economic activities. Nearly one-third of Austria's total national income is earned in ther capital Vienna. There is no other central region comparable in population or income to Vienna, though the same tendency of concentration of income can be observed in the other eight provinces of Austria. In general only two districts of a province form a central region, in which between 57 % and 73 % of the provincial income is earned (Geldner-Jeglitsch 1976).

References

Atkinson, A.B., (1970), On the Measurement of Inequality, *Journal of Economic Theory, 2*, 244 − 263.

Atkinson, A.B., (1976), *The Personal Distribution of Incomes*, London: Allen & Unwin, 1976.

Champernowne, D.G., (1974), A Comparison of Measures of Inequality of Income Distribution, *Economic Journal, 84*, 787 − 817.

Geldner, N. − Jeglitsch H., (1976), Das Inlandsprodukt nach politischen Bezirken im Jahre 1971, *Monatsberichte 2/1976*, 54 − 63.

Mincer, J., (1976), Progress in Human Capital Analysis of the Distribution of Earnings, in: Atkinson, ed. 1976, 136 − 176.

Sawyer, M., (1976), Income Distribution in OECD-Countries, *Occasional Studies, July 1976*, 1 − 36.

Suppanz, H. − Robinson D., *Prices and Incomes Policy:* The Austrian Experience, Paris: OECD.

Theil, H., (1967), *Economics and Information Theory*, Amsterdam: North-Holland, 1967.

Weissel, E., (1969), *Lebensalter, Arbeitszeit und Lohn:* Eine Untersuchung über die Lohnstruktur in der Wiener Industrie, Wien: ÖGB, 1969.

Jiri Sláma
A Cross-Country Regression Model of Social Inequality

In this paper* we shall present several variants of an econometric model used to explain national differences in the degree of social inequality. Probably the most crucial variable in our model is the Gini Coefficient — which measures the degree of inequality in the distribution of personal income. However, the inequality in income may be a consequence, as well as a cause of inequality in other areas of social life, such as education, health, etc. Our aim is to investigate how inequalities in economic and non-economic areas are related, and to determine the main factors responsible for international differences in the degree of social inequality.

The model is based on cross-country regressions, and includes countries with different economic and social systems at various levels of development. Out of the 41 countries covered in this study, (see Appendix II), 16 are developed market economies, 5 are East European socialist countries, and 20 are less-developed countries.

Although it would be desirable to investigate social inequality in many mutually interrelated areas, this would entail the inclusion of a very large number of endogenous and exogenous variables. Because of the severe restrictions imposed by the unavailability of data, the model is restricted to three primary equations with three corresponding endogenous variables, and four to seven exogenous variables, (in some variants a fourth equation and endogenous variable are added to the model.)

The three primary equations of the model are specified so as to capture the impact and interaction of three basic factors which influence the life and relative well-being of a person in a given country.

These factors are:

1. Personal income distribution measured by the *Gini-Coefficient: GINI*

2. The quality of health represented by the proxy variable of *Life Expectancy at Birth (Females): LIFEXP,* and

3. The quality of education represented by the proxy variable of *Median of Educational Attainment* for the population (age group 25 - 34 years): *EDUCAT.*

The Gini Coeffient is a well-known measure of the degree of inequality in personal income distribution. Despite its deficiencies, it is probably the least controversial variable in the model. The choice of the other two variables clearly requires some justification.

---

* The author wish to thank Franz-Lothar Altmann, Oldřich Kýn, and Ruth Polak for useful comments and criticism in the stage of specification and estimation of the model and for considerable help with editing the final version of this paper. I am also grateful to Economics Department of Boston University, which provided necessary facilities for my econometric work.

The variable of female life expectancy at birth as a proxy for the quality of health was chosen for several reasons. The most obvious reason is the availability of this measure for a wide variety of countries. As a single, and simply constructed variable with unambiguous meaning, it does not pose any problems for international comparisons. The life expectancy at *birth*, rather than some alternative measure (such as the mean age of the population) was chosen, because it is not sensitive to the relative weights of different cohorts in the population, and because it reflects more purely the current, rather than the past, quality of health.

Although life expectancy is a measure of central tendency, it may also reflect cross-country variations in the degree of inequality in the distribution of health among various population groups within a country. This is based on the assumption that the purely biologically determined life-span is approximately the same for all countries, or at least, that it is much more equally distributed than the actual life expectancy. It can be observed that in all countries, the most affluent population groups, which do not suffer from malnutrition and inadequate health care, have an approximately equal life expectancy which is quite close to the biological life-span. In some countries, the mean life expectancy of the entire population is very close to the life expectancy of the most affluent group, and this implies only a small dispersion among groups. In other countries, the mean life expectancy is considerably lower than the life expectancy of the most affluent group. This is apparently due to the fact that different social groups have radically different life expectancies, or, in other words the »chances of survival« in such countries are unequally distributed.

One might, of course, consider creating a special variable which would directly measure the degree of inequality in the »chances of survival«. Such a variable could be constructed, for example, in a manner similar to the Gini Coefficient, which measures the inequality of the income distribution. However, from the above argument, it follows that such a coefficient would be highly negatively correlated with the mean life expectancy.

To demonstrate this correlation, we have calculated a concentration coefficient which measures the life-span distribution among different cohorts of females (App. I). It was .02 for Sweden, .07 for Hungary and .62 for Tunisia. The life expectancy at birth for females was 77.4 years in Sweden, 72,6 years in Hungary, and 52,8 in Tunisia. It is evident then, that our variable LIFEXP can serve not only as a good proxy for the mean levels of the quality of health in different countries, but also for the degrees of inequality in the distribution of health among population groups within each country.

Finally, the life expectancy for females, rather than for males or for the general population was chosen, because it gives higher cross-country variation and is apparently more sensitive to intra-country inequalities.

The reasons for choosing EDUCAT (median of educational attainment for the population in age group 25 - 34) as a proxy variable for the quality of education are similar to those given above. The selection of one age group eliminates the unwanted influence of differences in the age composition of the population. The fact that the selected age group is the youngest group above the age required to complete a college education, guarantees that the variable reflects the most recently attained quality of education.

Finally, it is apparent that this variable reflects different degrees of inequality in the distribution of education among population groups within countries, and not only inter-country differences in the attained level of education. The argument here is similar to that presented for the variable LIFEXP. It can be assumed that the most affluent population groups in all countries attain roughly similar levels of education. Thus, if some countries have a substantially lower median of education attainment than other countries, it must be due to the greater disparities in the education level of different social groups in the former.

Having selected GINI, LIFEXP, and EDUCAT as the primary endogenous variables, we must now specify their mutual interdependencies in the model. Of course, we might begin with the assumption that each of the three variables directly influences the other two. The degree of income inequality undoubtedly has an impact both on the quality of health and the educational attainment in any country. Education may influence both the income distribution and the quality of health, and so on.

It is quite obvious, however, that it would be quite difficult to get reasonable estimates for such a model. It is therefore desirable to impose some restriction on the dependencies among the endogenous variables, and focus only on the most important ones.

Results of two types of models will be reported here. The first contains recursive models with only a partial dependency among endogenous variables. The second type includes models with full simultaneity, i.e. with closed-loop dependency among endogenous variables.

The most obvious is the dependency of life expectancy on income distribution. The more unequal the income distribution — the more unequal is the distribution of the quality of health and the chances of survival: That is, the higher GINI — the lower LIFEXP should be. Thus, we may expect a negative regression coefficient for GINI in an equation explaining LIFEXP.

The second most obvious dependency is that of income distribution on the level of educational attainment. Because higher levels of EDUCAT imply, as argued above, a more equal distribution of human capital, we expect that it will partly eliminate one of the sources of income inequality. Thus, in regression equations for GINI, we may expect a negative sign for the variable EDUCAT.

Somewhat less obvious is the dependency of educational attainment and life expectancy. Although the causal link between the two variables may very well work in both directions, we prefer to include only a one-directional relation in the model, namely, to consider variation in life expectancy to be a cause of variation in educational attainment.

The reason again is based in human capital theory: if education is considered to be an investment in human capital, then obviously the efficiency of such an investment depends on the expected length of productive life after the education process is completed. In countries with a higher life expectancy, more is likely to be invested in education so that we may expect a positive coefficient for the variable EDUCAT in an equation explaining LIFEXP.

Among the other explanatory variables in the model, we include first, social security costs (SOCSEC), defined as the share of social security expenditures (health, welfare, pensions and other transfer payments etc.) in national income. (The source is the ILO publication; *Social Security Costs,* 1972).

This variable is expected to be important for explaining international variations in the quality of health and attained levels of education, but relatively unimportant in explaining variations in income inequality. Because of the importance of this variable, it entered as an endogenous variable in some variants of the model. As a right-hand variable it entered either in the equation for LIFEXP or EDUCAT or both.

Next in importance as right-hand variables, are two dummy variables designed to capture the effects of international differences in the type of economic system and in the level of development. These are:

1. Dummy variable for East European socialist countries: DSOC, and

2. dummy variable for less developed countries: DLDC.

The systemic differences between socialist and nonsocialist countries are expected to be important in all three areas (i.e. income distribution, health, and education), so that DSOC appears on the right-hand side of all three equations in the model. However, the dummy variable for less developed countries DLDC appears only in the equations for GINI.

The next explanatory variable is GNP per capita: GP, which should clearly have a positive influence on the attained level of education EDUCAT, and possible a negative effect on GINI. (the higher the GNP per capita the more equal the distribution of income.)

Two other variables, the rate of growth of GNP: RG, and the investment ratio: INVR were used alternatively in the equation for LIFEXP under the assumption that the quality of health may differ in more and less dynamic societies. This rationale is admittedly not very strong, so that both variables were consequently dropped from simultaneous models.

Finally, two variables representing the structural characteristics of the population entered the equation for social security costs in recursive models. These are:

1. The share of old people (over 65) in·the population: OLDS, and

2. The share of salaried employees in the population: SALEM.

The positive relation between social security costs and the share of old people in the population appears to be indisputable. The share of salaried employees is also expected to have a positive influence on SOCSEC, and may also have some influence on GINI.

Tables 1 and 2 report estimations of six variants of our model. The three versions of table 1 represent four-equation recursive models with four endogenous and seven exogenous variables. Variant AI differs from BI and CI only slightly in specification, while variants BI and CI differ only in the use of alternative measurements for the variables (eq. in the use of Jain's GINI 2 instead of Paukert's GINI·1.) All of the variables discussed above entered the equations in a linear form, except for LIFEXP which was transformed by:**

$$\text{TLIFEXP} = \frac{1}{\ln (90\text{-LIFEXP})}$$

The three variants of the simultaneous models in table II all have identical specification with three endogenous and four exogenous variables. They differ only in alternative measurements of the variables. All three variants were estimated by the three-stage least squares method.

** This transformation was suggested by Prof. Champernowne to whom we express our gratitude.

Table 1 Recursive Models (OLSQ)

Variables: explanatory	Dependent	Variant A I				Variant B I				Variant C I			
		SOCSEC	EDUCAT	GINI 1	TLIFEXP	SOCSEC (A)	GINI 1	TLIFEXP	EDUCAT	SOCSEC (A)	GINI 2	TLIFEXP	EDUCAT (B)
Endogenous x)	SOCSEC							.0060 (6.72)				.0062 (7.09)	
	EDUCAT	-.083 (-.82)											
	GINI		-.0073 (-1.69)		-.2171 (-3.98)			-.0544 (-1.40)				-.3674 (-.93)	
	TLIFEXP								36.21 (2.05)				36.21 (2.05)
	Constant	-2.06 (-2.05)	2.44 (4.47)	.4472 (12.59)	.3457 (8.49)	-2.06 (-2.05)	.3451 (5.99)	.2941 (10.29)	-7.46 (-1.56)	-2.06 (-2.05)	.3691 (5.85)	.2821 (10.04)	-7.46 (-1.56)
Exogenous x)	OLDS	1.03 (6.10)				1.03 (6.10)			-.197 (-1.14)	1.03 (6.10)			-1.197 (-1.14)
	SALEM	.077 (1.28)				.077 (1.28)	.0036 (1.55)			.077 (1.28)	.0015 (.58)		
	GP		.017 (5.40)				-.000021 (-1.19)		.0011 (2.71)		-.000006 (-.29)		.0011 (2.71)
	DSOC		4.25 (3.72)	-.168 (-5.05)	-.076 (-4.05)		-.220 (-4.37)		3.37 (3.06)		-.192 (-3.48)		3.37 (3.06)
	DLDC			.099 (3.48)			.130 (3.07)				.121 (2.59)		
	INVR				.0042 (3.72)								
	RG							.0027 (1.15)				.0031 (1.31)	
Statistics	R² ($_F$-Stat)	.786 (68.78)	.651 (22.99)	.735 (34.27)	.604 (18.78)	.786 (68.78)	.733 (24.72)	.713 (30.68)	.682 (19.27)	.786 (68.78)	.665 (17.83)	.705 (29.49)	.682 (19.27)
	SER	2.49	2.00	.064	.027	2.49	.065	.023	1.94	2.49	.072	.024	1.94
	MEAN (St. Dev.)	7.41 (5.19)	5.31 (3.21)	.4361 (.1190)	.3296 (.0420)	7.41 (5.19)	.4361 (.1190)	.3296 (.0420)	5.31 (3.21)	7.41 (5.19)	.4320 (.1163)	.3296 (.0420)	5.31 (3.21)

x) in brackets t-statistics

Table 2 Simultaneous Models (Three Stage LSQ)

Variables: explanatory	Variant A II GINI 1	Variant A II LIFEXP	Variant A II EDUCAT	Variant B II GINI 1	Variant B II TLIFEXP	Variant B II EDUCAT	Variant C II GINI 2	Variant C II TLIFEXP	Variant C II EDUCAT
Endogenous [x]									
GINI		-90.81 (-3.79)			-.4357 (-5.23)			-.4930 (-4.02)	
LIFEXP			.044 (4.72)						
TLIFEXP	-.0050 (-.94)					8.70 (4.58)			8.65 (4.57)
EDUCAT				-.0089 (-2.34)			-.0077 (-2.23)		
Exogenous [x]									
Constant	.4304 (10.31)	103.16 (8.38)		.4593 (14.70)	.5127 (12.44)		.4504 (14.69)	.5371 (9.01)	
DSOC	-.170 (-5.07)	-18.59 (-2.89)	4.01 (3.74)	-.167 (-5.02)	-.0975 (-4.00)	4.17 (3.75)	-.172 (-4.91)	-.1093 (-3.32)	4.23 (3.82)
DLDC	.109 (3.55)			.091 (3.51)			.081 (2.91)		
SOCSEC		.661 (2.56)	-.109 (-1.11)		.0025 (3.49)	-.113 (-1.12)		.0025 (3.18)	-.121 (-1.21)
GP			.0016 (5.21)			.0016 (5.15)			.0016 (5.33)
Statistics									
R²	.733	.490		.734	.498		.689	.293	
SER	.061	7.40	1.78	.061	.0294	1.84	.065	.0349	1.85
MEAN (St. Dev.)	.4361 (.1190)	66.19 (10.36)	5.31 (3.21)	.4361 (.1190)	.3296 (.0420)	5.31 (3.21)	.4320 (.1163)	.3296 (.0420)	5.31 (3.21)

x) in brackets t-statistics

Considering the relatively simple structure and the small number of explanatory variables, the model performed quite well. It explained about 70 percent of intercountry differences in income inequality, attained levels of education and social security costs, and about 50 - 60 per cent of the differences in life expectation.

Most of the estimated coefficients appeared to be significant (expecially in the simultaneous variants) and had the appropriate signs. The joint explanatory power of right-hand variables was quite high in all cases, as can be seen from the F-statistics (Table 1) which range from 20 to 70.

According to our expectations EDUCAT was shown to have a negative influence on GINI, i.e. a higher attained level of education implies less inequality in the distribution of income. This effect, although it appeared with approximately equal magnitude, was statistically significant in models BII and CII, but not significant in models AI and AII.

All six variants of the model also confirmed our expectation that GINI has a negative impact on LIFEXP. That is, a lower degree of income inequality implies better and more equally distributed quality of health, and thus a longer life expectancy for the population.

Surprisingly, our expectation that EDUCAT would be positively related to LIFEXP (or its transformed version TLIFEXP), was also confirmed in models BI, CI, and very significantly in the three simultaneous variants AII, BII and CII.

The variable SOCSEC gave mixed results. Its positive sign and high statistical significance in variants BI, CI, AII and CII, lends support to our hypothesis that the quality of health and therefore life-expectancy is positively influenced by a country's expenditures on social security. On the other hand, the SOCSEC variable consistently appeared as insignificant and with an unexpected negative sign in the explanation of EDUCAT.

The dummy variable for socialist countries DSOC, was consistently significant. Not unexpectedly, it showed that socialist countries have a considerably more equal income distribution than non-socialist industrially developed countries. After controlling for the level of educational attainment, the mean value of the Gini coefficient for socialist countries was .26 − .28, for developed market economies .43 − .45, and for less developed countries it was .54 − .55. The positive coefficient of DSOC in the equations for EDUCAT showed that after controlling for life-expectancy, social security costs and GNP per capita, socialist countries show a significantly higher (by 3.5 to 4.3 years) level of educational attainment.

In the equation for life-expectancy, the socialist dummy DSOC showed rather unexpectedly, that after controlling for other variables (GINI, SOCSEC) the mean life expectancy in socialist economies is significantly shorter (by almost 20 years) than in other countries. But this results from the fact that DSOC counteracts exceptionally low or high values of GINI and SOCSEC in socialist countries. Because this behavior of the dummy variable may imply a misspecification of the regression equation, we therefore attempted to estimate variants BI and CI without DSOC. The results however, were not satisfactory.

The dummy variable for less-developed countries DLDC was added only to the equations for GINI, and it proved to be significant in all six variants − indicating a higher degree of income inequality in less-developed countries.

In all six variants, GNP per capita (GP) appeared to have a positive and highly significant influence on the level of education. However, it did not prove to be significant as an explanatory variable for GINI (variants BI and CI).

The share of old people in the population (OLDS) gave a highly significant and positive coefficient as expected, in equations for SOCSEC (variants AI, BI and CI), but it was negative and insignificant in equations for EDUCAT (BI, CI).

The share of salaried employees (SALEM) was insignificant in equations for SOCSEC, as well as in equations for GINI. The attempt to use RG (the rate of growth of GNP) for explaining life-expectancy was unsuccessful (BI, CI), while INVR (the investment ratio) gave a significant (AI) but not easily interpretable coefficient.

Conclusions

This study aimed to investigate relations between unequal distribution of certain economic and non-economic characteristics of population in different countries. For this purpose we constructed several variants of an econometric model which was to capture mutual interdependencies among income differentials, levels of education and chances to survive. In addition to that the model attempted to show the dependency of the three mentioned aspects of inequality on other national characteristics such as the level of economic development, the type of socio-economic system etc.

The empirical results based on data for 41 countries (16 developed market economies, 5 East European socialist countries and 20 less developed countries) revealed a close interrelationship between the variables of social inequality. It was shown that better education diminishes the inequality in income distribution, the increased equality in income distribution improves significantly the quality of health as measured by life expectancy and finally that the improved health and increased life expectancy contributes to the improvement of education. The empirical results also showed that the level of development and the type of socio-economic system play very important role in determining the degree of social inequality in individual countries.

	Columbia 1971				Hungary 1973			
	Town		Country – side		Town		Country · side	
	male	female	male	female	male	female	male	female
–1	19176	15284	3445	7179	1455	1028	1626	1170
1–4	9640	9501	5613	5787	113	73	178	133
5–9	2450	2096	1454	1400	54	32	77	51
10–14	1569	956	673	565	66	28	88	57
15–19	1888	1363	720	482	220	82	253	92
20–24	2349	1435	901	523	260	106	341	110
25–29	2051	1403	876	486	300	140	293	122
30–34	2027	1416	839	542	334	187	373	142
35–39	2057	1910	693	690	388	252	519	242
40–44	2129	1990	912	654	705	429	827	419
45–49	2304	2153	846	602	1019	712	1299	685
50–54	2960	2595	904	708	1431	972	1562	980
55–59	3315	2671	1064	694	1701	1201	1618	1094
60–64	4308	3759	1318	978	3322	2278	3566	2357
65–69	4339	3841	1357	1034	4114	3272	4791	3376
70–74	4971	4736	1700	1365	4720	4365	5936	4848
75–79	3654	3609	1152	988	4061	5271	5212	5754
80–84	2964	3329	1048	1077	2786	4372	3683	4781
85 +	3144	5312	1129	1553	1974	3884	2721	4112
unknown	570	377	215	130	–	2	3	4
total	77865	69736	31859	27437	29023	28686	34966	30529

	Tunesia 1971			Sveden 1973	Netherlands 1973		Sri Lanka 1968	
	females			females	females			
	total	Town	C.s.		Town	C.s.	females	males
–1	6311	4164	2025	473	444	264	8610	10702
1–4	3889	1715	2235	78	121	91	4627	4315
5–9	511	218	289	74	77	53	1561	1587
10–14	357	171	178	65	66	40	750	964
15–19	408	183	223	98	114	77	943	930
20–24	414	170	249	128	131	43	1031	1127
25–29	372	157	214	166	153	50	983	1006
30–34	444	207	244	192	159	54	827	963
35–39	496	200	300	236	203	81	1146	1428
40–44	462	219	250	348	337	142	893	1306
45–49	482	247	232	604	626	204	1183	2077
50–54	592	316	279	1024	857	280	1096	2110
55–59	738	387	339	1392	1145	363	1409	2601
60–64	1312	758	556	2238	1711	504	1626	2906
65–69	975	574	391	3500	2571	902	2451	3902
70–74	1263	985	753	5161	3779	1238	2718	3747
75–79	687	415	271	6814	4831	1652	2200	2830
80–84	1482	984	472	7142	4854	1764	2718	3064
85 +	?	?	?	8780	5537	2060	5264	5276
unknown	464						8	10
total	21659	12070	9500	38513	27716	9862	42044	52859

App. II Basic Data (endogenous)

	GINI 1	GINI 2	EDUCAT	LIFEXP	SOCSEC
1 Tunisia	0.5019	0.53	1.60	52.80	3.7
2 Sri Lanka	0.3771	0.44	6.09	66.90	3.6
3 Zambia	0.5226	0.48	0.97	44.90	1.9
4 Brazil	0.5744	0.54	2.81	61.10	6.7
5 El Salvador	0.4653	0.53	1.60	60.42	2.4
6 Colombia	0.5557	0.62	2.57	45.95	1.2
7 Costa Rica	0.4445	0.50	5.64	64.83	2.6
8 Panama	0.4258	0.48	4.26	60.88	6.2
9 Greece	0.3814	0.38	6.16	70.70	10.4
10 Japan	0.4223	0.39	7.84	75.92	6.0
11 United Kingdom	0.3385	0.38	9.73	75.10	12.6
12 Netherlands	0.4493	0.42	4.72	76.80	16.7
13 Germany (FR)	0.3939	0.45	6.98	73.83	17.4
14 France	0.5176	0.50	5.01	76.40	15.6
15 Finland	0.4729	0.46	4.11	74.21	11.6
16 Italy	0.4000	0.40	4.05	74.88	16.2
17 Norway	0.3622	0.35	5.55	77.43	11.3
18 Australia	0.3185	0.30	8.99	74.18	8.2
19 Denmark	0.3673	0.37	6.00	76.10	13.2
20 Sweden	0.3872	0.39	12.75	77.41	15.6
21 USA	0.4042	0.34	12.54	75.10	7.2
22 Czechoslovakia	0.2100	0.21	10.49	72.94	17.0
23 Poland	0.2200	0.22	8.61	73.76	9.4
24 Hungary	0.2500	0.25	8.55	72.59	11.2
25 Yugoslavia	0.2100	0.21	5.46	70.42	12.3
26 Canada	0.3933	0.3933	10.06	75.18	9.6
27 Ecuador	0.6826	0.6826	3.42	53.67	2.9
28 Quyana	0.4192	0.4192	6.04	63.01	4.2
29 Honduras	0.6188	0.6188	0.87	49.70	1.0
30 India	0.4755	0.4755	0.70	40.55	1.7
31 Iraq	0.6288	0.6288	0.55	51.60	1.3
32 Israel	0.3840	0.3840	7.72	72.96	7.1
33 Jamaica	0.5766	0.5766	6.51	66.63	2.9
34 Malaysia	0.5545	0.5545	2.27	66.73	3.0
35 Mexico	0.5243	0.5243	4.13	63.73	2.9
36 Pakistan	0.3359	0.3359	0.58	48.80	0.5
37 Spain	0.3930	0.3930	4.35	71.90	4.0
38 Turkey	0.5679	0.5679	0.97	53.70	1.7
39 Uruquay	0.4279	0.4279	5.95	71.56	7.5
40 Venezuela	0.5445	0.5445	3.16	65.90	3.5
41 Bulgaria	0.2118	0.2118	7.15	72.67	10.0

	GP	OLDS	SALEM	INVR	RG
1 Tunisia	408	3.55	14.89	22.0	4.3
2 Sri Lanka	177	4.32	18.89	15.0	5.5
3 Zambia	386	2.19	8.01	16.0	7.1
4 Brazil	609	3.34	17.39	18.0	4.8
5 El Salvador	307	3.44	17.95	12.0	5.9
6 Colombia	474	3.00	16.81	19.0	5.1
7 Costa Rica	674	3.73	22.44	21.0	5.1
8 Panama	854	3.71	18.91	17.0	7.8
9 Greece	1377	11.15	15.65	19.0	7.6
10 Japan	2786	7.06	32.39	32.0	10.5
11 United Kingdom	2787	13.16	40.36	17.0	2.8
12 Netherlands	3442	10.26	30.30	24.0	5.5
13 Germany (FR)	4245	12.97	37.39	26.0	4.6
14 France	3749	13.42	34.98	22.0	5.7
15 Finland	2849	9.29	35.93	26.0	4.6
16 Italy	2159	11.27	25.62	24.0	5.3
17 Norway	3916	13.06	35.21	30.0	4.9
18 Australia	3834	8.35	35.69	25.0	5.4
19 Denmark	4170	12.35	37.59	20.0	4.7
20 Sweden	5149	13.90	41.18	23.0	4.2
21 USA	5563	9.89	40.43	17.0	4.6
22 Czechoslovakia	2300	11.70	44.55	31.1	4.2
23 Poland	1500	8.80	34.29	31.6	6.5
24 Hungary	1500	12.00	36.39	28.9	5.4
25 Yugoslavia	800	7.87	21.43	29.9	6.6
26 Canada	4814	7.70	40.01	22.0	5.6
27 Ecuador	306	1.68	19.00	15.0	5.5
28 Quyana	382	4.00	13.75	18.0	4.4
29 Honduras	304	3.00	19.00	16.0	5.1
30 India	0.99	4.00	5.70	16.0	3.8
31 Iraq	429	5.29	13.00	19.0	3.4
32 Israel	2088	8.00	28.14	26.0	8.4
33 Jamaica	819	5.56	23.00	18.0	4.7
34 Malaysia	370	3.16	18.00	16.0	5.9
35 Mexico	782	3.73	16.46	17.0	7.3
36 Pakistan	116	4.00	5.32	16.0	5.4
37 Spain	1354	9.67	25.73	21.0	7.2
38 Turkey	445	3.96	12.36	16.0	6.0
39 Uruquay	794	7.55	24.44	14.0	1.2
40 Venezuela	1316	2.94	25.00	16.0	5.7
41 Bulgaria	800	10.10	37.97	32.3	8.2

App. III Correlation Matrix

	GINI 1	GINI 2	EDUCAT	LIFEXP	SOCSEC	GP
GINI 1	1					
GINI 2	0.9709	1				
EDUCAT	-0.6312	-0.6121	1			
LIFEXP	-0.5894	-0.5586	0.7662	1		
SOCSEC	-0.5733	-0.5542	0.5991	0.7686	1	
GP	-0.3826	-0.3168	0.7074	0.7194	0.7052	1

	OLDS	SALEM	INVR	RG	DSOC	DLDC
GINI 1	-0.6294	-0.5496	-0.6856	-0.1665	-0.6753	0.7195
GINI 2	-0.6035	-0.5271	-0.6525	-0.1395	-0.6780	0.6646
EDUCAT	0.6645	0.8252	0.4812	-0.0085	0.3185	-0.6894
LIFEXP	0.7901	0.8417	0.5610	0.0944	0.2260	-0.8028
SOCSEC	0.8813	0.7591	0.6035	-0.1032	0.3278	-0.8168
GP	0.7548	0.8140	0.3952	-0.0801	-0.0842	-0.7624
OLDS	1	0.7951	0.5888	-0.1065	0.2775	-0.8917
SALEM		1	0.6130	-0.0540	0.3314	-0.8101
INVR			1	0.3222	0.6442	-0.7403
RG				1	0.1518	-0.1967
DSOC					1	-0.3636
DLDC						1

1. TLIFEXP/LIFEXP

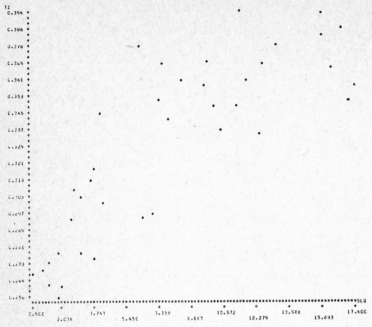

2. LIFEXP/GINI 1

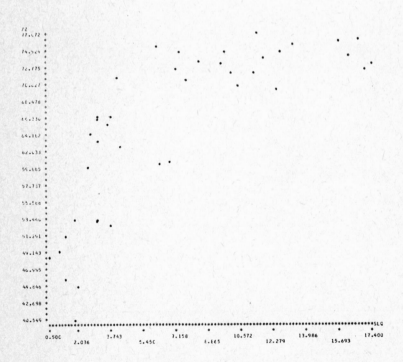

3. TLIFEXP/GINI 1

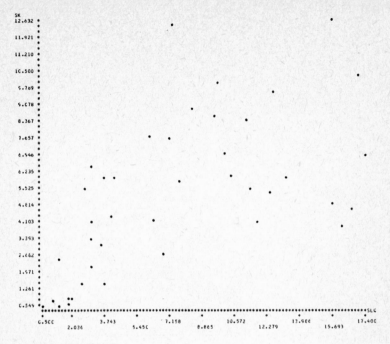

4. EDUCAT/LIFEXP

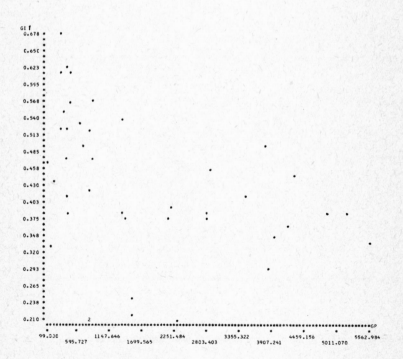

5. EDUCAT/TLIFEXP

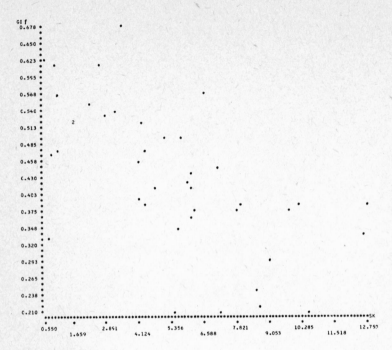

6. GINI 1/EDUCAT

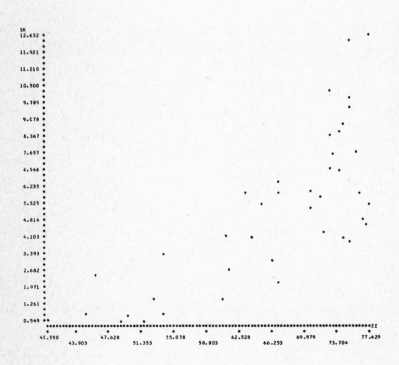

7. GINI 1/GP

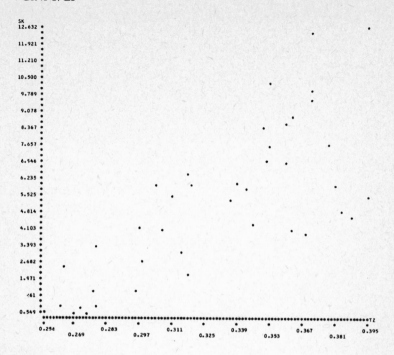

8. EDUCAT/SOCSEC

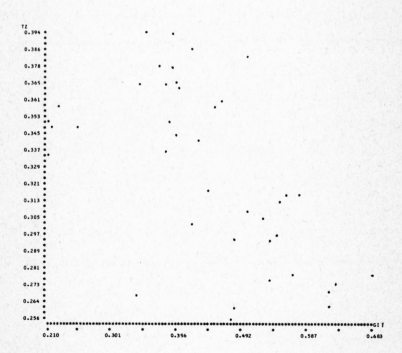

9. LIFEXP/SOCSEC

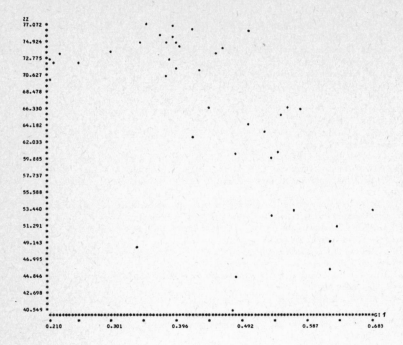

10. TLIFEXP/SOCSEC

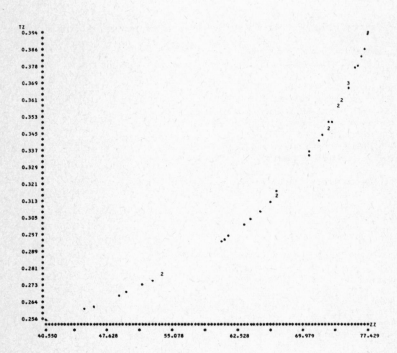

References

Ahluwalia, M.S., Income Distribution and Development: Some Stylized Facts, American Economic Review, May 1976

Brus, W., Income Distribution and Economic Reforms in Poland, in: Politico 1/1974

Carnoy, M., Can Educational Policy of Ilo's World Employment Programme Research Equalize Latin American Income Structures?, Ilo-Working Paper No. 22

Cassel, D./Thieme, H.J., Einkommensverteilung im Systemvergleich, Gustav Fischer Verlag, Stuttgart 1976

Askanas, B./Askanas, H./Levcik, F., Entwicklung und Niveau der Löhne in den RgW-Ländern, in: WIFO-Monatsberichte 1/1976

Hedtkamp, G., Internationale Finanz- und Steuerbelastungsvergleiche, in: Handbuch der Finanzwissenschaft, Tübingen, 1976

ILO, The Cost of Social Security, 7th International Inquiry 1964 – 1966, Geneva 1972

Jain, S., Size Distribution of Income, Compilation of Data, Washington, 1976

Kuznets, S., Modern Economic Growth: Rate, Structure and Spread, Yale University Press, New Haven 1969

Levcik, F., Wirtschaftsreform und Lohndifferenzierung. Auswirkungen der Lohnbildung in einer dezentralisierten Planwirtschaft. Unveröffentlichtes Manuskript

Matthews, M., Top Incomes in the USSR. Towards a Definition of the Soviet Elite, in: NATO, Economic Aspects of life in the USSR, Brussels 1975

Paukert, F., Income Distribution at Different Levels of Development: A Survey of Evidence, in: International Labour Review, Aug. – Sept. 1973, pp. 97 – 125

Rabkina, N.E./Rimashevskaya, N.M., Osnovy differenciacii zarabotnoi platy i dokhodov naseleniya, Moscow 1972

Stevens, C., Health, Employment and Income Distribution, ILO-Working Paper of ILO's World Employment Porgramme Research, No. 21

Wiles, P., Recent Data on Soviet Income Distribution, in: NATO, Economic Aspects of Life in the USSR, Brussels, 1975

Wiles, P., The Distribution of Income in East and West, Amsterdam 1974

Source of Data:*

GI 1	F. Paukert, ILO, 1973, National statistical Yearbooks (for socialist countries – own computation)
GI 2	S. Jain, World Bank, 1975
SLQ	ILO, Social Security Cost 1972
EQ	ILO, Yearbook of Labour Statistics 1974
IQ	UN, Statistical Yearbook 1974
AQ	ILO, Yearbook of Labour Statistics 1974
GP	UN, Yearbook of national accounts Statistics. 1974
RGP	UN, Yearbook of national accounts Statistics. 1974
ZM	UN, Demographic Yearbook 1974
ZZ	UN, Demographic Yearbook, 1974
SK	UNESCO, Statistical Yearbook of Science and Education 1974

* The variables refer to the 1960's or the first years of the 1970's.

Frank Klanberg
**Facts, Figures, and Syndromes of Income Distribution:
Some Notes in Retrospect.**

The essays in this volume cover a wide range of topics in considerable depth; to summarize them and the lively discussion which they kindled is a task beyond my capacity. My proposition is rather to add a few comments reflecting my own views on the broader issues which permeate and surround the papers in the book. To begin with, it is well worth opening one's mind to the contention that the distributive aspects of economic performance did in fact receive relatively minor attention from economists in the past, notwithstanding Ricardo's dictum that income distribution theory is »the principal problem in Political Economy«. Moreover, from the vantage point of an observer in hindsight, there appears a highly disproportionate amount of professional input into the development of the two principal strands of income distribution theory, namely functional and personal distribution theory, until a short while ago; likewise, the intellectual gulf separating the two approaches seemed almost unbridgeable. They moved along practically independently of each other, with minimal crossfertilization of results obtained and questions asked, and with evolutionary traits of largely peripheral value to one another.

Let us delineate this assessment in somewhat greater detail. Using the first appearance (1962) of Krelle's »Verteilungstheorie«[1] as a convenient point of reference, the proportion of space devoted to functional and personal distribution, respectively, in a textbook of some 300 pages was roughly 10:1. The gist of the theoretical argument in the chapter on personal distribution centered around Champernowne's stochastic theory stemming from his 1936 dissertation in which the author sought to explain what he considered to be a remarkable degree of conformity of published income tax statistics with Pareto's law.[2] Yet it is worth remembering that in the same year in which Krelle's book appeared, James Morgan[3] published his seminal article »The Anatomy of Income Distribution« in which it was argued very effectively that most money income data usually represent a mixture of rewards of individuals for productive effort, as well as individual claims to goods and services of society in relation to some measure of need. Put into terms more fashionable nowadays, a case was made for a multidimensional evaluation of the objectives of the distributive system, and implicitly it was asserted that one should try to explain macrophenomena from considerations of decisions on the micro level.

The proportion of papers devoted to questions of income distribution on the macro and on the micro level has changed substantially during the last 10 years and the borderline between them is today in flux. Of course, a mere shift in weights would not necessarily have to be very significant in itself. But something else has happened on the way. A profound change of the underlying thought pattern has occured to which lasting significance can be ascribed because it has affected our way of appreciation of a theory, and influenced our way of structuring research.

Consider the two chief contenders in the realm of functional distribution theory: the marginal productivity theory and Kaldor's »Keynesian« theory as a case in point. At first sight, the equations constituting these two »alternative« theories appear to provide the basis for independent theories of distribution imparting a differing causality to an explanation of the size of factor shares and, with plausible assumptions about the magnitude of the elasticity of substitution between capital and labor, giving rise to opposing results as to the effect of investment on the share of profit.[4] Yet it is easy to show that each theory rests on a singular behavioral assumption, a production function in the case of the neoclassical theory, and a modified Keynesian consumption function in the case of Kaldor's version. Now put this into the framework of an econometric model and consider a model in which there is only a sole behavioral equation, everything else being exogenous or consisting of income identities. The point to be made here is that the state of the art of econometric model building already has so shaped our visions of theoretical interrelatedness that today we would simply refuse to spend much time to quarrel about the explanatory power of perhaps academically pure, but behaviorally simplistic models.

A seemingly paradoxical fact of research activity is the rapidity with which the flood of papers wilted away that treated distribution as an appendix to growth theory, particularly after the flurry of excitement caused by endogeneously explained technical progress. Admittedly, a certain shift in research philosophy is partly attributable to the fact that major technical advances have occurred in the meantime. As experimental techniques increase in their sophistication and probing capacity, as large computer facilities become available and complicated software becomes exchangeable, so also does it become increasingly possible to execute empirical research on a scale which was formerly simply out of reach.

But hard practical realities, a growing awareness that some response was required to the challenges posed by a changing economic environment, have left their marks, too. For there has been, and there continues to be, a gradual process throughout the western — and not only western — world reflecting a syndrome which may be aptly epitomized as »la rivoluzione delle aspettative crescenti«. Probably for the first time in history, a large stratum of society becomes increasingly aware of actual income shares accruing to a respective group. Besides, very effective and sometimes quite unconventional (to put it mildly) means were found to press relative group advantages through the political process. As such tactics become universal, it is not too difficult to hypothesize that the outcome will be generally destabilizing to the economy — the first obvious result will be inflation — and that, after all, the actual income distribution is not bound to change much. And the inevitable frictions that are generated in the process contribute in many instances to sharp political dissent and political instability.

It is under these circumstances that terms such as income distribution and inequality find themselves in the unfamiliar position of being in the focus of political concern, and that guidance is expected from facts and figures related to income distribution for the shaping of national policies which can at this stage hardly be furnished without serious qualms. Thus, while most observers would agree that the answers obtained by using the old capitalist-worker epithets are useless and often misleading, it is by no means clear nor easy to decide what notions we should put into their place. The general answer would be that it depends on the goals one has in mind. For instance, it would make little sense to assess the impact of a specific educational policy on a level other than that of the addressees of that policy, that is individuals. This is also the line taken by the »earnings approach« of current human capital theory to which I shall come back later. On the other hand, if one emphasizes consumption possibilities, the distributive pattern cannot adequately be discussed unless the fact that people live together in families and share common expenses is taken into account. Tax policies provide a borderline case by virtue of institutional setting. Consequently, the very terms income distribution and inequality have assumed a new aura of ambiguity, and a meaningful application of them renders their precise prior definition a real necessity.

Much of what has already been said has also a bearing on the theory of wage structure in collective bargaining developed by von Weizsäcker in his contribution. The term »collective bargaining« is a portmanteau term in this context in the sense that it embodies three separate but related questions: how is the packet of substantive demands arrived at which the union puts before the employers, what happens in the negotiations after the initial conditions have been set, and what is likely to occur after some agreement has been reached between the two principal players.

On the first question observations from many countries suggest that it is not unusual for union rank and file to be in disfavor of settlements which would make the wage structure more homogeneous. In other words, they prefer visible distances of economic rewards accruing to their own more fragmented group rather that greater equality of wage structure among workers or union members at large. The resistance against flat rises seems to be the more articulate, the higher the degree of unionization among skilled craftsmen. In fact, it is often prudent policy for union negotiators to reestablish inequality between groups where distances have been narrowed by »leapfrogging« of competing groups or by some other mechanism. The underlying hypothesis, commonly refered to as wage contour hypothesis, implies a strong dependence of subjective welfare evaluations on the maintenance of earnings differentials with the result that existing relative welfare positions show a tendency toward entrenchment.[5]

Whatever validity is ascribed to this explanation, it is only part of the story. For there is also, and perhaps more importantly, the fact that employers have a keen interest to maintain earnings differentials and to reestablish them whenever union or government policies have been partly successful in making existing disparities less pungent. Employers act from a profit-maximization motif since they expect a more efficient work-effort from their employees in this way. The process usually takes the form of granting all kind of bonus payments and fringe benefits and has reached a stage which has provoked German court decisions ruling that beyond-contract payments are not allowed to be grossly out of tune with the stipulations of the existing contract. Clearly the practices castigated are adverse to every effort to change the wage structure, and they can thwart attempts to reduce inequality of earnings to a considerable extent. In view of these forces, big external shocks to the economy, or really strong and convincing ethical precepts, such as distaste for racial or sexual discrimination, would be required before any lasting change can be expected to take hold.

The wage contour hypothesis is vulnerable to the charge that views held by employees about wage differentials are not exogeneous, and that it cannot readily account for modifications required by technological developments, i.e. by the demand side of the labor market. Similar objections can be levelled against the human capital approach where the acquisition of that type of capital by individuals is the key factor in explaining their subsequent earnings. A supplementary theory of the demand for human capital is in a much cruder state and, as far as it can be said to exist, leads to serious difficulties in econometric testing.[6]

It is not possible here to review the current status of human capital theory in any comprehensiveness.[7] Instead, a few issues will be selected which are the focal point of much current debate. The first basic question is: Why do people spend money and forego earnings in post-compulsory education, and must such expenses be viewed as consumption or as investment? In the pre-1960 days, the consumption view was widely accepted. But after the work of Schultz, Becker and especially Mincer the investment model became clearly favored. According to the tenets of the model, people act as if they were rational investors of capital whose »rate of return« they try to maximize. Analytically, the model is much richer in substantive contents than the older stochastic models. In the last model temporary variations in earnings are interpreted as chance variations. The human capital model views such variations as a result of rational, cumulative efforts to invest. It can therefore be visualized as another manifestation of the »investment matters« syndrome of neoclassical growth theories.

Notwithstanding many different empirical specifications, the promulgation of an implicit human capital production function tended also to reinforce widespread public beliefs that a higher amount of schooling was not only favorable to lifetime earnings, but was also instrumental in achieving greater job security. Although this conclusion cannot be derived from human capital models in a rigorous fashion, it would be injudicious to deny that the whole approach did not in fact corroborate existing misconceptions.[8] The crisis in professional employment which began around 1970, particularly among scientists and engineers in the United States after the cutback of the NASA program, did not altogehter conform to that genteel mythology. Doubts arose as to the »worth« of demands for more and better education, and the once almost unassailable doctrine »The better the education, the safer the job« lost much of its previous luster.

Such labor market failures give rise to several issues. First, they serve as a reminder of the severe informational requirements inherent in the human capital approach. Judgements are needed on the expected increase in earnings for each year of the working life of an individual as well as on the effect of on-the-job training, or of learning-by-doing, in any occupation. Additionally, the risk factor associated with the choice of a particular occupation and, maybe more import-antly, with a particular school must be estimated. Forecasts of demographic developments, in principle the least uncertain elements in this array, must also be taken into account. Wrong guesses must therefore be expected to be the rule rather than the expection, and the theory offers little comfort to anybody falling victim to his own guesswork.

Although misjudgements of career opportunities must be conceded in principle, however, the coefficients of the earnings equation usually come out with the right sign in empirical work, i.e. the private rate of return to additional schooling is positive. This can be interpreted that expenditures of time and resources on schooling or other training do pay off. The empirical estimates are therefore not at all inconsistent with the basic assumptions of the investment model. This does not mean, however, that people can always be treated as rational investors in the sense that they are guided solely by financial considerations. Many jobs offer also nonpecuniary rewards and people may aspire to them in preference to higher pay.[9] To test such propositions within a human capital framework makes extra-ordinarily heavy demands on the data base and requires a good deal of ingenuity in converting nonmonetary rewards into monetary equivalents.

Besides, the role of ability needs to be reassessed. Intuitively, one may imagine situations where personal qualities such as »energy«, »drive« or »initiative« and the ability to transfer knowledge from one job to another count much more than formal schooling. Empirical estimates on the effect of those variables show substantial differences as to its conclusions. Mincer's various studies, partly echoed in his present paper with Borjas, seem to deemphasize the influence of personal and background characteristics on the earnings profile of an incividual. Taubman and his associates, on the other hand, find the coefficient of the variable on education in the earnings function substantially biased if family background and genetic endowments are not controlled for. These papers underline the ne-cessity to be extremely judicious in comparing the findings of differently specified models to one another.[10] Moreover, a critical reader often has great difficulties to be certain if and how the conclusions depend on the use of specific data sets. There is mounting evidence, though, which demonstrates that the effect of the educational system upon the earnings profiles is both direct and indirect. It affects status and earnings directly in accordance with the predictions of the human capital schooling model; and it serves indirectly as a catalyst to convert inherited cognitive skills and personality traits into »marketable assets«.[11]

To sum up, the human capital paradigm offers ample ground to delve deeper into the unresolved questions. But there is also a danger apparent in such ever more sophisticated studies, for a growing attention toward personal characteristics of individuals may to some extent blur a perception of fundamental societal scarcity relationships which would be a prerequisite to sensible educational planning. Thus, desirable levels of educational facilities to be provided by a society will continue to be normative issues, and we must still look for alternative means to judge the relative merits of specific educational proposals.

After this necessarily sketchy account of some problems in current human capital theory I turn briefly to some questions of international comparisons of inequality. The conventional wisdom, originally due to Kuznet's pioneering work and later »validated« by many others, was if a country starts from a low level of economic development, the initial effect of economic growth were to render the income distribution more unequal inspite of a perhaps rising living standard of the poor. Many development strategists have wondered what could be done to overcome or circumvent this unwelcome relation between growth on the one hand and inequality on the other hand.[12] Papanek's results now show that this concern was largely unwarranted. His evidence leads to no firm conclusion except that the relationship between economic growth and inequality of income can take almost any form. This finding, it may be added, is not too dissimilar from what we know about the relationship between the rate of real economic growth and the rate of inflation in various countries.

Papanek's thesis makes sense without really vitiating the reasons advanced in support of an inverted U-shaped curve of inequality of income versus the growth of per capita income. Suppose we have a high level of economic activity and at the same time a rapid growth of population. Per capita income may then well stagnate while inequality may worsen in some sense. This points to the role population growth plays in perpetuating inequality and highlights the somewhat dubious assumptions underlying a comparison of a unit of per capita income in country X versus the seemingly idential unit in country Y. The problem is compounded by the difficulties concerning a valuation of income in the subsistence sector in developing countries, spurring suggestions that considerations of inequality should preferably be based on measurements of consumption as a measuring rod of living standards rather than on income. Theoretically there is something to be said for this;[13] and statistically the consumption alternative appears to have some appeal considering the wellknown expenditure surplus phenomenon one encounters in cross-section data of advanced countries. But in international comparisons of income data one can easily overshoot the mark with such worries. Besides, the consumption alternative is not without some theoretical defects of its own. It would carry things too far to list them here, but I may point out that it is not possible to base unambiguous poverty standards on consumption patterns even when international data of some quality are available.

The question of income evaluation assumes yet another dimension depending on whether income in kind is omitted or (partly) included. Numerous studies in the United States and in Western Europe point to the intricacies of this problem. In political systems akin to dictatorships the problem becomes intractable, however, since the host of latent or open priviliges accruing to state or party officials is not even dimly recorded in statistics of money wages. It is an intriguing question how their inclusion would affect the general shape of the income distribution curve, and particularly its upper tail.

Another point having a direct bearing on cross-country comparisons is the degree of »moonlighting« which is apparently tolerated by the authorities in various countries with a varying degree of acquiesence. The quantification of such variables is surely not an easy task, and often a political impossibility. But my feeling is that it is not merely the potential disortion of published figures of income distribution that may bias analytical values. Another consequence of greater import may be the development of habits to conceal real income in response to government-imposed strictures stemming from real or purportedly egalitarian ideology-firmed systems. Twenty years ago, J. K. Galbraith[14] attempted to describe the system of American capitalism by introducing the concept of countervailing power. Today, the best defense of ordinary citizens against the zeal of government regulations is not seldom to develop a counterveiling prowess to adjust income figures in accordance to whatever the »Zeitgeist« is liable to educe.

In the general context of inequality and income distribution, it may now be appropriate to present a few concrete figures. Table 1 (see page 331) shows some summary statistics of income distribution in Germany in the year 1969. I selected this particular array of data to emphasize a few points. The first appears almost trivial but is nevertheless worth making. By skilful arrangement of statistical data many tables of this kind can be produced. But to make meaningful deductions from one-dimensional arrays of this sort is never easy and sometimes downright impossible. For example, it appears from table 1 that economic well-being is positively correlated with family size in a rather straightforward fashion. Yet the figures hide practically all the diverse reasons behind this phenomenon. To mention only a few: high incomes of head of households proper, varying labor force participation of wives and adult children in the household, pooling of factor and transfer incomes. Quintessentially the figures would suggest that family composition and changes in family »fortunes« — which can range from the extraordinary to the mundane — play an exceedingly powerful role in shaping economic well-being, sometimes to the point where earnings differentials between employed adults loose the impact they may have had in the past.

However in affirming such a viewpoint, today one is not far from becoming entangled in a quasi-ideological issue because there are those who prefer to advance explications of personal income distribution on a strictly individual or per-capita basis.[15] Again, neither view offers a panacea for all questions; the use of families, households or persons has its specific advantages and drawbacks, and the seemingly elegant method of constructing equivalent adult units in families or households circumvents those difficulties only in part since it is contingent on normative value judgements concerning the fraction of total unit expenditures ascribable as shared within the spending units. The best way to avoid the difficulties of selecting an appropriate decision unit is to have a data base with sufficient flexibility capable of yielding answers independently of specific grouping requirements. The design of existing microanalytic models such as DYNASIM in the United States and SPES in Germany attempts to capture this very flexibility.

There are two other issues which have so far been glossed over or left unanswered. In the first place, it should have become abvious that the role of the population module within a microanalytic simulation model is an absolutely crucial one. The composition of the input population has to be determined with utmost precision. Errors in the probability vectors (marriage, dissolution of existing units, disability, etc.), although quite small in the initial period, may propagate themselves with highly detrimental consequences through the system in medium-range (e.g. 15 years) simulations. Nevertheless I do not think there is reason for undue pessimism in this area. Many initially seemingly intractable problems have already been successfully solved or are at the point of becoming technically manageable.

The other issue relates to a more fundamental matter. Operational examples of microanalytic approaches fully document the fact that auxiliary models of the

Table 1: Net Household Income in the Federal Republic of Germany 1969 as a Function of Household Composition

Income class (DM p.m.)	Percentage of all Households	Average number of children per household	Proportion of children living in household of parents in age class					Average number of persons per household receiving factor income
			under 8	8–12	12–16	16–22	22–27	
Less than 500	11.6	0.01	.01	–	–	–	–	.22
500 – 600	3.9	0.05	.02	.02	.01	.01	–	.29
600 – 700	5.0	0.10	.04	.02	.02	.01	.01	.46
700 – 800	4.6	0.22	.10	.04	.04	.03	.01	.51
800 – 900	5.9	0.35	.18	.05	.05	.04	.03	.65
900 – 1000	6.2	0.57	.30	.11	.08	.05	.03	.77
1000 – 1100	6.0	0.85	.45	.17	.12	.08	.03	.83
1100 – 1200	6.3	0.97	.46	.21	.15	.10	.05	.92
1200 – 1300	6.0	1.05	.47	.23	.17	.13	.05	.98
1300 – 1400	5.7	1.14	.48	.28	.19	.15	.04	1.06
1400 – 1500	5.5	1.18	.47	.24	.21	.19	.07	1.17
1500 – 1750	10.1	1.29	.45	.27	.23	.26	.08	1.22
1750 – 2000	7.2	1.42	.42	.28	.27	.34	.09	1.32
2000 – 2250	4.7	1.50	.40	.28	.28	.40	.14	1.39
2250 – 2500	3.3	1.63	.43	.28	.30	.44	.18	1.39
2500 – 2750	2.1	1.68	.42	.32	.30	.44	.20	1.42
2750 – 3000	1.4	1.77	.44	.29	.30	.49	.25	1.40
3000 – 4000	2.6	1.70	.40	.31	.31	.44	.24	1.39
4000 – 5000	0.8	1.76	.47	.35	.34	.40	.20	1.35
Greater 5000	1.0	1.76	.45	.33	.40	.42	.16	1.19
Total	100.0	0.87	.32	.17	.15	.17	.06	.90

Source: Calculations by the author based on the Integrated Microdatafile (IMDAF 1969) of the SPES-Project Frankfurt. Population in Institutions and Non-German Nationals included.

macroeconomy are an indispensable component of a fully interactive model of the entire economy.[16] While this linkage approach has advantages for specific purposes in generating predictions relating to real policy alternatives, it must be born in mind that its theoretical justifications deserve further scrutiny. The charge could be raised that the entire microanalytic approach is really no more than a phantastically complex adornment to the existing theoretical framework of macromodels where the »market« acts as an equilibrator to impose order on the chaotic interplay of microdecisions.

One of the main points Krupp is making in his paper, is therefore to stress the ambivalency of the above argument. The real methodological question is the question of the empirical content of each model. If one finds a model that works, in the sense that it establishes a reasonable relationship between predictive performance and particular aspects of the world, one may have done good research or just have been plain lucky, but one may not necessarily have established an eternal truth. But this predicament exists in any kind of model-building. It is certainly no specific fallacy in microanalytic modeling.

There can thus be no mechanical answers to the questions raised. Even the shrewdest manipulation of statistical data cannot reveal with certainly whether there is a direct causal link between variables, whether there are systematic sampling errors in the data, or whether there are other hidden predictors operating. A certain dose of scepticism against the political utility of present day predictive power of existing models should, on the other hand, not distract our view from the fact that great strides forward have already been made. The need to base policy decisions upon more reliable data concerning individuals and institutions, as a basis for more intelligent and informed public decisions, has already begun to exert its influence on the way national accounts are handled by official statistical agencies. Data bases are continually extended and expanded, the most promising example being the availability of Public Use Samples of survey data in the United States.

Yet one must never forget how deeply our modeling paradigms as potential policy tools are embedded into the fashions of our time and into ideological slants that may be particularly forceful or current. There are examples in other sciences where existing paradigms in society proved to be obstacles to the dissemination of new ideas — the theory of relativity and anthropoligical relativism are cases in point[17] — which today seem self-evident. The gradual evolution of an integrated framework for modelbuilding suitable for answering questions about social inequality cannot, according to all experience hithertho accumulated, proceed but in slow steps, and it will be prone to many, perhaps serious errors. But it is the only alternative to groping in the dark, and hopefully the most effective defense against obstinate opinionatedness of policy makers.

Notes

[1] Krelle (1962)
[2] See also Champernowne (1973)
[3] Morgan (1962)
[4] This is elaborated, for instance, in Eltis, Growth and Distribution (1973), p. 300 ff., as well as in many other similar texts.
[5] See also Thurow (1975), p. 104 ff.

[6] Some of which are outlined in Griliches' review of econometric problems (1977). References to comprehensive models are given there.

[7] Authoritative accounts of recent origin are Mincer (1974) and Taubman (1975). For an overview see also the »slightly jaundiced« survey by Blaug (1976).

[8] Which were explicitly noticeable in the concurrently developed models of the »labor scrappage« variety. The conclusion of these models was that the scrappage, i.e. unemployment, occurred at the bottom end of the educational stratum. See Akerlof (1969).

[9] There is empirical evidence which shows that preferences for nonmonetary returns shows up as a reduction of earnings. See Taubman (1975), p. 49.

[10] The point is expounded by Griliches (1977).

[11] Fägerlind (1975).

[12] On the possibilities for such action, the reader is referred to the delightful but slightly facetious-sounding account by Peter Wiles (1974), Lecture. IV.

[13] Some arguments are summarized in Pyatt (1977).

[14] Galbraith, J. K., American Capitalism (1957).

[15] Perhaps most forcefully by Wiles (1974).

[16] In Germany, linkages of the Krelle macromodel to the Krupp micromodel have been used in preliminary work. See the paper by Krupp for further details. As regards the situation in the United States, see Orcutt, Caldwell and Wertheimer II, (1976), Chapter 1.

[17] I became aware of those examples through the excellent exposition by John Ziman, The Force of Knowledge, 1976, p.300.

References

1. Akerlof, G. A. (1969): Structural Unemployment in a Neoclassical Framework, *Journal of Political Economy*, Vol. 77, p. 399, 1969.

2. Blaug, M., (1976): The Empirical Status of Human Capital Theory: A Slightly Jaundiced Survey, *Journal of Economic Literature*, Vol. 14, 1976, p. 827.

3. Champernowne, D. G. (1973): *The Distribution of Income Between Persons.* Cambridge University Press, Cambridge.

4. Eltis, W. A. (1973): *Growth and Distribution*, The McMillan Press Ltd., London.

5. Fägerlind, I., (1975): *Formal education and adult earnings.* Almquist & Wicksell International, Stockholm (1975).

6. Galbraith, J. K. (1957): *American Capitalism: The Concept of Countervailing Power.* Hamish Hamilton, London 1957.

7. Griliches, Zvi (1977): *Estimating the Return to Schooling: Some Econometric Problems.* Econometrica 45, (1977), p. 1.

8. Krelle, W. (1962): *Verteilungstheorie*, J. C. B. Mohr (P. Siebeck), Tübingen 1962.

9. Mincer, J. (1974): *Schooling, Experience and Earnings*, National Bureau of Economic Research, New York.

10. Morgan, J. B. (1962): *The Anatomy of Income Distribution*, The Review of Economics and Statistics, Vol. 64, p. 270 (1962).

11. Orcutt, G., Caldwell, S., and Wertheimer II, R. (1976): *Policy Exploration through Microeconomic Simulation*, The Urban Institute, Washington D. C., 1976.

12. Pyatt, G. (1977): *On International Comparisons of Inequality*, American Economic Review, Papers and Proceedings, Vol. 67, p. 71, 1977.

13. Taubman, P. J. (1975): *Sources of Inequality in Earnings*, North Holland Publishing Co., Amsterdam 1975.

14. Thurow, L. C. (1975): *Generating Inequality*, The McMillan Press Ltd., London 1975.

15. Wiles, P. (1974): *Distribution of Income: East and West*, North Holland Publishing Co., Amsterdam, 1974..

16. Ziman, J. (1976): *The Force of Knowledge; The Scientific Dimension of Society.* Cambridge University Press, Cambridge (1976).

List Of Contributors

Horst Albach
Institut für Wirtschafts- und
Gesellschaftswissenschaften
Betriebswirtschaftliche Abt. I
Universität Bonn
Adenauerallee 24–42
5300 Bonn

Wolfgang Asam
INIFES
Haldenweg 23
8901 Leitershofen

J. Behrman
University of Pennsylvania
Department of Economics
3718 Locust Walk CR
Philadelphia   1974

George J. Borjas
The University of Chicago
Department of Economics
1126 E. 59th Street
Chicago, Ill. 60637

Edward C. Budd
The Pennsylvania State University
College of the Liberal Arts
Department of Economics
613 Kern Graduate Building
University Park, Pa. 16802

Dennis W. Carlton
Massachusetts Institute of Technology
Department of Economics
Cambridge, Mass. 02139

D. G. Champernowne, F. B. A.
Trinity College
Cambridge
England

Richard B. Freeman
Department of Economics
Harvard University
Cambridge, Mass. 02138

Thomas Fues
Institut für Wirtschafts- und
Gesellschaftswissenschaften
Betriebswirtschaftliche Abt. I
Universität Bonn
Adenauerallee 24–42
5300 Bonn

Bernd Geisen
Institut für Wirtschafts- und
Gesellschaftswissenschaften
Betriebswirtschaftliche Abt. I
Universität Bonn
Adenauerallee 24–42
5300 Bonn

Zvi Griliches
Harvard University
Department of Economics
1737 Cambridge St., Room 414
Cambridge, Mass. 02138

Rober E. Hall
Center for Advanced Study in the
Behavioral Sciences
202 Junipero Serra Boulevard
Stanford, California 94305

Frank Klanberg
Transfer-Enquête-Kommission
Hamburger Allee 26–28
6000 Frankfurt am Main 90

Wilhelm Krelle
Institut für Wirtschafts- und
Gesellschaftswissenschaften
Wirtschaftstheoretische Abt. I
Universität Bonn
Adenauerallee 24–42
5300 Bonn

Hans-Jürgen Krupp
Johann Wolfgang Goethe-Universität
Senckenberganlage 31
6000 Frankfurt am Main 1

Oldrich Kýn
Boston University
College of Liberal Arts
226 Bay State Road
Boston, Mass. 02215

Robert E. B. Lucas
Boston University
College of Liberal Arts
226 Bay State Road
Boston, Mass. 02215

Gustav F. Papanek
Boston University
College of Liberal Arts
226 Bay State Road
Boston, Mass. 02215

Ralf Pauly
Institut für Ökonometrie
und Operations Research
Universität Bonn
Adenauerallee 24–42
5300 Bonn

Jan Pen
Faculteit der Rechtsgeleerdheid
Rijksuniversiteit Groningen
Broerstraat 7
Groningen

Martin Pfaff
Lehrstuhl für Makroökonomie
Universität Augsburg
Memmingerstraße 14
8900 Augsburg

Jiri Sláma
Osteuropa-Institut München
Scheinerstraße 11
8000 München

Paul Taubman
University of Pennsylvania
Department of Economics
3718 Locust Walk CR
Philadelphia, Pa. 19174

Michael Wagner
Institut für höhere Studien und
wissenschaftliche Forschung
Stumpergasse 56
1060 Wien

Terence Wales
University of Pennsylvania
Department of Economics
3718 Locust Walk CR
Philadelphia, Pa. 19174

Carl Christian von Weizsäcker
Institut für Wirtschafts- und
Gesellschaftswissenschaften
Universität Bonn
Adenauerallee 24–42
5300 Bonn

T. C. Whiteman
The Pennsylvania State University
College of the Liberal Arts
Department of Economics
613 Kern Graduate Building
University Park, Pa. 16802